EVERYDAY LIFE IN THE ICE AGE

EVERYDAY LIFE IN THE ICE AGE

A New Study of Our Ancestors

Elle Clifford

Paul Bahn

ARCHAEOPRESS ARCHAEOLOGY

ARCHAEOPRESS PUBLISHING LTD
Summertown Pavilion
18-24 Middle Way
Summertown
Oxford OX2 7LG
www.archaeopress.com

ISBN 978-1-80327-258-0
ISBN 978-1-80327-259-7 (e-Pdf)

Front cover: Reconstruction of a Solutrean woman and child by Elisabeth Daynès.
Inside front cover: A group of Magdalenians, reconstructions by Elisabeth Daynès.

Contents

Preface

Don Johanson

As a paleoanthropologist, I have a deep interest in the human career, from the first fossil traces dating back millions of years to the emergence of modern *Homo sapiens*. My research has focused on Africa's Great Rift Valley, largely in the Afar region of Ethiopia where I discovered the Lucy skeleton in 1974.

What sparked my captivation with the Ice Age, that period between roughly 40,000 and 12,000 years ago, was a visit to southwest France in the summer of 1982, when I accompanied a group of people to the Périgord to view some of the painted caves of the Dordogne region. I have the most wonderful memories of my arrival in the quaint little town of Les Eyzies, the epicenter of French prehistory, and can recall admiring the Hotel Cro-Magnon, a stone building covered in ivy and topped with a red tiled roof. Going inside, I was amazed to see that the hotel was actually nestled into the cliff close to the Cro-Magnon Abri, which is how the early residents of that time (ancient but anatomically identical to modern *Homo sapiens*) got their name.

We seated ourselves in an intimate dining room perfumed with enticing kitchen aromas and were treated to a splendid meal: a silky *pâté de foie gras* with triangles of toast, followed by a *magret de canard*, then onto a traditional vinaigrette salad, a mind-boggling selection of cheese, and finally an *ile flottante*, all washed down with a brilliant Pécharmant.

The next morning began with a visit to the spot just a few steps from the hotel where roadworkers uncovered flint tools and human bones in 1868. At that time, before the modern museum was built, a small plaque attached to the stone wall of the Abri Cro-Magnon was all that remained; the original human skeletons, grave goods, and artifacts are now displayed in museums elsewhere. As I photographed the site, I thought what a modest homage it was to this important discovery for French prehistory.

We then made our way slowly through the town eastwards, along the Avenue de la Préhistoire, for my first visit to a real *grotte ornée*, Font-de-Gaume. I was enthralled by the polychrome paintings of bison, horses, and other creatures portrayed by Magdalenian people, but it was the poignant depiction of a male reindeer licking the forehead of a kneeling female that made the deepest impression on me.

As the tour continued, I was surprised that each cave had its own distinctive character and flavor: each offered a unique variety of depictions of the bison, reindeer, mammoths, woolly rhinos, and horses who walked the landscape with our ancestors tens of thousands of years ago.

The final destination on the tour was the *pièce de résistance*, 'the Sistine Chapel of Prehistory' – Lascaux. Making the visit even more remarkable was that our guide was none other than Jacques Marsal, who with some boyhood pals had found the cave in 1940. It was clear his excitement had not diminished in the years since, and he said that from the moment he saw the paintings on the ceiling he knew the cave would always be a part of his life; he did, in fact, dedicate his life to protecting and preserving it.

My excitement grew as we followed Jacques to the imposing, art deco-like bronze door that stood between the modern and the ancient worlds. Before entering, we were instructed to dip our shoes in a disinfectant so as not to bring in spores or pollen that might grow on the walls and harm the precious art. Inside, the floor was compacted cave earth, and the air a little musty. Jacques gave us a moment for our eyes to adjust to the darkness, and with his flashlight, slowly illuminated the walls. I know my jaw wasn't the only one that dropped open! We stood in hushed reverence while he pointed out the bulls and horses, and details such as the black bear hidden in the belly of a large bull, and a mythical figure with two straight horns shooting out of its head, perhaps a human in an animal skin, who Jacques speculated was commanding the cavalcade of animals.

I felt an oddly powerful connection to the group of Cro-Magnon artists who had long ago stood where I was – squinting in the faint light flickering from crude oil lamps, they must have surveyed their stone canvas while deciding what to depict: A hunt? A death? Something otherworldly?

We followed Jacques deeper in, the ground sloping downward through a narrow opening which led to a gallery. In a whisper, he told us to look up. Then he flipped a switch and light shone upon stunning polychrome paintings on the ceiling that could only have been created if a scaffold had been built in the cave. Up to the right was a large black stag, heavily antlered, with a look of fear in its eye. Deer were also drawn in a sequence of images suggesting they were fording a stream. At the bottom of the narrow gallery was a screaming horse falling over a cliff.

I would love to have stayed for hours, but 40 minutes was the limit, and I exited the cave feeling a profound shift in my thoughts. I was intensely aware of the wind gently moving the top branches of the pine trees, and again I felt a sense of what these Ice Age artists must have felt after putting in a day's work. I will never ever forget that feeling.

Over time, my friendship with Jacques deepened, and he showed me the rarely-seen sections of the cave. One day, he crouched down, dug out a chunk of ocher from the wall, the very ocher used in some of the images, and gave it to me: '*Un petit cadeau pour toi.*'So who, exactly, were these ancient artists? Where did they come from? Did they have language like modern humans? Did they fall in love, did they grieve, did they create music, did they laugh? And what happened to them? Why did they become the dominant species, effectively wiping out their closest relatives, the Neanderthals?

To answer these questions, we need to review our human story. Research has shown that Neanderthals (*Homo sapiens neanderthalensis*) and modern humans (*Homo sapiens sapiens*) had a common ancestor (*Homo heidelbergensis*). The two lineages lived and evolved in reproductive isolation, Neanderthals in Europe and modern humans in Africa. The distinctive anatomy of Neanderthals developed in response to an Arctic-like landscape, where heat conservation promoted short, squat bodies, rugged, projecting faces, and elongated, oval skulls, while the tall, linear bodies of modern humans responded to the tropical conditions where heat dissipation was favored.

Both Neanderthals and modern humans were hunter-gatherers, but their tool kits were very different. Over roughly 400,000 years, the stone tool technology associated with Neanderthals demonstrated little advancement. In contrast, modern humans, as the result of a cognitively enhanced brain, invented a variety of specialized tools and weapons that were employed in highly successful subsistence strategies.

Shortly after modern humans arrived in Europe from Africa around 45,000 years ago with a superior technology, Neanderthals began a decline that culminated in their extinction. The details of that extinction are becoming better understood with continued exploration and discovery. The behaviorally and cognitively advanced moderns outcompeted Neanderthals, but not before there was some hybridization with moderns, as is witnessed in the human genome of today. Maybe the smaller and more sparsely distributed populations of Neanderthals were assimilated into modern humans and bred out into extinction.

In any event, they are gone and we are still here, asking questions, seeking answers. I will always have a passion for understanding how our Paleolithic ancestors lived, and I'm sure to refer often to this well-researched volume by Elle Clifford and Paul Bahn. We are all fascinated with this story because it is our story; it was our ancestors who celebrated their world through complex technology and boundless creativity. No matter what 'modern times' bring 'modern humans,' we must keep that creativity flowing.

Acknowledgements

The teachers, friends and colleagues who have helped us over the years with information, publications and site-visits are far too numerous to mention, but they have all contributed to this book in different ways.

We are enormously grateful to João Zilhão, who read our entire manuscript and made invaluable criticisms, comments and suggestions which improved it considerably and saved us from some errors. We would also like to thank Margherita Mussi and Lawrence Straus for reading and commenting on parts of our text, and Erik Trinkaus, Jim Enloe and Helen Fenwick for help with documentation. Needless to say, we alone are responsible for any shortcomings in the work. We are honoured that Don Johanson agreed to write a preface for the book.

For providing illustrations we are particularly grateful to Robert Bégouën, Bruno Caland, Elisabeth Daynès, Brigitte and the late Gilles Delluc, Lyudmila Lbova, the late Arlette Leroi-Gourhan, the late Alex Marshack, Pedro Saura, Lawrence Straus and the late Jean Vertut.

Illustrations were also kindly provided by James Adovasio, the late Nikolai Bader, Rodrigo de Balbín, Matthew Bennett (Bournemouth University), Yaniv Berman, Gerhard Bosinski, Francesco d'Errico, Sergey Fedorov, David Frayer, Philippe Froesch (Visualforensic), Michel Girard, Khaled Hakami, Joel Irish, the late Jan Jelínek, Nandita Jhaveri, Alice Kehoe, Miroslav Králík and the journal *Anthropologie* (editor-in-chief, Zdeňka Nerudová), Stéphane Lancelot, Landesmuseum Hanover, Jean-Daniel Larribau, Lysianna Ledoux, the late André Leroi-Gourhan, Michel Lorblanchet, the late Frank Marlowe, Evgeny Mashchenko, Alessia Nava, Christine Neugebauer-Maresch, Pavel Nikolskiy, Geneviève Pinçon, Mario Reis, the late Alain Roussot, Dominique Sacchi, Romualdo Seva, the University of Tübingen, Ulm Museum, Eligio Vacca, Marian Vanhaeren, Luc Vanrell and João Zilhão.

At Archaeopress we would like to thank David Davison, Ben Heaney and Mike Schurer.

Introduction

'These people are the forgotten us' – Hugh Brody, *The Other Side of Eden*, 2000.

When reading *Everyday Life in the Ice Age*, you have to imagine a world without a written language – writing was invented thousands of years later. A world with only the most rudimentary scientific understanding. You also need to envisage ways of counting, measuring or telling the time that were very different from those we take for granted in the modern Western world. You might wonder how people managed to communicate, organise themselves, record their ideas and knowledge, predict the future, and teach their young everything they needed to know. We asked the same questions, and they became the starting point for this book.

We also wondered how our ancestors, living tens of thousands of years ago, survived the enormous challenges of the last ice age. How did they manage their everyday lives? It is important to stress from the outset that we are dealing with biologically modern people who were identical to ourselves both physically and (as far as we can tell) psychologically and behaviourally – they had the same intellectual abilities as us, but lacked our thousands of years of accumulated knowledge. Of course this applies equally well to their predecessors such as the Neanderthals!

It is safe to assume that Palaeolithic communities that existed by hunting and gathering were absorbed with watching animals, and learning everything about them – not only their habits, but observing them in every situation – as their survival depended on this very intimate knowledge. These very early versions of us also **must** have had a way of thinking and comprehending the world, and predicting the future in a clear and orderly manner. They also had to be able to communicate their thoughts and beliefs about the world they inhabited to each other and especially to their offspring. Only through doing this could they share experiences and knowledge, beliefs about causality, and establish agreed rules by which their communities and cultures could live.

The sharing and spreading of ideas are things we now take for granted – an idea can be transmitted across the world in a matter of seconds these days. But when long-distance communication began, it would have been a huge step for mankind, and it may have started well before the last ice age. Likewise, the most significant and dramatic changes in human cognition and behaviour seem to have appeared during this protracted period.

All cultures have their own 'world reality,' and most of us have never experienced *a way of life* other than our own. As a consequence, it is difficult for us to imagine how it feels to live a hunter-gatherer lifestyle. In this regard, we owe a debt to a number of anthropologists who have spent years – even decades – living with indigenous groups whose lives are very different from our own. Their commitment to understanding another culture's beliefs about the world is invaluable to our understanding of our early ancestors' existence in small hunting and gathering communities. Not surprisingly, anthropologists report how difficult it is to convey to us, with our 21st-century perspective, how indigenous people see their world. This is in no small part because their way of life, and their understanding of reality, are beyond what most of us in Western society – with our own beliefs, values, social norms, traditions, politics and technology – can grasp intellectually. It is nevertheless important for us to try and understand their viewpoint, as it is central to who we are as human beings, and to the cultural development of our early ancestors over these early millennia.

Thanks to the dedicated work of generations of archaeologists, we now have a wealth of evidence to help us understand those ancestors, and to open a virtual window into our deep past. What we have attempted to do in this book is piece together the (inevitably somewhat incomplete) picture of how ice age people lived. From the physical evidence archaeologists have discovered, we have endeavoured to make plausible, but cautious deductions as to how our early ancestors thought and behaved during this period of our cultural evolution. Where we don't know, we say so; and where we are speculating, we make it clear. We strive to be as honest as possible.

The book incorporates four different kinds of evidence – 1) archaeological data of all kinds – sites, features, artifacts, art objects, human skeletal material, and animal and plant remains; 2) ethnographic data from historic and modern hunter-gatherers, to fill in some gaps in our knowledge of prehistoric life; 3) knowledge of basic human behaviour, needs and anatomy; 4) knowledge of the behaviour and tolerances of animals and plants.

This is the first work of its kind ever published in English, and offers readers an exhaustive and realistic picture of life during the last ice age, with its many problems and challenges. We hope that it will dispel some of the many myths and assumptions about our early ancestors.

There have been a number of popular books on Neanderthals, who preceded us in Europe and elsewhere, but far fewer on our own species. Our book takes a different approach to presenting the way humankind developed socially and psychologically. It looks at every aspect of the lives of biologically modern humans in Europe, from circa 40,000 to 12,000 years ago – a time of radical changes in climate and environment. It explores how people were able to cope with and adapt to sometimes rapid changes. The way communities developed had a great deal to do with their resources in the geographical areas they settled in: the climate, landscape, vegetation, and animal life. These variables were pivotal to the development of these early groups – their social structures, economic activities and practices and (although they remain elusive) their ideas and beliefs about the meaning of life.

Humans have always needed to process information about the world around them, they need to be 'efficient' at remembering important stuff, and they need cooperation from other members of their group and community. During the ice age – particularly in the severest conditions – survival would have been a daily operation, and organising their lives as extended families, in groups, and coordinating and learning from each other's experiences, would have required a sophisticated level of social intelligence. Consequently, our early ancestors would have been pushed to the limits of human potential and ability just in order to survive!

The Upper Palaeolithic may have been one of the most important stages in human history. This period has produced evidence for a dramatic change in human thinking and behaviour, although we still have much to discover about the origins of human psychology – and this crucial stage of our development. Psychologists predict human behaviour, but rarely do they look back and engage with history to understand the origins of our behaviour. Appreciating our ice age past can help us understand what it means to be human.

We hope that the book will encourage more specialists to examine aspects of prehistory other than the minutiae of stone tool typology – in other words what Upper Palaeolithic tools might have been used for, and the lives of the people who made and used them. We would also like to encourage debate in order to produce a more rounded view of ice age life and behaviour.

Although the book focuses almost entirely on Europe, much of what we present is equally applicable to other parts of the world during the same period. It is worth bearing in mind that from 40,000 to 12,000 years ago represents about 1200 generations – and is 15 times longer than the period separating us from the year 1!

It goes without saying that our book cannot be exhaustive. Many hundreds of sites of the period are known throughout Europe, containing thousands of artifacts and probably millions of stone tools. From this mass, we have selected examples that we feel to be of major importance or interest and that shed significant light on ice age ways of life. Many of them are in the French Pyrenees, partly because this region has been studied for 150 years and one of us studied its prehistory for a doctoral thesis, but also because it presents particularly good or important examples of some of the aspects of ice age life. And whereas most studies of the last ice age focus on a catalogue of tool types, we prefer to concentrate on what tools were used for!

Similarly, out of a vast bibliography in many languages, we have only been able to highlight those works which we have found most useful, important or informative.

We have chosen not to present things in chronological order, as most aspects – unless specified otherwise – are applicable to the whole period. Precise dates are of little use, and are distracting to the general reader, so we have not systematically standardised or calibrated them.

CHRONOLOGY

Upper Palaeolithic – the Upper Old Stone Age.

Pleistocene: the period from c. 2.5 million years ago to c. 12,000 years ago. This book covers the last part of the Pleistocene.

Much of our book deals with aspects that apply to the whole period, but occasionally we will refer to specific phases, so it is important to present their names and timespans here in calibrated years. Bp means 'Before present'.

Aurignacian:	*c.* 38,000 bp (cal. 41.5 – 35 ka, though earlier in some areas)
Gravettian:	*c.* 30,000 bp (cal. 35 – 25 ka)
Solutrean:	*c.* 23,000 bp (cal. 25 – 22.5 ka)
Early Magdalenian:	*c.* 21,500 bp (cal. 22.5 – 20 ka)
Middle Magdalenian:	*c.* 17,500 bp (cal. 20 – 15 ka)
Late Magdalenian:	*c.* 14,000 bp (cal. 15 – 13 ka)

Chapter 1

Introducing the People: Appearance, Abilities and Disabilities

In this chapter we attempt to give the reader an accurate idea of what our ice age ancestors might have looked like, and the particular skills they had. At the same time we will demolish some of the many widespread myths about them.

For example, it is commonly claimed that they were small when compared to modern humans – but this is not so. The skeletons from the Cro-Magnon rock-shelter (France), along with many others, show that – within the sample of skeletons discovered so far – men averaged 1.8 m (5 ft 9 in) in height, and women 1.66 m (5 ft 4 in). Their cranial capacity was the same as our own, around 1500 cc. They were also very robust, with well-developed musculature, especially in the legs, as one would expect in mobile hunter-gatherers.

Another myth, constantly proclaimed not only by journalists but also by popular books and even some prehistorians, is that they had short lives – for example, that their average age at death was 32. This is nonsense. The truth is that we do not have the slightest idea what their average life expectancy was. We do know that some individuals of both sexes reached their 60s; but the main problem is lack of information. Consider that for the whole of the Eurasian Upper Palaeolithic – a period of about 30,000 years – we have the remains of fewer than 200 human skeletons, many of which are simply fragments or no more than a single tooth! For Spain and Portugal we only know the Lagar Velho hybrid child (see p. 2), the Red Lady of El Mirón (see pp. 257-58) and a few bones from the cave of Parpalló. For the same timespan on the vast Russian plain, all we have are the remains of ten people at Sunghir (pp. 24-28) and four bodies at Kostenki. For the whole of Siberia, we have the two badly-preserved child skeletons from a grave at Mal'ta, and a few bones from Afontova Gora 2. How can we possibly calculate life expectancy with such a tiny sample? Even in countries with rather more burials (France, Italy, Czech Republic), they are still relatively scarce; they are not evenly distributed through the period, and many of them – as we shall see (p. 200) – seem to be very special individuals who may have been given extraordinary funerary treatment. So we are utterly ignorant about how representative or unrepresentative a sample of the general population they may be. It is quite possible that some categories of people – perhaps of a certain clan, totem, age, status, occupation or degree of initiation – may have been treated differently, or buried far from settlements, and thus are completely absent from the archaeological record.

THE LAPEDO CHILD

The 'Lapedo child' was found in the rockshelter of Lagar Velho, Portugal, in December 1998. Although the human remains themselves could not be dated, the animal bones and charcoal found with them place the burial firmly at c. 29,000 years ago, the 'Gravettian period'. The evidence indicates that a shallow pit was dug at the back of the shelter, and a branch of Scots pine was burned at the bottom. Then the child was placed in the pit; the fact that red ochre stains both the upper and lower surfaces of the bones and forms a clear boundary with the surrounding whitish sediment suggests strongly that the body was wrapped in an ochre-painted shroud. It lay in an extended position, with a young, dead rabbit placed across its lower legs, and with two red deer pelvises (perhaps meat offerings) by its shoulder and its feet. Round its neck was a perforated-shell pendant, while on its forehead was some kind of headdress made up of four canines from two different red deer stags and two hinds. Different methods of determining dental age at death give a mean of 4.7 years, and the skeletal age at death corresponds with this assessment.

Figure 1.1. a: The Lapedo burial in situ.

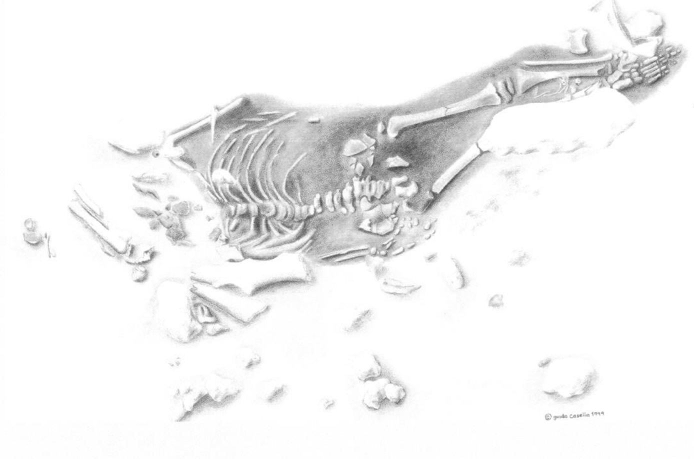

Figure 1.1. b: Drawing of the Lapedo burial.

From the start it was clear that this was an anatomically modern child – it has a chin and other modern features – but the bodily proportions, especially those of the legs, suggested some Neanderthal input. Overall, this child is clearly not a normal biologically modern human, and it displays an unusual mosaic of postcranial characteristics – especially in the lower limbs, but also in some features of the upper. In addition, it has a pitting of the occipital bone in the skull which some specialists consider virtually diagnostic of Neanderthals. Possible alternative explanations, such as nutritional or climatic factors, have been put forward for the child's odd proportions, but there is no evidence at all for malnutrition having stunted its growth, while exposure to a far colder climate had no similar effect on the proportions of the youngsters buried at Sunghir (pp. 24-28). No hypothesis fits the data better than the 'hybridisation' theory – that this child was part of a population descended from admixture between Neanderthals and Cro-Magnons (a name traditionally applied to modern humans) at the time of contact between them more than five millennia earlier.

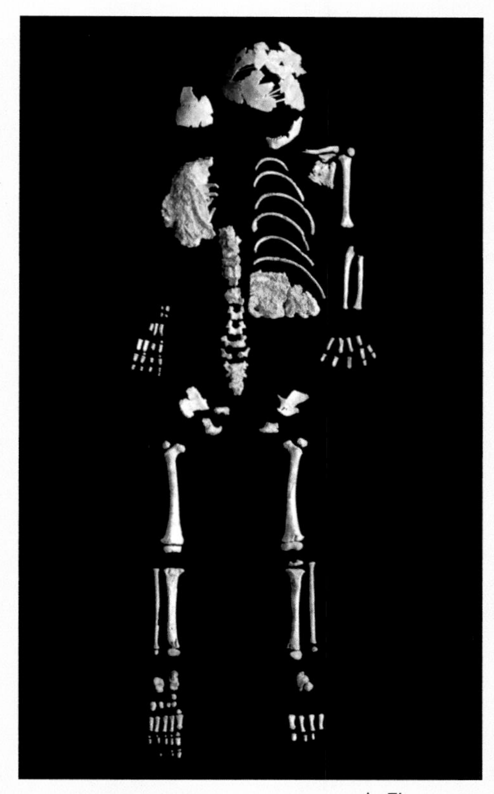

▲ *Figure 1.1. c: The Lapedo skeleton.*

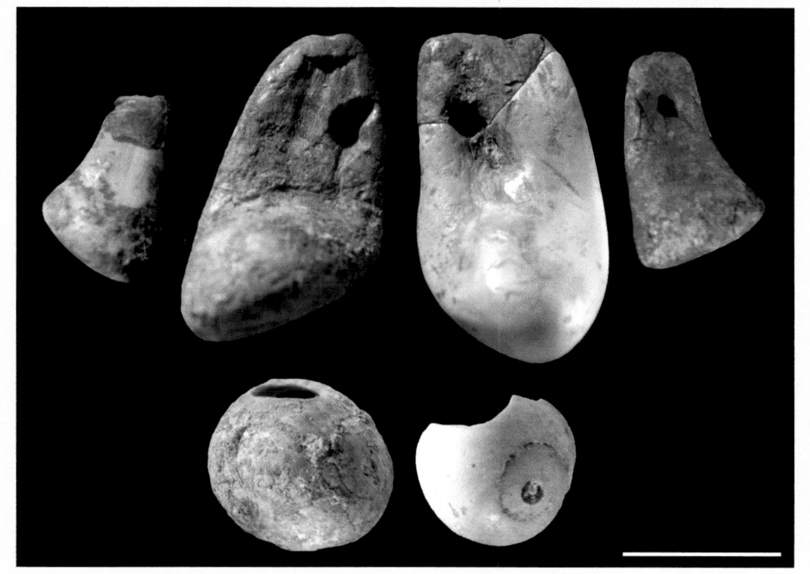

Figure 1.1. d: Some of the jewellery from the Lapedo burial.

In short, whenever you see a claim for life expectancy in the ice age, it's fake news! And the same applies to estimates of population in any period of the ice age or any region, let alone for Europe as a whole. We can only estimate how many people lived together as a group. Different ways of life will have required hunting territories of widely differing sizes, and we cannot simply assume that any region was completely and uniformly occupied by people, or that Europe was 'full' at any time. There must have been some very sparsely occupied areas, as there are today. At times, parts of south-west Europe clearly constituted refugia which became more densely occupied as other areas were depopulated due to extreme aridity and cold.

Based on numbers of sites known, there seems to have been an increase in population through the period, especially towards the end, in the Magdalenian – but even so, our methods of dating are still so imperfect that we cannot be sure how many of the sites are truly contemporaneous.

Cooperation must have been of crucial importance to ice age hunters, and – based on modern hunter-gatherers – it is usually assumed that the average hunting band comprised about five men, who stayed together and knew each other's strengths and weaknesses. So the band as a whole would have 10-12 adults, and 8-13 children – in short, a total of 20 to 25 people. But these figures are derived from historic and modern groups in often marginal environments. Are they applicable to the Upper Palaeolithic?

Occasionally we can be reasonably sure of numbers – for example, at Pincevent (p. 59), if there were four to six people in each of the 11 tents, then this group comprised several dozen people. At Mezhirich (p. 66), if each of the big huts housed one family, then there must have been at least 25 people in the village. But even these figures are tentative – after all, ten people will produce as much garbage in two months as five people in four, and in any case it is very hard to determine how long a site was inhabited for.

But where regions or periods are concerned, estimates differ so hugely that they are clearly no better than guesswork. For the Magdalenian of the Cantabrian coast, claims have ranged from 1000 to 22,000 people, whereas a recent study of Cantabria in the Solutrean has speculated that the population could have been as low as 500. For France in the Upper Palaeolithic, estimates range from 8000 to 50,000 or even 200,000! For the whole of Europe a total of 14,000 people has been put forward, or a minimum of 2300 and a maximum of 37,700; while one researcher suggested 500,000 for Iberia alone! Some of these figures are based on number of people per square kilometre (estimates vary from 0.1 to 6). Others are derived from the number of sites – but how many remain unknown to us? We have no idea what percentage has been found, or how many have been destroyed by nature or people, nor do we know which were occupied at the same time, or for how long. Finally, some figures are based on simulations of carrying capacity derived from climatic and vegetation models; or on a calculation that each individual hunter-gatherer would need 5-10 square kilometres for subsistence. All such figures depend on numerous variables that cannot really be factored in with any accuracy or confidence, and of course there will have been major fluctuations through time, especially in phases of climate change. In short, we have no true idea of population sizes for any region or period in the ice age.

It is thought that biologically modern humans arrived in Central Europe from the East, starting perhaps 46,000 years ago. Is there any way of knowing what they looked like? We have two sources of information: depictions produced during the ice age, and the reconstruction of faces based on skulls from the period. The latter technique has been much improved in recent decades, and gives us a reasonably accurate idea of how they looked – although, of course, details such as nose shape, skin and eye colour, and hair length and colour can only be guesswork (see the Cap Blanc lady, pp. 12-13). In the future, DNA analysis will help to elucidate some of these details – for example, it has already revealed that the young boy buried at Mal'ta (Siberia) 24,000 years ago had brown hair, brown eyes and freckled skin!

Humans were depicted rarely in the ice age, in comparison with the many hundreds of animal figures. And most images interpreted as humans are undetailed or exaggerated (many are prognathous, i.e. have faces that jut forwards), or are so sketchy that they are best described as 'anthropomorphs' or 'humanoids'. However, at one site in particular, the rock-shelter of La Marche, numerous human images are known, which seem to be portraits, caricatures and sketches (see Box).

Figure 1.2. The Magdalenian engraved, painted and sculpted head of a bearded man, fallen from the sculpted frieze at Angles-sur-l'Anglin (Vienne, France). 48 x 35 cm.

For decades, despite the steadily growing number of 'Venus figurines' (p. 9), it was believed that depictions of humans were rare in ice age imagery, and that they were badly done (even though many animal figures were equally incomplete or sketchy!). But the discoveries at La Marche showed that they are not so rare; their quality, together with that of the figures at nearby Angles-sur-l'Anglin, and that of the ivory head from Dolní Vestonice (p. 42), shows that realistic images of people were by no means taboo, as had often been supposed. Since it is clear that the artists could have depicted humans, had they wished to, the most plausible explanation for their scarcity is simply that such depictions were irrelevant to their purpose. One may suppose that the artists who produce the figures of Christ, the Virgin and saints for Christian churches could also make excellent animal images, but they do not do so because they are irrelevant to this religion.

Genitalia are rarely depicted on Palaeolithic humans, even on figurines, and pubic hair is

LA MARCHE

The great rock-shelter of La Marche (Vienne, France) is one of the most renowned sites of ice age imagery, thanks to the more than 2000 stone plaquettes and blocks bearing magnificent engravings of animals but also, and especially, of humans. Indeed, this gallery of human portraits and caricatures of about 17,000 years ago is unique and of huge importance. At least 115 quite realistic human figures are known among the engravings at the site, outnumbering all other species depicted here. The great scholar Léon Pales spent more than 25 years deciphering the site's engravings, which were published in four remarkable volumes.

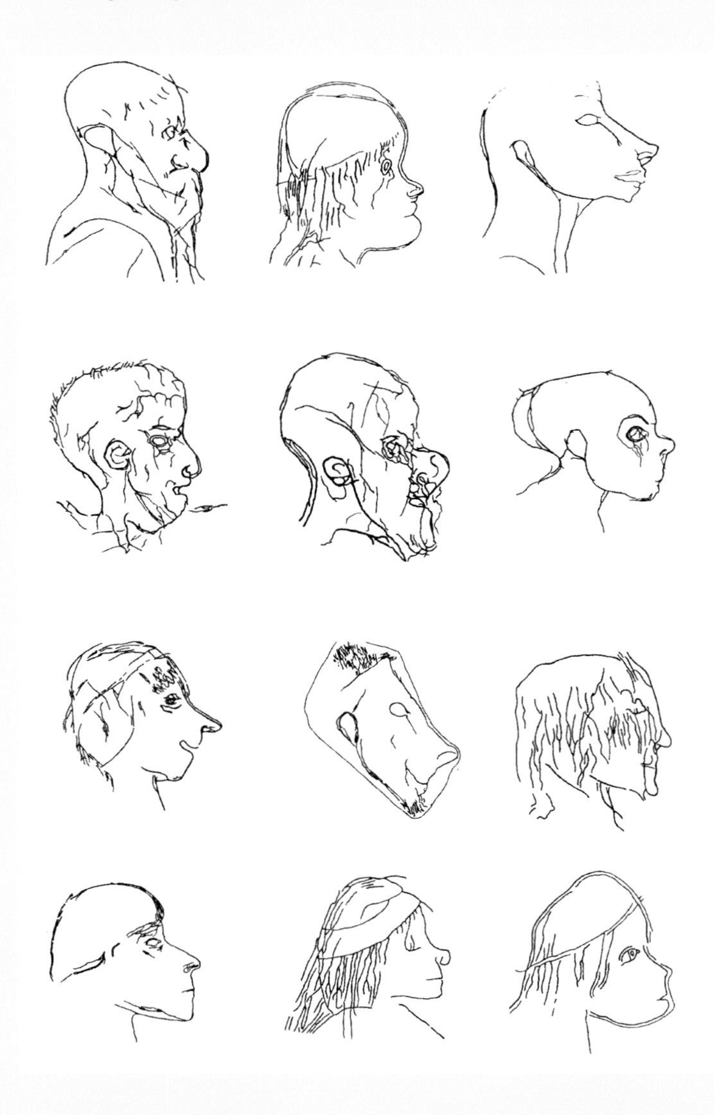

Figure 1.3. a: A selection of the human heads in profile, engraved on stone plaquettes at La Marche. Here they have been standardised for size and orientation. Note the variety of facial hair, hairstyles, headgear and facial expressions, and the wide range of nose- and face-shapes. The sixth head is thought to be that of a young infant.

Figure 1.3. b: Another engraved head from La Marche, showing a frontal view of a bald, bearded man. On the left is the complete recording of lines engraved on the plaquette, from which the head has been 'extracted'.

never shown. On bodies drawn in profile, the phallus can be seen, but the vulva cannot. A study of over 70 depictions of supposed males found that about one third were ithyphallic. Where genitals are absent, or on isolated heads, males can still be confidently recognised from beards and moustaches, whereas breasts denote females (assuming that bearded ladies and hermaphrodites were as rare in the Palaeolithic as they are today). At La Marche, using these criteria, there are 13 definite males (including 11 with beards). Three heads are seen full face at La Marche; all the others, together with 90% of the bodies, are in profile. Of 51 bodies drawn at the site, four are definitely male, but only 27 of the rest can confidently be seen as female: eight of these have breasts; the others have been identified on the basis of the size of hips and buttocks. Clear beards are also depicted on human figures at Les Espélugues (Fig. 1.4) and Vado all'Arancio in Italy (Fig. 1.5). We have no idea if men shaved, though sharp-edged flints could certainly have done the job. Depicted heads without facial hair have to be left 'neutral' – length of hair is not a sure guide. La Marche also shows us that baldness existed. We have a few indications of hairstyles, not only at La Marche, but also, for example, in the 'bun' on the ivory head from Dolní Vestonice (p. 42), and the long hair on the ivory head of Brassempouy (although, sadly, the authenticity of the latter carving is not certain).

◀ *Figure 1.4. The bearded man from Les Espélugues (Hautes-Pyrénées)*

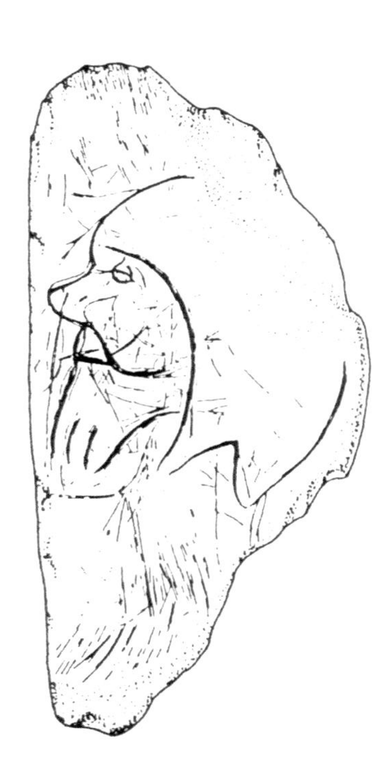

Figure 1.5. Tracing of an engraving of a bearded male profile on a small limestone plaque from Riparo di Vado all'Arancio (Grosseto, Italy). Final Epigravettian (c. 14,000 years old). It measures 40 mm high, 33 mm wide.

In Palaeolithic depictions of humans as a whole, details such as eyebrows, nostrils, navels, and nipples are extremely rare. The legs are often too short (as in the art of many later cultures), the legs and/or feet of figurines are held together or slightly apart, and the female figurines of the Russian Plain usually have bent knees. Few figures have hands or fingers drawn in any detail (examples include La Marche, the 'Venuses' of Laussel [p. 232] and Willendorf [p. 107], the man in the Lascaux shaft-scene [p. 115], etc). More than 75% of female statuettes have arms depicted, usually held close to the body for technical reasons (most are symmetrical, a few asymmetrical), and in more than 70% of these the arms are directed to specific points rather than just hanging at the sides – only four have the arms directed to the breasts, while in 28 the arms rest on the abdomen. Since it would be more normal to have the hands clasped at the pubic level, this has been seen as significant, and perhaps links these particular figurines to pregnancy (see below). On other figures, the arms may be at the sides, raised horizontally (as on the Sous-Grand-Lac man), or up in the air – all these poses are represented at La Marche.

Except for the two ivory heads mentioned above, very few statuettes (apart from those of Siberia) have any kind of facial detail; their heads are held erect or tilt forward slightly (though one from Kostenki tilts upward). Many Palaeolithic humans are headless; in some cases, as in the female bas-reliefs of Angles-sur-l'Anglin (p. 160), it is clear that they never had heads. The same is true of 9

FEMALE FIGURINES

The (mostly Gravettian) female figurines, irritatingly and erroneously nicknamed 'Venuses', and found from France to Russia, have been presented in so many art histories and popular works on prehistory that they have come to characterise the ice age and its depiction of women. This is unfortunate, partly because such statuettes are rare when seen against the timescale of 30 millennia, and because the constant display of a few specimens with extreme proportions presents a distorted view.

Early scholars tried to use them as evidence of different races during the period, interpreting the obese ones as steatopygous, i.e. having the special fatty deposits which produce the massive, high and wide buttocks of some female 'Bushmen' and 'Hottentots'. In fact most of them merely present proportions which one can see anytime anywhere on women who have produced lots of children, or even on women who have never given birth! In short, the figurines have no value whatsoever as indicators of race.

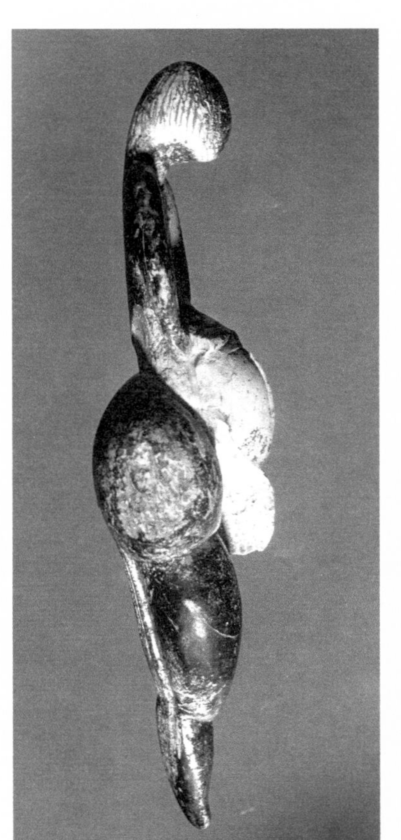

Only four (Lespugue, and one each from Willendorf, Grimaldi and Gagarino) have really extreme proportions, and only Lespugue has truly monumental breasts. On the whole, the obese carvings are not anatomically abnormal – they are simply bodies worn and altered by age and childbearing. They seem well-nourished, with their adipose tissue concentrated in discrete areas rather than spread out as a continuous layer. The depiction of fat women has been

Figure 1.6. ◀ a: The 'Venus' of Lespugue (Haute-Garonne) seen from the side. Ivory, probably Gravettian. Height: 14.7 cm.
▼ b: Big fragment of a limestone female figure from Kostenki I (Russia), measuring 13.5 cm. Her bracelets are joined at the front like handcuffs.

argued to represent an imaginary and 'idealized' female – stressing desirability and fecundity – or, alternatively, to correspond to reality. The realistic folds of tissue do suggest the artists were very familiar with these conditions.

One theory is that a genetic anomaly occurred, and that the resulting corpulent women held a fascination for our ancestors. On the other hand, the extensive distribution of such images in Eurasia strongly implies that obese women were not uncommon. But how could women in active, highly mobile hunter-gatherer communities achieve such proportions? It has been suggested that this may have been due to semi-sedentism and short-term high caloric input, if these depictions are accurate. Ethnographic studies overwhelmingly describe hunter-gatherer women as highly active, and the idea that women in prehistory sat around a fire all day raising children and cooking and eating so much that they became obese – an ice age version of a pandemic lockdown! – is unlikely to be a realistic one. However, girls and women do require a certain amount of body fat to start menstruating and to reproduce, and both obesity and severe malnutrition make it far harder to become pregnant.

It is clear that the numerous figurines vary widely, and appear to depict women throughout their adult life – though one cannot accurately estimate the age of the females represented – and with a wide range of physiological conditions, often involving pregnancy or, in a few cases,

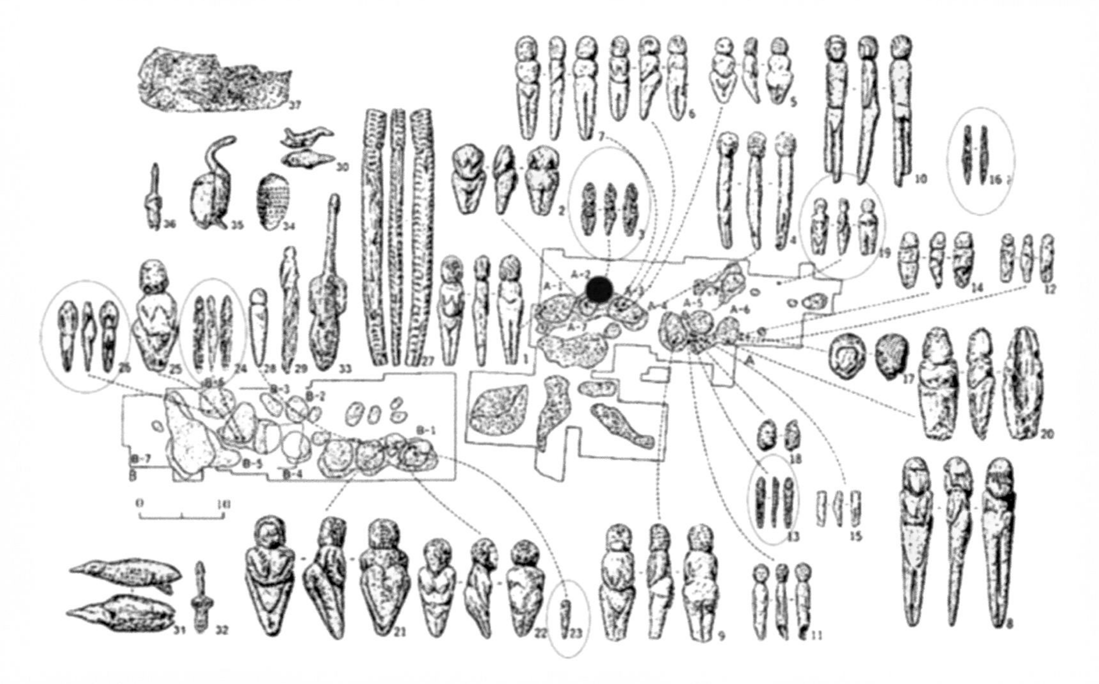

Figure 1.6. c: Plan of the Mal'ta excavation. The central dot marks the child burial, and child figurines are circled in red.

possibly childbirth (e.g. a figurine from Kostenki XIII). This would help explain why the breasts and abdomen are constantly emphasised, but not the thighs and buttocks (except in some west European examples), let alone the head and extremities. The small, slim Siberian figurines, on the other hand, are utterly different, with a total absence of any accentuation of the female anatomy.

Some researchers have seen the carvings as anatomically realistic, and have even attempted to assess whether they are pregnant or not, or whether they have had children in the past and even how many. However, one needs to bear in mind that the notion that each figure was meant to represent a female of a precise age and physical state is a theory, a possibility, not an accepted fact. Indeed some female researchers have cautioned against over-interpretation and treating the depictions as photographically accurate. Besides, it has been shown that these physical features can be found in non-pregnant women and in non-mothers, i.e. that one cannot distinguish mothers from non-mothers by shape, and that one cannot generalise in this way about the female form, such is its enormous physical variation and such is the stylisation of these little carvings.

Overall, it is extremely unlikely that – contrary to the beliefs of some male researchers – the figurines were the equivalent of *Playboy* pinups and made to titillate adolescent boys. Although sexual attributes dominate in some of the figures, these are sexual attributes to our modern western eyes. Not all societies see women in the same way, and modesty is culture specific, as can be seen in the covering of hair and the use of veils; for example, breasts have a primary function and are not seen as sexual in many cultures.

engraved humans at La Marche, but others at this site and elsewhere may have had their heads broken off, either purposely or accidentally.

Children are very rarely depicted in Palaeolithic art (perhaps even non-existent apart from the supposed baby of Gönnersdorf, p. 180), though some specialists believe that a few of the humans of La Marche (pp. 6-7) may be infants on the basis of head shape and bodily proportions, and that some of the small human figurines from Mal'ta may represent different stages of childhood. Gönnersdorf may also have yielded the oldest known depiction of childbirth, although it is very sketchy (p. 174).

Many more people today are right-handed than left-handed, but can we trace this same pattern far back in prehistory? Once again, ice age imagery can be of some help. On cave walls there are hundreds of hand stencils – where a left hand has been stencilled, one would think that this implies the artist was right-handed, and vice versa, but only if we assume the hand was stencilled palm-downwards! Even though the paint was often sprayed from the mouth, one can suppose that the dominant hand assisted in the operation. Of 158 hand stencils in the French Pyrenean cave of Gargas, 136 have been identified as left and only 22 as right. Moreover, in the few cases where ice age figures are depicted holding something, it is mostly, though not always, in the right hand.

In most cases, fine engravings on cave walls are almost invisible when lit from the front, but 'leap out' when lit from the side. This fact is of some importance, for it also provides an indication of whether the artist was right- or left-handed. Right-handed artists tend to have their light-source on the left, to prevent the shadow of their hand falling on the burin (engraving tool) or brush, and accordingly the majority of Palaeolithic parietal engravings are best lit from the left (in portable engravings, too, the proportion of right- and left-handers is similar to that of today). Occasionally, however, one comes across the work of a southpaw – for example, Gargas cave has many engravings, including a fine, detailed pair of front legs of a horse. These had been known and admired for decades, but one day, when visiting scholars lit the figure from the right instead of the left, they were suddenly confronted with the rest of the horse, which nobody had seen before!

At the reindeer-hunters' camp of Pincevent (p. 59), the distribution of flint-knapping debris can indicate whether the knappers were right- or left-handed. Sometimes, skeletal evidence is available – for example, in the boy known as Sunghir 2 (pp. 24-28), whose musculature clearly showed that he was right-handed and had probably done a great deal of throwing spears or harpoons. The

CAP BLANC

Another intriguing example of handedness is the Magdalenian sculpted frieze of Cap Blanc (Dordogne), which comprises six horses, several bison and one or two deer heads. Close examination of the carvings and the direction of tool-blows had suggested to some researchers that the artist had been left-handed. An adult skeleton was found buried beneath the centre

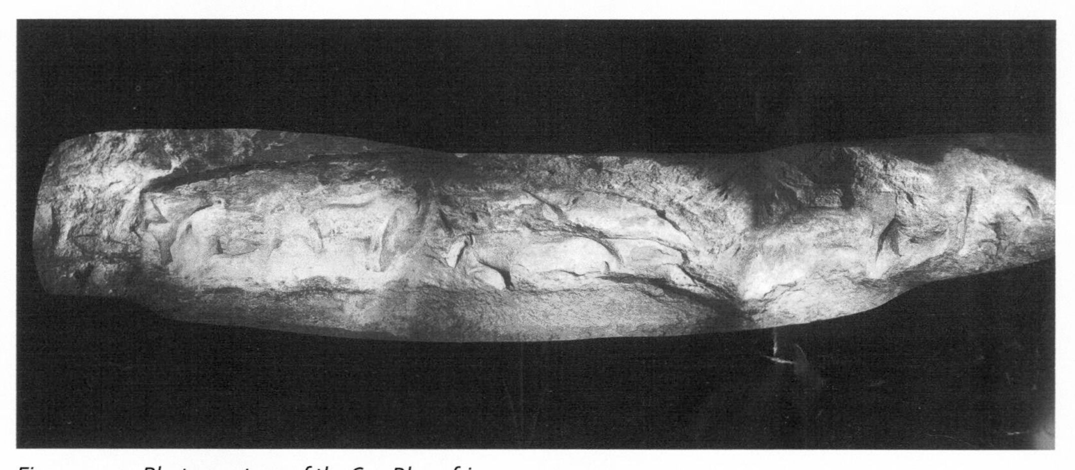

Figure 1.7. a: Photomontage of the Cap Blanc frieze.

of the frieze; it was dug up in 1911, and subsequently sold to the Field Museum in Chicago. Long thought to be a male, it was subsequently identified by more detailed analysis as a female, probably aged between 25 and 35. In 2001 a cast of her skeleton was acquired and placed in its rightful location beneath the frieze; the anthropologist who positioned the cast noticed that she had greater muscular development on the left and was thus left-handed. So it is possible that she was the sculptor, buried in a place of honour in front of her work. A fine facial reconstruction of this young woman was produced a few years ago.

Figure 1.7. b: Cast of the Cap Blanc skeleton in front of the sculpted frieze's central horse.

Figure 1.7. c: Reconstruction of the woman's head by Elisabeth Daynès

adult male (Sunghir 1) and the other child (Sunghir 3) were also right-handed. A study of 'thrower's elbow' (see below, p. 17) found that it was far more common in the right elbow than in the left.

Artifacts can also sometimes provide clues; for example, the bit of ice age rope found in Lascaux cave (p. 91) consisted of fibres spiralling to the right, and was therefore tressed by a right-hander.

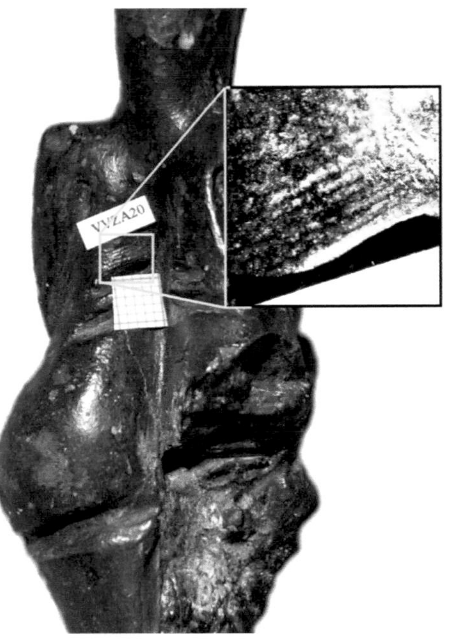

Figure 1.8. a: The terracotta 'venus' from Dolní Vestonice (Czech Republic). b: Child's fingerprint on the figurine's back.

Tracks and traces

It is quite possible that tattoos, body paint and scarification may have existed, but until soft tissue is found on a frozen corpse (like that of the tattooed Copper Age Iceman or those from Scythian burial mounds), we cannot know. Outside of depictions and hand prints/stencils, our only knowledge of ice age soft tissue comes from footprints, and also a few fingerprints preserved on pieces of fired clay of c. 26,000 years ago from Dolní Vestonice and Pavlov – it is interesting that some of these belong to children (about 10 years of age), as well as subadults and women; no adult males have yet been detected.

One child's fingerprint has been detected on the back of the famous fired-clay figurine known as the 'Venus of Dolní Vestonice' from Moravia (Czech Republic), dating to about 25,000 years ago. Analysis suggests that the finger belonged to a child aged between seven and 15, most likely around 11. But the analysts understandably deny that such a masterful work of art could have been produced by that child.

Ice age prints of bare feet (as well as occasional hands and knees) are known from many caves (especially in France), where they can provide intriguing information (see pp. 192-195); but they have also been found preserved in the open-air in Australia and New Mexico.

In Australia, in the Willandra Lakes region of New South Wales, a series of 124 prints have been found, dating to 19,000 - 23,000 years ago, and covering an area of 700 sq m. They were made by at least eight individuals – adults, adolescents and children – crossing what was then a moist muddy surface in an arid region at the height of the last ice age. They were moving in all directions, some running and others walking. Aboriginal trackers were asked to examine the site, and they revealed that some prints were those of a man without a left foot or leg. Since he could not have hopped for any distance, he must have had a support pole, and a number of small circular or oval impressions are indeed thought to have been made by implements, such as the base of spears used as support poles or walking sticks – one never puts a spear in the ground point first because that blunts it. The trackers interpreted other marks as made by the dragging of sticks or a branch, possibly to build a fire somewhere.

In New Mexico, one set of tracks in White Sands National Monument appears to have been made by humans stalking or harassing (and possibly hunting) giant ground sloths, whose tracks are also present [Fig. 1.9]. Another set in the same area constitutes the longest Late Pleistocene-age double trackway known, with an out- and return-journey of more than 1.5 km. It seems to have been made by an adolescent or small adult female who was carrying a young child in at least one direction at a steady but fast pace, but the child – probably under 3 years of age – also walked at times. Occasionally their bare feet slipped and slid in the mud. Between the two journeys, their tracks were overprinted by giant ground sloth and mammoth.

Ice age people probably had an excellent sense of direction, like hunter-gatherers today. They were almost certainly fitter than most of us – as shown

Figure 1.9. Human footprint inside that of a giant sloth, White Sands (New Mexico).

by their living up steep slopes, their rock climbing, and their exploration of physically strenuous, difficult and inaccessible parts of deep caves (pp. 184-186). Did they perhaps have senses superior to ours – such as more acute hearing, better discrimination of smells, or keener eyesight, especially in the dark? Even today, in any population, a small number of people are hypersensitive to colour, smell and taste. It is known that some modern Australian Aborigines can detect the presence of other humans up to 2 km away from the smell of faeces around their camp. They were certainly far more used to moving around and carrying out activities in semi-darkness than we are today, but where their senses are concerned, like their feelings and emotions, we can only speculate. These aspects of ice age people do not fossilize!

Similarly, can we assume that they had better memories than ours (pp. 215-19)? Theirs was an oral culture with no external storage of information (except in imagery), and hence they must have relied on stories and myths. Since they lacked our knowledge, they were unable to explain scientifically the phenomena around them – rainbows, clouds, echoes, tides, weather patterns, reflections in water, and everything in the sky, etc. We have in our possession the accumulated and documented knowledge of all the civilisations that came before us. Their oral culture did not have these benefits, but needed stories and myths to be handed down successfully from one generation to the next.

What we can safely say about ice age people is that they were not just hugely knowledgeable about the natural world, but they also displayed tremendous manual and technical skills, together with immense patience and endurance. They had remarkable powers of physical and psychological adaptation to their very particular environmental conditions. They applied their considerable intelligence to surviving in a frequently hostile world.

The division of labour – did women hunt?

It has been a long-accepted tradition that men and women were assigned different economic roles in prehistory. Man was the hunter, the protector of women, and had the most important role, and women did their bit by raising offspring and roasting the meat that the ice age hero brought home. It was a long time before this view was seriously disputed.

In the late 1980s a number of female researchers challenged the assumption that 'hunting' was solely the domain of males; they argued that the importance of hunting for meat had long been exaggerated while the contribution of foraging and fishing had been neglected. Gradually the idea grew that a 'cooperative food-collecting approach' would have been more successful than assigning sex-appropriate roles to different activities.

The near universal division of labour in modern hunter-gatherer societies may not have emerged during, or until after the end of the ice age – in part due to the small population numbers. Or it may have varied depending on a number of factors over time or across the vast area of Eurasia. Consequently, as gender differences in the past remain invisible, we cannot confidently assume anything about the roles of men and women in prehistoric cultures. What is more likely than assigned roles is that men and women gained 'status' that was earned by fulfilling their obligations to their own family's or group's survival. This would be especially so if men were frequently absent either hunting, exploring or trading. It does, however, seem highly probable that, even if women were 'house bound' when child rearing became a priority, they would have been capable of hunting and butchering animals – particularly smaller species – and manufacturing their own tool kit. If their partners failed to return from their excursions they would soon need to fall back on being self-sufficient in order to survive. The logical conclusion is that ice age women could hunt and make tools, even if these activities declined during times of pregnancy and rearing their young.

One may assume that strong, agile women would have been just as capable of hunting as men. However, among modern hunter-gatherers the hunting of big game is almost entirely a male pursuit, and it is highly probable that the same applied in the past. One study of a small number of ice age human skeletons has found that evidence of 'thrower's elbow' – i.e. lesions of tendon attachments at the elbow – occurs almost exclusively in males, indicating that they preferentially employed movements involving the strenuous throwing of projectiles. It seems that women did not.

Pursuing big game is likely to have been a predominantly male activity for a number of reasons, most importantly because hunting as a family would have put the children at risk; and if carrying a child in a sling or cradleboard (see p. 106), the women would presumably have been slower chasing down an animal and even vulnerable during such an activity – as we shall see (p. 29), this may explain the infant with a flint in its backbone.

One could argue that it would have been the accompanying infants and children who would have made both tracking and hunting extremely difficult – particularly when trying to ensure that they remained quiet. These practicalities, and the desire to protect their youngsters, would have been the most likely driver for this traditional division of labour, which is frequently observed in modern hunter-gatherers. This was not because women lacked the necessary skill-set or the desire; nor does it mean that women were always restricted to the campsite or domestic space and never participated in hunting – especially those women who were either too young or too old to be nursing infants or caring for children. It also makes sense that if women were without the support of men, as may well have occurred at times, they had the prerequisite skills to be self-sufficient in every way.

A final consideration is the force required to kill a large animal such as a wild reindeer or bison. Moreover, after the animal has been wounded and brought down, there is still the matter of slaughtering a (perhaps struggling) beast, and then butchering and transporting the carcass. The strength required for

GENDERS – RIGID OR FLUID?

In the last 50 years our views have radically altered regarding gender and gender roles, and these have recently become a much discussed topic, moving beyond the roles of men and women in our modern society to a dialogue about the individual's gender identity – i.e. an inner feeling of being male or female, both or neither. This may be the same as the sex a person was assigned at birth, or not.

Since there is little in the archaeological record that can shed light on whether 'gendering' was an issue in the Upper Palaeolithic, we are reliant again on ethnographic data to enlighten us as to the possibility of this having a long history, and if 'identity' as an issue was something that mattered to our early ancestors.

Early 19th-century chroniclers noted that several North American tribes, including the Sioux, recognised the possibility of an individual not being male or female but of having a third gender. These individuals were called Berdaches or two-spirit people, and were considered to have shaman status. It was also observed that amongst the Chumash, Mono, Yokuts and Tübatulabal tribes of California there was a small group of men who lived 'like women' – with the same clothing, jewellery and adornments as their female counterparts. These Indian (men), who were called Joyas (jewels in Spanish), were specialists in funeral and mourning rituals; and it was believed they had spiritual powers. Their existence was also recorded by Catholic Church officials who wrote that the Joyas' 'carnal acts' with same-sex partners were a sin against God!

Some cultures recognise the ability of an individual to change gender. Among the Chukchi of Siberia seven gender categories are identified, and gender transformations can take place when shamans enter 'trance states' to perform ceremonies. Divine actions can result in a change of gender or gender fluidity: the rainbow serpent god Ungud (the creator of life) in the mythology of several Aboriginal groups of northwestern Australia is described as sometimes male, and sometimes female. It is also worth noting that a number of ancient folk heroes from a variety of cultures can be both men and women at the same time. In Norse mythology, Loki is a trickster who has the ability to shape-shift and change sex.

In the past, some Palaeolithic skeletons were simply misidentified as to their sex – the famous 'Red Lady of Paviland' was in fact a man, while the Cap Blanc man turned out to be a woman (pp. 12-13). But in a few cases, the anatomical sex was hard to determine – most notably the younger child at Sunghir (p. 19), and the central skeleton at Dolní Vestonice (p. 42). In both cases, only genetics could finally prove that these supposed females were in fact males. These were clearly unusual individuals, and this was presumably reflected in their appearance and behaviour. Some modern societies such as the Inuit, Native Americans and Siberians are very sensitive to such differences, and any physical or psychological peculiarities are believed to have some purpose and can evoke respect and/or fear.

As we have shown (p. 16), early investigators – who were mostly male – had deeply entrenched views about gender roles in the past.

undertaking these tasks should not be underestimated; and, although ice age women were no doubt fit and strong, ice age men would certainly have been even more suited to these physical demands as either individuals or small bands.

Recent claims have been made by feminist scholars that males were not dominant in the last ice age, and that females were emancipated 'working women' with the same rights as men, and performing the same economic activities as them. There is very little ethnographic support for this view. However, what is generally ignored in this debate is the likelihood that, if men were engaged in hunting away from the home base, women would have shouldered the crucial role of teaching children the important skills they needed for survival (see p. 187), and this may have been considered the more important role in these early communities.

Although they are very much the exception rather than the rule, Agta hunter-gatherer women in the Philippines are known to participate in hunting large game. Even though Agta men hunt and fish full-time, Agta women often bring home half the meat consumed by the group, and many women participate in activities associated with hunting, such as tracking animals. Both young and older women hunt, and those with youngsters carry them in slings. This keeps their infants safe, and close enough to feed, while their arms remain free to use hunting spears. They also report pregnancy is in no way a disadvantage, and they have no trouble running up hills to chase animals!

One recent publication has challenged the 'man-the-hunter' hypothesis, but does it provide any concrete evidence that women hunted in prehistory, and hence that such activities were not necessarily sexually differentiated? The 9000-year-old remains of a young adult were excavated at the Andean highland site of Wilamaya Patjxa (Peru), buried with a 'hunter's tool kit' comprising projectile points and animal-processing tools. Osteological analysis revealed this young person had been around 18 years old at death, but the claim that it is a female remains inconclusive.

This discovery raised the issue of whether any graves in antiquity have unjustifiably and automatically been assumed to be male, as was the case for the two Sunghir children (see pp. 24-28) – Sunghir 2 aged 11-13, and Sunghir 3 aged 9-10. Initially they were both thought to be male, and this assumption was probably due in part to the presence of weapons in their grave. Certainly, early genetic analysis claimed that Sunghir 2 was a boy and Sunghir 3 a girl; more recent DNA testing, however, has strongly indicated that both are male. So the Sunghir case is a valuable object lesson in being cautious before jumping to conclusions of any kind.

An even more extreme example of this type of erroneous bias is the recent discovery that a Viking Age burial from Birka, Sweden – an extraordinarily rich grave filled with weapons – is that of a woman. Since its excavation in 1878 it had always been seen as the grave of a high-status professional male warrior, but osteological and especially genetic analyses have proved conclusively that this was a woman. Of course, one cannot be sure that she actually used the weapons. But bearing in mind such widespread myths as 'amazons' and 'valkyries' one inevitably wonders how many other graves containing weapons and hunting equipment have been similarly misattributed to males!

Where insights into the possible division of labour are concerned, we are forced to turn to ethnographic sources, and some of the best analogies for ice age Europe are to be found in subarctic reindeer hunters. For example, in some Canadian Indian communities both men and women hunt and fish, but men spend more time hunting big game, while women spend more time fishing and snaring small game – they rarely take caribou, even though no taboo restricts them. The difference is probably a result of the rule that child care tends to restrict women to repetitive, interruptible, non-dangerous tasks that do not require extensive excursions. There is a notable contrast between the attachment of women (and children and old men) to the domestic space of the camp, and the journeys undertaken by the men hunting big game.

In and around camp, the women spend a great deal of time preparing skins, sewing garments, cutting and drying meat or fish, cooking meals, and tending their families. Men make and repair equipment, split firewood, skin animals (especially for furs), and do a variety of home-oriented jobs. Among the Cree, both boys and girls are expected and encouraged to extract necessities from the wild beyond the home.

In subarctic Canadian Indian communities, every adult has to be skilled in meeting all the necessities of life, but men and women have different powers. There are male and female domains within their lodges, and male and female possessions. But the separations are symbolic, relative, shifting and ephemeral.

Figure 1.10. Aymara woman in 1988, Lakaya village, Lake Titicaca, Bolivia. She is working on a horizontal loom using a pick made from a llama legbone.

Every adult woman has her own cooking fire; the hearth marks the woman's gender and age status. Men make cooking fires for themselves when out in the bush. In many cases, men work with hard materials while women work with soft, pliable and perishable materials.

If one can assume that this was also often the case in the ice age, it helps explain why women's activities have been hard to detect in the archaeological record, because soft organic materials disintegrate and do not usually survive, unlike stone, bone, antler and ivory. In subarctic Alaska, almost two-thirds of Ingalik products are (or include) cords and lines which are essential for snares and traps, nets, packing, and sewing. Making lines is an interruptible, repetitive, safe, in-camp activity that is compatible with child care. The women probably also wove baskets, bags and mats, and sewed birch-bark and skin containers (see pp. 98-99).

However, it is important to note that such a division of materials is too simplistic, since we know in modern hunter-gatherer societies that women can and do make tools of stone and other hard materials, while men are equally capable of making lines and nets. Similarly, where cave and rock art is concerned, it was traditionally assumed – by the almost exclusively male scholars – that only men were artists, and that the imagery reflected male preoccupations of hunting and sex. We now know that this is nonsense, and since women do produce rock art in other cultures – such as in Australia – there is no reason whatsoever to assume that all, or even most, ice age imagery was created by men. There are, however, rare instances where the sex of the artist can be assumed; for example, the great bison on the Altamira ceiling were drawn with such extensive and sweeping lines and domination of space that the artist was almost certainly a man (although one cannot rule out the possibility that it was an unusually big woman).

Figure 1.11. A now lost painting by Paul-Joseph Jamin (1853-1903) showing an early 20th-century view of a Cro-Magnon artist at work – in such works, the artist is always a white bearded male while female admirers are topless or naked!

Contrary to some recent claims, it is by no means easy to 'sex' the hand stencils in ice age caves – modern studies of hand stencils made by Australian Aborigines, European students and other groups have all shown that there is a tremendous overlap between those made by females, adolescents and small males. It is therefore yet another myth that the ice age hand stencils were made either by predominantly men or predominantly women. It is very hard to obtain reliable measurements of Palaeolithic hand stencils, and the sexing of hands is also difficult due to differences caused by the technique, the position of the hand and the wall, etc. Experiments in making hand stencils have resulted in varied measurements which might suggest different sexes – in short, one individual can produce very different stencils!

Feeding the ice age family

Life in the Upper Palaeolithic could be harsh or pleasant, depending on climatic and environmental fluctuations. At times there would have been plenty of food even in the areas close to glaciers, since periglacial environments are rich in flora and fauna. For example the Gravettian campsite of Dolní Vestonice in Moravia lay in a broad valley with grasslands, forests and the river Danube housing small herds of reindeer and horses. Yet a thousand kilometres to the north lay a 300 m high great wall of ice.

Despite the idyllic image often presented of ice age life, it is not unusual for the skeletons from this period to display evidence of phases of slow growth caused by starvation or illness during childhood and later. Reconstructing the diet patterns and what foodstuffs these early communities consumed can tell us a great deal about their health. However, it's impossible to know how stable the food supply was from one season to the next, or year on year, and we can only imagine the stress and anxiety caused by food shortages. These might suddenly happen as a consequence of the climate deteriorating, animals changing their migratory pattern, or plants and tubers failing to materialise, leaving whole communities with a dire lack of food.

Whether or not Palaeolithic populations were healthier than we are now – that is, before the onset of agriculture and the subsequent changes in diet that it brought – has been a frequently debated topic.

Dietary requirements

It is worth considering what the requirements are for a healthy diet, and how many calories a day an individual would need in order to stay in good condition. Today, a Western man needs 2700 kcal per day, and a woman 2000; these figures vary depending on age, weight and way of life, and certainly decrease as they grow old. But ice age people – in view of the often stringent climate, their physical exertions, and the lack of modern conveniences and heating – must have needed more, so for them one can perhaps estimate 3000 per day as an average: perhaps only 1300-1600 on rest days, but 3600 on hunting days. A pregnant woman would also have needed more, because breastfeeding needs another 500 per day for a daily production of 800 ml of milk.

It has been calculated that a family of seven (adults and children) at 0° C would need a minimum of 15,000 - 20,000 calories a day, which is the equivalent of 25 lbs of meat. A tundra reindeer, for example, would yield 75 lbs of meat, so it's likely they would need at least one carcass every 3 - 4 days if it was supplemented with other foods. Thus it goes without saying that it requires a large animal population to support a community of hunter-gatherers.

However, resources in their habitats were always finite, and guaranteeing a long-term food supply before farming arose would have been difficult if not impossible. Periods of starvation are very likely to have occurred over the twenty or so millennia of the last ice age.

It is certain that there were a great number of variations in the ice age diet, and even 'back-up' strategies, but it has also been suggested that these early human populations were able to tolerate a reduced-calorie diet as an adaptive response when food resources were limited. Over the millennia people may have evolved through natural selection to tolerate a restricted diet, and this enabled later populations to remain strong, fit and healthy even through long periods of food shortages. Moreover, by co-operating as extended families and communities, they would have been better equipped to survive the unexpected and highly diverse living conditions during the ice age.

Any discussion about dietary and nutritional requirements must consider that people around the world have adapted to a multitude of specialised diets, some influenced by cultural tradition and others by the availability of produce and livestock. For example, some diets are high in protein, especially in colder climates; a traditional Inuit diet, for example, derives 50% of its calorific intake from fat, and 30-35% from protein through eating raw meat. Breadfruit, which is high in carbohydrates like potatoes, has been the staple food in the Pacific for more than 3000 years and is now widely cultivated in the Caribbean and other tropical regions. Populations living in regions at high altitude or in other colder climates need food rich in calories derived from fat and protein, whereas populations in low latitudes use carbohydrates and eat less fat and protein.

So it seems that around the world people have found many alternatives in order to create a sustainable diet, and our ice age ancestors, no doubt, ate everything that was available and possible to eat.

Health, of course, is not just dependent on diet, but also on a suite of factors that include fitness, fertility, longevity, population growth, environmental stresses, disease, adequate shelter, etc. What evidence from the ice age can shed light on some of these factors?

SUNGHIR

Sunghir is an open-air seasonal site on the banks of the Klyasma River near the town of Vladimir, about 320 km northeast of Moscow. It was excavated several times between 1956 and 1977, under the guidance of Otto Bader, and appears to have been occupied for extensive periods – perhaps even as long as 2000 - 3000 years – between 30,000 and 22,000 bp.

The archaeological material recovered from the site indicates that its communities were well adapted to living there, even in severe conditions, as they had suitable dwellings and appropriate clothing, and at times the climate may have been relatively mild. The Sunghirians, it seems, were physically fit and well developed, indicating that they walked or even ran long distances over rugged terrain.

During the warmer periods, the earth would have been soft enough for people to dig pits and graves into what otherwise would have been frozen ground. The full glacial conditions that followed seem to have protected the graves in the permafrost (permanently frozen soil). Excavations revealed that at least ten of its occupants perished at Sunghir, and were buried at the site with variable treatment, revealing signs that a clan social system could have evolved for these prehistoric hunters.

In 1964, the first human remains were discovered: a female skull (Sunghir 5) and, below this, a grave containing an almost complete skeleton of a tall male (approaching 1.82 cm) with very broad shoulders and a heavy build. In all probability he was right-handed. His teeth were healthy, and he

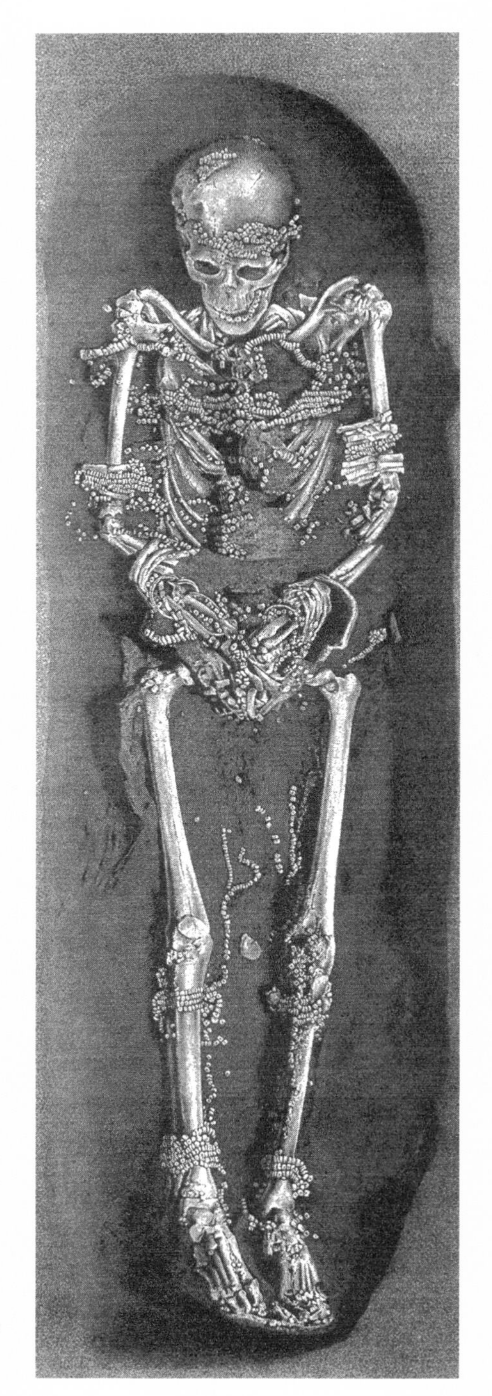

Figure 1.12. a: Drawing of Sunghir 1.

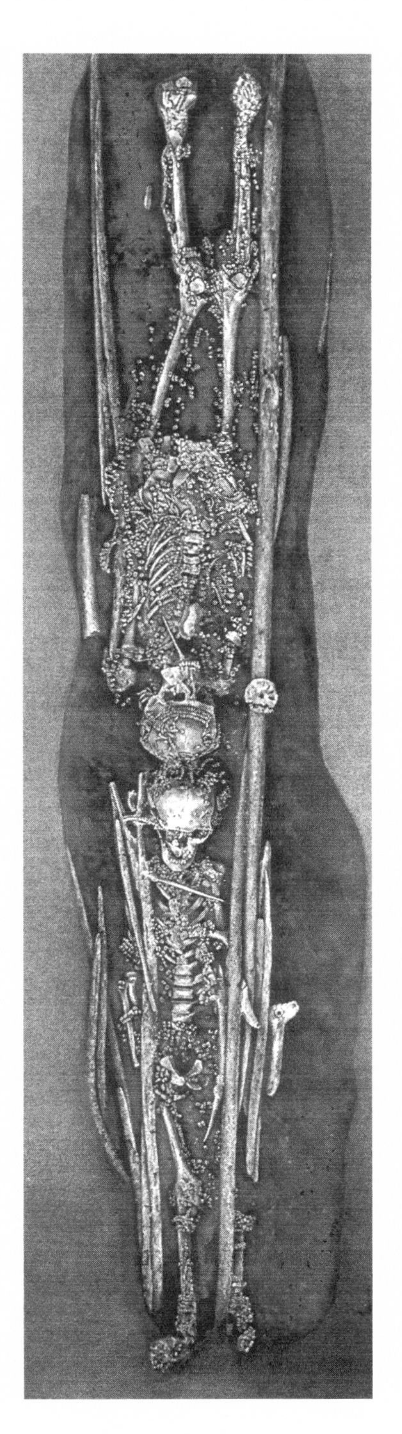

was at least 45 years of age or even older at death. Sunghir 1, as he became known, appears to have died from an incision in the lower neck into the first thoracic vertebra (see p. 29).

He was placed in an extended position in a shallow grave; his head and upper body were extensively covered in red ochre. The burial included rich grave goods and around 3500 mammoth ivory beads on the skeleton – indicating either that he wore decorated clothing, or that the beads had been strung around his chest, shoulders, elbows, wrists and ankles – along with 25 mammoth ivory armbands, a pebble pendant and 12 pierced fox canines on his forehead. According to Bader's reconstruction of his attire, Sunghir man was wearing fur coats resembling those of modern Arctic people with long trousers, moccasin-type footwear and a poncho-type overcoat (pp. 110-11). This individual must have been a significant person in his community, considering his fine apparel, and the richness of the grave goods.

Five years after Sunghir 1 was discovered, and about 3 m away, the badly preserved remains of an adult male (Sunghir 10) were uncovered. Underneath his remains, excavators found a long shallow grave, containing the well-preserved remains of two children in what is considered one of the richest, most spectacular, and complex burials from the Upper Palaeolithic period.

The children had been placed head-to-head on their backs and, like Sunghir 1, with their hands positioned across their pelvic region; their remains were covered in red ochre. As mentioned earlier, their ages were estimated to be around 11-13 years for the older child (Sunghir 2), and around 9-10 years for the younger (Sunghir 3). These ages were estimated on the basis of their dental development and long bones, but should be taken as approximations.

Figure 1.12. b: Drawing of Sunghir 2/3.

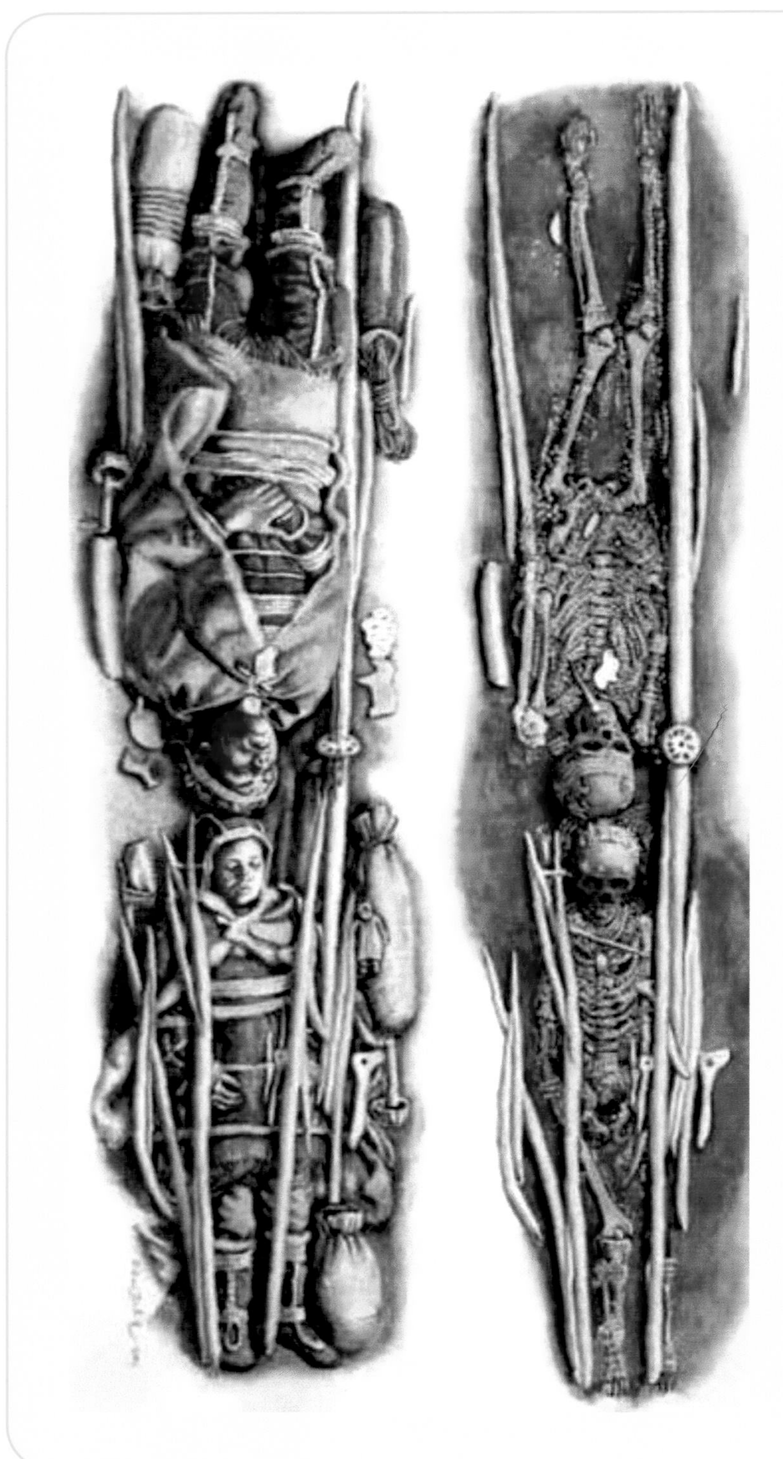

The children's almost intact remains were dressed in clothing and headgear that had been elaborately decorated with thousands of mammoth ivory beads, and hundreds of perforated fox canines. Sunghir 2's clothing was ornamented with almost 5000 beads and over 250 arctic fox canines around the waist – possibly a belt of some kind. Also in the grave were ivory pins that may have secured his clothing in some way, an ivory figure of a possible horse placed on his chest, and a larger ivory figure of a mammoth beneath his left shoulder. At his right side lay a long 'spear' or 'lance' of straightened mammoth ivory, probably too small to have been used as a weapon, and next to it a small 'wheel' of beautifully carved ivory had been placed. Sunghir 2's left forearm and hand were missing from the grave; as this was noted at the time of excavation, they are unlikely to have been displaced after burial.

Figure 1.12. c: Reconstruction of Sunghir 2/3.

However, the most intriguing addition to the children's grave is the inclusion of an adult human femur of indeterminate sex; the epiphyses had been chopped off and the inside had been packed with red ochre and placed alongside Sunghir 2's left arm. This is the only modified human bone known to have been deliberately included within a grave in this period. It suggests there must have been some special connection between the individual it belonged to and the children – otherwise, presumably an animal bone packed with ochre would have sufficed. Alternatively, the bone may have been an important 'relic' within the Sunghirian community.

Sunghir 3 was ornamented with even more beads than the older child. At least 5400 mammoth ivory beads were arranged in bands across the clothing (but no fox teeth); there was an ivory pin at the throat, and a number of small lances of ivory (at least ten) alongside the skeleton. Three ivory wheels (like Sunghir 2) lay at the left side of the head, and two perforated batons, one of which was decorated with incised dots.

Bone chemistry and tooth-wear combine to show that Sunghir 1 and 3 ate a normal diet for the period, rich in animal protein. However, the boy known as Sunghir 2 had almost no tooth wear, and clearly had a different diet, which was more vegetarian, with little grit. This is curious, in view of the location and the period, and one can speculate that he may have had difficulty chewing animal meat – the muscle markings around his jaw were not robust, indicating that he had little bite-force, although analysis of his long bones revealed he did not lack protein in his diet. The only other protein available to Sunghirians must have come from invertebrates such as earthworms, insects, spiders, snails and slugs – not a diet of preference for many folk, although in Thailand people eat wasps, grasshoppers and bamboo worms. In Japan silk worms are a delicacy, and locusts and centipedes are just a few of the 'bugs' in the Chinese diet. Indeed the world's leading chefs are causing a gastronomic revolution by including 'creepy-crawlies' like spiders and insects on their à-la-carte tasting menus!

The Sunghirian community specialised in hunting mammoth, but they also consumed a variety of other mammals that were available, resulting in a diet rich in protein and fats. However, a pure meat diet is inadequate to supply some of the essential vitamins (A and C) that humans require to stay healthy. Fortunately, the Sunghirians (along with other ice age communities) also had plant material available to eat, as their skeletal remains indicated they were not deficient in vitamin C (reserves can be kept in the human body for 3 months), nor were they deficient in Vitamin B, which can be found in plant seeds and bone marrow. Vitamin C is found in an animal's kidneys, liver, tripe and eyes, and in plant leaves and shoots – eaten either raw or boiled, or as juice.

It is difficult to imagine how the Sunghir children could have died at the same time, and this has led to the suggestion that they may have been considered significant or special in some way, and were selected for a sacrificial or ritual purpose. We will never know, but it is certain that a great deal of time and effort went into these three burials, and there must have been either a good reason or a compelling belief that led to the elaborate treatment of these three individuals after their death.

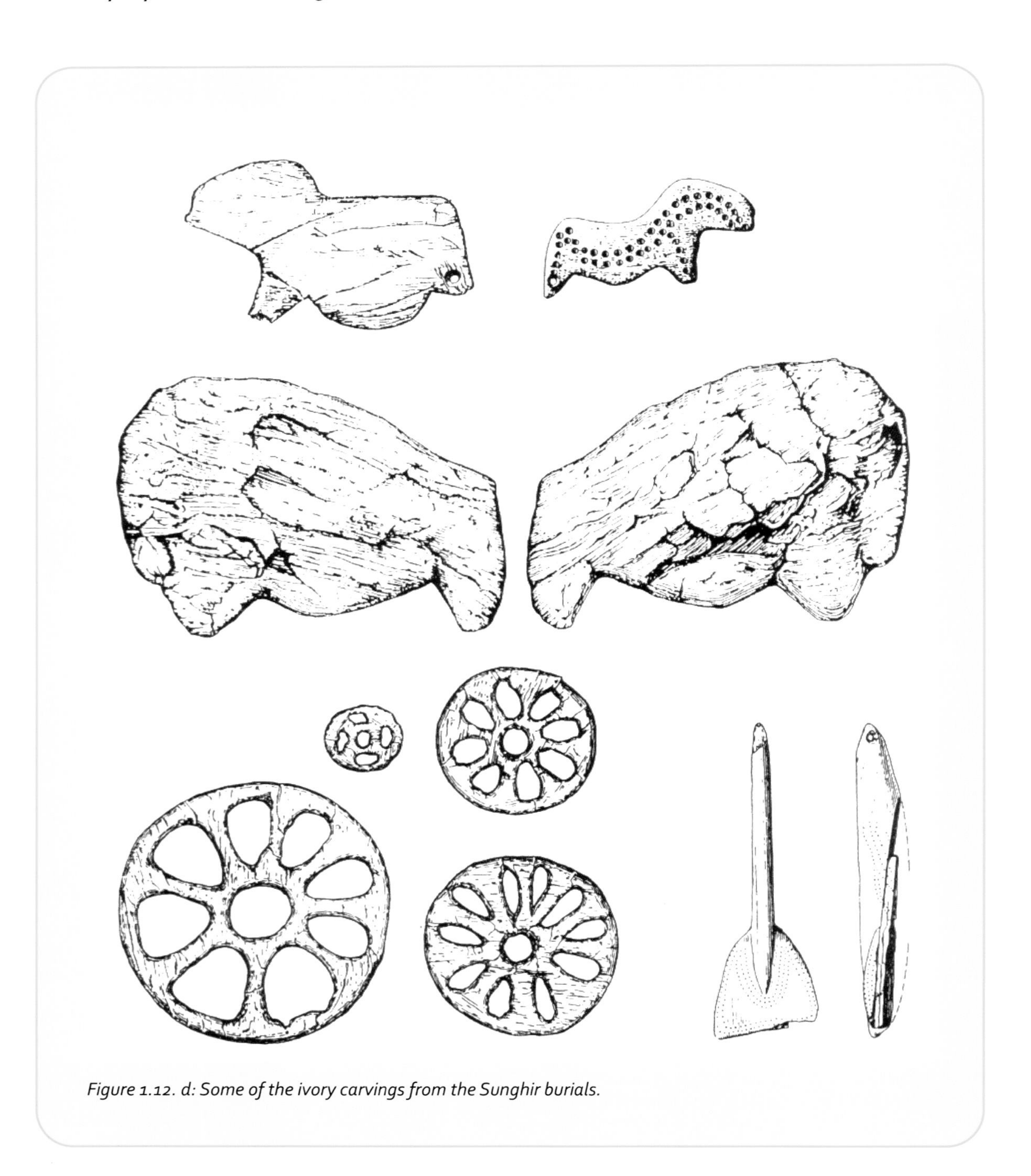

Figure 1.12. d: Some of the ivory carvings from the Sunghir burials.

Fitness and violence

Regardless of their nutritional status, Palaeolithic men, women and children were highly active and had to be physically fit in order to survive. They were extremely mobile people and they probably walked a great many more than the 10,000 steps a day we are recommended in order to stay fit! They had robust physiques with strong bones and powerful muscles – the result of the intense physical exercise required to support their lifestyle. We can assume they regularly performed duties such as chasing down prey, and running and walking fast over rugged landscapes. They would have had to carry or drag heavy loads, such as carcasses, wood, stone for tools, or camp equipment, over rough and hilly terrain. They also had to undertake hard manual labour – for example, digging frozen ground, butchering meat, and processing animal hides. Skins need pummelling and pounding, which is tough work and may be one reason why women had well-developed physiques too.

There is no evidence of osteoporosis during the ice age. Although it is an age-associated disease, it would have been an unlikely pathology, due to their high mobility over rough, uneven terrain. This would have built up bone mass from an early age – tarmac roads and pavements are not good for the human skeleton! These tireless walkers must have often been weighed down by heavy loads, which explains the degenerative wear and tear seen on many bones.

Not only is there evidence of strong musculature on the skeletal remains of Palaeolithic humans, but their ability to explore the dangerous cave systems without the help of modern lighting and equipment (or a map) is a testament to their athleticism, courage and audaciousness. Speleologists are usually at the top of their game in terms of fitness, and need strong nerves! The narrow crawlways in many caves (e.g. only 35 cm wide in Fronsac cave, France) also suggest that some explorers were very slim – or surprisingly young given the danger involved (see pp. 184-86)!

On the whole, Upper Palaeolithic people were fit and healthy; little evidence has been found for arm or leg fractures, and there are only a few indications of any violence in this period in Europe (apart from the alleged 'pierced humanoids' depicted in the caves of Cougnac and Pech Merle). A piece of flint – probably an arrowhead – is embedded in the pelvis of an adult woman from San Teodoro Cave, Sicily. A fragment of a retouched flint bladelet was found embedded in a thoracic vertebra of an 18-month old child buried in the Grotte des Enfants at Balzi Rossi, Italy, and probably caused its death (p. 17) – one can only wonder if this was caused by a hunting accident, and therefore does it imply that the child's mother was out hunting with the infant on her back?

At Dolní Vestonice (Moravia), a fragment of a frontal bone of an adult male, dating to c. 27,660 bp, was found with a large wound above the eye, which had healed – it seems to have been caused by a large blunt instrument, wielded with some strength, and thus represents one of the rare indications of violence in the period in Europe. Another example is the adult male at Sunghir, who has a perforation in a thoracic vertebra (p. 25) – he seems to have been stabbed in the neck, and the wound did not heal. The cause could have been either a projectile or a handheld blade, which severed a vein or artery and he doubtless bled to death. What we cannot know, of course, is whether this episode was accidental or intentional.

There is similar evidence in other parts of the world: the Kamikuroiwa rock-shelter in Japan, dating to 14,500 bp, contained an adult female hipbone with a bone point embedded in it – she was stabbed twice, and the point was left in; seven skulls from the upper cave of Zhoukoudian in China have enigmatic depressed fractures; in Israel, a Natufian adult male of 14,500 - 13,000 bp from Kebara Cave has a stone projectile embedded in his spine. He did not survive the wound for long. Most dramatic of all is the cemetery of Jebel Sahaba, in the Sudan, dating to at least 13,400 bp, which yielded numerous bodies that had been speared or clubbed – about 67% of the 61 men, women and children died violently. Some men were riddled with marks from bone points, while others, including some children, have small stone points embedded in their skulls – these flakes doubtless formed part of composite hafted weapons. Most of the trauma seems to have been caused by projectiles. However, the fact that there are numerous healed lesions indicates that the cemetery does not represent a single warfare event, but sporadic and recurrent episodes of violence, perhaps triggered by major climatic and environmental changes in this region.

Nevertheless, these are rare exceptions, and it therefore appears that, on the whole, life was peaceful in the Upper Palaeolithic, although we have no idea how often death by interhuman violence occurred. Certainly, no depictions are known of it, and the few images interpreted as men holding weapons are confronting animals, not people. Many people often assume that our ancestors were all cannibals, but there is very little evidence for this at all in the period that concerns us here. One exception is Gough's Cave, Cheddar (England), where human bones dating to 14,700 years ago display traces of defleshing, disarticulation, chewing, marrow extraction, and even what are claimed to be human toothmarks! What we cannot know, of course, is whether this was starvation cannibalism, an act of aggression or a ritual act. At this site, three human skulls were carefully made into cups – such cups are also known at other sites, such as Le Placard (France) where eight were found, one of which had contained ochre or was painted red. It is thought they would not have been very useful for drinking due to the holes and sutures in them!

Apart from the few examples cited above, there is very little evidence of causes of death. There are any number of possibilities – hunting or other accidents, falls, drowning, cold, burning, wild animals – and sacrifice, quarrels or inter-group conflict. But in addition, there must have been many diseases and ailments that proved fatal.

Analysis of ice age skeletons has also revealed a wide variety of non-fatal conditions, although of course we can only detect ailments that leave traces

CRO-MAGNON

The 'old man' of Cro-Magnon (Dordogne, France), unearthed in 1868, has undergone analyses for 150 years, with differing results. A rounded lesion above his right eye was first thought to be physical damage caused after death, while a depression on one femur was believed to have been caused by a missile from a sling, or by an animal horn or tusk. Other researchers claimed that the brow lesion could have many causes, while the wound on the femur was attributed to a club, and a different lesion on the pelvis was thought to have been made by a spear. A later analysis attributed the brow lesion to water drops falling onto a partially exposed skull. The most complete anthropological examination, in 1965, estimated the man's age to be only about 50. It confirmed the diagnosis of the spear-wound on the pelvis, but attributed the lesion on the femur to localized inflammation. Traces of chronic osteoarthritis were found on five lumbar vertebrae. More recent analyses of the lesion on the skull have pointed to an actinomycosis (an inflamed abscess) or to Langerhans cell histiocytosis (causing a proliferation of abnormal cells). The latest diagnosis, based on a micro-CAT scan, is neurofibromatosis (a subcutaneous tumour with progressive bone erosion).

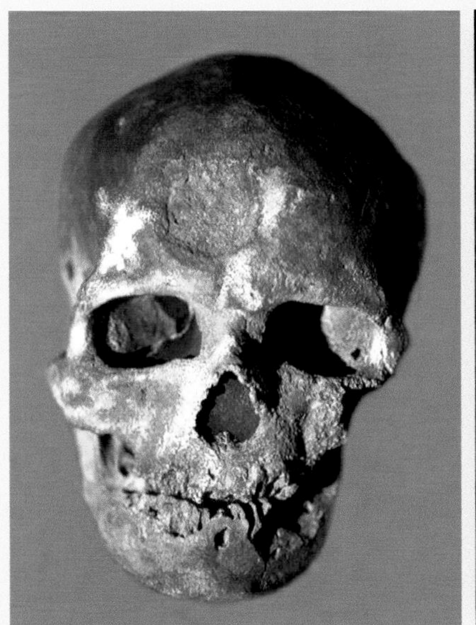

Figure 1.13. a: The skull of the 'old man' of Cro-Magnon. b: Reconstruction of the 'old man' showing the benign tumour.

on bones. One example is the 'old man of Cro-Magnon' who may have had bone actinomycosis, a parasitic illness. Other skeletons from Cro-Magnon and Chancelade had cervical arthritis, while that from Combe Capelle had pronounced scoliosis. Such pathologies suggest that these individuals were limited to having sedentary lives and spending a lot of time in a sitting position.

The young child known as Sunghir 3 had exceptionally short and bowed femurs, but they do not seem to have affected his gait, since the tibias were normal and symmetrical. Opinions differ among specialists as to the cause of this condition – partly because it has not been observed among recent humans. Some attribute it to a rare genetic abnormality or mutation, or the effects of inbreeding. Others have proposed that the deformity was most likely due to rickets as a result of Vitamin D deficiency, despite the lack of other abnormalities in the skeleton linked to that condition. Analysis of the male adult known as Sunghir 1 indicated that he had moderate rickets at an early age, but this did not produce deformities and was later overcome.

At the Arene Candide necropolis in Italy (p. 201), osteological analysis of two skeletons showed one individual with pathological bowing of the limbs, and another with a milder form of the same disease.

At the open-air site of Ohalo II, Israel (pp. 153-54), a grave dating to 19,300 bp contained a 35-year-old man, buried on his back, with his hands folded on his chest. Analysis of the bones revealed that he was disabled, perhaps due to a degenerative disease on one side of his body.

Some cases of arthrosis – disease of the joints (spondylosis) and degenerative vertebrae – are also found in the Upper Palaeolithic, and may be the result of a number of unfavourable factors such as poor nutrition, excessive load bearing and general life conditions. At the site of Afalou Bou Rhummel (Algeria), a man had rheumatoid polyarthritis, which locked his elbows in permanent extension, so he probably couldn't feed himself.

At Rochereil (Dordogne), a child of 2-3 years had a skull corresponding in size to that of a 7 - 8-year-old because it was hydrocephalic. It features the only known Palaeolithic trepanation, where a bone disc has been cut out of the frontal bone. However, since this was done from inside, it was clearly done after death.

VITAMIN D

Calcium absorption for bones is dependent on Vitamin D, and the calcium concentrations were not high in the Sunghir bones. Vitamin D can be found in animal liver, eggs and oil from fish – but only coastal people with a diet high in fish oils would obtain a sufficient supply from that source. Vitamin D is synthesized by ultra-violet rays and is more successfully absorbed in light-skinned people. Thus rickets can be caused by either a deficiency in diet or a lack of sunlight. As we shall see later (pp. 110-12), the Sunghir community may have wrapped their infants and children in fur pelts and skin-clothing which would have impeded their vitamin D production during the winter months when sunlight was much reduced.

All these examples provide insights into some of the varied disabilities found in the last ice age, and how the individuals concerned were clearly recognised as 'different' *but were cared for*. We can only speculate as to how epileptics or the mentally ill were treated by the group. But we do have one extraordinary example of a disadvantaged individual who was not only cared for but also given a very special burial – the world's earliest known dwarf, from Romito (Italy).

THE ROMITO DWARF

This remarkable burial was found in the 1960s in a large rock shelter near the village of Papasidero, in northern Calabria, Italy. The grave, dated to around 11,000 years bp, contained not one, but two skeletons in a shallow, oval pit. They are known as Romito 1, a middle aged, small, and slightly built woman; and Romito 2, thought to be a young male, of short stature (1.3m or 4' 2') around 16-18 years of age.

It is not certain the two individuals died and were interred at the same time, as the exact disposition of the remains was not documented sufficiently well. However, the closeness of their positions (his skull on her cheek and her arm around him) seems to indicate they were. Two large fragments of bovid horn were found with the bodies.

Romito 1's skeleton was the less complete of the two, but her remains, being normally proportioned and of small stature, indicated she was most probably female. Analysis of her tooth-wear suggests she was at least 35, or possibly even 40-50 years old when she died. In the absence of a DNA test it is not known if the two were related, although a number of anatomical features of both their skulls and teeth show many similarities.

Romito 2 is now considered to be the earliest known dwarf, as well as the only dwarf found in an ice age hunter-gatherer society, preceding other specimens by 5000 years. Analysis showed that all of his long bones, especially the radius and ulna, were bowed and deformed, and about half the size of normal limbs. His skull showed a bulging forehead, compressed cranial base and jutting lower jaw.

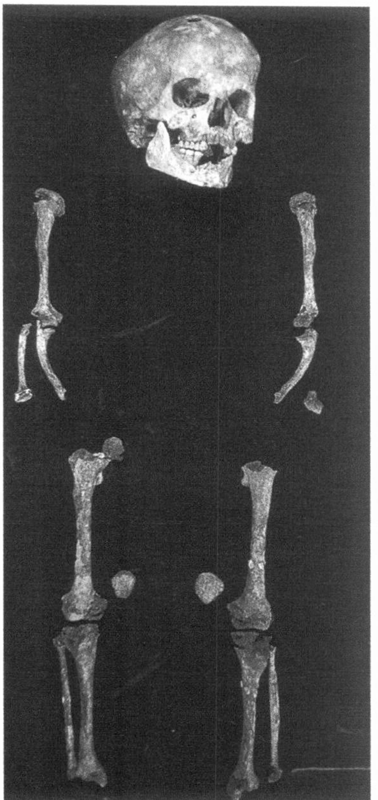

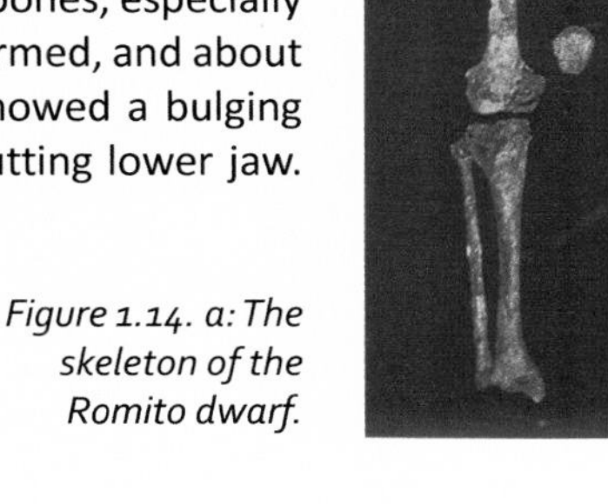

Figure 1.14. a: The skeleton of the Romito dwarf.

The hands and feet were missing, as was the pelvis, making accurate sexing difficult, although several features of the muscle attachment lean towards him being male.

It is thought that the most likely cause of the young man's dwarfism was *Acromesomelic dysplasia*, a genetic mutation. One would expect this to be a very rare condition 11,000 years ago, and given the small population sizes around at the time, it's unlikely to have been encountered often.

Romito 2 would undoubtedly have had limited mobility, and been unlikely to travel any distance without assistance. Activities such as hunting would have been challenging, as his forearms were extremely short and bowed, with reduced flexibility at the elbows. However, his inability to participate to any great extent in his community's economic activities would not have precluded him from contributing in other important ways. Even a role as the group's resident child-minder would have given the women freedom for other tasks.

For a mobile hunter-gatherer group, migrating to other sites is a necessity, and it cannot have been easy for Romito 2 to keep up with the others, walking over mountainous terrain, without enduring a great deal of pain. So it is likely he was transported in some way, be it on a wooden sledge, or even on horseback (pp. 123-28)! One would imagine that, in order to survive, he must from early childhood have been given a great deal of support to overcome his disabilities. Was he considered a liability, or valued as 'special' in some way by his social group? We can only guess

Figure 1.14. b: The two engraved aurochs of Romito. The large one is 1.2 m long.

what skills and talents he may have developed to make himself less of a burden, and there is no reason to suppose his intelligence was impaired.

We have no way of knowing how, or why he died so young, and no evidence of trauma or violence was apparent on his skeletal remains. Nor indeed can we be sure of what his relationship with Romito 1 might have been – was she his mother, a significant other, his carer, or just a local woman that died around the same time? Her 'special' place in the burial would suggest that she was of importance. What is clear is that, despite his formidable handicaps, Romito 2 managed to survive into early adulthood, and this surely came at some cost to his extended group. Nevertheless they protected and supported him throughout his lifetime.

The Romito burial site itself features a remarkable decorated rock on which three aurochs (wild cattle) were deeply engraved, most notably a great bull nearly four feet in length. As at Cap Blanc (pp. 12-13), the fact that the burials were placed in front of the art implies that these individuals were very special people within their community.

Teeth, mouth and gum infections

The ice age diet clearly did not lack mineral salts, fluorine and calcium, but had almost no sweets and sugars, and consequently the teeth from the period seem generally healthy, with a low incidence of caries. One example is the Algerian site of Afalou Bou Rhummel where, out of 800 teeth (from 26 men, 14 women and 5 children), only 3.4% had decay. One remarkable exception, also in North Africa, is the Grotte des Pigeons at Taforalt (Morocco) where excavations of layers dating to 15,000 - 13,700 years ago unearthed evidence of the systematic harvesting and processing of edible wild plants, primarily acorns and pine nuts. The adult teeth from 52 individuals recovered at the site display an exceptionally high occurrence of caries (51.2%) which is comparable to modern industrialized populations with a diet high in refined sugars and processed cereals. Only 3 adults had no caries at all. It seems that an increased reliance on wild plants and changes in food processing caused this early example of oral disease. In addition, more than 90% of the Taforalt adults had had their upper central incisors removed, a cultural practice characteristic of the period in that region, which must have limited the masticatory use of the front teeth.

The teeth of Upper Palaeolithic people normally display little wear on the incisors but considerable abrasion on the crowns of molars and premolars, both for young children (e.g. a 7-year-old Magdalenian at Lortet, France) and adults. Some Magdalenian teeth have wear patterns similar to those of today. But we can't assume that heavily worn molars and premolars are due solely to a plant-based diet, since those of (e.g.) female Eskimoan people can be equally worn. So the wear can also be due to abrasives in food, as opposed to the texture of food, and teeth will often have been used as a 'third hand' in many tasks, or as tools to crack bones. Some gum disease, abscesses, injuries and infections may also have been caused by the processing of skins or plant materials. One adult at Le Placard had a lesion in the jaw and had lost a tooth, while the young woman from the Abri Pataud (see pp. 166-67) had an impacted molar and two supernumerary teeth in the upper molar region – this congenital abnormality had caused complications such as inflammation, periodontal disease, and perhaps septicaemia and may have led to her death.

The fact that such conditions are so rare in the skeletons known to us from the last ice age suggests that overall their dental hygiene must have been reasonably good – it is known from grooves and striations on their teeth that even the Neanderthals of Krapina (Croatia) used toothpicks, so this must certainly be true of the Upper Palaeolithic.

Diseases and infections

Relatively low population levels would limit the incidence of transmitting infections. In all probability our ice age ancestors had none of the diseases that we acquired with farming, although that is not to say they were not at risk from injuries or illness linked to butchering animals and especially sick animals. There are a number of pathogens that can be transmitted from infected animals, plants, and the soil that could be spread within communities living and sleeping in close proximity; it seems, however, that these diseases are not characteristic for the Upper Palaeolithic.

However, living in cold conditions made it necessary for these populations to be continuously attired in animal-hide clothing, and staying alive by keeping well wrapped-up is not without possible health hazards! Even slight inflammatory conditions can leave traces on an individual's bones – especially children, and the boy known as Sunghir 2 had traces of infection on his spine. The most likely candidate is *Mycosis fungoides* that began with a skin infection. If it was inhaled or entered through a wound, it could trigger sepsis. Mycotic infection can affect people working with animals such as vets, or those working in abattoirs or as gravediggers – one study in Poland showed that 20% of farmers had been infected with mycoses. Zoophilic and geophilic fungi that are found in soil are also known to cause skin disease.

The diseases found among contemporary hunter-gatherers provide insights into those which may have affected ice age people. One class of disease would be caused by those organisms that had adapted to our pre-hominid ancestors, and persisted with them as they evolved into humans – for example, head and body lice. As humans lost their body hair, lice (*Pediculus*) migrated to human heads, making way for pubic lice (*Phthirus*) to take up residence. Lice like to hang out on clothing, hair and beards and even eyebrows!

Pinworms or threadworms, and most of the internal protozoa and bacteria such as salmonella, would be in the second class of diseases, although early animal domestication may have passed many of them from animals to humans, and they were not present when we were exclusively hunting and foraging.

THE ARCY PARASITE

The remains of one specifically human parasite have been discovered in the sediments of the decorated Grande Grotte at Arcy-sur-Cure in northern France. Radiocarbon analysis of organic material in the thin Palaeolithic living-floor – containing a fireplace, lamps, blocks of pigment, grinders, and animal bones including cave-bear – has produced results from 24,660 to 30,160 bp. The cave-bear bones – which include newborn specimens, abundant youngsters and general disarticulation – are characteristic of hibernation caves. The investigators therefore believe that occupation by humans and bears may have been essentially contemporaneous, but alternating – the people in summer, the bears in winter.

Samples of sediment from the occupation layer were subjected to a palaeo-parasitological analysis, and some of them produced concentrations of the eggs of parasitic intestinal roundworms – *Ascaris sp.* – from faecal material.

It is difficult to determine the species because the host is unknown. On the basis of modern parasitological data, there are two candidates: *Ascaris summ*, which infests pigs and wild boars; and *A. lumbricoides*, which infests humans. The pig option can safely be discarded, since the climatic context of this period makes the presence of a wild suid highly improbable – the Grande Grotte's flora and fauna point clearly to cold steppic conditions, featuring reindeer, mammoth, rhino, marmot, chamois and arctic fox. Moreover, one would not expect to find a wild pig deep inside a cave!

It is therefore almost certain that the eggs lay in human excrement. There remains a slight possibility that the omnipresent cave-bear might be the source, but on present evidence bears are never associated with *Ascaris* – they tend to be infested with a totally different parasite, *Baylascaris transfuga*, whose eggs are extremely dissimilar to those of *Ascaris* in shape and size.

The conclusion, therefore, is that the people who occupied the cave during the last ice age suffered from ascaridiose, a parasite that was transmitted orally either by eating food tainted with faecal material, or simply from unwashed hands.

Zoonotic diseases have animals as their primary host and only incidentally infect humans. Humans can be infected by zoonoses through insect bites, by preparation and consumption of contaminated flesh, and from wounds inflicted by animals.

Some parasitic infections can enter the digestive systems of humans: for example, helminths are organisms that can live outside or inside a host's body. Helminths are invertebrates characterized by elongated, flat or round bodies such as flatworms, flukes and tapeworms. Helminth eggs are present in animals' intestines, especially those hunted for their pelts such as fox, wolf or bear, and can be present on plant leaves or berries, or a sick animal's carcass or faeces. Once ingested the larva hatches from the egg into the host's digestive system and travels through the blood to any organ in the body including the bone. As mentioned above (p. 27), it is probable that the boy known as Sunghir 2 acquired his protein from invertebrates, and this would have significantly increased his chances of parasitic infections.

Tuberculosis (TB), caused by the microbe *Mycobacterium tuberculosis* complex may well have emerged around 70,000 years ago during the Palaeolithic, and originated in *H. sapiens.* It is thought that the modern form of TB developed around 40,000 years ago when the population may have grown and was living a more settled life in small communities. We can only speculate as to how our ancestors survived this devastating disease, and why women are more resistant to it than men. TB has been linked to the onset of controlled fire use, smoke exposure and increased physical contact among individuals sitting around the hearth.

There must have been other dire consequences of smoke inhalation from drying meat and sitting around a fire in a confined space. Cave fires are carcinogenic, and frequent exposure to smoke, even for brief periods, can cause sub-optimal long-term effects. The smoke, ash, and dust from fires (and torches) – especially fires that were burning bones – would have been bad for their health, and especially for infants, children and young adults. Smoke is filthy as it clings to clothing and hair. Perhaps this is one reason why they didn't live inside caves but preferred cave mouths and rock shelters.

Waste matter and sanitation

Would our ice age ancestors have found each other malodorous? We can probably assume they smelled differently from ourselves! To a great extent they would smell of the skins and furs they wore which would have carried a strong pungent odour, but in all probability they either didn't notice, or were simply habituated to the smell or, alternatively, they may have found it attractive! Personal hygiene probably wasn't high on their list of priorities, but they may have washed in rivers or used snow to clean themselves when available. There is some evidence (pp. 249-50) that they utilized hot thermal springs where available, but this could also have been for 'internal cleansing' rather than simply for bathing.

Foraging exposed our ancestors to many bacteria in the soil and decaying plant matter (including sewage excrement in waste water). Botulism can be fatal – *Clostridium botulinum* is a bacterium found in soils that feeds on dead and decaying organic matter, and although not poisonous itself, under certain conditions like stagnant swamp water it produces a toxin called botulin. This is known to kill water birds, which were definitely in our ancestors' diet. One can presume, however, that trial-and-error learning would have taught them to avoid eating birds and animals that they hadn't killed themselves. Present-day Australian Aborigines never eat road-kill!

What happened to the rubbish left behind after a camp was abandoned? Presumably animal remains would be left to rot, as would the accumulated human waste. However, this would quickly attract animals, birds and mice that would remove rotting food remains, especially any fat and bones. But the question remains as to what they did with their human waste and any human corpses that were not afforded a burial!

Immunity and treatments

We remain largely ignorant of the specific diseases that may have affected our ice age ancestors – for instance, we have no clue about the existence or prevalence of sexually transmitted diseases, even though many STDs have had a long association with primates and humans. Where population density is low and people are sparsely distributed, having minimal social interaction with other communities, it is much harder for pathogens to propagate and survive, and most STD pathogens are not long-lived in the environment outside of a 'body'.

What can we assume about possible immunity to disease in the period? Our bodies have evolved ways of fighting disease: one example is a mother's milk which provides antibodies that are transmitted directly to the infant's gut to protect it against a range of parasitic and harmful infections – and it's probably safe to assume that parasites would have been present in our ancestors' guts (see p. 37)! They ate animals, and not all of the meat they ingested would have been cooked sufficiently to kill bacteria. It's likely that they ate the contents of

Figure 1.15. A Himba chief's daughter coating herself with ochre. Namibia, 2012.

various animals' stomachs too and, as they also wore animal skins, parasites or fungal infections could have been transferred to humans in a variety of ways.

Even though we don't know how much immunity these people had to infections, or what germs were around, it's highly unlikely that they suffered from the whole range of food allergies known today, or that they were allergic to animals or 'cave dust'. This is partly due to modern hygiene: our practice of using disinfectants has resulted in many people having overactive immune systems.

It is highly probable that these early communities had worked out the medicinal benefits of some plants, and had remedies for a number of ailments. Of course, this would be dependent on the availability of suitable plants in their local environment. Certainly iodine can easily be extracted from seaweed, and stored indefinitely, and the iron-rich rock haematite (red ochre) was used extensively throughout prehistory – even before *H. sapiens* came on the scene.

Apart from its symbolic value and use as paint, ochre has cleaning and disinfectant properties that are exploited by many indigenous societies. For example the Himba women of Namibia use it to protect their skin from the sun and to repel insects – and they believe it enhances their appearance! Ochre has a powerful astringent effect, can arrest haemorrhage (which could have been crucial during and after childbirth, p. 164), and has antiseptic and deodorizing properties. Generally it seems to promote healing. In medieval times, it was used for washing and purging, in eye remedies, and for drying malignant ulcers. Some Australian Aborigines use it as medicine: a wound may be covered with chewed red ochre and then with leaves. Ochre moistened with water is used on sores on any part of the body, even when the pains are internal. Red ochre and water, followed by cold ashes, are also used to treat burns.

As we shall see in later chapters, archaeologists have found evidence of widespread ochre use on tools, weapons and ornamental artifacts, in caves and on dwelling floors. It was also much used in burial pits – possibly for purification (to reduce the smell of a decomposing body) or embalming purposes.

Burials

A great deal of varied evidence can be obtained from the ice age burials discovered so far, as we show throughout this book – about physical types, clothing, grave goods, etc – but some also provide evidence that relatives were sometimes buried together. For example, the Magdalenian burial of Oberkassel (Germany) contained a 50-60 year old male and a 20-25 year old female, who were interred simultaneously. Analysis of their skulls showed numerous similarities and coincidences in characteristic features, which pointed to a high degree of kinship: they were probably father and daughter or even grand-daughter. Similarly, some anomalies in skulls at Predmostí (Moravia) were interpreted as

THE DOLNÍ VESTONICE TRIO

In 1986 a remarkable triple burial was unearthed at Dolní Vestonice, a Gravettian open-air site in Moravia. Initial assessments of its contents became a classic example of how misinterpretation can produce enduring myths in prehistory.

The skeletons were in a shallow pit, in an extended position, side by side, with their heads towards the south. All three were young, between 17 and 20 years of age. The eldest, lying supine in the centre, was very gracile; this, together with the shape of the pelvis, led to it being identified as a female. On her left was a big, robust skeleton, more than 175 cm tall, a 17-year old male, lying on his stomach, with his head turned away to the west. His left arm covered the female's hand, as if holding her. On her right was a smaller robust male, aged 18 or 19, lying on his left side and facing the female. Both of his arms touched her pelvis. The three skulls were in a soil impregnated with red pigment (the bigger man's skull also had a coating of white powder), and the red crust around their frontals contained the remains of diadems of wolf and fox teeth and small ivory beads. There was also ochre under the pelvis and between the thighs of the woman, and on the hands of the man touching her pelvis.

A quantity of fragments of carbonised wood, up to 56 cm long and 10 cm wide, lay directly on the skeletons as well as near them. These may be the remains of some sort of tomb cover, a replacement for the covering of mammoth shoulder-blades usually found on Upper Palaeolithic graves in this region. It was perhaps burned as part of the funerary ritual, as the greatest mass of carbonised wood (a funeral pyre?) lay immediately west of the grave. The corpses themselves were not burned, but the presence of brick-red burnt loess soil just above the wood suggests that the fire was extinguished by having earth heaped over it.

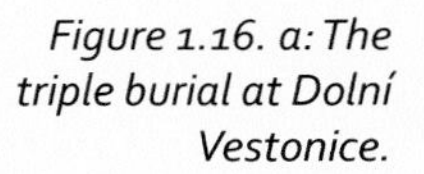

Figure 1.16. a: The triple burial at Dolní Vestonice.

Wood from the grave produced a radiocarbon date of 25,640 years ago. The three skeletons had clearly been buried at the same time (the female was put in first). Are they there because of an accident, an epidemic or for some other reason? One clue is that the female's bones show several pathological abnormalities, most recently attributed to a congenital dysplasia – e.g. shortening of the leg bones, and anterior bowing and torsion of the right femur. Analysis also points to periods of growth inhibition and systemic stress during early childhood.

Her skull is strikingly asymmetrical, so she must have had some facial paralysis. In her mouth was a fragment of burnt reindeer pelvis, which may have been used as a clamp to bite on during times of great pain, as it shows traces of scratches and pressure.

One proposed explanation was that the burial was a reproduction of a real event – a failed birth. The man on the female's left holds her arm to give comfort but cannot bear to look, while the man on her right – perhaps a medicine man – tries to help the delivery, but in vain. The ochre round the female's pelvis supposedly marked the location of a newborn child's skeleton whose bones had disintegrated.

Figure 1.16. b: Ivory carving of a human head from Dolní Vestonice.

It was an appealing and melodramatic idea, but the complete disappearance of the baby's remains was highly dubious due to the good preservation and virtually complete state of the three adults. In addition, there are other enigmas; for example, the male with his hand on the female's pelvis was skewered to his sacrum by a large piece of wood, while the other male's skull was smashed. It is possible that these two apparently healthy and powerful males met violent deaths, perhaps sacrificed to accompany the dead female.

However, the primary objection to the scenario was that some specialists were convinced that the central figure is not a female but rather an effeminate, gracile male. The pelvis has both male and female distinctive features, so the sex of the central skeleton remained ambiguous and uncertain – but recent genetic analysis has now proved it to be male! Moreover, it appears that the male to the right was a relation, perhaps even a sibling, but the one to the left was not a relation.

A realistic thumb-sized ivory carving of a human head from Dolní Vestonice is usually (but unjustifiably) assumed to be a woman because of its elaborate hairstyle (p. 7). The asymmetry of its face has led some researchers to link it with the enigmatic individual at the centre of the triple burial.

heritable family structures. Some researchers also saw certain morphological details in the Dolní Vestonice triple burial as indicators of a close genetic relationship, and this has now been confirmed for two of the skeletons (p. 42).

The great majority of ice age burials discovered so far are in, or very close to, dwelling sites. But we have no idea if this was a privilege reserved for a few special people. Where are the others? One possibility is that some people may have been cremated: the earliest known cremation is that of Mungo Woman in Australia, dating to c. 25,000 years ago, so this practice may well have existed elsewhere – but as yet we have absolutely no evidence for it in ice age Eurasia.

The most likely explanation for this is the sheer quantity of dry wood needed for the task – about 146 kg are required to efficiently cremate a dead body. Would this quantity have been available, and would people have been prepared to squander it for such a purpose? The pyre would have needed tending for several hours to stay above the 600° C needed for cremation.

Some burials, as we have seen, contain enormous quantities of grave goods (e.g. Sunghir, pp. 24-28), while others have none or a few (e.g. Lagar Velho, p. 2). Certain grave goods were clearly important and precious – for example, in the triple burial of Barma Grande (Italy), all three skeletons had extraordinarily long flint tools: an adult male had a blade 22x4 cm in his left hand, an adolescent in the centre had one 26x4 cm in the right hand, while the other adolescent had a big scraper under the head. DNA analysis has shown that both these adolescents were female. Similarly, at Arene Candide (Italy), the young male skeleton known as the 'Prince' held a 25x4 cm blade in his hand, like a dagger, and was also accompanied by four perforated batons of moose antler (pp. 201-202).

There is a great variety of grave-pit construction – some were covered by bones such as mammoth scapulas, others by heavy stones or slabs, and some by branches which were set alight (Dolní Vestonice, p. 41). At Villabruna (Italy) some stones covering the pit had painted motifs. The woman of St Germain-la-Rivière was inside a miniature dolmen. Some of the skeletons in the Gravettian decorated cave of Cussac (Dordogne) lie in bear hollows.

Most are single burials, but a few doubles and triples are also known. There appears to be no standard rule on orientation, and no apparent difference between the sexes in terms of wealth of jewellery or the presence of tools.

In a number of sites – most notably Dolní Vestonice and Pavlov in Moravia – isolated human bones and teeth have been found scattered through the occupation areas. As mentioned earlier, an adult human femur, filled with ochre, was placed alongside the older child buried at Sunghir (p. 27).

Occasional examples are known of very unusual treatment of human bones – most notably at Le Mas d'Azil (Ariège) where the skull of a young adult was found isolated on its right side, its base turned to the cave wall. There were no teeth or jawbone. The left eye socket contained an oval bone blade, 4 cm by 2 cm, cut from a deer vertebra. A similar one, found nearby, was presumably for the right eye.

The use of skulls as cups has already been mentioned (p. 30), and perforated fragments of human skulls have also been found – the Magdalenians put two holes into a newborn's parietal bone from the abri du Veyrier, and an adult one from Le Rond du Barry. There are also a few perforated human teeth (e.g. six found close to each other at the far end of Bédeilhac cave). The Pyrenean cave of Enlène yielded a perforated fragment of a child's mandible (p. 199).

Figure 1.17. The skull from the Mas d'Azil with its bone cut-outs.

Conclusion

So far, we have presented the available evidence regarding the appearance, and the physical abilities, disabilities and ailments of our ice age ancestors. The likelihood that men and women had different economic roles has also been explored. In the next chapter we shall examine what is known about the climates and environments in which they lived, the resources available to them, how people adapted to changing conditions, and their choice of living sites. Location, we will discover, was extremely important to our ancestors when choosing an ideal home; and we will discover how, once accommodated, they provided themselves with heating, lighting, and a surprising array of home comforts!

Chapter 2

Setting the Scene: Ice Age Environments and Home Comforts

The changing climate

What kind of world did our ice age ancestors inhabit? Numerous scientific techniques have been brought to bear for decades on this question – and thanks to sedimentology, pollen analysis, and the detailed study of fauna and flora, together with dating methods, we now have a detailed picture of the environments and how they changed.

The period known as the Quaternary started c. 2.6 million years ago, and had about a dozen climatic cycles, each of which lasted c. 115, 000 years. In each, a warm period was followed by a cold period of roughly the same length. The last full interglacial-glacial cycle (often designated in late 20th- century literature as the Riss-Würm interglacial and the Würm glaciation) started c. 130,000 years ago and ended 11,000 years ago, but it contained oscillations of temperature at every stage. We are currently in a warm phase, the Holocene or Postglacial.

The last glacial period featured cold, dry stadial episodes separated by relatively mild, humid interstadials. In the period that concerns us here, there were about twelve warm phases between c. 41,000 and 13,000 years ago, with a period of maximal cold at c. 22,000 - 20,000. But the ensuing warming was not continuous: there were more cold phases, but shorter, and progressively less severe. Each cold episode was preceded by intense precipitation, with more snow falling in the winter than was melted in the summer – hence glaciers extended southwards and downwards. The result was dry cold episodes, with little vegetation other than grass and coniferous trees. The soil dried out, and was pulverised by freezing, and then winds deposited it on plains and plateaux as 'loess'. In some regions, however, such as western Iberia and some of the Mediterranean regions, the last glacial maximum was cold but humid. In the milder phases, rains returned, along with lusher vegetation – grassy steppes with shrubs and more trees – and different animals.

In that period of maximal cold, known as the Last Glacial Maximum (LGM), the winters must have been long and rigorous, while summers were short and mild. It is very hard to estimate temperatures, as there were a wide variety of micro-climates. Close to the ice, the coldest times must have been 10° to 15° C lower than today. In western Europe, it is unlikely that average temperatures were lower than -10° to -15° C in the very coldest phase, while the average summer maximum must have been between 5° and 10° C. The extremes were something like -20° in winter and +17° in July. In other words, the winters must have been as severe as those of present-day Lapland, but the summers were longer and warmer. Rainfall must have been 30 to 70 cm per year. But this is all approximation. Magdalenian temperatures in Europe are thought to have been about 5° C lower than today, similar to Norway. This would have raised caloric requirements by a few dozen a day, as long as the people had warm clothing (see below, p. 95).

In the coldest phases, masses of ice several kilometres thick extended over northern Europe as far down as the south coast of Ireland, northern Germany and southern Sweden. The volume of glaciers in mountains also increased – in the Alps they came down to 600 m (to the Lyon area and the northern Italian lakes), and the Pyrenees were also covered. In the temperate phases these glaciers retreated almost to their present positions. In the coldest phases, so much water was trapped in ice that the seas retreated and were lowered – the Atlantic coasts of Brittany and Aquitaine were in places almost 100 km farther out. There was no Channel, and Britain was joined to mainland Europe. The Mediterranean coast was also farther out, depending on the depth of the sea bed – c. 50 km at Agde, more than 10 km at Marseilles. The entrance to Cosquer cave is now hidden 30 m below sea-level. In the LGM, sea level was at its minimum 120-135 m down.

In warmer phases the levels rose again and coasts were drowned. Consequently, we have lost numerous coastal sites and a huge amount of evidence from the coldest phases. Changes in shoreline would have made marine resources more or less accessible. There were huge variations within and between regions – for example the Atlantic coastline of SW France and the Mediterranean coastline of Iberia. In other words, the landscapes were never uniform. As mentioned above, in cold phases forest disappeared and grassy steppe took over, while the temperate phases saw the partial return of trees. Close to the ice were arid, inhospitable, windswept plains, like tundra. Farther south, local climates depended on longitude, latitude, altitude, distance from the sea, and exposure. Microclimates also varied with orientation, relief, the presence of lakes and rivers, etc.

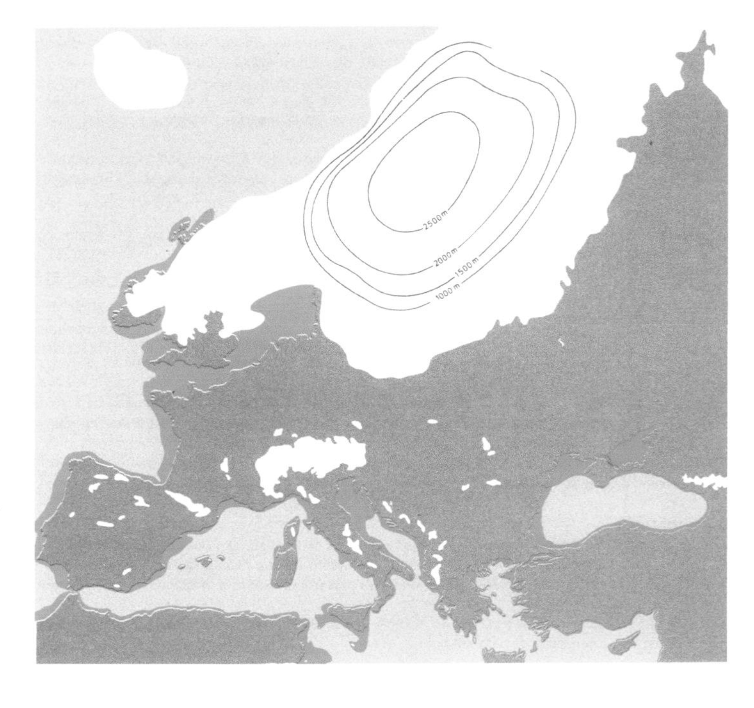

Figure 2.1. Europe at the height of the last glacial maximum. Glaciers are in white; coastal areas now drowned are in dark blue.

The plains had a steppe of grasses and lichens. In the uplands, vegetation differed in valleys and plateaux – limestone plateaux were windswept and steppic, while valleys had a mosaic of landscapes featuring meadows and clusters of trees. But it is crucial to note that the landscapes of Europe have changed – we are not seeing what Palaeolithic people saw. For example, when one is in the Dordogne it is very tempting to imagine ice age people in those precise settings – but many aspects have changed, particularly the route of rivers, their levels and the location of fords. The Pleistocene environment has gone, and has no equivalent today – so there is little point in seeking close parallels elsewhere, and this in turn limits the validity of looking to Australian Aborigines or Bushmen for ethnographic information. Probably the closest analogy is to be found in precolonial North America and southern Canada.

Flora and fauna

The changing conditions could make some areas inaccessible to habitation, and had huge effects on the vegetation, which in turn affected the types of animals available. The Pleistocene low latitude tundras and forest tundras probably carried a greater biomass than their modern counterparts in high latitudes because the midsummer angle of incidence of solar radiation is much higher in (e.g.) France than in the Far North, leading to more effective photosynthesis and plant growth favoured by the warmer summers. We have already stressed (p. 22) the richness of periglacial systems.

Figure 2.2. Impression of a hazel leaf, Lascaux cave.

Dry zones were dominated by pines (38,000 - 22,000 years ago), and then the birch in the Alps and Germany after 20,000. More humid valleys had alder and willow. But in interstadials, which were humid and temperate, pine and birch were replaced by hazel, oak, lime, elm, maple, walnut, hornbeam and ash. There were also shrubs like ivy and boxwood, and an undergrowth of ferns. Our evidence for all this comes primarily from pollen, but occasionally charcoals can be identified – and residues in lamps (pp. 74-76) are usually from juniper. In Lascaux cave we not only have charcoals from oak, fir and juniper, but also a hazelnut and a few leaf impressions! Pollen from the cave has revealed the presence in the area of walnuts, hazelnuts, acorns, beechnuts, currants, and perhaps rhubarb.

Burnt walnut and hazelnut shells have been recovered from many sites. At the Magdalenian site of Miesenheim (Germany), dating to 11,040 bp, evidence has been found for chicory, willow shoots, clematis and pimpernel, as well as birch

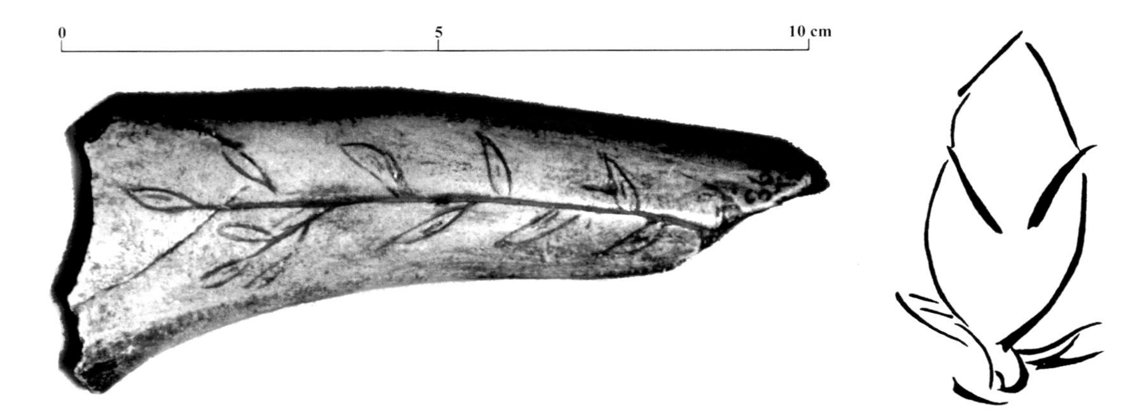

Figure 2.3. a: Engraving on bone of a leafy branch. Grotte du Trilobite, Arcy-sur-Cure (France). b: Plant-like motif on the engraved baton of Montgaudier, France (see also p. 150).

sap. In addition there were little ephedra berries, barberries and currants, and later little plums and blackberries. The inhabitants also had hazelnuts, and dropwort tubers which can make a tasty flour. At the Magdalenian site of Aurensan, in the French Pyrenees, an early method of flotation found carbonised seeds of raspberry and strawberry in the sediments, while El Juyo yielded raspberries and blackberries. The Gravettian and Solutrean levels of the Cova de les Cendres (Alicante, Spain) have yielded remains of crowberries (*Corema album*), a fruit with a high vitamin C content. Some parts of Europe also had chestnuts during interstadials. At Nerja (Spain), pine nuts were consumed, and their importance in the diet seems to have increased with time. Despite a total lack of direct evidence, one assumes that ice age people must also have eaten juniper berries, sorrel, dandelions, nettles, roots, bark and fungi.

Similarly, we have no evidence for consumption of honey, probably because bees need warmth and a blossoming season of sufficient duration to survive without human assistance. The absence of such sweet foodstuffs helps explain the lack of caries in most ice age people's teeth! Various berries can naturally ferment, and dozens of indigenous cultures (including the Inuit, San, Aborigines, etc) make slightly alcoholic drinks from this fermentation in the relevant season. It seems safe to assume that ice age people were no different in view of their doubtless vast knowledge of the properties of plants – some Australian Aborigines can identify 300 plants! In Utah, evidence has recently been found that Native Americans were already using (probably chewing) tobacco about 12,300 years ago.

Where animals are concerned, micromammals (moles, shrews, dormice, rats, hedgehogs, bats) were numerous and varied, and because they evolve rapidly and adapt ecologically, they are excellent indicators of climate. Consequently, much has been learned about changing conditions from their remains in different sites and periods.

Figure 2.4. A reindeer engraved in the cave of Altxerri (Guipúzcoa, N. Spain); it has a small fox, 25 cm long, engraved on its neck.

Larger herbivores also changed with the vegetation. In temperate and humid phases, or times of moderate cold, the animals which lived in valley bottoms and woodland or clearings included the red deer and the Megaloceros (extinct giant deer) with its three metre antlers. Moose flourished in North Germany.

In the cold, dry glacial times, animals like the ibex and chamois came down from the high peaks, and horse, bison and reindeer flourished on the steppes. The horses were small and sturdy, resembling the modern Przewalski and tarpan. The steppe bison of ice age Europe is now extinct – it was bigger than the modern European bison, and could reach 2 m at the shoulder and weigh almost a ton. The aurochs (wild ox) was of similar size and weight.

Reindeer were migratory: in temperate phases they went north, but they never got south of Northern Spain. Some of the finest depictions of reindeer are found in the North Spanish caves, which perhaps reflects their novelty value in the region. They were rarely depicted in France, where they were far more numerous!

In the coldest phases, the saiga antelope was also to be found on the steppes, as were the mammoth and woolly rhino. Like reindeer, mammoths never got south of Northern Spain (with only a handful of depictions known there) and no rhino depictions have yet been found in Iberia.

There were plenty of carnivores to prey on the herbivores – the omnivorous cave bear reached more than 2.5 m standing and weighed c. 400 kg. The smaller brown bear was better adapted to cold phases but also to forests. The cave lion

Figure 2.5. Three birds drawn in the Cosquer Cave (Bouches-du-Rhône, France), interpreted as great auks. They are each c. 27 cm long.

was much bigger than present-day species, but was not well adapted to great cold, unlike the wolverine and arctic fox. The wolf and fox could adapt to any conditions. Other cold animals or high-altitude species included the arctic hare, weasel, lemming, snow vole and marmot.

In cold phases, there were birds such as ptarmigan, willow grouse (pp. 143-44) and snowy owl. In temperate phases there were clearly a wide variety of birds and fowl – most depictions of birds are of water species – and eggs were certainly consumed (hen-egg size shells have been recovered at Pincevent, p. 143, and elsewhere), providing protein and lipids.

On the coast there were also sea birds and auks (the latter seem to be depicted in Cosquer Cave, as well as on a plaquette from Italy's Grotta Paglicci), as well as seals, marine fish, crustaceans, shellfish and seaweed. On the North Spanish coast, sites such as Tito Bustillo and El Juyo had crab claws, shells and sea urchin spines on their occupation floors. Many kinds of molluscs were consumed – thousands of specimens are known from Altamira and El Juyo, the most common being limpets and periwinkles. At La Riera, starting c. 21,000 years

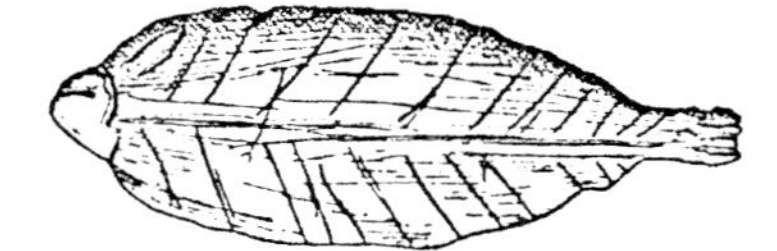
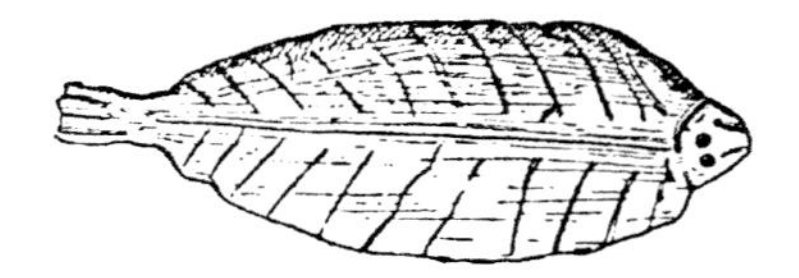

► *Figure 2.6. Bone cut-out of a marine flatfish, Lespugue (France).*

▲ *Figure 2.7. Engraving of a whale on a whale tooth from Las Caldas (Asturias). 52 mm in length. A bison is engraved on the other side.*

ago, over 19,000 relatively intact mollusc shells were recovered from 21 species, but 92% of the edible ones were limpets. At Cueva Morín there are also oysters, clams and mussels. On the southern Spanish coast, many tens of thousands of marine mollusc shells were found at Nerja Cave (see p. 145).

We have a few depictions of flat sea fish as well as a couple of whales which were perhaps seen out at sea, but presumably more often when washed up on beaches. At Le Mas d'Azil an ibex was carved on a cachalot tooth while the tooth was still fresh, while at Las Caldas (Asturias) a whale was actually engraved on a whale tooth! We also have some fine seal depictions, as well as a few seal bones from animals which may have swum upriver. Inland there were river fish, especially salmon and trout, of which we have hundreds of depictions and numerous remains.

Who would live in a place like this?

Despite persisting popular belief, fuelled by the best efforts of movie-makers and cartoonists, it is yet another myth that people during the late ice age were 'cave men' who habitually lived in caves. Over the last 150 years, archaeological investigation has made it clear that they primarily occupied cave-mouths, sunny rock-shelters, and tents or huts in the open air. This is hardly surprising, since caves are not the most pleasant choice of habitat – they are usually dark, wet, slippery, and full of rocks and jagged concretions.

Nevertheless there are cases, some of them in the French Pyrenees (e.g. Bédeilhac, Enlène), where hearths and other signs of occupation have been found far inside very deep caverns, and even hundreds of metres from the entrance (assuming that the present entrance was also the main one in prehistory). The cave of La Garma in northern Spain, one of the greatest finds of recent decades, comprises an intact Upper Palaeolithic gallery, whose entrance was blocked towards the end of the ice age. It contains not only a great deal of wall art, both paintings and engravings, but also more than 500 square metres of occupation debris (such as animal bones, shells, bone implements, and portable art objects)

Figure 2.8. Structure made of erected slabs of stalagmite floor, deep inside La Garma cave (Cantabria, N. Spain).

located in the first 70 m but also at 90 and 130 m from the entrance; there are even stone structures.

In some cases people may have sought refuge in caves during particularly harsh conditions: at present the caves of southern France and northern Spain maintain a fairly constant temperature (usually *c.* 14° C) which makes them pleasantly cool in summer and mild in winter. However, work by geophysicists has established that during the last ice age it was not merely mild but quite warm inside the caves – a fact which helps to explain why the Palaeolithic footprints found in their depths are almost all of bare feet and have no sign of frostbite or amputated toes.

In many regions of Europe it is far easier to find cave- and rock-shelter sites, so our picture of the ice age is very skewed towards such places. Open-air living sites of the period are generally far harder to find, but they provide crucial information of many kinds.

Where cave-mouths are concerned, they probably preferred 'ouvertures soufflantes' (blower openings) which brought warmer air to the entrance. Even today, hunters, shepherds and mountaineers seek them out in cold weather. As for rock-shelters, there was a clear preference for those which faced south, which were better for warmth, solar radiation, and as protection from north winds. They kept the heat of the day longer, and their higher degree of evaporation would have facilitated the drying of meat and hides.

As one can see at shelters such as Pataud (Dordogne, France) or Asprochaliko (Greece), hearths were often arranged against the rear wall, thus using the heat storage and radiant properties of rock to best advantage. In addition, they would

USE OF DEEP CAVES

In some cases temporary encampments deep inside caves seem to be linked to the creation of decoration on the walls. For example, in the cave of Tito Bustillo in northern Spain, people lived at the entrance, making weapons and tools, and preparing pigments and crayons, but they lit a big fire in front of the great decorated frieze, 150 m inside. Excavations here found occupation debris and colouring materials, as well as several meals of ibex meat, and evidence of resharpening flints for engraving. So they clearly spent quite some time here (this huge cave was decorated throughout, over different periods, not only in the main galleries but also in side chambers).

In two cases, both discovered relatively recently in France, and both dating to the Gravettian, skeletons of the period were deposited deep inside decorated caves: at Cussac, several individuals were found, some of them inside cave-bear hollows with ochre, and one was dated to c. 29,000 bp; while at Vilhonneur, the partial remains of a young male have been dated to c. 31,000 years ago.

It is a tragedy that we have irretrievably lost huge amounts of fascinating information from cave-floors: in some cases, the caverns were frequented throughout history, and thus any prehistoric traces on the floors were destroyed centuries ago; in others, the prehistoric galleries were

Figure 2.9. Skeleton in the decorated cave of Cussac (Dordogne).

discovered during modern times, but the discoverers inadvertently obliterated the precious evidence because (no doubt with their attention focused on the decorated cave-walls) they simply did not notice the footprints, objects and even engravings at their feet. With one important exception – the Tuc d'Audoubert – it is only in recently discovered caves such as Fontanet, Erberua, Chauvet, La Garma and Cussac that the floors have been carefully preserved intact.

The Tuc d'Audoubert's inner depths were first explored in 1912; as the cave is privately owned by the Bégouën family, visits have been kept to a strict minimum ever since, and nothing has been disturbed. Thus the cave not only has artistic treasures (above all, the unique clay bison figures (p. 195), as well as engravings), it is also a treasure-house for all manner of evidence about the activities of the Palaeolithic visitors: flint tools, teeth or pieces of bone were carefully placed in rock-crevices or stuck into the floor; stalagmites were deliberately broken; cave-bear jaws were picked up, their canines were removed (presumably for use in necklaces) and then the jaws were thrown down again (p. 207); and simple structures were made of pieces of stalagmite floor. In short, since no one visited these galleries between the last ice age and 1912, one can actually follow the traces left by Magdalenian people and reconstruct many of their actions.

The same applies at Fontanet, a gallery blocked during the Magdalenian period and only rediscovered in 1972. Here, the back part of the cave has no traces of occupation but does have numerous prints. The front part near the blocked entrance has no prints, but it has engravings and paintings on the walls, and, on the floor, a series of hearths around which are the animal bones that the occupants probably tossed over their shoulders. Here again, the vestiges and prints are so fresh that one would think they were made a few minutes ago rather than 13,000 or 14,000 years ago. Chauvet Cave has many varied traces of human and animal visitors; in particular, numerous bones of cave-bear are present naturally, but one bear skull is on a natural, isolated rock (see p. 195). Chauvet also contains at least three man-made structures.

sometimes build huts against the rear wall – in the abri Pataud, one Gravettian hut of c. 25,000 years ago, was 3.5 m long and 2.5 m deep (i.e. 10 sq m), and contained three hearths and lots of flints. It is probable that a whole series of beams or poles were leaned against the wall, their bases wedged in place with stones, and were then covered with hides.

Similarly, at the shelter of Flageolet I (Dordogne), the Gravettians carved hollows, 15 cm in diameter, in a huge block, into which they seem to have wedged tree trunks that leaned against the wall as a framework for a covering. At Bourdeilles (Dordogne), traces of three postholes were found, 40 cm deep and 10-20 cm in diameter, which may have supported a barrier of hides or branches to close off the site.

In the great shelters they always had to adapt to the space available between fallen blocks and the wall – as the climate changed, the episodes of freezing and thawing caused blocks constantly to fall from the ceiling, and also caused the rear wall to gradually retreat backwards. At Pataud the space available for dwelling varied enormously from period to period.

Figure 2.10. Reconstruction in the abri Pataud museum of one type of shelter made against the back wall.

Over time, rock-shelters and cave mouths filled up through accumulation of material (e.g. toolworking debris), bones, earth brought in on feet, plus wind-blown sediment, as well as the rock falling from walls and ceilings. Hence Pataud had to be abandoned in the Solutrean period, because by then it had filled up almost to the ceiling.

Favourable shelters were sometimes used for many millennia – e.g. Laugerie and Pataud in the Dordogne. Obviously, the most vital necessity for any dwelling place was proximity to a reliable water supply – rivers, streams or springs. As we shall see (pp. 249-50) they were clearly aware of the existence of thermal springs which must have puzzled them, but which must also have been most welcome, for warmth and also perhaps for medicinal properties. There were advantages in being close to fords and places where herds had to pass. Sites at some altitude not only provided a good view of the landscape but also meant floods could be avoided.

CAVE COMFORTS

Apart from boulders which may have been used as seats, no cave 'furniture' has survived. Presumably it was all made of wood and has therefore disintegrated through time – as yet, no one has been fortunate enough to find a waterlogged Palaeolithic site with preserved wood; only a few Palaeolithic wooden objects, including a few spears, have survived in Europe and elsewhere (see pp. 87-88). But we know that Palaeolithic people were perfectly capable of working wood – as we shall see, some of the decorated cave-walls definitely required ladders or scaffolding, and the actual sockets for scaffolding-beams survive in Lascaux.

In addition, other forms of evidence show us some improvements and amenities which were brought to the caves: at Enlène (Ariège), for example, thousands of small sandstone and limestone slabs were brought in from local sources and laid down as a kind of pavement; many of them were engraved. The cave's Salle des Morts has 320 kg of plaquettes – almost 7000 of them – but only a few are engraved. The Salle du Fond had a real paving of plaquettes – a minimum of 23,504 (with only c. 2.5% engraved); they could cover an area of 235 sq m – not the whole chamber, just different parts of it.

Such plaquettes have been found in numerous sites, and many have been broken or burned. One theory suggests that they represent a kind of heating device – sandstone has thermal qualities and a resistance to tension which make it suitable for a function of this kind (although, being brittle, it tends to break very easily). In France, old peasants in some areas still use heated sandstone plaquettes, wrapped in cloth, as bed-warmers!

Pollen analysis of sediments in caves such as Lascaux and Fontanet has revealed that great clumps of grasses and summer flowers were brought in, presumably for bedding and seating. In Lascaux these clusters seem to have been laid down in places – especially in the Passage – where they had to sit to engrave and paint. The grasses brought into Fontanet were placed around a hearth, but not too close so as to avoid burning! On the north Spanish coast, at Tito Bustillo cave, seaweed was brought in; while at Parpalló cave, in Valencia, lots of little shells with no nutritional value were doubtless brought in attached to algae/seaweed.

Figure 2.11. Paving of slabs inside Enlène cave (Ariège).

In South Africa, in the back of Border Cave, between 60,000 and 40,000 years ago, there was grass bedding on insulating layers of ash that would have protected against insects; similar evidence exists in the South African rock-shelter of Sibudu, at 77,000 bp. It is possible that some groups lived in filth – many still do today – but it's likely that most kept their living areas fairly clean and burned soiled bedding.

So even though few caves were actually inhabited by late ice age people for any length of time, it seems they knew well how to adapt this environment to their advantage and comfort.

Sediments analyzed at the German cave of Geissenklösterle showed such a huge proportion of fat that it suggests the floor was probably covered in the skins of large mammals. In La Garma,

Figure 2.12. a: Diagram showing the position of some of the many stone rings in the sculpted frieze of Angles-sur-l'Anglin.

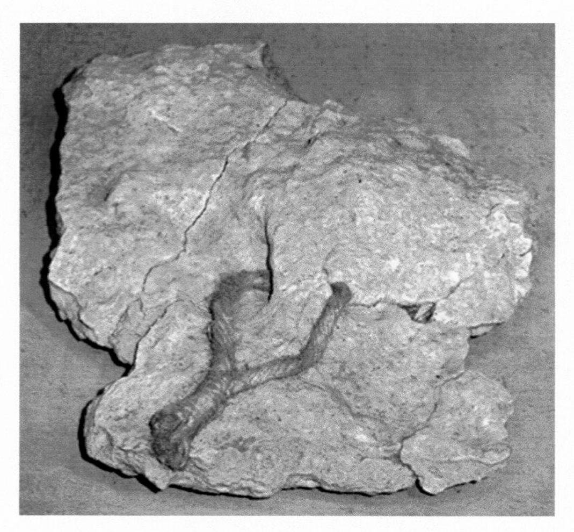

Figure 2.12. b: Fallen fragment of shelter wall, in the abri Pataud museum, showing its stone ring with a modern rope.

dating to c. 14,000 bp, the distribution of some distal phalanges (end bones of toes) indicates that the skin of a cave lion was used as a mat – the ice age equivalent of the tiger-skin rug!

One noteworthy feature of some ice age occupied caves and shelters is the making of rings in the rock. These are still in situ in sculpted friezes (at Cap Blanc and especially Angles-sur-l'Anglin, which has 51, mostly on vertical ridges) but also occur in the ceiling of Pair-non-Pair and in fallen wall fragments at Pataud. Such rings would have been extremely useful for attaching hides, or perhaps suspending food or other materials out of the reach of animals or children.

It has often been claimed that fragments of bone found stuck into cracks in cave walls were attempts to pierce the supposed 'veil' between our world and the spirit world, but in fact many of them are more plausibly seen as 'nails' used for hanging things out of the way of damp floors, or – again – out of the reach of children or animals. Wood would rot very quickly in the caves, but bone does not; and such 'pegs' are well known in rock-shelters in both North and South Africa. It is true that many of the Palaeolithic examples do not protrude from the cave wall. However, it is noteworthy that, in the Tuc d'Audoubert, there are no bits of bone in the walls of the upper (decorated) network; they are only found in the lower network around the Magdalenian dwelling areas, close to the river – which argues against them being ritual or symbolic in nature. Similarly, in the Enlène/Trois Frères complex, such bones abound in the domestic cave (Enlène) but are totally absent in the 'sanctuary cave' (Trois Frères). In Enlène almost 100 objects were stuck into cracks in walls and ceiling: 98% are bone, the rest reindeer antler. Most are single rather than grouped. In the cave as a whole, about half must have been inserted by people over 12, but the rest could have been placed by people of any age. It has been suggested that they might be supports for cords or strings, but this is unclear as there is no pattern to them.

Even more enigmatic in Enlène is that about 70 objects were stuck into the cave floor – mostly big bone fragments (average length up to 9 cm), spearpoints and other bone tools, some teeth and flints, and a couple of sandstone plaquettes. Once again, they are very diffuse, with no pattern, so it seems they were not holding down skins or something similar.

In Gargas, 230 bone fragments have been found in wall-fissures in the lower cave, close to the occupation area with its domestic activities, displaying no link to the hand stencils, and once again with no perceptible organisation or grouping. In El Castillo, not only bits of bone but also teeth, pebbles, stone tools and even fragments of eggshell have been found in such fissures, so obviously not all were 'pegs', and other motives are clearly needed to explain them (p. 248).

Figure 2.13. Possible campsite plan from the Magdalenian rockshelter of Molí del Salt, Catalonia (Spain).

Carry on camping

The people of the last ice age clearly had both base camps (some seasonal, others permanent) and also hunting camps. An engraving on a schist slab from Molí del Salt (north-east Spain), dating to 13,800 years ago, has even been interpreted – somewhat imaginatively – as the depiction of a camp comprising seven dome-shaped huts.

Some sites were like little villages, and one of the best examples we have is the large Magdalenian reindeer-hunters' camp at Pincevent. Located in northern France (Seine-et-Marne), on the left bank of the Seine, it was discovered in 1964 during gravel extraction work. The site seems to have been occupied around 13,000 years ago at least 15 times – analysis of reindeer teeth and antlers shows that the people were here between April and October, leaving in the early winter just before the river's annual flood gently covered everything with up to 50 cm of fine silt and sand. Each such layer disturbed nothing, but neatly separated the episodes of occupation. It also meant that the next arrivals would not always have seen traces of the previous camp. We do not know if the same group came every year, but the consistency of location suggests that the people knew and remembered this landscape. The precise frequency and duration of the visits remain uncertain.

Estimates of the site's extent vary – level IV-20 was excavated over almost 5000 sq m. Even today, rain affects the terrain badly, so the fine condition of the abandoned camps suggests short stays in the dry season. The winter floods would have made the place uninhabitable, and the group cannot have left their dwellings here – there are no postholes, and nothing was dug into the ground or given foundations. Consequently the dwellings must have been light and movable. Their positions and size have been determined by hearths at the entrance and areas of ochre. They appear to have been round or elliptical – c. 4.4 m by 3 m. The complete absence of traces of their structure means that only ethnography can help us envisage what they comprised. The few charcoals at the site (mostly pine and willow) indicate that there was not much woodland

Figure 2.14. ◄ a: Reconstruction drawing of part of Pincevent;
▼ b: Reconstructed tent, hearth and debris scatter at Pincevent.

around, so they were unlikely to be wooden huts or made only of vegetation. The most likely solution is that a few wooden poles would have formed a cone shape, which was then covered with reindeer hides – in other words, these were light conical tents, resembling tepees.

Experiments have shown that putting clay along the bottom of such tents would have made them stable and able to withstand violent squalls, so no pegs were necessary. It is reckoned that at least 8 poles were needed, the longest 4 m and the shortest 3 m, to make a tent about 2.7 m high. The weight would depend on the type of wood used. Roughly 35 reindeer hides would be needed for each tent's covering – these were probably hairless to reduce their weight. Some hides may have been sewn together, but not too many or they would have been too heavy to transport (unless animals helped – see pp. 123-28).

Since each tent was c. 10 sq m it could shelter four or five people. It is thought that about 11 tents were occupied at the

Figure 2.15. Hearth and debris scatter, Pincevent.

same time (as shown by the fact that flints from different dwellings can be fitted together), which would suggest a village of up to 50 people. Each tent had one entrance and a circular hearth, 50 cm across, at the edge – so it was outside when the tent was open and inside when closed. What is known as Dwelling 1 was bigger and contained a line of 3 hearths, 2 m apart and 50 cm in diameter; they were in hollows, 20-25 cm deep. It is likely that one of these was for cooking, the others for crafts. The floors often had lots of ochre: once seen as a ritual purification, it is now interpreted as a way of cleaning the floor or the result of some work – probably extensive skin-working. This is likely in view of the variable quantity of patches, which seems to correspond to the intensity of activity carried out: ochre occurs in small heaps and 'areolas' around the hearths. Sometimes the floors were not specially prepared, but simply hardened and flattened by foot traffic. The red areas inside the dwellings contain numerous tools, whereas areas with no remains or ochre form crescents at the back of some tents and were probably where beds or hides lay.

At Pincevent, domestic refuse from activities around the fire was ejected to an area up to 7 m in front of the tent entrance – this is where one finds heaps of soot and ash from the hearths, used tools, fragments of heated stones, flints and bones. This material becomes more dispersed the farther you go from the tent. The bigger pieces – reindeer antlers, bones and big flints – were thrown a few metres from the dwelling. It is clear that flint was worked inside the tents, and pieces of knapping debris seem to have been carried in or on a kind of mat, from which they were slid off to make a heap. Some of the detritus may also have been pushed to the edges to form draught excluders or (outside) to help hold down the hides.

Why did these people use Pincevent so often? Just downstream from the site, at the confluence of the Seine and Loing, there is a narrowing of the valley which could have helped them trap migrating reindeer. Certainly the basis of their way of life seems to have been the exploitation of big reindeer herds in their autumn migration. More than 90% of the bones in the site are of this species; they clearly ate some immediately, but prepared others for drying. The butchery was systematic and efficient, and all parts of the carcass were used (see below, pp. 129-30). Repeated finds of hyoid bones and upper canines at hearth edges suggest that reindeer heads were cooked and eaten in the tents. However, despite the immediate proximity of the Seine, the site has almost no fish remains or bird bones.

Other similar Magdalenian camps are known in northern France – most notably Etiolles, where the preservation is equally outstanding, thanks to the deposition of flood-silts from the Seine which likewise separate the occupations. Here the major factor in the choice of site appears to have been the proximity to a source of excellent flint in the valley, while the occupants of the site of Verberie settled at the intersection of a reindeer migration route and an area of good flint outcrops. There are some differences with Pincevent – e.g. at Etiolles, the tents had two or perhaps even three entrances, the hearth was at the centre of the interior, and all activities took place around it: not only food preparation but also toolmaking and repairs. Most fireplaces were hollows with a stone edging; some had stone slabs at the base and the fire was lit on them. Some big slabs and blocks were also used to wedge the posts that held up the two big tents, which measured 6 m in diameter at the base.

In some sites it is not clear whether tents or light huts were erected. For example, in the Dordogne a number of such Magdalenian open-air sites have been found, especially in the vallée de l'Isle. At Le Breuil, located on a river terrace, a line of four quadrangular dwellings – either tent or hut bases – was found, each of about 4 sq m. At this site, and many others like it, the dwellings were paved with local pebbles, mostly of quartz, but also of sandstone, schists, granites, gneiss and dolerites. The majority are intact, and are 5-25 cm long, 4-15 cm wide and 10 cm thick. The inhabitants never used angular or irregular pebbles. The stones always formed a quadrangle. Some of them may have served as duckboards, designed to keep hides and bedding above the floor – in other words, to protect against cold and humidity and avoid a layer of mud. Some pebbles had been heated, perhaps to soften frozen ground. In some cases, channels or gutters were dug to evacuate water from slopes or the tent/hut's sides. Sand seems to have been brought in to level, regularize and clean the floors.

At Duruthy, a Magdalenian open-air site by a cliff in the Pyrenean foothills, occupied in the winter, the humid environment led the occupants to lay down a very extensive pebble 'pavement' to consolidate the soil – hundreds of thousands of river cobbles were laid down at the foot of the cliff, one of the biggest such operations in the Palaeolithic.

We can occasionally have a clearer idea of constructions; for example, at Moravany-Zakowska, in Slovakia, Gravettians built a rectangular half-buried structure of wood, 8 m by 4 m. Here the interlocked beams – possibly a living floor – were found carbonised. However, perhaps the clearest evidence we have of wooden huts is that from Gönnersdorf, a Magdalenian open-air site in northern Germany. Located on a small promontory, protected by a relief from the wind, it dominated the Rhine, 40 m below.

Preservation of the site is excellent due to a covering of pumice after a volcanic eruption c. 12,900 bp.

This site comprised several round huts, paved with schist plaquettes. Regularly spaced post-holes mark the outline of each hut, while a deep one held the central post – so they may have resembled yurts. Charcoal and pollen revealed that the commonest tree here at the time was the Scots pine, but experiments in using it to make a hut found that the wood was breakable, bent and crooked, and so useless for the purpose. However alder was also present, and it yields straight and regular timbers that are well suited to the task. A reconstruction of a stable framework of alder was able to carry a roof and walls – these required about 40 horse hides, 23 of which formed the roof (the horse was the dominant species in the site's faunal remains). It is interesting that the posts were 1.2 m apart, which is the width of a hide of a Przewalski-type horse. The weight was 5.5 kg per sq m. It was found that such a roof could withstand a weight of snow of c. 45 kg/sq m. The total weight of horse hides was 250 kg, so it is highly probable that these were not transported but left at the site between stays.

The dwelling area was powdered with ochre – it was found under the plaquettes and also in pits. The entrance at the south-east was paved with big schist slabs, and postholes there suggest a windbreak. There was a second entrance at the west, facing the prevailing winds – probably to help the fire to draw or for getting rid of smoke through a hole in the ceiling. The diameter of the huts is 6 – 8 m, and the position of the entrances is very like those at Mezin/Mezhirich (see below, p. 66).

Figure 2.16. Reconstructed hut at Gönnersdorf.

Some huts were repeatedly occupied – as shown by several layers of paving. They must have been left standing, rather than dismantled and transported.

Faunal remains in the huts point to seasonality – one was occupied in the winter, as shown by the bones of horse foetuses. This means that pregnant mares were killed, who would have been impregnated in the spring. There were also the remains of lots of fur-bearing animals like arctic fox and variable hare. Another was occupied in the summer (it contained lots of foal hooves). Yet their architecture is identical.

These huts were used repeatedly. Each one contains different raw materials from different sources – quartzite, chalcedony and flint – so it is clear that the same groups kept using them. One group travelled to a region with Baltic flint (the Ruhr basin), while another was in the Meuse region when it was not at Gönnersdorf. Both of these regions are more than 100 km away, to the north-west and north-east. So they clearly lived elsewhere in other seasons. They came from different areas and had different traditions, but at times they came together in this place. They all engraved on plaquettes, but the paving of one winter hut (occupied by people from the north-east) had lots of mammoth engravings, while a summer hut (people from the north-west) had lots of bird drawings.

Figure 2.17. Reconstructed fireplace in the Gönnersdorf hut.

On the basis of ethnography, it has been suggested that people used big fixed houses in winter and transportable tents in the summer – and indeed there are traces of tents at Gönnersdorf which were clearly short-stay habitations and were taken down and carried away afterwards. But as mentioned above, at least one permanent hut at the site was a summer dwelling.

Next to one Gönnersdorf hearth was a mammoth femur stuck in the floor, presumably for supporting a grill (see fig. 2.17). But mammoths were rare here in the final Pleiastocene, so the other side of the hearth had a posthole. Unlike at Mezin/Mezhirich, there were numerous little

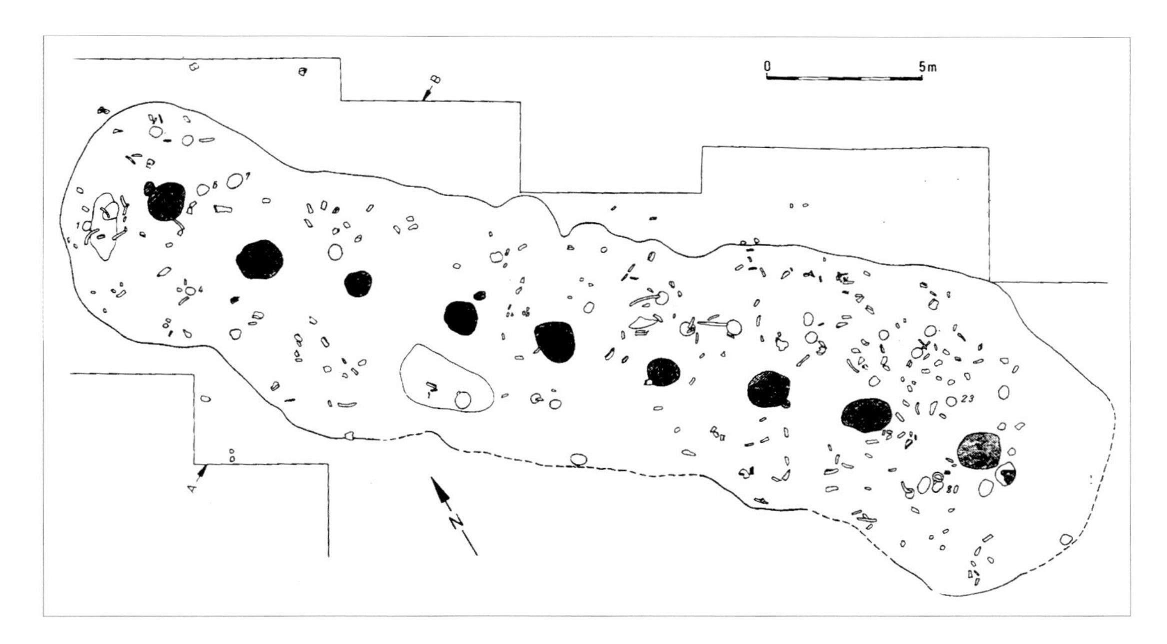

Figure 2.18. Plan of the dwelling with 9 hearths at Kostenki IV.

cooking pits. The heated and shattered quartz pebbles were later dumped in front of the hut. The great number of pits – 30 to 40 in one of the huts – plus the repeated reconstructions of hearths and pavings and the abundant material indicate the intensive and prolonged use of these dwellings.

Some of these features also exist at sites on the Russian Plain, but here the dwellings were often much bigger – for example at Kostenki IV, on the river Don, numerous little pits, 20-40 cm in diameter, were found inside two long huts, 23-35 m long and 5-6 m wide. Their floors were coloured with ochre and charcoal. One had a line of 9 hearths inside, and the pits were close to these, and some presumably played a role in cooking. It has been suggested that they had hides inside, could be filled with liquid, and heated by hot stones (quartz pebbles) from the fire. However, there are far too many pits in these dwellings (about 20 in the upper layer) for them all to be used in cooking at the same time; and after use, lots of things were placed in them – fox and hare legs in anatomical connection, spears and other bone/ivory objects, human and animal figurines. Perhaps things were simply less vulnerable in the pits than on the surface? Judging by the remains of variable hare and arctic fox, Kostenki IV seems to have been used repeatedly in the winter, around 23,000 years ago.

In the same period, there were also round dwellings – for example at sites such as Kostenki, Gagarino, Dolní Vestonice, etc. These were c. 6 m in diameter, 30 sq m, and each probably housed a family. We don't know if the long houses preceded them, or if both types existed together in the same site. The round houses have a central hearth as well as cooking pits.

Building with mammoths

Probably the best-known and certainly the most evocative huts of the last ice age are those made of mammoth bones. Many examples exist in Central and Eastern Europe, but some of the best known are in Ukraine – particularly Mezin and Mezhirich, which date to c. 16,000 years ago. On the vast plains of these regions, timber must often have been scarce, so mammoth bones and tusks were used as building materials.

Most huts were round, but some were elongated with several hearths inside; for example, the Pushkari I [**Fig. 19**] dwelling was 12 m long and 4.5 m wide, with 3 hearths equally spaced inside along the main axis. A pit 60-80 cm wide was filled with burnt fuel – only bone, not wood. There were also groups of little cooking pits. Bones and tusks from at least 60 mammoths were used in the construction. They formed a vaulted structure, probably with a central opening for smoke. This was just one house, but the site was very extensive, so there was probably a whole collection of such structures here.

At Kostenki I, an even bigger structure was found – 35 m long, 17 m wide – 425 sq m – with a straight line of 8 hearths inside. In fact it is hard to believe it was all one structure, and some researchers see it as a whole village of elongated, irregularly shaped huts, 80 cm-120 cm deep and 2-4 m in diameter, forming an oval shape around the line of hearths. Their superstructure was of mammoth bones and tusks. As at Kostenki IV, the floor was coloured by ochre and charcoal, and there were numerous small pits inside – some could be for cooking, but others might be post holes and storage pits. Mammoth femurs were stuck into the floor, apparently to act as little worktops or anvils. An even bigger structure at Avdeevo was at least 45 m long, 21 m wide – i.e. 950 sq m! Once again, it contained hearths and pits. At both sites, around the edge were bigger pits that seem to be semi-subterranean entrances to the big dwelling. Other huts are at ground level, c. 5 m in diameter or even – as at Kostenki XI – 8 m. The base of the walls was big mammoth bones, often skulls.

At Mezhirich it took the bones of 150 mammoths to make four huts. At hut 1, 25 skulls formed the base – they were buried with their cavities on the ground and

Figure 2.19. Reconstruction drawing of the long dwelling at Pushkari I.

the forehead facing inwards. The spaces between them were filled with smaller bones. The hut was c. 7 m in diameter, so covered 16-35 sq m. A second row of bones, mostly scapulas and pelvic bones, rested on the skulls. Higher still were 35 tusks which perhaps formed a dome, or served to hold down skins stretched over a framework of wooden poles. Reindeer antlers were found inside, on top of the rest, and may have formed part of an opening in the roof for smoke. So overall it was probably a conical or beehive-shaped construction of bone, hides and possibly timber.

Figure 2.20. a: The remains of mammoth-bone hut 4 at Mezhirich (Ukraine).

Figure 2.20. b: Modern reconstruction of hut 1 at Mezhirich.

Hut 1 also had 95 mammoth jawbones arranged on each other like chevrons, nested together in 24 columns – these may have formed a supporting or retaining wall around the foundation, or were perhaps merely decorative. Another Mezhirich hut has long bones aligned vertically and sometimes stuck in skulls. Other bones like bits of spine, skulls or shoulder-blades were used as reinforcement.

At both Mezhirich and Mezin, some hut entrances were formed by two tusks of the same size – there was a skull at either side, with its cavity uppermost and the forehead facing away. The tusks were placed in the skull cavities to form pillars. In one hut at Mezin, the two tusk points were joined together by a thick piece of tusk. The hut entrances mostly faced south-west or south-east, depending on the terrain and the prevailing winds. Inside, the hearths were shallow pits with no protective stones. They were repeatedly emptied, and the ashes were discarded outside, near the entrance. These waste areas comprised burned bones, as well as unburned bones and stone tools.

At Gontsy, six huts of different sizes were found (the biggest 6 m in diameter), with up to ten pits around each of them. Recent excavations have also revealed large working areas with hearths; dumping areas with remains of hearth cleaning and flint-knapping; butchering areas for reindeer, carnivores and rodents; and, in a nearby ravine, a major mammoth bone bed containing artifacts (presumably for butchering) and numerous hearths (doubtless for defrosting, drying and

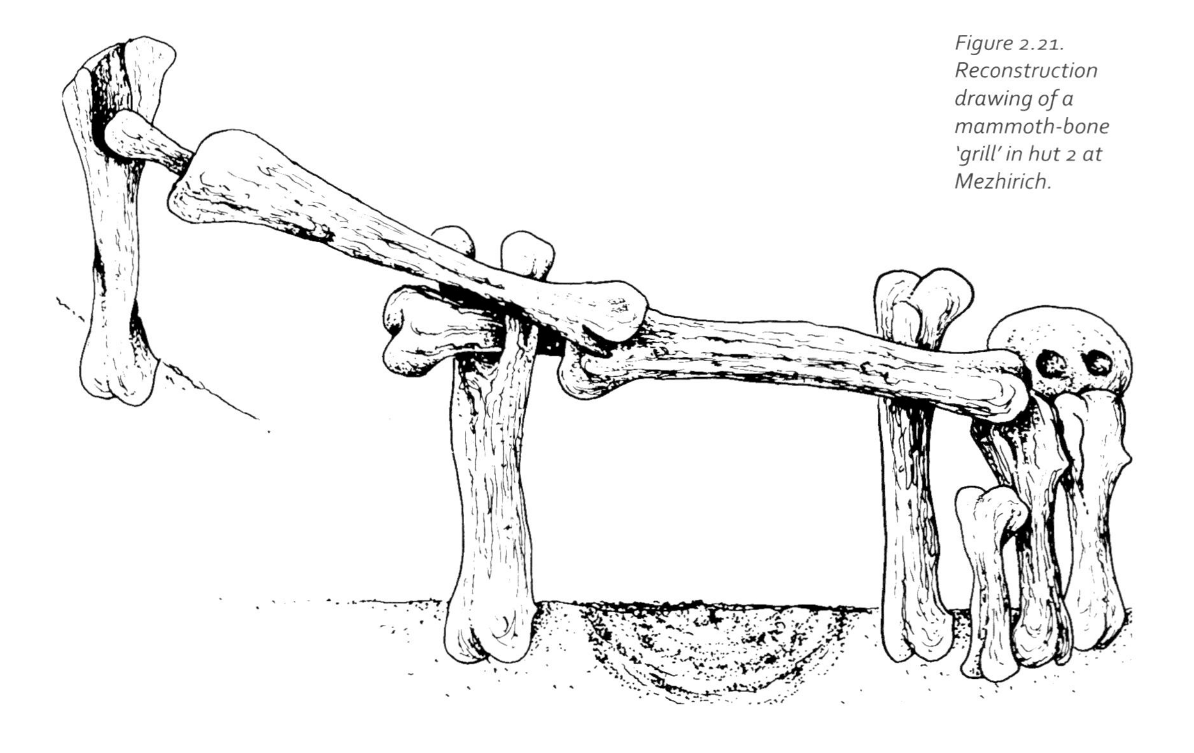

Figure 2.21. Reconstruction drawing of a mammoth-bone 'grill' in hut 2 at Mezhirich.

smoking meat). This bed comprises mostly ribs, vertebrae and distal leg bones – scapulae, pelvises, skulls, tusks, long bones and jaws are under-represented, since these are the bones found in the huts.

In some constructions there was a clear quest for aesthetic effect – at Yudinovo spine fragments alternate with skulls, while one Mezhirich hut has a rhythmic repetition of bone series. The roofs were sometimes domes made of complete tusks or wooden beams. Flat bones like the pelvis and scapula were often pierced for branches or ropes to go through to consolidate the structures. The whole thing could be covered with hides, sometimes held down by interlocked reindeer antlers. There was sometimes a draught excluder of earth to keep it impermeable and stable. Sometimes there was even interior decoration – at Mezhirich and Mezin, some mammoth bones bear zigzags, meanders, and other motifs painted in red ochre.

In the huts, mammoth long bones were often stuck in the ground near the hearth, probably as the support for a grill or barbecue. In hut 2 at Mezhirich, there were two mammoth femurs at either side of the fireplace. Cooking pits are not usually found in these dwellings; perhaps, in addition to the grills, they used skin vessels hanging from tripods, in which hot stones could boil food (see p. 156).

Needless to say, mammoth-bone structures required a huge amount of work and effort. Contrary to popular myth, people rarely hunted the animal (see pp. 134-35), and radiocarbon dating has shown the mammoth huts often comprise bones of very different ages, and in widely differing states of weathering and preservation. Many had been gnawed by carnivores. In short, the people must have scavenged and collected from skeletons produced by natural deaths and encountered in the landscape. They were brought back to camp as building materials or fuel. But even so, it was no easy task to gather the bones: a defleshed and dried mammoth skull weighs a minimum of c. 100 kg, or 300 kg if both tusks are attached, and moving one would not have been straightforward – it takes four men to lift one, so they cannot have been moved over big distances, unless people used sledges or even animals for the purpose (see pp. 123-28).

The sheer quantities of mammoth bones are overwhelming, especially in Moravia. For example, at Milovice, dating to 22,000 - 24,000 years ago, 98% of bones at the site are mammoth, and 64,000 bones were unearthed from the 700 sq m excavated (about 80% of the site). This may seem a lot, but in fact Dolní Vestonice and Pavlov produced more than twice as many from half that area, even though they were excavated much earlier and hence less carefully. The Milovice bone accumulation cannot be natural, as the site is not in a valley that formed a passage or a natural trap, and it is far from the river. And the presence of so many heavy, non-meaty bones such as scapulae, jaws and pelvises, as well as isolated molars, tusks and skulls, argues against them being the result of hunting (see pp. 134-35).

At Mezhirich, it is reckoned that to assemble and construct each of the four big huts needed at least 10 people working for 5 or 6 days! Estimates for huts at other sites are similar – e.g. 2.3 days for dwelling 1 at Dobranichevka and 3.3 days for each hut at Gontsy.

Obviously, these dwellings could not possibly be dismantled and transported. Unfortunately we know very little of the duration or seasonality of the stays in them. There were probably repeated seasonal stays, and in some sites the abundant remains of arctic fox and variable hare point to winter occupation. At Mezin and Dobranichevka, there are no newborn or very young reindeer, suggesting that neither site was occupied in the summer – they also have almost no game birds or fish. We are equally uncertain about the full size of these villages. Mezin had five houses, and we know at least four huts at Mezhirich (though there were probably more), but unlike at Pincevent (see above pp. 59-62) we cannot be sure if they were all occupied at once.

Some of these villages also contain big pits – for example, at Dobranichevka, over an area of several hundred square metres, there were four round huts, each about 4 m in diameter and never less than 20 m apart. But there were also ten large pits: one was filled with stone tools, ochre, pieces of amber (including beads), and bone splinters; but the other nine were filled with bones. One such pit was 2 m across at the top and 1.2 m deep! So it seems obvious that bones were collected or kept for fuel, and certainly small bits of charred bone are very common in many of these sites, especially in regions and periods with few trees, so little timber was available for shelters and fuel.

Fire

Humans may have achieved the controlled use of fire at least a million years ago. If so, then by the last ice age there must have been tremendous expertise in making fire, maintaining it, and transporting it. Fire afforded warmth, protection, lighting, and a means of cooking, as well as smoking, meat, fish and hides. It makes starches and animal protein more digestible, detoxifies many foods, and kills worms and parasites. Fire can also be used for heating flints and changing the colours of pigments, and, of course, for keeping threatening animals at a distance! It would also be relatively easy to build the kind of specialized fire needed to send smoke signals in order to pass information.

Contrary to widespread popular myth, one can't make fire by hitting two flints or quartzites together – any sparks produced are too weak and short-lived. But it can be done by striking flint and iron pyrites together, and directing the resulting sparks at tinder or dried fungus. The Magdalenian site of Trou de Chaleux (Belgium) yielded a fist-sized nodule of pyrites with a deep groove in it from repeated percussion, which suggests that

Figure 2.22. Drawing of the nodule of pyrites from Le Trou de Chaleux (Belgium).

this method was known and used. The rock-shelter of Laussel (Dordogne) contained a similar nodule with marked striations attributable to percussion by hard stones. This method became common in the Mesolithic and Neolithic periods, and was still being used in the 18th/19th centuries by some Eskimoan and North American Indian groups.

Instead of percussion, the commonest way of making fire was by friction. Some 19th-century prehistorians thought that cupmarks in stones in the Magdalenian shelter of La Madeleine (Dordogne) might have been used for this, but that method does not work -- the sand produced smothers any ignition. Other prehistorians interpreted some bone implements as firemakers, but there is no ethnographic evidence for bone being used in this way, and experiments show that it does not work. To make fire one needs wood: if you have the right wooden implements (firesticks) and some tinder, it takes between 20 seconds and a minute to obtain a flame. Normally a vertical piece of wood is placed into a hollow on a horizontal piece, and twirled rapidly by hand or with a bow. Soft woods are best, though hard varieties can also be used – among the best are lime, laurel and ivy. The method produces not sparks but embers; you have to place them onto dried grass, straw or lichens, and then blow! Unfortunately, since wood does not normally survive in ice age sites (see pp. 87-90), we have no direct evidence of the practice. Moss, birch bark and some kinds of fungus make good tinder for igniting fire.

It can safely be assumed that it was always important to gather suitable firewood and kindling, so it was crucial to have the knowledge and ability to distinguish trees (not all kinds of wood ignite easily) and know where to go to find them. It was also necessary to store a sufficient quantity of wood and kindling in a dry place – cave-mouths and rock-shelters were ideal for this. It was also crucial to keep the fire going – this job may perhaps have been assigned to children – as it would be difficult to relight it in humid conditions. Obviously, wherever possible fires would have been built out of the wind and rain.

Surprisingly, fire can be easy to transport – some Australian Aborigines carried burning embers around, wrapped in leaves or hide; and Patagonian Indians would travel with a fire in the bottom of their canoes, on a bed of gravel and wet moss, so that they could immediately light one on arrival. In this case it was the children who looked after it, as the adults were steering and paddling.

We know from charcoal that wood was the main fuel in most places and periods. They may also have burned dried animal dung, grasses, peat, brush, or dried seaweed, but these have left no traces. But we do know that bones were a major source of fuel, especially on the Russian plain, but also sometimes in western Europe in periods when timber was scarce – for example, in the Pyrenean cave of Enlène, where some hearths in hollows contained bones, and a third of bone fragments recovered were burned. Experiments show that fresh bone can be a decent fuel, but – apart from the smell and smoke (especially in caves like Enlène with no natural chimneys to evacuate the smoke), there are other

Figure 2.23. Some of the hearths deep inside the cave of Enlène (Ariège).

disadvantages. It takes a lot of time and effort to get it burning; this probably needs wood at the start – dried grass and brush are not sufficient. Bone does not burn for long – a cow scapula lasts about 30 minutes – and it stops burning suddenly, so great quantities are needed (15 kg of bovid bones provide about 90 minutes of feeble flames). The highest temperatures obtained are 650-680° C, whereas 800° C is easily attainable with wood such as pine or oak. But 200° is enough to carbonise a steak. So burnt bone found in a hearth may just be from cooking or use as a subsidiary fuel.

As we have already seen, ice age hearths had a wide variety of shapes and sizes. Some were flat, others in hollows, with or without a stone edging or a base of slabs. It must have been necessary to clear ashes away regularly, as at Pincevent (see above pp. 59-62) where they probably used reindeer shoulder-blades as shovels. At the Swiss Magdalenian open-air site of Hauterive-Champréveyres, 12 apparently contemporaneous areas of charcoal were found, c. 1.7 m apart, and varying in size from 0.4 to 4 sq m. These flat hearths had up to 3 cm depth of ash, and 99% of the charcoal was willow, plus some birch. They seem to have burnt small branches and twigs, but there were some burnt bones, eggshell fragments, and fish scales, presumably from cooking. In open-air sites, wind is an especially important factor for fires; the dominant winds in the Neuchâtel region are west and south-west, and in the site 80% of remains are on the west/south-west edges of the hearths, so that people could avoid smoke – which suggests that there were no tents here.

The efficient use of fire demands that some of the heat produced in combustion be retained – but in the open-air this is impossible, and even in light and poorly insulated structures, such as skin tents, it is not easy to achieve. In structures of this kind used by the Athabascan Indians, the interior remained cold in spite of the use of a large fire, and frost would rapidly form on surfaces not exposed to the direct radiant heat. So, although a tent prevents exposure to direct wind cooling, the amount of heating within may be very limited. In complete contrast, the well-insulated snow houses of Eskimoan people are tropical or sub-tropical inside when it's -45° C outside! Other cold-exposed peoples attempt to reduce heat loss from their dwellings by the use of a double-walled construction – the large skin houses of the Siberian Chukchi contain an inner sleeping compartment, also of skin, which contains a fire in the winter. This may be the case with some of the ice age house plans at Kostenki, for example, and being semi-subterranean also helped!

As mentioned above, fire was used not only for cooking, but also for the processing of raw materials. Where flint is concerned, heat improves the possibilities of pressure retouch, and also retouch by percussion. The technique was clearly used by the Solutreans, the greatest flint-knappers of the ice age – for example at the Spanish cave of Parpalló. Experiments have shown that it is a very complex technique: the flint has to be at a constant temperature of over 200° C for 20 to 70 hours, and is then cooled very slowly. This modifies the internal structure, and makes it much easier to detach fine blades by pressure or percussion. In the Magdalenian of Etiolles (see below), they could obtain blades 30-40 cm long. Heat was probably also used for hardening wooden implements – this is known thanks to a yew spear from the Middle Paleolithic site of Lehringen, Germany, dating to c. 125,000 years ago.

The main mineral pigments used in the last ice age were ochre and manganese, both of which are fairly ubiquitous in limestone country. It is clear that Upper Palaeolithic people knew that the colour of ochre is modified by heat, and fragments at different stages of oxidation have been found in hearths. Yellow ochre, when heated beyond 250° C, passes through different shades of red as it oxidises into haematite. A further stage in pigment preparation, used in the cave of Lascaux, involved the mixing of different powdered minerals. Chemical analysis of 10 samples produced some surprising results; for instance, one pigment contained calcium-phosphate, a substance obtained by heating animal bone to 400° C. It was then mixed with calcite, and heated again to 1000°, thus transforming the mix into tetracalcite phosphate.

HAVE YOU GOT A LIGHT?

Fire was also used for lighting, which is one reason why hearths are found inside caves. But how did they light themselves when moving around at night or inside deep caves? There were two kinds of portable systems: burning torches and stone lamps.

In one experiment, a researcher went barefoot to the farthest depths of the Pyrenean cave of Niaux (2 km into the mountain), carrying six pine torches, each 80 cm long and impregnated with beeswax and a reserve of 200 gm of soft wax. One torch was lit before entering. Walking slowly, he did the 4 km round trip in 3 hours, before he ran out of illumination. He found that each torch gave off an orangey-yellow flame which provided quite enough light for walking – pine torches emit very bright light but their resin also produces dense black smoke. Juniper, on the other hand, is good for duration, light-intensity and an absence of smoke.

Torches have some major advantages: they are easy and rapid to light, especially if birch bark is used for ignition, and they radiate light in all directions. They need continuous oxygenation and supervision – it used to be thought that charcoal marks on cave walls were made when people tried to revive dying torches, but experiments have shown that the best way to do this is simply to move them around. Just walking fast keeps them burning, as long as they are made of several branches rather than a single stick. Impregnating them with resin or animal fat extends the light's intensity and duration – they can normally last up to an hour.

Lamps, on the other hand, can produce stable lighting for over an hour, but it is not multi-directional – mostly upwards and laterally, but very little downwards. So torches were best for crossing wide spaces and exploring caves, since they lit floor, ceiling and walls, with an action area of c. 6 m, whereas lamps were needed for prolonged stays in enclosed spaces with little ventilation and allowed an action area of c. 3 m. Lamps are not good for difficult passages due to possible fuel spillage, so the two lighting methods were clearly complementary.

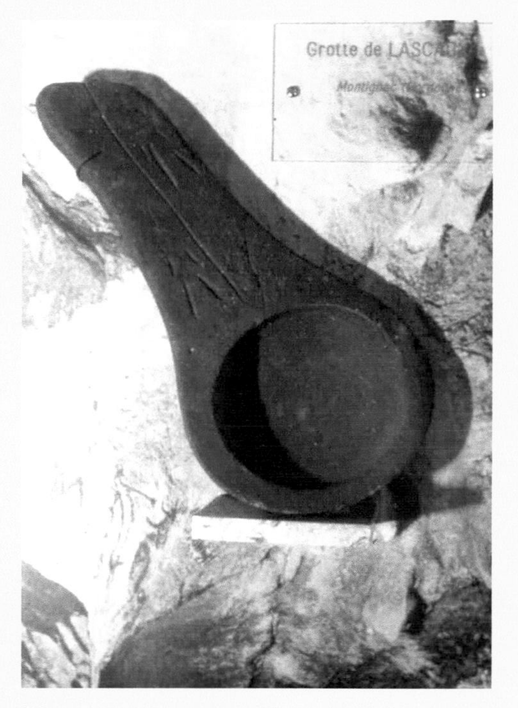

Figure 2.24. The engraved lamp found in Lascaux (Dordogne).

Sometimes big shells and fossil shells were used as lamps, but most were flat or slightly hollowed stones. There are a few beautifully carved stone lamps, and some such as those from La Mouthe or Lascaux even have engravings on them. Many are of a red sandstone from the Corrèze region of France, and their manufacture therefore seems

Figure 2.25. An experimental Ice Age stone lamp, burning animal fat.

to have been a regional speciality. Combustion residues in some specimens have been subjected to analysis, which indicated that they were fatty acids of animal origin – e.g. the La Mouthe lamp contained black material which proved to be carbonised animal fat; while remains of resinous wood or of non-woody material clearly come from the wicks (residues in the carved Lascaux specimen proved to be burned juniper leaves). In one experiment to make a lamp like that of La Mouthe, a piece of sandstone was worked with picks and choppers, then finished with scrapers and burins – the work took almost 5 hours. Other experiments have been carried out with replica lamps of different types, different fuels (cow lard, horse grease, deer marrow, seal fat), and a variety of wicks (lichen, dried moss, birch bark, juniper wood, pine needles, dried mushrooms, and kindling). The results led to a number of interesting insights, which were confirmed by study of the lamps used by Eskimoan people.

Firstly, a good fuel needs to be fluid, and easy to light. The initial melting of the animal fat needs to absorb the wick material which, by burning, continues to melt the fuel. This cycle can continue for hours providing both wick and fuel are replenished from time to time: one estimate is that 500 gm of fat will keep a lamp going for 24 hours. It would have been easy to carry extra fuel, as animal fat is not heavy or bulky – a mere 40 gm would give an hour's light. The flame is conditioned by the number of wicks and the degree of liquefaction of the fat. It is worth bearing in mind that it may have been difficult to obtain sufficient fat from lean animals in the winter.

Since they must have understood the importance of fat, particularly for children, they presumably devised ways of storing it.

There are two basic types of lamp: the open-circuit model, in which the fuel is evacuated as it melts; and the closed-circuit, where the fuel is kept in a cavity. The open type seems very rare in the ice age, although many simple slabs of stone may have been used like this (about 130 limestone slabs at Lascaux were interpreted in this way, although many are now lost, and only about 36 seem likely lamps); most recognisable Palaeolithic lamps are of closed-circuit type. In Eskimoan communities, the open types are for occasional use, while the closed types – in which far more work has been invested – are used daily.

But how bright are these lamps? The answer, surprisingly, is that they are pretty dim even in comparison with a modern candle. The power of the light given off depends on the quality and quantity of fuel; the flame is usually unstable and trembling. Experiments with a stone lamp using horse fat produced a flame of one-sixth the power of a candle, according to measurements with a photometer.

With such limited radiance, it would have been necessary for ice age people to use several lamps at once, or to resort to burning torches (which have an average light intensity that is five times greater than a fat lamp with two wicks). For example, Pech Merle's spotted horse frieze is four metres in length, so could not all be lit with one lamp – it would have required several at once, and the same, of course, applies in many other cases, such as the Altamira ceiling, while Lascaux's Hall of the Bulls would have needed dozens at once. In Chauvet some figures were drawn while balancing with some difficulty on rocks or stalagmites – one hand was used to hold oneself and the other for drawing – and so the light source must have been elsewhere – probably someone holding a torch or lamp. In some decorated caves in southern Spain, there were 'fixed lamps' that burned on the top of big stalagmites.

We, of course, are spoiled by artificial light, and are no longer accustomed to dimmer sources. But in fact it is surprising how much can be seen by the light of a single candle, and a large cave-chamber could be lit adequately with two or three. It has been found that with only one lamp one can move around a cave, read, and even sew if one is close enough to the light – the eye cannot really tell that the flame is weaker than a candle. Indeed it is best to visit the decorated caves with weak light, because these images were never intended to be seen in a strong electric glare.

Conclusion

In this second chapter we have learned about the geography, landscapes and changing climates of our ice age ancestors. We also showed that these early hunter-gatherers harvested everything available to them in the landscape in order to make ends meet – and to endure the frequently brutal conditions the ice age brought. A clear picture is now emerging of just how resourceful these prehistoric communities were, and in Chapter 3 we will learn how they made use of every available resource to enhance their chances of survival and success in such a challenging world.

Chapter 3

Our Crafty Ancestors

Toolmaking

Ice age toolmakers have almost always been depicted as men and their weapons and implements have generally been linked with men – for example harpoons for fishing were assigned to the male tool kit, while women were thought to have fished with hooks or nets!

Women as both toolmakers and users have been well documented ethnographically, and there are many examples of indigenous men and women carrying their own tools in a leather bag around their waist; it is probably safe to assume that this was also a common practice during the ice age. It is also highly likely that women would not only have carried their own tools but also been responsible for making them – so that if their tools broke they did not have to wait for their men to mend or replace them, when they could get around to it! Young adults would have also needed to learn how to make tools, and someone – male or female – would have needed to teach them.

There is absolutely no biological basis for a belief that women are not suited to using 'tools', and ice age women would certainly have used the most

Figure 3.1. Henri Breuil, in a book of 1949, was one of the few scholars to depict ice age women making stone tools.

appropriate implement for a particular job. What remains an open question is which specific jobs were assigned to men or women in the community. Many tools – such as some scrapers and knives – that were once thought to have been used for hunting now look more like implements that could have been used for skin processing. Skinning animals for food and fur, and de-skinning fish, were tasks which required sharp cutting tools, and women doubtless carried a variety of them in their tool kit.

Women will certainly also have used 'sticks' for simple tasks, and of course these have perished. But for gathering plant materials, underground roots and tough vegetation like bracken, something sharp was needed to do the job – a simple stick, sharp or otherwise, would be useless.

Weapons and tools made of hard materials are those which survive in the archaeological record, and they are generally associated (not necessarily correctly) with men, while those made of soft materials have mostly disintegrated, and are generally associated (not necessarily correctly) with women.

The flint stones

The best known remains from the ice age – because they are indestructible – are the countless stone tools made in the period. Palaeolithic people developed tremendous knowledge of the properties of different rocks, especially flint. They worked some kinds of hard stone (limestone, granite) with picks or hammers, while soft stones such as steatite or sandstone were abraded and polished to make lamps, figurines, pendants, beads, etc. Even chalk was sometimes worked, as in the Gravettian site of Amiens-Renancourt (northern France), where no less than 15 female figurines in this material have recently been found, as well

Figure 3.2. One of the recently discovered chalk female figurines from Amiens-Renancourt (Somme, France).

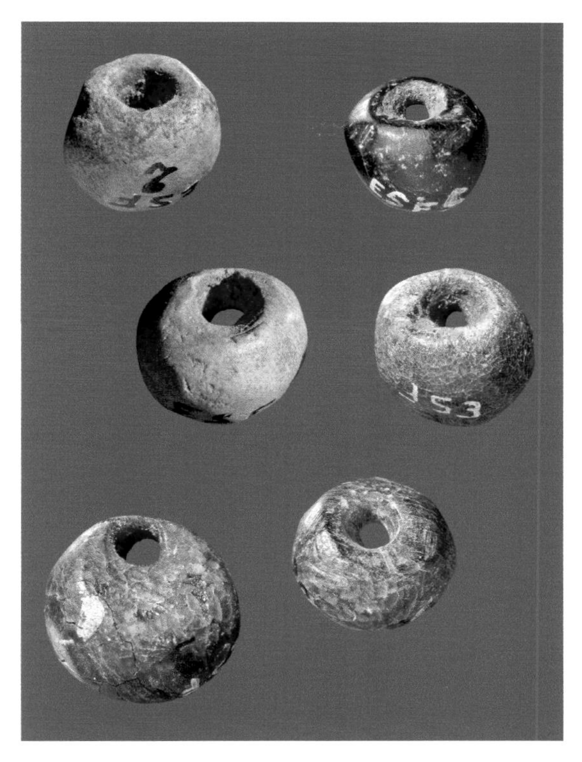

Figure 3.3. In the Pyrenean cave of Enlène, almost 250 small beads were found – 153 in lignite, 50 in amber, and a few of limestone, schist and talc. The beads were clearly made here since various stages of manufacture are present, as well as waste fragments; the traces of ochre, present at every stage, especially in perforations, show that it was probably used as an abrasive.

as chalk jewellery – it seems to have been a regional speciality – perhaps even a production centre for such statuettes. Tough pebbles and cobbles were multi-purpose, being used as anvils, grinders, pounders, smoothers and sharpeners. Our predecessors in Europe, the Neanderthals, had developed about 60 kinds of stone tools, but the people of the last ice age had more than 200, as well as lots of bone and antler implements (see below).

They could accurately predict the forms of flakes and blades that could be struck off nodules of flint. They could also produce large series of regular blades from a block, which could then be turned into all kinds of tools (for cutting, scraping and piercing, and some multi-purpose) by striking it with a stone, wooden or antler hammer. In this way a great deal of cutting edge could be obtained.

Where flint is concerned, they knew the very best sources. For example, the huge decorated cave of Rouffignac (Dordogne) has countless nodules of flint protruding from its walls, but they are of terrible quality so were completely ignored by ice age people, who were well aware of where they could obtain better-quality material – such as at Bergerac, not too far away. At La Combe Saunière (Dordogne), the Solutreans made two-thirds of their tools from mediocre flint obtained less than 20 km away, but the rest from excellent flint brought in from at least 20-30 km and even from more than 70 km. The good flint was not worked at the site but brought in as blades or finished tools.

An idea of the lengths people would go to for good flint can be seen in some high-altitude camps in Italy. At Monte Avena, in the eastern Alps, they were extracting flint at 1450 m; the first rough knapping and selection was done there, and a few tools made. At Val Lastari, at 1060 m, another camp next to a rock wall, flint was extracted, knapped and stocked. Two structures here contained flint blocks that had undergone testing for workability. A third structure, 100 x 40 cm, by the wall, was 25 cm deep, and filled with intact blocks, nuclei, and hundreds of pieces of knapping debris. This workshop was devoted to producing blades and bladelets for export and use in tools and weapons. Both sites were also dwellings, located along seasonal migration routes.

At Pincevent (see above, pp. 59-62), the quality of the preserved evidence is such that one can actually see where flint-knappers worked outside the tents – either because there was more room, or because they were practising. The

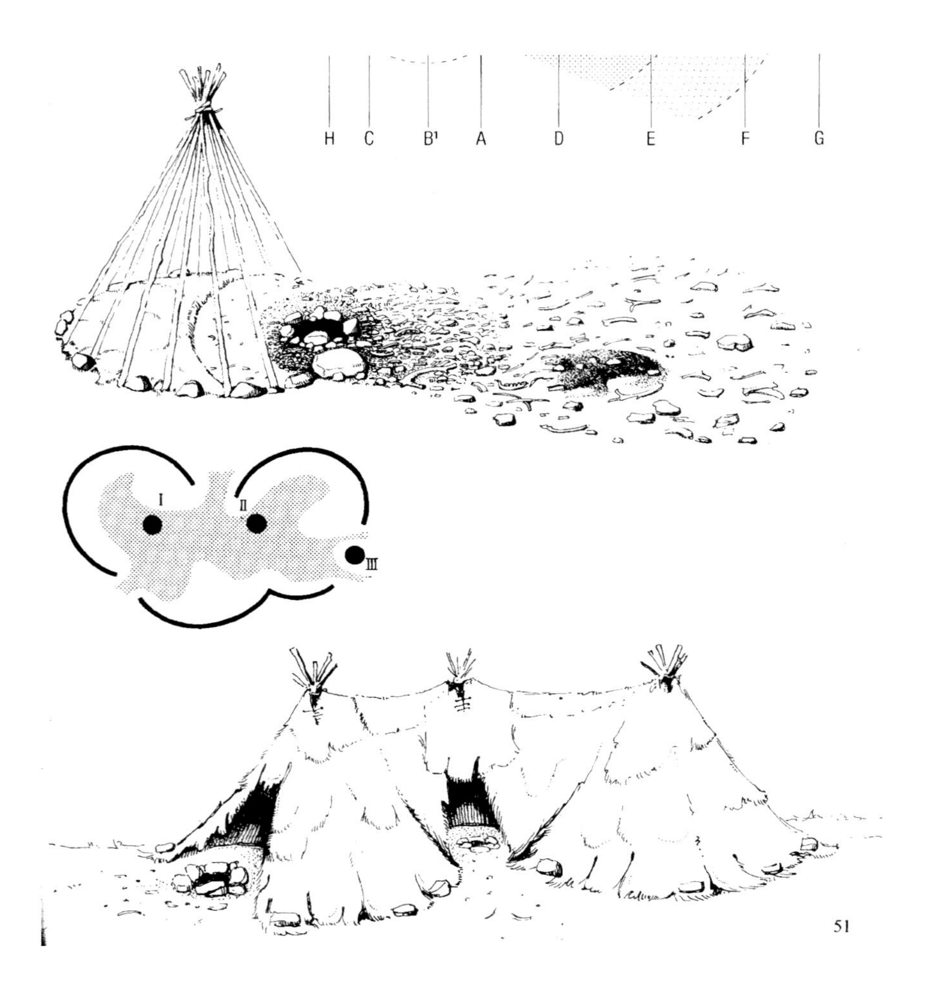

Figure 3.4. Reconstruction drawings of Pincevent dwellings, hearths and debris scatters.

distribution of the debris sometimes even shows if they were right- or left-handed, sitting on the ground or on a block, or if the knees were protected by a leather apron. By fitting flints together and thus reassembling the original nodules, researchers have learned about the knapping techniques, and the distribution of implements to different tents.

Refitting, or conjoining as it is sometimes called, entails attempting to put tools and flakes back together again, like a 3D jigsaw puzzle. The work is tedious and time-consuming, but can produce spectacular results. One refitted stone, designated N103, from the Magdalenian site of Etiolles includes 124 pieces, some of which are blades over 30 cm long.

Why do archaeologists devote so many hours of hard work to refitting exercises? Very broadly because refitting makes it possible to follow the stages of the knapper's craft and – where pieces from one core have been found in different areas – even the knapper's (or the core's) movements around the site. Of course,

Figure 3.5. A refitted terminal Gravettian flint core (made from 141 flints) from Lapa do Anecrial, Portugal.

displacement of flakes may have nothing to do with the changing location of the knapper: a burin spall, for example, can jump seven metres when struck off! And it should not be assumed automatically that each core was processed in one episode of work: it is known from ethnography that a core can be reused after a short or long period of absence.

Most of the Pincevent lithic material came from the river or nearby, but some flints are from elsewhere (e.g. 40 km to the north-east). They used mediocre local nodules from the river banks, and did not even bother to get the better flint available from cliffs on the other bank! So clearly, flint work was not important to them. The inhabitants probably spent little time on flint knapping – in one stay of three to four weeks, a group of four to five people probably didn't spend more than 15 hours on it; this was adequate to make the implements and weapons needed for hunting and processing the reindeer. Blades, bladelets, scrapers, awls and burins were made around the hearths. But they did not use fire in making flints. One particular stone core was found to have had a dozen blades removed from it beside one hearth, and eight of the blades had been retouched. The same core was later moved to a different hearth and work recommenced; some of the flakes struck off here were made into tools such as burins, all of which were used to work reindeer antler.

At one hearth, L115, one excellent knapper produced around 15 big regular blades, some of which went to four other hearths located 10, 25, 40 and 70 m away; and some blades from them came to L115. So it seems that some experts had group responsibilities or social roles.

At the Swiss open-air site of Hauterive-Champréveyres (see above, p. 72), there was intense flint-knapping around each flat hearth – mainly producing tools known as burins and backed bladelets. In one place there were what appear to be two stone-block seats with lots of knapping debris at their base.

At Etiolles (see above, p. 62), the best knappers worked by the main hearth in the centre of the tent; the others were on the periphery. At Pincevent, on the other hand, knappers of average skill sometimes worked round the main hearths. The best flint was reserved for the best knappers, while the others worked with inferior material. Etiolles has more than a dozen hearths from occupations in November and late winter/early spring, and there are thousands of pieces of knapping debris around them. This site has a particularly high level of production from flint of top quality – being close to a source, the inhabitants could bring whole blocks in to work on. Some of these nodules were 40-50 cm long, even 90-100 cm. They also brought some tools of non-local flint into the site. The richest dwellings contained 300-500 kg of knapping debris (not including the blades that were taken away). One knapper in unit U5 obtained at least 500 blades, 20-40 cm long, from 25 nuclei. That goes way beyond individual needs and must have been done for the group or even for trade.

Curiously, alongside the really masterly blade production, unit U5 also contained some clumsy knapping debris, highly grouped – which can presumably be attributed to apprentices. As mentioned above, the really good knapping was done close to the central hearth; there was occasional knapping behind this, and the really clumsy knapping was done farthest away. The excavators detected at least 11 bad episodes, showing different degrees of skill or progress, and using nuclei that had already been worked by the experts.

The Solutreans were by far the greatest flintworkers of the ice age. At the French cave of Le Placard (Charente) they made about 5000 shouldered points, as well as numerous willow-leaf points. One might see this as mass production, but of course it depends on the timespan of occupation at the site. At the open-air knapping site of Montaut (Landes), they created large quantities of identical and 'bizarre' fine flints, which implies a high output by a small number of gifted craftsmen, or even by a single talented individual. Thanks to cases like this, one wonders whether some really expert flintworkers were itinerant, travelling around the regions, and earning their keep by making tools for the different groups. It is likely that most people in a group were capable of making a basic set of tools, but in each group – or perhaps in each generation – there will have been one or more gifted individuals who had far greater expertise. And it is the best of these experts who could have made their living this way – offering their skills in exchange for food and board.

How can we assess what stone tools were used for? One way is to compare them with similar implements from historically documented cultures, where tool functions are known. But in recent decades, microscopic analysis of microwear on the edges of stone tools can be compared with traces left by experimental use of replica tools on different materials. For example, the wear on some flint tools suggests that bone-working had an important role at Pincevent.

Establishing the function of a set of tools can produce unexpected results that transform our picture of activity at a site. For example, the Magdalenian site of Verberie, near Paris, yielded only one bone tool; yet studies of microwear on the site's flint tools show the great importance of boneworking: an entire area of the site seems to have been devoted to the working of bone and antler.

Mastic

We are sure that hafting materials were used in the last ice age since traces of them have been found in even earlier periods – for example, what seems to be a mastic made of heated bitumen has been found on several stone tools from the Middle Palaeolithic site of Umm el-Tlel in Syria. This has been confirmed by the discovery in Germany of a complex birch pitch, dating to 80,000 years ago, which is thought to have served as a glue for securing wooden shafts to stone blades.

Figure 3.6. a: the antler spearpoint from Pincevent with flints still attached; ► b: an antler spearpoint with backed bladelets from Ostrovskaya (Perm, Russia).

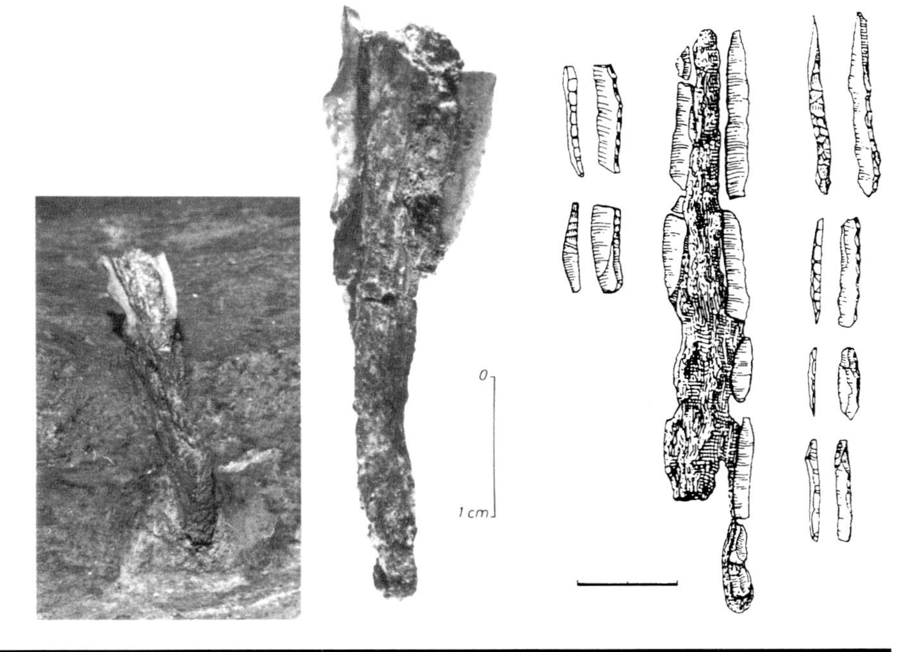

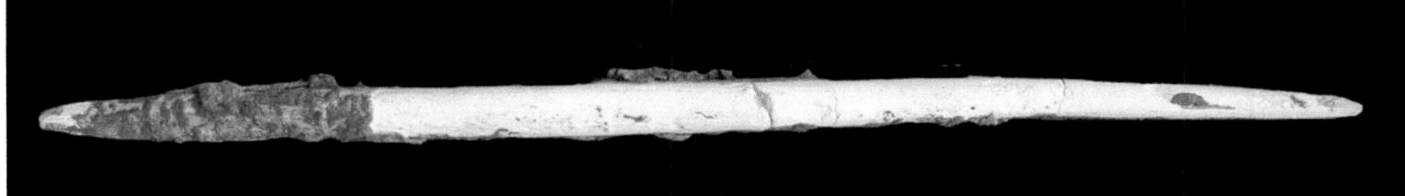

Figure 3.6. ▲c/ ► d: a spearpoint from Lascaux with traces of hafting.

During the last ice age many small flint tools must have been hafted or inserted into supports, most of which have not survived. They were probably fixed to shafts with materials such as those mentioned above, or pine resin or beeswax. The Villabruna shelter (Italy) yielded the 12,000 bp burial of a young adult male with what seems to be a hunter's kit which comprised not only tools but also a tennis-ball-sized lump of propolis (bee glue) and ochre. It is known from ethnography that powdered ochre mixed with fish glue (especially that from sturgeon bladders) could also be used for hafting. At Lascaux, for example, one flint bladelet had traces along one edge of a mastic made of sap or resin and red ochre. In 1982, at Pincevent, a 43 mm fragment of a spearhead, made of reindeer antler, was found stuck almost vertically into the ground, 30 cm from a hearth. It had two finely retouched flint bladelets stuck into grooves, one on either side. Similar spearpoints with grooves down them had been found at many other sites, and it had often been thought that they were for poison, but thanks to the Pincevent specimen it is clearly far more probable that they were for mini-flint barbs.

Feats of clay

Did ice age people know how to make pottery? Obviously they did: any fire lit in a cave-floor will have hardened the clay around it; indeed, lumps of fired clay around hearths bear a marked resemblance to crude potsherds. The recent discovery that pottery in Japan, China and eastern Siberia dates back at least 13,000 - 21,000 years merely underlines the fact that, if ice age people did not make pottery, it was through lack of need rather than through ignorance. Pottery vessels are heavy and fragile, and of little use to mobile hunter-gatherers.

Nevertheless, a number of terracotta figurines have survived and been recovered in different areas: a few examples are known from the Pyrenees, North Africa and Siberia, but considerable quantities – 77 fairly intact, together with over 10,000 fragments (and others poorly fired, which have disintegrated) – have been found in the Czech Republic at the open-air sites of Dolní Vestonice (more than 5700 fragments), Pavlov (more than 3500) and Predmostí and Petrkovice (a handful each), where they are securely dated to the Gravettian, *c.* 28,000 bp. They comprise small figurines of animals and a few humans and display some spatial differentiation (i.e. herbivores in one hut, but human figurines in the centre of another, together with carnivores); a hearth or 'oven' for their manufacture has also been found. The best known of these figurines is the 'Venus' of Dolní Vestonice, made, like the rest, of wetted local loess soil (see above, p. 14). Fragments of three terracotta animal figures have also been reported from the Gravettian of Wachtberg, Austria (c. 32,000 bp), 36 from Vela Spila cave in Croatia (c. 21,000 - 18,000 bp) and others from Kostenki I (Russia).

Experimentation has been carried out on the manufacture of the terracotta figurines as well as of the 'oven' or 'kiln' in which they were baked. Tests on the Czech figurines indicate that they were fired at temperatures from 500° to 800 °C, and the shape of their fractures implies that they were broken by

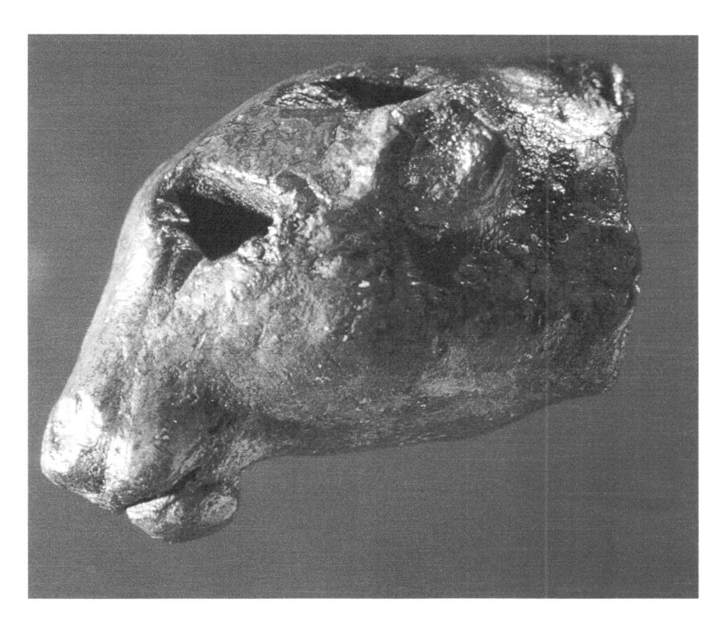

Figure 3.7. Terracotta lion head from Dolní Vestonice.

thermal shock – in other words they were placed, while still wet, in the hottest part of the fire, and thus deliberately caused to explode – though it should be noted that they would merely have shattered, not popped! Rather than carefully made art objects, therefore, their lack of finish and the manner of their breakage suggest that they may have been used in some special ritual.

Using hard bits of animals

Bone, antler and mammoth ivory were used for numerous kinds of tools and weapons, from spearthrowers to harpoons, and from needles to spearpoints. Ice age people cut and sawed limb bones, ribs, phalanges, etc, and turned them into a wide range of implements. Antlers were also used to make a variety of implements, including perforated batons (see below, pp. 94-95). Bird bones were sometimes used to make needles, as well as musical instruments (see below, p. 230). Ivory was transformed into a remarkable array of tools, spears, daggers, knives, as well as figurines, bracelets, beads, etc.

As we have already seen (see above, p. 85), large quantities of bones were stocked at some sites. In the cave of Le Mas d'Azil (Ariège) – one of the two 'supersites' of the Pyrenees – early excavators found intact deer bones and antlers carefully arranged along the walls, and numerous heads of horse and reindeer and jaws of other animals had been deposited together. There were also large accumulations of reindeer antlers, including many 'very young' animals. In the other Pyrenean supersite, the cave of Isturitz, the northern chamber had accumulations in two places of worked and unworked reindeer and red deer antlers – probably a reserve stock – while the vertebrae and ribs of large herbivores were common around the cave entrance but not further inside.

Antlers were mostly collected when shed – those of big males seem to have been chosen for size and thickness (e.g. in the north Spanish caves of El Juyo and Rascaño); but one perforated baton at Tito Bustillo was made from an antler that was cut from the skull. At French sites such as La Madeleine, La Vache or Pincevent, antlers on killed females were present, but little used.

Strips of antler were detached by the groove-and-splinter technique. Experiments have shown that first the antler had to be soaked in water for hours to soften it, then two parallel incisions were cut with sharp flints through the compact outer tissue, after which the strip between the incisions could be prised off. Reindeer antlers could yield 'baguettes' or rods of 50 cm length or more.

The eyed needle was invented during the last ice age. The earliest known occur in Siberia, more than 40,000 years ago, but in Western and Southern Europe they appear to be an invention of the Solutreans, c. 26,000 - 23,000 bp. Specimens are known of different sizes: the Magdalenian cave of Enlène contained no fewer than 369, mostly made from the metacarpal bones of reindeer or bison due to their density and robustness. The needles' high degree of polish show they had been intensively used. However, most needles were so fine and delicate that they must have been far too fragile for penetrating skins or sewing leather and furs. The holes must have been made with robust flint or bone awls, and then the needles were simply used to carry thread through them. They were also appropriate for woven material, or for sewing beads and shells onto lighter textiles; for example, the diameter of the eyed needles found at the site of La Madeleine (Dordogne) was probably determined by the task of stitching *Dentalium* shells onto clothing. Since we know from marks on their teeth that Neanderthals used toothpicks, it is perfectly possible that some of the smallest Upper Palaeolithic needles may also have served this purpose!

One implement characteristic of the European Magdalenian (more than 3000 are known) is the antler or bone 'harpoon' – some with barbs on one side, others with barbs on both. They have traditionally been seen as tools for fishing, and this may have been true at times, but many have no sharp point and they have also been found in sites with no fish remains. Similar implements are known from recent cultures in North America and among the Eskimoan peoples – they were attached to belts, and objects were hung from them.

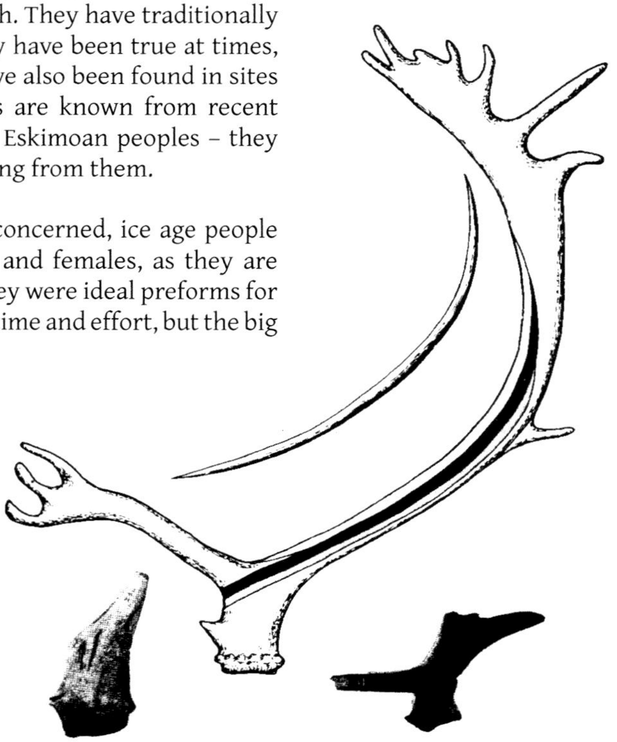

Figure 3.8. The groove-and-splinter technique.

Where the working of mammoth ivory is concerned, ice age people will have preferred the tusks of juveniles and females, as they are relatively thin, long and straight – hence they were ideal preforms for making rods, etc. Straightening tusks takes time and effort, but the big ivory spears with the Sunghir children (pp. 26-27) – one of 2 m, the other 1.6 m – appear to have been straightened by heat! Experiments have shown that, if one wraps three layers of wet hide around a tusk, and then places it all on a hearth, then after 1 hour 45 minutes the hides are burnt, but the tusk has become soft and can be worked and reshaped in all kinds of ways. Alternatively, successive cycles of immersion in water until the ivory is saturated make it possible to straighten it.

Figure 3.9. One of the hundreds of eyed needles from the cave of Enlène (Ariège), still trapped in sediment.

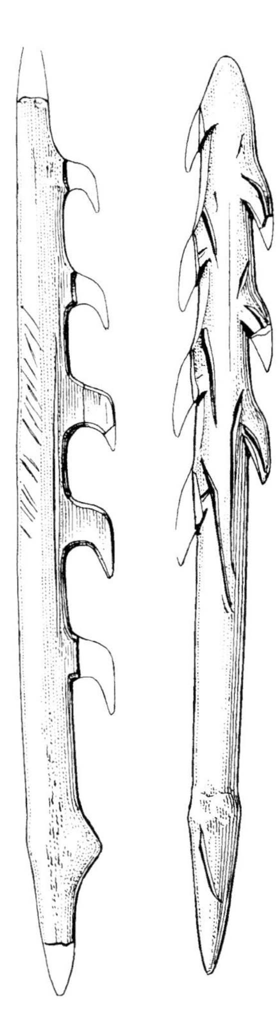

Figure 3.10. a/ ► b: 'Harpoons' with unilateral and bilateral barbs. La Madeleine (Dordogne).

Huge quantities of beads were carved from ivory – for example at Sunghir (pp. 25-26). It has been estimated that each bead took 15 minutes to produce (after making ivory blanks, cutting preforms, cutting and drilling holes), so the c. 14,000 beads in the three main burials represent over 3500 hours of labour. If one assumes a six-hour workday, that means 583 days for one person, or 58 for 10 people. It is clear that the beads were made at the site, as blanks were found on the living floor. The standardisation of bead shapes and sizes also argues for manufacture by a limited number of makers. However, the 3500 hours for the beads represents just a small fragment of the time devoted to ivory working at Sunghir – the spears, figurines, tools, bracelets, rings, pins, etc, must also have required a huge amount of time, labour and effort.

Woodwork

Wood is one of the most important organic materials, and must have been used to make tools for as long as stone and bone. However, wood technology is greatly under-represented in the archaeological record, since few pieces have survived. Ironically, we have far more evidence from more remote periods than from the last ice age itself; in particular, the German site of Schöningen has yielded – from an airtight layer of mud – no less than eight spears, dating to more than 300,000 years ago. Seven are made from slim straight spruce stems, and one is of pine. They are 1.8 to 2.2 m long, and display highly developed workmanship: their centre of gravity is in the front third, and the tips are worked symmetrically. Their throwing qualities are equal to modern tournament javelins: replicas have been thrown up to 70 m. The site also contained a charred wooden staff (skewer?), a possible throwing stick, and some grooved wooden tools (made from the very hard branch-bases of silver fir), incised at one end, which may have had stone blades mounted in them.

As mentioned above (p. 73), a well-made yew spear with the bark scraped off was found at the Middle Paleolithic site of Lehringen, Germany, dating to c. 125,000 years ago. And further evidence of Neanderthal woodworking has been discovered in the Spanish rock-shelter of Romani, where a 'pseudomorph' (i.e. hollow) of a decayed pointed wooden stick, 1 m long and dating to almost 50,000 years ago, has been found in sediment, as well as traces of juniper receptacles. The stick has been interpreted by some as a digging stick, and other possible Neanderthal examples have been found at Poggetti Vecchi (Central Italy) and Aranbaltza III (Basque country).

Therefore, despite an almost total lack of direct evidence, it is obvious that the people of the last ice age must have had tremendous skills in woodworking. For example, at Boomplaas Cave in South Africa, replicas of the site's later Stone Age tools were made and then used to chisel and plane wood. When the resulting use-wear was compared with that on 51 tools from the site, dating back to 14,200 years ago, it was found that all the prehistoric specimens had the same polish, thus confirming the early importance of woodworking here. Indeed, so many early stone tools must have been used in the procurement and working of wood that the period has arguably been given the wrong name and, instead of Palaeolithic, should be called the Palaeoxylic!

Figure 3.11. Early photo of Lascaux's Axial Gallery showing the holes for scaffolding in the clay walls.

It is not really known how trees were felled, since there are few real axes or adzes known in the European Upper Palaeolithic. Perhaps they concentrated on trees that fell naturally, or set fires at the base. But we still have no idea how they tackled major woodworking projects. One can assume that they must have made ladders, and also – in some caves – scaffolding. This is the case in

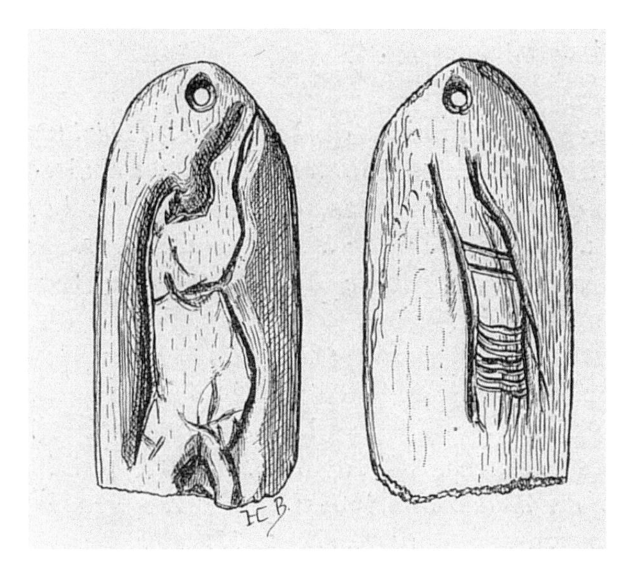

▲ *Figure 3.12. Tracing of the engravings on a bone pendant from Saint-Marcel (Indre). On one side is a galloping animal; on the other a motif which Arthur Evans interpreted as a sledge, and Henri Breuil accepted this view.*

► *Figure 3.13. The Shigir 'idol' in 1894.*

Lascaux, where there are sockets for 17 planks in the clay walls of the Axial Gallery, and remaining fragments show that they were of oak. Branches were doubtless used as frames for huts, tents and skin boats. Planks could have made rafts, while hollowed logs would have been dugout canoes. Wood must also have been used for sledges. However, we have absolutely no evidence for the making of skis or snowshoes. There must have been a wide variety of wooden artifacts and containers, but also works of art. The most startling example, from the end of the ice age, is the Shigir idol, found in a peat bog in Russia's Urals in 1890. Dating to c. 12,000 years ago, this monumental sculpture, made from a larch trunk, was 5.3 m high, with a head carved in 3D. It is a remarkable indicator of the countless works in wood (as well as bark) that we must have lost throughout Eurasia and beyond.

Finally, there remains the question of whether the bow and arrow existed in the last ice age. It is known that spearthrowers existed and were much used in Western Europe – those which survive are mostly elaborately carved in antler, but many of them are more likely to have been prestige items (or even, in some cases, toys – see p. 191) rather than functional. Instead, spearthrowers for everyday use are more likely to have been made of wood. A good spearthrower increases the distance, speed and force of the throw, and with it a goat-size animal can be brought down from 20 m away.

The people of the last ice age were so intelligent that it is possible that they invented the bow and arrow – perhaps in multiple places and times, but solid evidence is lacking and ambiguous; for example, quartz points older than 60,000 bp found at Sibudu (South Africa) have been interpreted by some researchers as arrow-heads; and a bow-and-arrow kit has been claimed at 48,000 bp at Fa-Hien Lena (Sri Lanka). Where Europe is concerned, a late Magdalenian bow was reported to have been found in the cave of Teyjat (Dordogne), but was destroyed during excavation. The site of Stellmoor (North Germany), dating to c. 11,000 bp, yielded two fragments of wooden bows and about a hundred arrows – some of them intact – with nocked or bifurcated bases. All were made of pine. Unfortunately they were destroyed in the last war, but they show clearly that the bow was in use by the end of the ice age.

However, there is possible indirect evidence for an earlier use of the bow in the morphology and technology of some stone projectile point types – most notably the barbed and tanged points from the Upper Solutrean of Parpalló cave, Spain. In terms of their size and shape, these certainly fit comfortably in the ranges displayed by ethnographic examples of arrowheads – but also of dart tips. The same can be said of some Gravettian Font-Robert points and Solutrean shouldered points. There is considerable overlap between arrowheads and dart points!

Innovations with fibres and plants

Most of the artifacts that have survived from the last ice age are made of stone, bone, antler and ivory, as they remain well-preserved over long time periods. On the other hand, very few examples of soft materials – those used for making baskets, cordage, rope and nets – have come down to us, as they are fragile and perish quickly, like wood. However, we do have some solid evidence that the people of the period had, at some point, developed fibre technology which would have given them a wide variety of ways to 'catch, hold and carry'.

Using plant fibres requires cutting the correct plant in the proper season to obtain the right fibres, and involves a complex understanding and a series of skills for preparing them, and then twining them into a string to use them as cord. People would have known where to gather the appropriate plant materials – for example rushes at riverside marshes – and which plant fibres maintained their strength throughout the year.

We have a few precious fragments of cordage. As mentioned earlier (p. 91) a bit of rope was found in Lascaux's 'Cabinet des Félins' (contrary to a common misconception, it was nowhere near the cave's famous shaft and was not used to go down there!). It was a 3-ply cord, 30 cm long, and 7-8 mm in diameter, and is probably of plant fibre. The Israeli site of Ohalo II, dating to c. 19,000 years ago (see p. 153), also yielded three fragments of twisted fibres which have been interpreted as the remains of cordage. Unsurprisingly, similar finds are known from elsewhere in the world with better conditions of preservation – for example Fort Rock Cave, Oregon, has yielded twined basketry, sandals, and cordage, probably more than 11,000 years old; a twined mat fragment from Fishbone Cave, Nevada, has been dated to 11,250 bp; and a remarkable basket

Figure 3.14. ▲ a/ ► b: The fragment of cord from Lascaux.

has recently been found at Muraba'at cave, Israel, dating to c. 10,500 years ago (p. 154).

Where Europe is concerned, even as long ago as the late 19th century a number of French archaeologists were interpreting some ice age implements in terms of weaving – for example in the Pyrenean Magdalenian cave of St Michel d'Arudy an object of reindeer antler was interpreted as a hook for making nets of fibre, while in Le Mas d'Azil so many apparent bone 'shuttles' were found that the excavator believed not only in Palaeolithic weaving but also in the cultivation of textile plants. A spindle and a spindle weight were later found in that same supersite. One pioneering early archaeologist, Gustave Chauvet, devoted no less than six pages of his 1910 book to ice age basketry and weaving – he even suggested that the multiple zigzag decorations on a point of reindeer antler and a bone fragment from the cave of Le Placard might depict basketry; and he presented ethnographic data on uses of birch bark and of basketry.

Unfortunately these early claims were generally spurned or ignored, and most prehistorians focused exclusively on the weapons and tools in hard materials that had survived in huge quantities. Yet it was always obvious that weaving and basketry must have been of great importance in the Upper Palaeolithic. Strong evidence eventually emerged in Moravia, where on some of the numerous fragments of fired and unfired clay at the Gravettian sites of Dolní Vestonice and Pavlov, c. 26,000 bp, (see above pp. 84-85) 79 impressions have been found of artifacts such as textiles and basketry, made from wild plants rather than animal fibres. It seems likely that these artifacts were manufactured at the sites, and they bear evidence to the sophisticated technologies being used, with eight different types of twine from plant materials. They show a wide variety of techniques and styles, and this varied inventory and the fine work point to long expertise. The types include single-ply, multiple-ply and braided cordage; knotted netting; plaited wicker-style basketry; and a wide variety of woven textiles.

However, it is less clear what these products were used for – perhaps matting for the floor, wall-hangings, blankets or for sleeping on, storage baskets and bags, or even textiles for clothing such as shawls, shirts, and skirts. Two pieces

Figure 3.15. ◀ a/ ▼ b: On a fragment of fired clay from a Pavlovian site in Moravia can be seen the imprint of a small mesh, with a fishnet knot. The netting diagram shows the technique used.

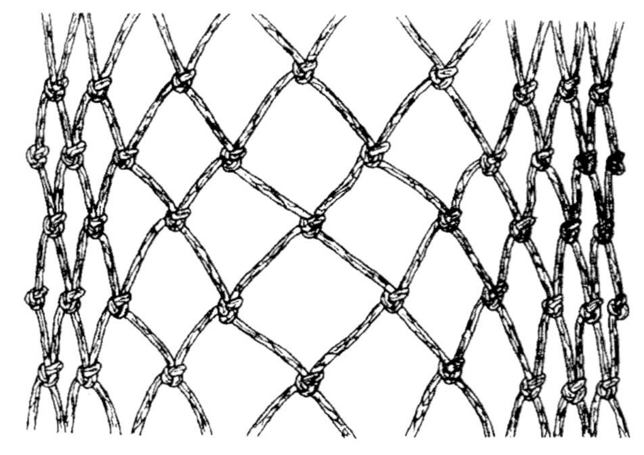

of fabric had been stitched together with a type of whipping stitch similar to one used today – such visible seams point to the making of more complex structures like clothing and bags. Four of the fragments found at these sites had impressions of cordage fastened together with 'weaver's' knots, suggesting that they were manufacturing nets for fishing and for catching small mammals such as rabbits. An abundance of small animal bones have been excavated at these campsites, and catching small animals in nets would be a more successful approach than trying to spear or club a small creature darting for cover! However, larger animals could also have been captured using nets and then killed once trapped. Likewise, nets could be attached to trees to capture birds.

Recently, what may be an impression of a textile has been discovered on the wall of Cosquer cave at shoulder height – perhaps caused by someone leaning on the wall or accidentally touching it with their shoulder.

A number of species would have provided suitable fibres – e.g. nettle, mugwort, alder, yew, lime, cattail, willow. Such plant fibres could have been made into cordage, which could then have been used for all sorts of things: cord can be wrapped and tied around things to bind them together, to tie up, hang up, wrap up, and so on. A length can be strung between two trees and then a skin thrown over to make a dry shelter, or just used to hang things from – including laundry! This type of 'A' frame den would provide shelter when a rock overhang or cave

Figure 3.16. Imprint of a textile on a wall in Cosquer cave.

was not available, and a pile of wood or foliage at one end and a fire just outside the other end would provide both warmth and a means of cooking, as well as relatively safe accommodation for the duration.

Plant material can likewise be turned into rope and used to make ladders to climb up or down in a cave, or to take bird eggs from their nests in trees or along a cliff face. A sturdy rope can also be used to make a bridge, or for tethering animals (see below, p. 126). As we shall see, cords and ropes could also make useful belts. Baskets could have been made from pliable hazel and willow branches or vines. Being light, they can be used for all manner of things, such as transporting – they are ideal for collecting fish and shellfish or plant material – and for storing pretty much anything!

All of these plant materials could have been worked by both sexes, as well as children. Making things from plants was probably a seasonal extended family affair, and not a job solely for women while the men were sharpening their tools! Of course women and men may have had their own traditions or made their own items for personal use, and gathered their own materials similarly. Or certain tasks could have been specific to either men or women, but if so, it's unlikely that any task that led to their mutual survival would have been considered a 'lesser' role in these early cultures.

Fibres could also have been obtained from a wide variety of animals – canine or wolf hair (or even discarded human hair!) can be spliced, plaited, finger-twined and thigh-rolled and put to use. Shed wool fibres could have been collected from mammoth or woolly rhino, and turned into felt-like material for clothing,

Figure 3.17. Reconstruction of a Solutrean woman and child by Elisabeth Daynès.

blankets and so forth. However, doubtless the best such material available would have been horse hair – from tails and manes – which can be turned into remarkably strong rope, far stronger than most plant fibre cords. And we have indirect evidence that this was done, in the form of the numerous perforated antler batons from the period. More than 70 different interpretations have been put forward over the years for these objects – the most widely accepted is that they were used to straighten the shafts of spears – but it seems quite clear that many of them were involved in the making of horse-hair rope by twisting single strands together. Not only do they closely resemble a wooden tool used by traditional US cowboy rope-makers, but the wear patterns in their perforations were mostly made by the rubbing of cordage; and on the many decorated specimens, the horse is the most common motif! Strong rope would have been

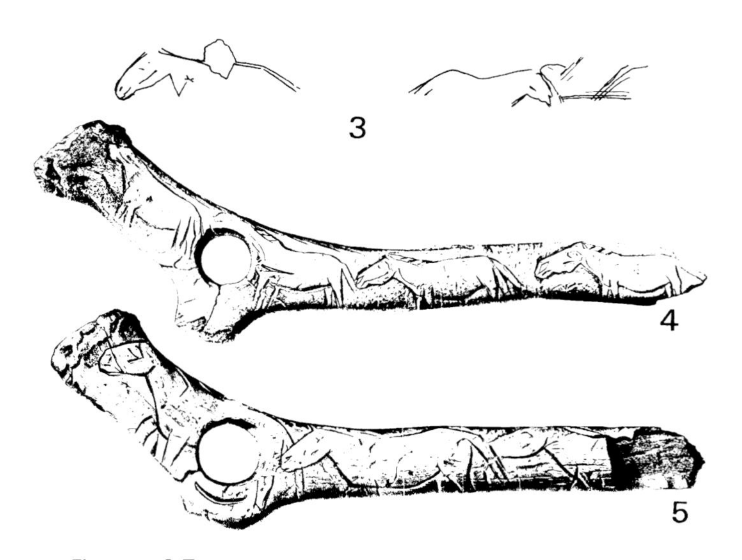

Figure 3.18. Two perforated antler batons from La Madeleine, decorated with horse images.

invaluable to hunter-gatherers for numerous purposes.

Animals also provided sinews, tendons and guts which can be removed after the kill and, while still fresh, divided into small parcels and twisted to make a fine thread. If used wet they regain their pliability and can be knotted to make long lengths that can be used for sewing or lashing things together, like spear-points and arrow-heads to wooden shafts. The long tendons from an animal's legs are particularly useful. For example, in the Solutrean site of Badegoule, eight complete reindeer feet were found under a block – since there is nothing to eat on them, they were interpreted as having been put aside as a precious source of tendons. An animal's bladder and stomach can be recycled as semi-permanent containers for liquids and can be inflated as line-floats for fishing, or pouches for containing fats or bone marrow. In addition, these organs, once dried, can be tightly stretched to make a cover for a musical instrument of drum or tom-tom type.

Animal skins and clothing

It is worth noting that there are often unusual wear-patterns on many of the women's teeth recovered from the Upper Palaeolithic, and some researchers have proposed that these dental marks could have been caused by the women using their teeth to pull and stretch fibrous material when performing tasks related to skin processing or even basketry. This type of wear pattern is often present on the teeth of Inuit women, who are known to perform this same activity when stretching animal skins. Many bone and antler tools were probably used for skinworking – spatulas, smoothers, shuttles, etc, – and doubtless also lots of wooden tools which have disappeared. It is highly probable that both men and women would have learned how to process skins and to produce effective garments and footwear. An ethnographic cross-cultural survey of 185 societies has shown that in Eurasia and the Americas skinning was mostly done by men, but skinworking was predominantly a female task. Even among the Ingalik of Alaska, where men made the hideworking awls, scrapers and knives, the tools were used by the women.

The main hunting season would be during the summer months, and it's most likely that the preparation and sewing of animal skins would have been a major job for the autumn, when hunting opportunities were more limited, other than trapping smaller mammals. The first job, of course, is to skin the animals, and with the right tools and practised hands, this can be done very quickly. An experimental butchering of a hyena carcass with ice age stone tools showed that the initial incision from chin to tail and along all limbs took 5 minutes! Skinning provided a square metre of hide in 10 minutes. Degutting and cutting the skeleton into pieces took 45 minutes (from the first incision at the chin). The claws could be left attached to the hide, or cut/smashed off.

Figure 3.19. A Nunavut woman in 1951, chewing seal skin to soften it for making boots.

The processing of animal skins into clothing was, by necessity, of huge importance to our early ancestors, and would undoubtedly have taken up a great deal of their time. It has been estimated that it takes 300 hours of work to treat the 27 reindeer (caribou) hides needed to make enough clothing for a family of five people. Ethnographic data show that for Eskimoan clothing it takes 12 reindeer hides to produce one complete outfit of inner and outer parka, mitts, boots, stockings, etc. Such an outfit would last two years at best, and is usually replaced every year due to wear and tear. So the family needs 84 reindeer per year just for clothing – or at least 42. This does not take into account hides needed for sleeping bags, or making sleighs, tents, etc. If clothing is made from small animals like foxes, a truly huge number of skins is needed, and this entails lots of work in trapping, skinning, tanning, sewing, and so on.

Skin preparation requires some sunlight, and the sewing would have been easier to perform in daylight rather than during the winter months when it would have been dark for long periods, with minimal light offered by the hearth fire. It's also likely that the winter would have been too cold for the processing treatment to be a success, and it's also worth noting that animal hides (and furs) would be at their thickest in the winter and hence involve more work.

Ethnographic data show that it is best to peg-out an animal skin, or tie it to a wooden frame to stretch it, before starting the first, defleshing stage of the process – scraping off all the muscle tissue, membranes and fat from the internal surface with the edge of a scraper, sometimes called an end-scraper. Next comes the job of removing all the hair from the skin. 'De-hairing' is achieved by 'sweating' the skin over a few days, as this allows the natural bacterial decay to loosen the hair at the roots. An alternative method which ice age people could have employed is 'liming', which involves using a mixture of wood-ash with water to get rid of the fat and loosen the hair. This is then followed by repeatedly soaking, washing and 'working' the skin.

The next step is placing the skin against a large log or stone, and scraping away the hairs with a blunt-edged tool. As mentioned above, the animal hairs recovered from hides could be turned into cords or felting – this involves working the hairs together with one's hands or feet, a task so simple even a child could do it. Alternatively the hairs could be made into strings for netting or cordage, and bristles could be used to make brushes, which were clearly used to make some cave paintings – experiments with a variety of materials have shown that the best results (i.e. solid, precise and regular marks) are produced by brushes of badger hair (human hair is too supple and fragile). Brushes of crushed or chewed vegetable fibre were next best.

Alternatively skins might have been putrefied; this involves applying a thin gruel of cooked animal brains, liver or fish-spawn and rubbing the mixture into the wrung-out skin until it is absorbed. The hide is then dried in the sun – or just sunlight – to 'cure', perhaps stretched on a wooden frame. Further soaking, working, wringing and drying are repeated until the material is soft. The working consists of pummelling, scraping, and pulling in all directions with the hands, and turning and twisting to keep the skin on the move as it dries. Preservation and drying might have been assisted by 'smoking' the skin over a slow, smouldering, fire made from rotten wood under a makeshift skin tent, and this has the effect of sterilizing it too. Waterproofing skins is a simple procedure – the surface is just rubbed or 'dressed' with pre-cooked animal fats. Soaking animal skins in urine – an Eskimoan method – also makes it easier to remove hair and any remaining flesh. Another technique, used by North American Indians, is to use ochre mixed with animal fat, brains or viscera. Ice age people clearly knew ochre's abrasive, antiseptic, and impermeabilizing properties – many of their smoothers, spatulas and scrapers have traces of it, and usewear marks on some flint scrapers also point to this. As we have already seen (p. 61), numerous ochre traces on habitation floors have been interpreted as working areas and evidence of skinworking.

Ice age communities may have also learned to treat skins with tannins, which can be extracted from tree bark, leaves, wood, and even berries and plant roots or decaying plant matter. Tanning is extremely effective – it makes skins impermeable, and protects against vermin and putrefaction, but they need to be dried quickly or they shrink and turn into rawhide, which is by no means as soft or comfortable to wear. Dry and clean skins have a tendency to go stiff like cardboard, so they had to be made supple and thinner by breaking the dermal fibres – i.e. currying, which means flattening, equalising and making supple the leather by rubbing it with a smoother, blade or scraper, and hammering it with a pebble. Smoking some skins can also make them supple.

Once treated, the skins would have been made into clothing and shoes, as well as used in tents and huts, as we have already seen. It is extremely probable that these early groups had a waste-not-want-not approach to their economy, as skin preparation involved a huge investment of time and effort. Indeed, it's likely that 'recycling' old goods probably started in the ice age – when clothing became worn-out or uncomfortable, or was infested with lice, the old hides would have probably been utilised in some other way. For example, old skins might be sewn together to make drapes to hang over a rock-shelter opening in order to keep out the wind and cold, as well as night predators. Other possibilities would be blankets, sleeping bags, roof covers and tents; slings for carrying infants or food (p. 179); and manufacturing small canoe-type boats, or vessels for liquids or cooking. Some animal viscera could have been used as impermeable linings, while bladders make excellent bags for carrying or storing liquids.

CONTAINERS: CACHE AND CARRY!

Water is essential for all life (we can survive an average of 3 days without it), and easy access to water, especially for nursing mothers, would have been a priority for our ice age ancestors. Unless they were living alongside riverbanks in semi-temporary huts or tents, they would probably have to walk daily to collect water – but collect it in what?

Containers were obviously invented at some point in the past, and most likely well before the early Upper Palaeolithic by our hominin ancestors who, it has been suggested, used both ostrich eggs and animal skulls for this purpose. Observing rainwater that has collected in anything would have been noticed so often that eventually the 'aha!' moment had to occur to someone – whose next thought would have been 'that could be useful for...', and the idea of using objects for putting things in would have developed.

Many of the everyday things we take for granted needed some bright spark in the deep past to invent them for the very first time, and each of these simple things – wooden cups, bowls and trays, a needle, a carry bag, a container and string (just to mention a few innovations) – would have been revolutionary at the time, enabling people to develop new behaviours, activities and skills that improved their living conditions.

Containers could have been made from animal hide or an appropriately shaped stone, or carved from solid wood, or manufactured from slices of bark, like birch (a common species during the last ice age), tied or glued together. These would have been useful for transporting and storing water (and blocks of ice), once they had been made watertight. They could be used for storing food like nuts and bone marrow and dried foodstuffs. Birch-bark containers were certainly evident by the Neolithic, and could even be used for transporting embers (see above, p. 71). The Native American people of New England have long known about the special uses of birch bark for all manner of items, from shoes (see below, p.112) to canoe construction and musical instruments.

Figure 3.20. Ojibwe women of Minnesota in c. 1930, making birch-bark containers for maple syrup.

Other types of containers might have been made from animal skins waterproofed with animal grease, or from animal stomachs and bladders, which can be used for storing liquids. Some small bone and ivory objects from ice age sites such as Combe-Capelle, Fourneau du Diable and Brassempouy have been interpreted as stoppers for such vessels, as they are similar to ones used by the Lapps and Inuit.

Wine and water are still carried in goatskin bags by shepherds in many parts of the world. Even tough plant materials, if plaited or woven, can be fashioned into waterproof receptacles and baskets. Animal horns may also have been put to use, as they are useful for storing and pouring, as drinking vessels, and for getting fires to take by blowing the horn gently into the fire to create a draught.

Certainly, food would have had to be stored to survive through the winter months, and storage methods (aside from pits, p. 65) would have had to be damp-proof and strong enough to deter scavenging animals.

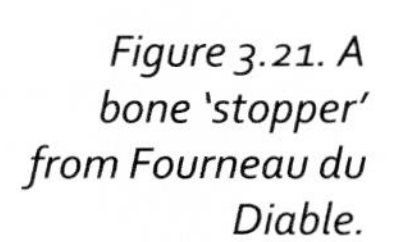

Figure 3.21. A bone 'stopper' from Fourneau du Diable.

Leather thongs would also have been very useful and could be used as harpoon lines. These strips can be cut spirally from a single piece of dried pelt under tension. If applied wet, the thongs would shrink when dry and hold a joint or two things firmly together, while leather laces would also have been useful for tying things together.

In trying to assess what kind of clothing existed in the last ice age, we have three kinds of evidence. First, actual depictions of garments in figurines and drawings; second, physical remains of clothing, mostly recovered from burials; and third, ethnographic information to fill in the many gaps in our knowledge.

Humans probably went naked – or decorated with body paint or ochre – when the global environment was much warmer than it is now. The invention of clothing would have come about as the climate grew colder and less stable, and humans needed thermal protection in order to survive. Although wearing clothing would have been a radical move for humans, this adaptation to the colder weather is likely to have come about gradually, from simple clothing like a cloak (draped, not fitted), worn when the climate was reasonably warm, to more complex garments to shield humans from the severest of weather conditions such as extreme cold and strong winds.

Inadequate clothing may have been the driving force behind populations migrating, and the desire – or need – to find a warmer refuge. So the manufacturing of complex, well-fitting, warm clothing was probably invented and developed as a way of coping with the ever-present problem for humans of 'climate change.' Apart from the coldest part of the Last Glacial Maximum, the earth has had 'in-between' periods of warming, and there may have been times during the summer months when simpler clothes were worn or abandoned altogether. But during the coldest glacial conditions, appropriate clothing would have meant the difference between life and death, especially for infants and children.

For ice age Europeans, warm clothing was definitely required as the average annual temperature was 5° or 6° C lower than today – as we have seen (p. 46) Magdalenian France's climate was like that of Scandinavia. We have no idea how hairy their bodies may have been – this is not a feature of the few naturalistic depictions available – but clothes were certainly needed in all seasons.

Although the actual clothing from the ice age has disintegrated, and is therefore (almost) invisible in the archaeological record (see below), the tools that were used to process hides and make clothes have survived in abundance, and specific tools seem to have been used to make different types of clothing in different climates. Microscopic analysis of these tools can show wear on their edges which identifies traces of contact with animal hide.

As mentioned earlier, the main Palaeolithic tools needed to make fitted clothing are awls and eyed needles – the former for piercing the skins to make holes, and the latter for sewing. When these tools are found together, it's likely they were used for making more complex clothing that traps in body heat and gives the wearer protection from the cold – and, during the coldest periods of the last ice age, protection from hypothermia and frostbite. Recent hunters living in the far north would take a few needles along with them on a trip, because torn clothing would let in the sub-zero temperatures, and a quick repair could mean the difference between life and death.

Finds of needles and other types of artifact associated with sewing at some Paleo-Indian sites in North America are generally interpreted as indicating domestic areas allocated to activities that were probably the 'duty of women'. As we have already argued (p. 21), this is a completely outdated assumption. For example, the Inuit form aggregations of 45-50 people (not just women) in 'finishing camps' to make new winter outfits from caribou hides. Nothing interferes with this period of sewing activity to make their 'survival suits' for the coming winter. Preparation for this activity starts in childhood. It is likely that the low population numbers in the Upper Palaeolithic would have meant that everyone – men, women and children – was involved in this activity.

Figure 3.22. Tracing of the engraving known as the 'femme à l'anorak' in Gabillou Cave (Dordogne).

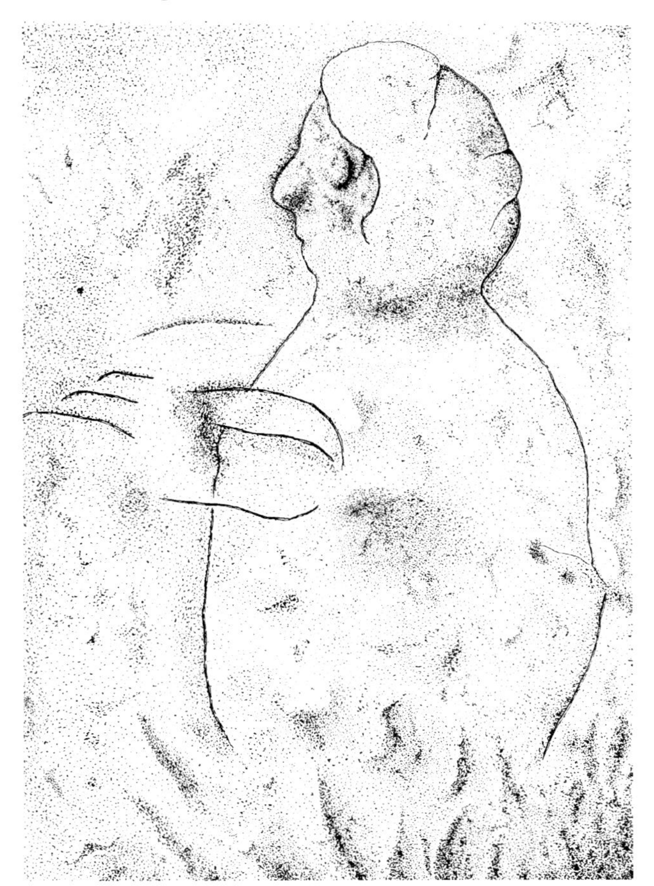

Clothing is rarely clear in ice age depictions; some engraved and highly stylized depictions of women at Gönnersdorf are totally covered with lines, but these could represent tattoos or body-paint rather than clothing (see p. 180). Other depictions are often open to a number of interpretations. For example, the engraving known as 'La femme à l'anorak' on the wall of Gabillou cave (Dordogne) is often seen as a woman wearing an anorak or a blouse with a hood, while other researchers have pointed out that the figure is unsexed and the 'hood' may simply be a hairline. A carved horse tooth from the Pyrenean cave of Bédeilhac also looks like a human wearing a hooded anorak. The bearded male, sculpted, engraved and painted at Angles-sur-l'Anglin, appears to be wearing a garment with a fur collar (see p. 5). The famous female ivory carving known as the 'Venus of Lespugue' (see p. 9) seems to have a garment of some kind showing at the back – this has been interpreted as a skirt made from 11 cords twined around a base cord which serves as a belt. Other researchers see it as a kind of loincloth, ending in a fringe that covers the back of the thighs – but either way, it is odd that this garment sits below the buttocks and has no front!

Some mid-Magdalenian perforated bone discs have been recovered: circular pieces cut out of thin bones (often scapulas). Some may be toys (see p. 192); others could be buttons, although they are not particularly robust, or just decorative pieces – a human engraved on a bone spatula from Bruniquel has a row of big circles from throat to crotch!

Figure 3.23. Bone spatula from Bruniquel bearing an engraving of a human with circles down the front.

Belts are certainly depicted occasionally (e.g. at La Marche, Enlène and Kostenki). Many female figurines from Russia (notably Kostenki and Avdeevo) have possible bandeaux, often with straps, usually on top of the breasts or around the waist – but these are not found on figurines in western Europe. They appear to be decorations rather than garments – for those, we need to look farther east, in Siberia, at the sites of Mal'ta and Buret (c. 23,000 - 19,000 bp) in the Lake Baikal region (see p. 103). None of these figurines is pregnant, and many are dressed rather than naked; unlike some of the figurines of Central and Western Europe, they are not usually interpreted as 'fertility' goddesses.

Some of them appear to have clothing engraved on the surface, while others have decorated heads. Microscopic analysis has revealed traces on the surface that were not previously observed, indicating that all of them are 'dressed' to some extent or 'accessorized' with bracelets, hats, shoes, bags and even backpacks! Some appear to be wearing fur 'coveralls' similar to the 'kerkery' outfits worn by women and children in the extreme North of Siberia. Judging by the proportions, some of the sculptures could even represent small children.

Other figurines seem to be wearing overalls and items that look very similar to clothing, bags, and everyday objects worn and used by Arctic people in more recent times – their wind- and water-proof parkas are made from fish skins or seal intestines and are worn during the summer months. Other Siberian figurines appear to have short parkas like those worn by

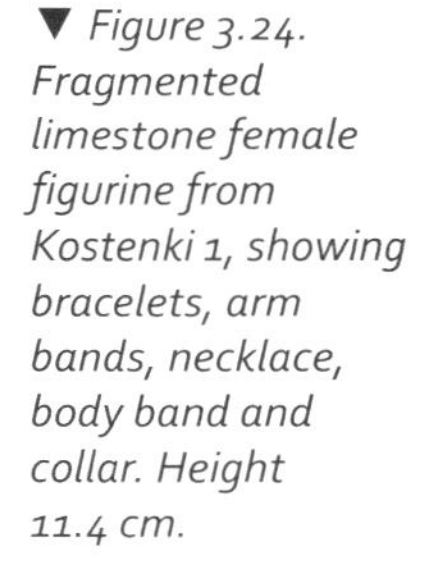

▼ Figure 3.24. Fragmented limestone female figurine from Kostenki 1, showing bracelets, arm bands, necklace, body band and collar. Height 11.4 cm.

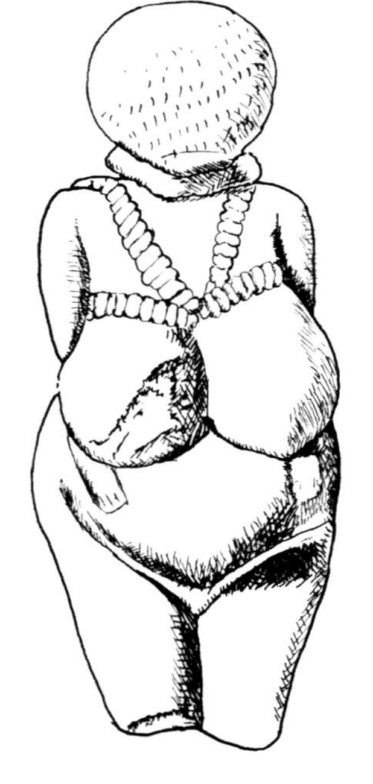

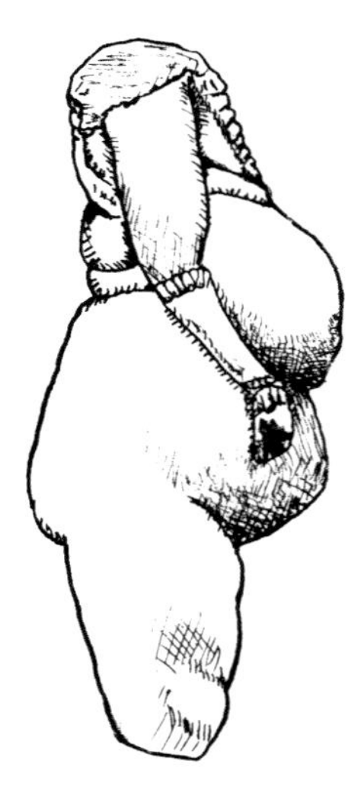

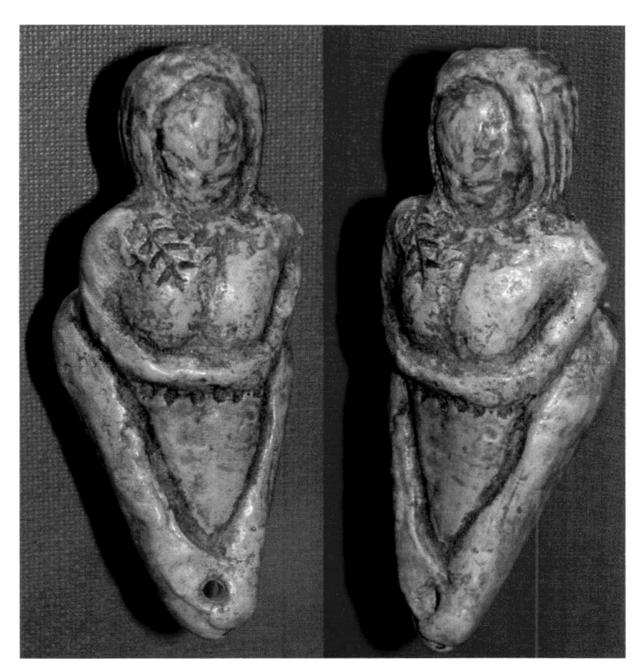

Figure 3.25. ▲a: Figurine from Mal'ta showing head covering; ► b: Figurines from Mal'ta and Buret; ▼ c: Figurine from Mal'ta of a child wearing a 'coverall' compared with drawing of a summer poncho made of seal intestines

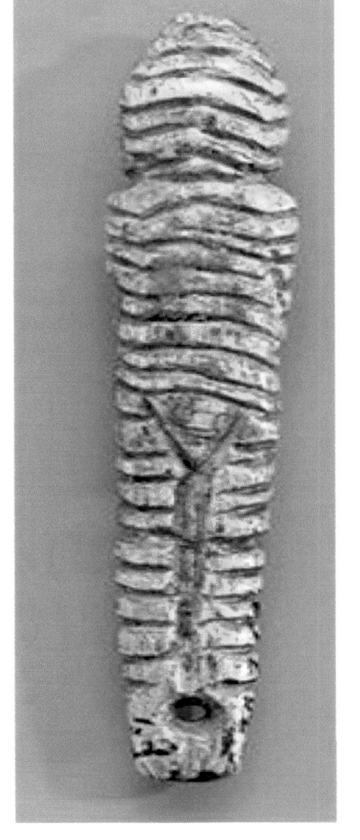

the Koryak and Itilmens indigenous populations who live today in northeastern Eurasia.

Figure 3.26. Long waterproof cape made of sea-mammal gut, from the Aleutian Islands.

Alternatively, those people living in sub-Polar or Arctic temperatures may have favoured an anorak cum all-in-one outfit made out of animal hide with, perhaps, the luxury of an additional fur lining or trimmings – not unlike the traditional outfits worn by the Eskimoan peoples living today. For example, everything the Orochon reindeer herder wears comes from the reindeer (Oro means reindeer and chon means man). The Nenets reindeer herders still rely on traditional clothing sewn by the women. A Nenets man wears a *malitsa* – a coat made of about four reindeer skins, the fur being closest to the skin on the inside, and the leather on the outside. The *malitsa* has an integrated hood and gloves and is similar to a poncho with no zips or buttons. New *malitsas* (just like all other fur clothing) are used in winter-time but they do begin to moult, and within several years have to be replaced, and the worn-out clothing used during milder weather. In extremely cold conditions men wear yet another layer of reindeer fur, known as a *gus*. Unlike the *malitsa* the *gus* has leather on the inside and fur on the outside and, equipped with these two layers, a man can stay outside overnight and sleep with the herd in temperatures down to -50° C and below. The women wear a *yagushka* which has a double layer of about eight reindeer skins, and which is buttoned at the front. Both men and women wear hip-high reindeer-skin boots that consist of an inner and outer boot that are worn together and tied up with a belt. The Sami of Lapland still make shoes and leggings from the hides of reindeer limbs, because snow does not stick to reindeer legs! In addition, the skin from the limbs is particularly strong, durable and impermeable. The pieces of fur at the bottom of a reindeer's foot are sometimes assembled to make soles for footwear – it can take the four feet of 14 reindeer to make the soles of a single pair of boots!

The numerous bones of arctic fox, red fox, wolverine and wolf found at Mal'ta imply that the inhabitants were hunting these animals for their fur – the warmest and most effective coverings for keeping out the cold. Eskimoan people and reindeer herders often take advantage of the thermal effects of fur and line their garments accordingly. Any leftover bits of fur could be made into gloves and mittens. The animals' tails may have been left on the skins to make them easy to tie or attach to clothing.

Where actual remains of ice age garments are concerned, our only real source lies in burials – but of course this immediately raises the important question of whether these were special funerary garments or if they represent everyday wear. The astonishing wealth of decoration on some burial outfits tends to suggest the former interpretation. It is hard to imagine hunters attempting to approach an animal or crawling through the undergrowth in garments adorned with hundreds of beads and shells!

CARRYING CHILDREN

Figure 3.27. Mal'ta figurine of an adult woman with one breast exposed, and a northern Chukchi woman in summer, with one breast uncovered for constant readiness for feeding her baby.

One statuette apparently has an engraved nude breast, and this has been compared with Chukchi women who typically keep one breast exposed when they are nursing infants. Inuit women such as the Chukchi, Koryak and Yupik have a pouch attached to the back of the parka (*amaut*) for carrying a baby. Dried grass and moss are placed at the bottom of the pouch and perform the job of a nappy!

Bags for carrying infants are ubiquitous in indigenous cultures, and more elaborate than a bag or sling is a cradleboard, the traditional Native American baby carrier. Infants are swaddled (wrapped tightly) and then placed and strapped onto a wooden plank or attached to a basket made from woven fibres. The cradleboard is as easy to carry as a backpack, and can be propped up against a tree or hard surface like a baby chair, or even hung from a rock shelter wall (using a bone peg, p. 58!) while adults work. The child's movements are restricted so it can't crawl off or get into danger, and is safe from predators if high above the ground. For journeys, larger travel baskets or cradleboards could be secured to a sled used to transport older children who were unable to walk quickly enough to keep up with the group.

Figure 3.28. Navajo woman with cradleboard, 1914.

HEAD COVERINGS

Elaborate hairstyling is extremely rare in ice age imagery – the small ivory head from Brassempouy is the best-known example, but alas that piece is not definitely authentic and may have been carved (albeit in ancient ivory) by an excavation labourer in the late 19th century. The limestone female figurine from Willendorf (Austria) may have elaborate hair, but since it covers the whole head, it is more often seen as a fibre-based woven cap or hat; other researchers have seen it as a cap decorated with rows of shells, as found in many burials. Some of the La Marche figures (p. 6) are wearing different kinds of headgear or hairstyles.

Figure 3.29. The limestone carving known as the 'venus' of Willendorf (Austria), 11 cm high.

THE LA MADELEINE BURIAL: THE CHILD OF AN ELITE FAMILY?

La Madeleine, on the banks of the Vézère river in the Dordogne (France), is one of the richest rock shelters in Europe. The wealth of occupation material and art objects excavated there led to the site giving its name to the late ice age culture of the Magdalenian.

Edouard Lartet and Henry Christy discovered the shelter in 1863, and it continued to be studied by a number of archaeologists and some amateur investigators throughout the following decades. Denis Peyrony started his excavations in 1911, uncovering a huge quantity of archaeological material. In 1926 he found a piece of bone that appeared human, and after three days of careful excavation the skeleton of a young child was uncovered in a grave heavily stained with ochre, and covered with remains of exquisite shell jewellery.

The burial pit was large but modest – a simple hollow in the sand and clay soil, some distance away from the main habitation area. The child had been laid on its back with its head facing south and arms extended along the body. Three stones had been placed in a semi-circle directly behind the child's head, perhaps to protect it. Many of the child's bones were connected and attached, apart from the skull. The head may have been somewhat raised and, if not covered sufficiently, might have been damaged by the comings and goings in the shelter.

The burial is dated to the very end of the Magdalenian period, around 11,500 bp. The child's age is estimated at between two and four years, as both milk and adult teeth were present. What is so spectacular about this child's burial is the exceptional personal ornamentation: the jewellery consisted of numerous small, perforated shells (around 1275 *Dentalium,* 99 *Neritina*, 25 *Turritella* and 13 *Cyclope*) and pendants of fox and deer canines – two of each. The shells were found around the ankles, knees, wrists, elbows, neck and the head. It seems this was not a burial garment, as the much-used shells indicate that it had often been worn beforehand while the child was alive. It must have been made of supple leather (like buckskin) because experiments show that fine bone needles break easily on hard leather. 186 needles were found at the site, some of which have a width compatible with this work – they are very fine, hard to produce and very easy to break.

The various shells on the child were from different sources: *Dentalia*, for example, were sourced from beaches along the Atlantic coast some considerable distance away from the Vézère valley, which shows that such materials were constantly being collected, or acquired through trade links.

Dentalium shells are tubular, and had been snapped or sawn into lengths of 6-7 mm (none was intact); traces of wear on them indicate that they were sewn individually onto the garment they were attached to. The sizes of the shells used for this burial are significantly smaller than those found at other sites, indicating that they were made to order for this very young child. This is not the only example of personal ornamentation appearing to be size-selected for the individual – it is similar, for example, to the smaller ivory beads of the Sunghir children (pp. 25-26) – and so it is probable that communities had their own style of clothing which enabled them to be recognised as a distinct social group.

However, making the shortened lengths of *Dentalia* was just the start of the work – the total length of shells on the garment comes to 9 m, and this indicates that the same amount of thread was needed for sewing the shells onto it! There were 2400 holes made by the sewing needles (of less than 2 mm diameter). Those examining the garments have estimated at least 30 hours for the sewing work alone.

Let's consider for a moment the time it must have taken to source, cut, and prepare the shells – over a thousand of them – and make the jewellery. Add to this the time involved in sewing the shells onto the child's clothing with a bone needle. The large number of ornaments and the substantial investment of time needed to make this single garment is staggering – but what does

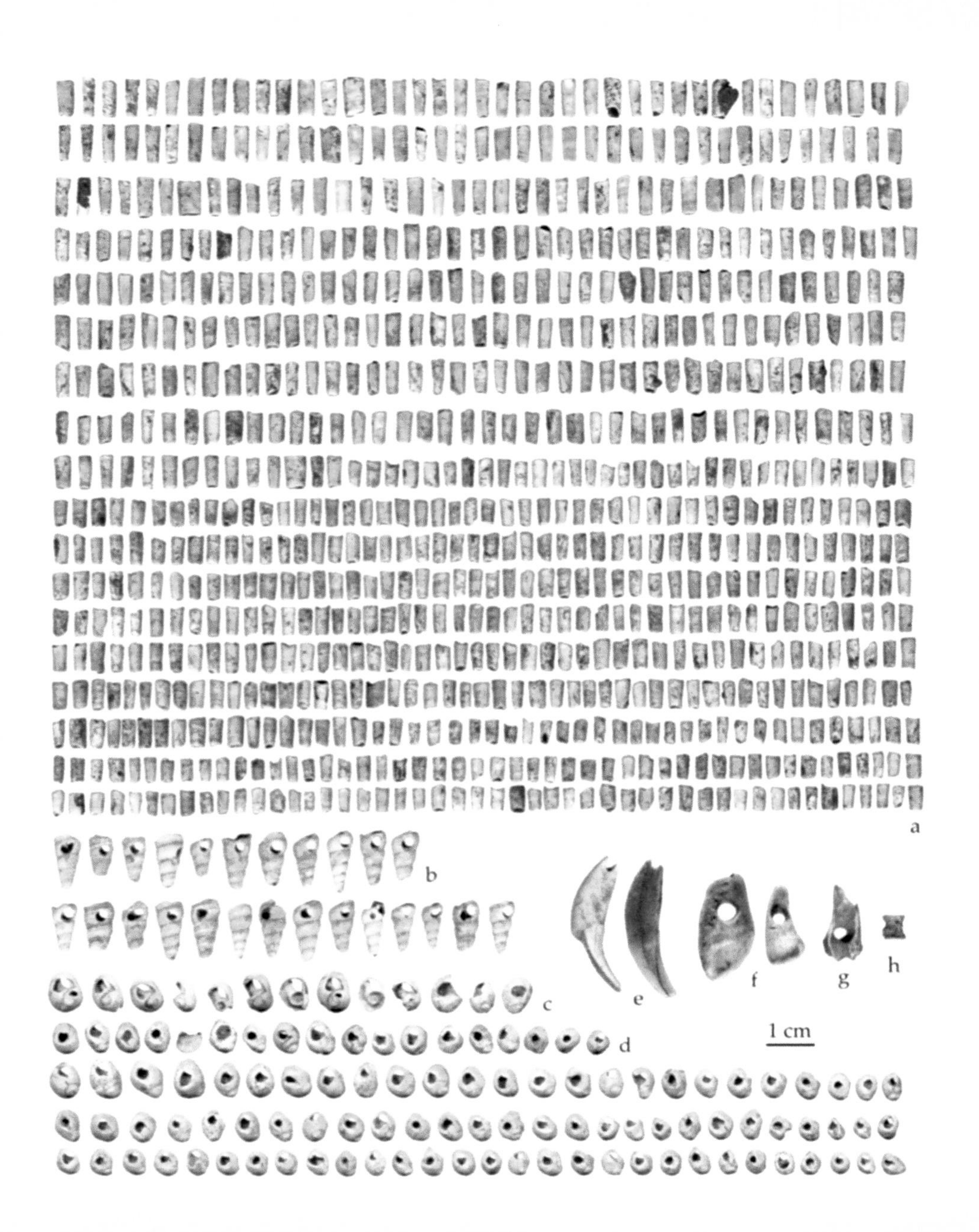

Figure 3.30. The jewellery from the La Madeleine child burial.

it tell us about the people that buried this child? Although we can only speculate, the effort involved may reflect more than just parental care, and indicate a hereditary ranking system. Was this a 'special' child of some kind, or the child of an 'elite' family? Since it would have been difficult for any child to achieve status through its own merits in such a short time, the latter explanation is more likely. However, the notion of social and inherited status, or hierarchies within hunting and foraging people and those living during the last ice age, certainly require us to modify our view of these early societies as being wholly egalitarian! On the other hand, as we shall see (p. 200), it is possible that *all* children were highly valued by these communities and given elaborate burials.

Another extraordinary kind of garment was found in the child burials of Arene Candide (see p. 201) where the numerous squirrel tail-vertebrae in perfect order on the chest have been interpreted as the remains of jackets made of red squirrel tails – would these have been normal or very special garments?

The position of the thousands of little shells on the two children buried at Grimaldi (p. 169), in parallel vertical lines between the waist and the upper thighs, suggest that they were sewn onto loincloths. The distribution of beads, shells and other ornaments on some bodies seems to indicate fully enveloping garments – e.g. the man known as Sunghir 1 has 3500 tiny ivory beads arranged in lines, which must have been sewn onto a garment of reindeer and/or arctic fox skins, the main staples at the site. As there was no opening at the front, it must have been put on over the head. Fox canines hung from the sleeves. More beads were sewn onto a bonnet or an anorak hood. Lines of beads along the legs, round the knees and ankles, and on the feet indicate that trousers were sewn to the shoes, which were doubtless of leather or skin.

Figure 3.31. Drawing of the two children in the Grotte des Enfants.

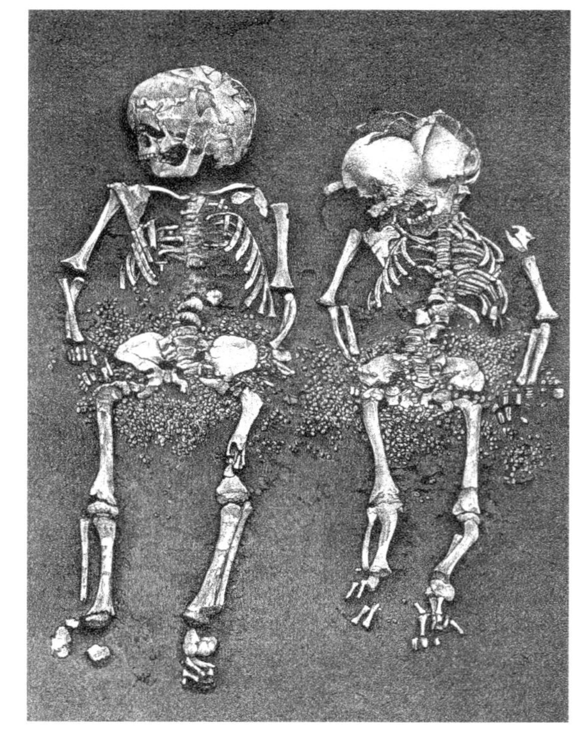

The Sunghir burial remains certainly show that these people had developed the technology required for complex clothing. If the Sunghir man had been buried in the customary attire of his community (rather than special grave clothes), these would presumably have comprised a shirt and trousers, a poncho, headwear and moccasin-like shoes. It's also quite possible that ice age people wore underwear made from the softest of animal

Figure 3.32. Reconstruction drawing of the Sunghir 1 man.

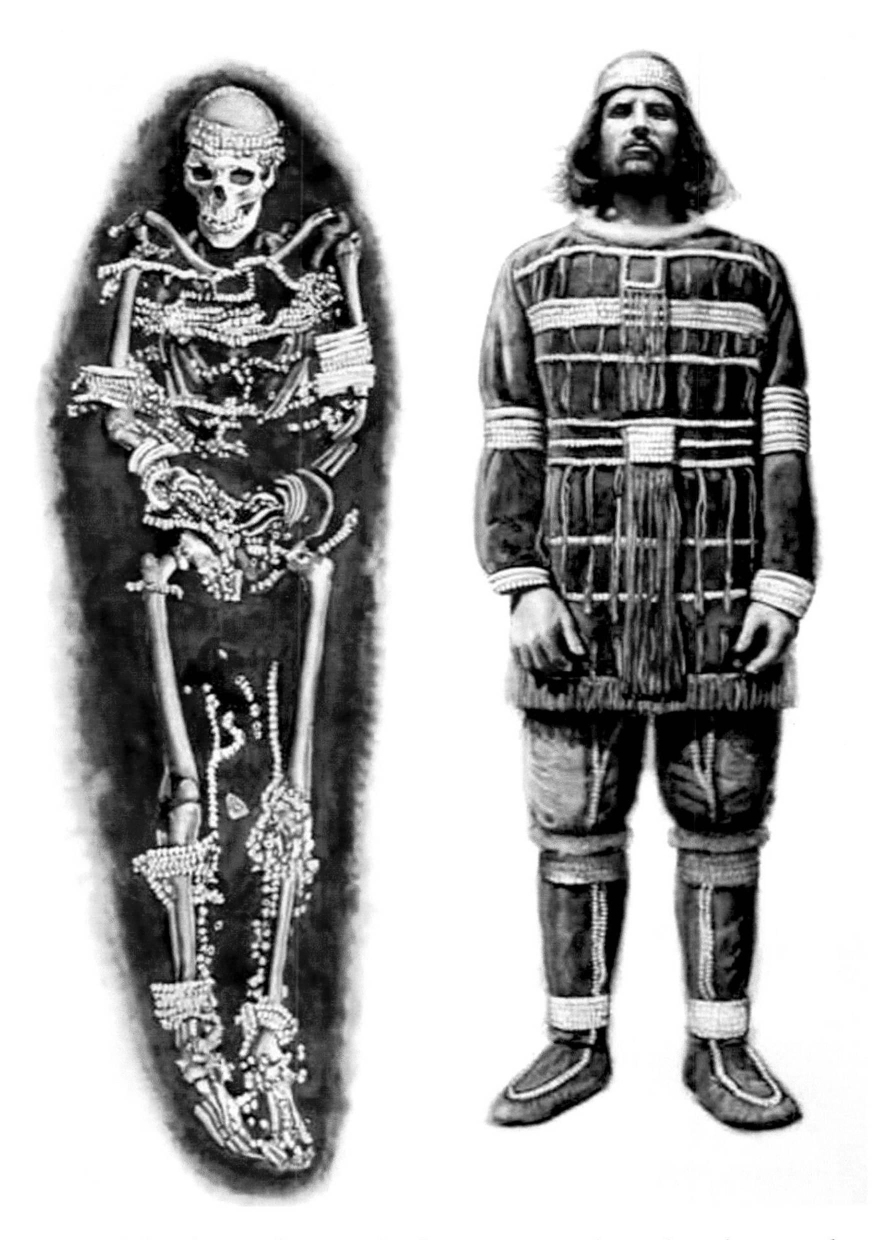

skins. Buckskin from a deer is soft after wetting, and may have been used as undergarments during particularly cold periods or for infants' and children's clothing. Warm air gets trapped between the layers of skin clothing and the body, providing excellent insulation against the cold. All these garments would have been made using hides such as reindeer, horse and bison – with different animal skins manufactured into different garments appropriate for different conditions. Alas, we can only speculate if they had skin or fur bikinis like Raquel Welch's in *One Million Years BC*!

Garments such as those worn by the Sunghir people would have required fairly advanced tailoring techniques, and would be far from easy to sew together with bone needles. It is probable that by the end of the ice age certain sites had become specialised in manufacturing clothing with an excellent standard of workmanship. Clothing might well have been painted or dyed, and judging by the effort put into cave and rock art and portable art objects, it is extremely probable that they decorated or painted everything they wore.

Considering the huge amount of time and effort that went into creating ice age clothing, it seems obvious that they must have worn different outfits for different activities – especially processes like butchering and skinning which would inevitably have spoiled and stained their garments.

Youngsters would presumably have served quite a long apprenticeship making simple items such as carry bags or containers until they were both physically strong enough and had the requisite skills to move onto custom-made clothing. It is certainly the case that the highly skilled, complicated and crucial tasks of manufacturing clothing have long been overshadowed in the archaeological literature by the mastery and dexterity of tool-making.

Best foot forward

It is very probable that outside caves and dwellings, and especially during cold events, people would have routinely worn semi-rigid to stiff-soled shoes, boots or sandals to protect their feet. There is some anatomical evidence for human footwear in the Palaeolithic (notably gracile phalanges below otherwise robust lower limbs), dating back to the Gravettian in Europe but even as long ago as 40,000 bp in China. As shown above, the existence of footwear can be inferred from beads around the feet and ankles in burials such as Sunghir – and the adult male buried there had noticeably gracile phalanges.

It is clear that footwear and warm clothing must have been invented perhaps hundreds of millennia earlier, as one cannot walk barefoot on ice and snow, and people would have needed to hunt in those conditions during the earlier ice ages in northern Europe.

Obviously we do not know precisely what Upper Palaeolithic shoes were made of or looked like. One possibility in some areas could have been rabbit skins, which can be turned inside out and are just the right size. Another possibility, known from ethnography, is fish-skin shoes. Footwear could also have been created from fallen bark, bark from dead trees, or bark that was carefully removed from the trunk so as not to damage it; this can be treated, then cut into narrow strips and woven into foot coverings (as well as non-leaky containers). Dry moss can be used to soften and protect the foot inside the shoe and absorb moisture.

It can safely be assumed that they had something like moccasins, whether made of hide or bark. It seems, however, that they did not usually wear them inside

Figure 3.33. Footprint in Fontanet cave, long thought to be wearing a moccasin, but now thought to be naked. A pattern of holes in the clay floor is next to it.

caves – doubtless they would quickly have been ruined by the wet and muddy conditions, and bare feet would also be far less slippery than wet footwear! This is why it was no surprise that all ice age footprints found in European caves are of bare feet – with one exception. In the Pyrenean decorated cave of Fontanet, one footprint was widely considered to be that of a foot encased in a moccasin. However, when three Namibian Bushman trackers were recently brought to the caves to study the footprints, they all declared that the Fontanet print was barefoot after all!

Conversely, in the huge Gravettian cave of Cussac (Dordogne), which contains the most recently discovered set of footprints, there is evidence of footwear for the first time. The human prints in the cave show no trace of toes, but bear prints do. Experiments have shown that unpadded footwear leaves traces of toes unless the ground is hard, and even padded footwear leaves traces of the big toe. This means that even some apparently naked prints in some caves could be shod, but the only explanation for the Cussac prints seems to be the wearing of footwear.

Conclusion

Once again we have learned how resourceful and innovative our ice age ancestors were in their production of tools and their use of all the materials available to them. Not only were they practical, but they were able to fashion goods and clothing that must have been considered creative and luxury items for the time. We have a plethora of evidence that they developed new behaviours, activities and skills that must have improved their living conditions considerably; indeed some communities may have developed enough expertise to establish manufacturing sites producing surplus goods that may have been traded with their neighbours, or via long-distance social networks. In Chapter 4 we will explore the evidence for the range of food resources available to ice age people, and how they used their knowledge to exploit them to the full. We also consider the possibility of control of animals, and how dogs may have been introduced as hunting partners.

Chapter 4

How to Make a Living: Survival and Subsistence

Hunting -vs - gathering

The last ice age was a period of hunter-gatherers, so it is now time to look at the evidence we have for the food resources available and how they were exploited. Obviously everything depended on the local topography and environment, as well as the climate and the seasons of occupation.

It should be remembered that ice age Eurasia could, for long periods of time, be an inhospitable place with bitter winds, freezing temperatures and waterlogged lands. Following the tracks of herds in such hostile environments would have been a formidable challenge – and not without risks – so having a variety of alternative food options would have been a vital lifeline for our hungry ancestors. On the other hand, both southern France and Iberia would have been pleasant regions in which to take refuge during the coldest phases of the ice age.

Although hunting was undoubtedly one of the principal activities of the period, we do not have a single clear depiction of it in the huge wealth of ice age imagery

Figure 4.1. Photomontage of the entire 'shaft scene' in Lascaux (Dordogne), showing rhinoceros, dots, apparently wounded bison, bird-headed ithyphallic man and 'bird-on-stick'. Probably Magdalenian. Total width: c. 2.75 m.

THE IVORY BOOMERANG

It always seemed extremely likely that boomerangs and throwing sticks (kylies) made of wood were used in the last ice age but, being made of wood, they have not survived. In Australia, however, three complete wooden boomerangs did survive in Wyrie Swamp and are up to 10,000 years old. Killing sticks probably predate the boomerang, and can be accurate up to about 200 m, much farther than a man can throw a stone or spear.

Figure 4.2. Paul Bahn with the Oblazowa boomerang.

Proof that this hunting technique also existed in ice age Europe came in 1987, when an ivory boomerang was unearthed in Oblazowa, a cave in southern Poland. Dating to c. 20,000 years ago this impressive object, made from the end of a young mammoth's tusk, has a span of 71 cm, is up to 6 cm wide and 1.5 cm thick. One side preserves the external, convex tusk-surface, whereas the other has been polished almost flat. It is certainly not a returning boomerang, but its shape clearly suggests that it was aerodynamic.

The object was far too precious to be used for throwing tests, so an exact replica was made in plexiglass, from which a copy was taken in plastic of the same specific gravity as mammoth ivory (1.8 to 1.9). The facsimile weighed about 800 gm. The first tester, an expert in the field of throwing implements, had difficulty in throwing the boomerang. Not only is 800 gm quite heavy for objects of this type, but the span and outline are unusual. The two ends are of different widths – the wider one is clearly the gripping end, and has transverse engraved lines on its underside which afford a better grip. The thinner end, on the other hand, because of its greater curvature and less favourable position in the hand, could injure the thrower as its point slides through the hand.

The boomerang can be thrown with either hand without loss of flight qualities. The tester threw the facsimile at an angle of 80-90°, almost horizontally. Its flight path proved extremely stable (whereas that of a wooden specimen, weighing only 200 gm and with a span of 50 cm, was influenced by wind conditions). Throwing the object horizontally prevents excessive lift which can hinder aiming, and which may also help game to spot it too soon. With a following wind, the average flight path was 25-30 m, but against the wind it was 35-40 m. In other words, wind propulsion from behind had less effect on the distance thrown than the aerodynamic lift from a facing wind. The same results were obtained in summer and winter, and in a variety of weather conditions. Throwing into the wind, of course, makes it harder for the prey to detect the hunter's scent.

Other tests were carried out by sport-boomerang enthusiasts. In a light breeze, various attempts confirmed that only a horizontal throw was practicable and sensible. The best throw achieved was 66 m, with a gentle facing wind. For comparison, a bent wooden cudgel, loaded with lead to weigh 800 gm, was tried, but travelled only 27 m at 18.5 m per second, whereas the boomerang went up to 66 m at 21.4 m per second.

Subtle details in the carving of the ivory, all apparently designed to improve its stability and ballistic qualities, indicate that its maker knew precisely what to do. Its ingenious form points to a long tradition of making weapons of this kind; the carver was clearly drawing on long-accumulated knowledge in the working of this difficult material and in the design of such weapons, which were probably used to bring down small game.

– with the possible exception of the highly enigmatic 'shaft scene' of Lascaux which appears to show a stick-figure human in front of a bison which may have been disembowelled by a spear. We therefore have to deduce hunting methods from the weapons and animal remains that have survived. As we have seen, the commonest are spearpoints and 'harpoons' of bone and antler, together with the spearthrower, and probably bows and arrows. But they also knew the killing stick (see Box).

As we shall see below (pp. 137-42), by the end of the period if not before, the hunters certainly had the assistance of dogs. We have no idea whether they also used ferrets or birds of prey. But we can be sure that thousands of years' experience must have made them expert trackers and also highly accomplished at finding and exploiting their prey, whose habits, behaviours, and movements were extremely well known to them. The game available depended on climate, topography and season. They were well aware that some animals may live alone (red deer, ibex), others in herds (horses, reindeer), and they knew the migrations of different species in different seasons. Any gaps in the hunting calendar could be filled with small game. We can also safely assume that a wide variety of hunting methods were used – chasing, approaching, stalking, ambushes, trapping, and game-drives (but not off cliffs – see Solutré box).

It is virtually impossible to quantify the animal resources that might have been available in different periods and regions, because there is a tremendous variety in habitat and population density and structure amongst the modern representatives of all the species we are concerned with here, and the range of *potential* environmental tolerance of each species is generally far broader than its present range. The fact that we lack modern analogues of the prehistoric plant communities and animal predator/prey communities is a further severe limitation, nor can we be sure that the ecological requirements of those species which do survive are unchanged. Of course, we also need to assume that human behaviour has not changed markedly since prehistoric times and that most hunter-gatherers led mobile lives. It is equally important to assume that the behaviour and tolerances of live resources are also broadly predictable for the past. One must further assume that, in general, when faced with a set of economic choices, people will consider the probable outcome of each choice, and then make a rational decision to adopt an economic strategy which will, in the long term, lead to an effective but not necessarily maximal exploitation of resources. And the desire to minimise effort underlies all economic decisions.

For decades, 'Man the Mighty Hunter' was the accepted, almost unconscious, one-sided view of how our early ancestors 'made it' through the ice age, and the period's imagery – mainly depictions of animals – led to the erroneous notion that the species portrayed on cave walls and portable objects were directly linked to hunting, which was therefore a major preoccupation of these early populations. The traditional notion of 'Man the Hunter' was further compounded by early investigators being a little too eager to see modern-day hunter-gatherers as living fossils whose lives could be compared with the activities of the ice age hunters.

For a very long time, and until recent decades, the less glamorous but more realistic picture – one of women, children and the elderly gathering plant foods like roots, tubers, edible shoots and lichens, nuts, berries, and fruits, and trapping small mammals to sustain the family – was generally neglected. And, as suggested earlier (p. 21), both sexes were probably involved in both activities – along with fishing and catching birds, gathering eggs, collecting insects, etc.

One can safely assume that observing what animals like deer and reindeer ate would over time have given people valuable information about edible vegetation (wild grasses and sedges, tree shoots and woody plants, along with fruits and berries). Small animals hoard nuts for future use and this is unlikely to have gone unnoticed by these shrewd observers of animal behaviour. In addition, having knowledge of where animals like red deer were browsing and grazing around the landscape might well have improved their foraging strategies, and knowing where animals go to eat or drink provides the canny hunter with good places to camouflage him or herself and lie in wait with a spear ready to strike. All these skills must have been taught to the next generation, out in the field.

We can likewise safely assume that they must have identified the reliable areas for gathering produce and the particular seasons of the year that would yield food that was ready for collecting. At the same time they will have acquired knowledge of those areas where it would be a waste of time and energy looking for resources when the soil or conditions were not likely to produce tubers, edible roots, fruiting shrubs etc. Even on the Russian plain – notably at Sunghir – they engaged in plant-gathering when the food was available. The people were often nomadic, moving to avoid driving herds to extinction, or exhausting local resources, especially plants.

In fact the traditional distinction between hunters and gatherers in the Upper Palaeolithic is probably a false one, and it is just as likely that, depending on the season, everyone went gathering or fishing together, or on a communal hunt. Certainly, when the salmon were running (pp. 159-62), it would have been all-hands-on, including children, to maximise the daily catch. Dividing up the labour between the sexes would have been a strategy to enhance their success, and flexibility, adaptability, and planning for the future would have been the hallmarks of their food-procurement strategies.

But how often did they need to hunt? And did women and children make a bigger contribution to the diet by gathering food? It has been calculated that 240 calories of plant food can be gathered in 1 hour, whereas hunting is hard, has a high failure rate and is estimated to produce only 100 calories for every hour of hunting activity. So was meat as significant a part of the ice age diet as has always been thought? It is known that some Australian Aboriginal men are dependent on their women folk for food, rather than the other way around.

In some modern hunter-gatherer groups, only men make weapons, but a hunter who kills an animal is not its owner – it is shared with everyone in the group, and even with other groups through a complex network of friendship, alliance and obligation. Sometimes in modern communities the hunters take the meat with the most fat, leaving the less nutritional parts for the women. Modern hunter-gatherers only need to spend three to five hours a day procuring food. Palaeolithic hunters may have only needed two hours a day to get one animal that would feed a group for several days.

It is certainly possible that hunting brought status – it is by no means a 'soft' option, and catching and butchering animals are hazardous and dangerous activities that can lead to injury. There can also be other impacts on health, as contaminated food and hides and parasites are all possible routes for infection and the spread of disease. Nevertheless, ethnohistoric and ethnographic evidence shows that rotted or putrefied meat, fish, fat and stomach contents have often served not as starvation foods but rather as desirable and nutritionally key dietary staples in northern environments. So perhaps the same was true in the ice age.

On the other hand, it is quite possible that ice age women were considered important members of their communities, and that they were accorded status not only through success at providing and preparing food but also and especially through childcare. Perhaps these activities, rather than hunting prowess, were the most highly valued – if indeed these matters were ever considered. We shall never know.

Hunting for clues to hunting

Depending on the particular economy, different-sized areas would have been needed for survival. Some groups must have all moved together, once or twice a year, following the seasons or the herds; or they had a permanent base camp, and some members undertook expeditions with little camps; or the group came together periodically and split up into smaller groups for the rest of the year. In most sites, the ages at death of the animals killed – deduced from bones and tooth growth – indicate the season(s) of occupation.

For example, most ice age sites in the Dordogne seem to have been primarily occupied in the winter. But at the Abri Pataud, the ages of the reindeer killed indicate that people were present in all seasons, and they brought whole animals back to the site, so they were not killed far away. At Pont d'Ambon the fishes and red deer also show year-round occupation. Supersites such as Isturitz and Le Mas d'Azil in the Pyrenees were almost certainly used for periodic gatherings of people from different areas.

SOLUTRÉ

One popular idea which must be quashed at the start is that ice age people sometimes drove herds of animals off cliffs. In 1866, excavations began at the open-air site of Solutré in central France, a very complex Palaeolithic occupation covering several hectares at the foot of a great cliff, with some sections up to 10 m thick, and containing material from almost every phase of the Upper Palaeolithic. It was used for about 25,000 years from the Aurignacian to the Magdalenian, and gave its name to the Solutrean period. Its most spectacular feature was a series of layers containing thousands of horse bones – the richest, dating to the Gravettian, was more than a metre thick and contained up to 100,000 horse bones. They were clearly killed in situ, as all parts of the skeleton are present, often in connection. The animals were systematically butchered and cut up, with marrow and brains always extracted. Some were burned – the occupants must have smoked the meat to preserve the enormous quantities obtained. Reindeer teeth show that the site was primarily occupied in the spring.

By the 1860s the notion of human antiquity was firmly established, and some scholars' minds were turning to the reconstruction of daily life in the Palaeolithic, based on archaeological evidence mixed with the early ethnography of 'savage' peoples. This led one of Solutré's excavators, the historian Adrien Arcelin, to produce the very first prehistoric novel, *Solutré ou les chasseurs de rennes de la France Centrale* (*Solutré or the reindeer hunters of Central France*, 1872), in order to bring the site's occupants to life. His worthy effort had the unfortunate consequence of creating, in only two pages, one of prehistory's most famous and durable myths – that horses had been driven to their death from the top of the precipice. He had never put this idea forward in his scientific articles on Solutré, since no such drive would have been possible there – the location of the horse bones meant they would have had to fly 100 m from cliff-top to site! Presumably the horse herds must always have used the same routes, and could be ambushed against some enormous fallen blocks near the base of the cliff.

In creating this dramatic image, Arcelin may have been influenced by some ethnography from the New World where bison herds were sometimes driven off precipices. The best-known site of this kind today is Canada's Head-Smashed-In, first described in the 1880s, which was in use for five millennia, starting c. 6000 years ago.

Figure 4.3. Postcard of the Solutré excavation, c. 1912.

Horses

The huge quantities of horse bones at Solutré are quite exceptional, but there are other sites where the horse was the main species exploited – for example at Gönnersdorf. As mentioned earlier (see above, p. 64) it is clear that pregnant mares were killed here. Similarly, in the Magdalenian period at Isturitz the horse bones apparently represent animals of all ages, including many young animals and even some newborn specimens. This is intriguing, as ethnographic data suggest that hunters would not normally kill a heavily pregnant mare, let alone a newborn foal, as this would endanger the future of the species. The heavy reliance on horse for many millennia at Isturitz therefore suggests very

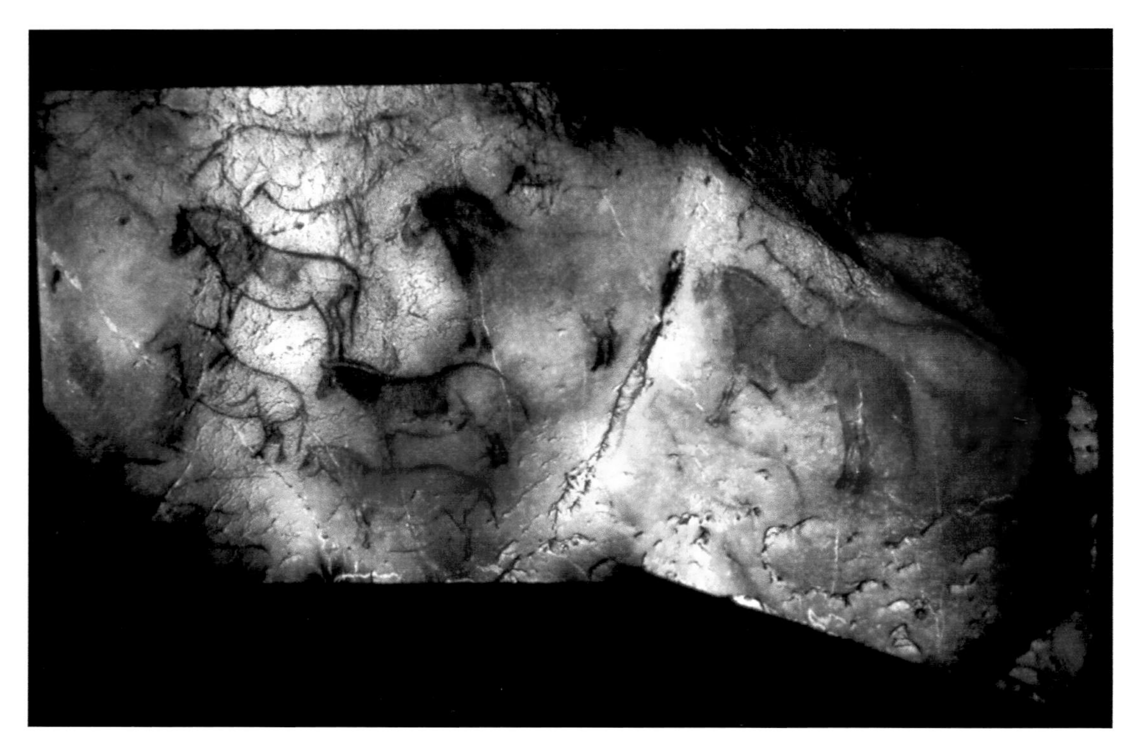

Figure 4.4. Photomontage of the horse panel at Ekain (Guipúzcoa, Spain), c. 4 m wide. Note the 'M' mark on the horse hides. Probably Magdalenian.

strongly that the exploitation was careful and efficient – going far beyond opportunistic hunting – and leads one to speculate about the possibility of some sort of management of horses at this site.

The horse was clearly of enormous importance throughout the last ice age, and not always as a food resource. For example, at Pincevent (pp. 59-62), the archetypal reindeer-hunters camp, several tents had an isolated horse tooth near the hearth, and a fragment of horse bone was found just outside other tents. This is clearly deliberate and can be compared with the isolated horse teeth or jaws found carefully placed inside Magdalenian hearths in some deep Pyrenean caves such as Labastide and Erberua.

The horse's importance is also evident in ice age imagery – the species is depicted in more than 75% of decorated caves, spanning all regions and periods. It dominates in a wide variety of sites such as Lascaux (whose 364 depictions far exceed any other animal), Ekain, Tito Bustillo, and the sculpted frieze of Cap Blanc. Moreover, the representations of what seem to be simple harnesses on some horse-heads – especially one from La Marche – and also in parietal figures at the caves of Erberua and Oxocelhaya indicate that the horse may well have been under close control during the Upper Palaeolithic.

It was long thought that modern Przewalski horses were 'living fossils' since they so closely resemble the ice age depictions: short stubby manes, long tails,

Figure 4.5. a: Tracing of horse head from La Marche;
► b: Tracing of horse engraved in Marsoulas cave (Haute Garonne);

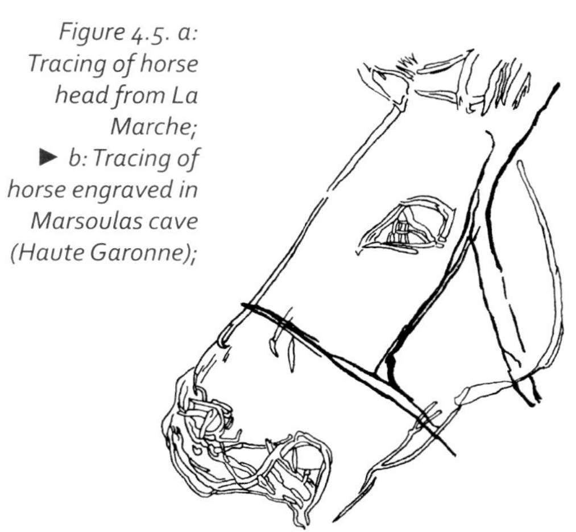

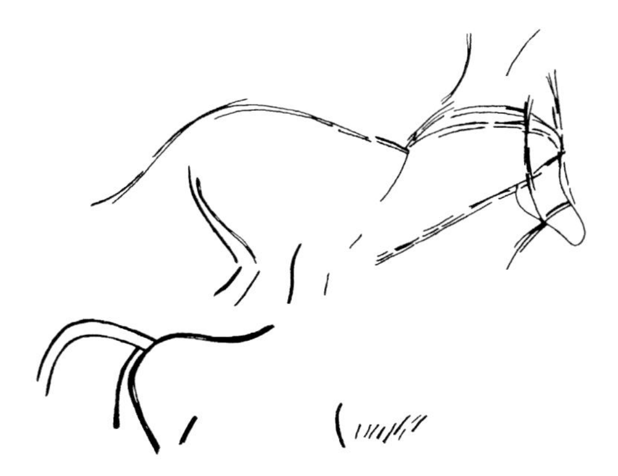

Figure 4.5 ▼c: detail of engraved/ scraped horse engraving from Oxocelhaya (Pyrénées Atlantiques);
► d: Drawing of the Oxocelhaya horse head, c. 25 cm long;

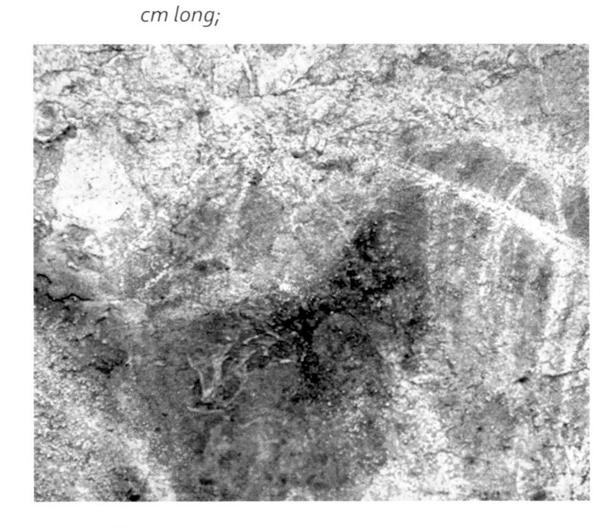

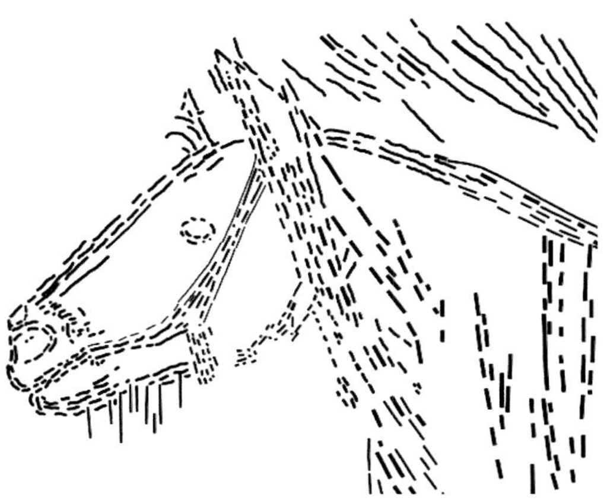

Figure 4.5.e: Tracing of possible horse head engraved on reindeer antler at Espèche (Hautes-Pyrénées).

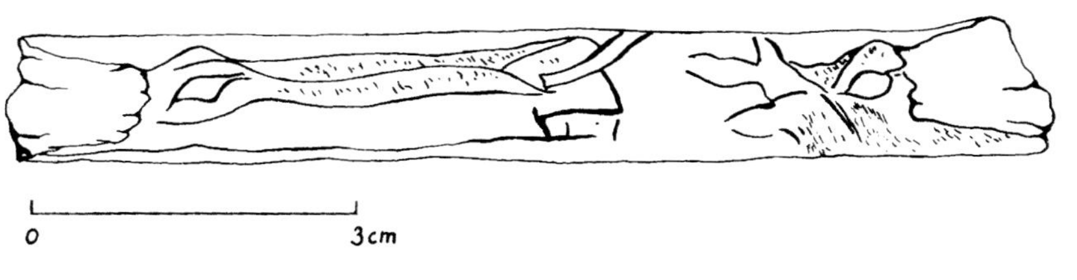

ANIMAL CONTROL

Archaeologists realized in the 1970s that 'wild' and 'domesticated' are an inadequate description of the status of animals within the complex spectrum of their possible relationships with people. Nineteenth-century scholars had been greatly hampered by this simplistic dichotomy, and when discussing ice age life some had resorted to intermediate animal husbandry terms such as 'semi-domestication' – i.e. not full subjugation, but possible taming, capture, herding, corralling and conservation. In short, a wide variety of forms of animal control.

Starting in the 19th century, prehistorians relied on two main hypotheses to decide whether animals were wild or domesticated. The first was the 'butchering theory' – here, the crucial criterion was the presence or absence of certain parts of the herbivore skeleton. If vertebrae, ribs and scapulae were absent, this suggested that killing and butchering had taken place at some distance from the living-site, so the animals were presumably wild. If they were domesticated, one would find all parts of the skeleton. Of course, this theory had no validity – the distance between butchering- and living-sites is an independent variable and need have no correlation with either skeletal remains or the existence of domestication. It is far easier to carry – or transport on a sled – a whole carcass than a series of pieces! In fact there many ice age sites which contained whole series of reindeer vertebrae, and, as we have seen (p. 120), Solutré had all parts of the horse skeleton, often in connection – which led some specialists to believe, in accordance with the theory, that the horses here were domesticated. But those who refused to accept any animal control in the Palaeolithic ignored these 'exceptions' and applied the theory with enormous inconsistency – for example, it was claimed that the Solutré horses had been lassoed, overpowered and brought to the site for slaughter, thus making a mockery of the butchery theory!

The second hypothesis, equally invalid, was the 'dog theory' – i.e. it was claimed that the dog was the first animal to be domesticated; no other domestication of any kind could take place without the presence and help of dogs, and there were no dogs in the ice age. However, many scholars pointed out that reindeer herders such as the Chukchi and Tungus manage perfectly well without dogs, and even in the late 19th century there were already finds of what seemed to be dog bones in ice age sites (see pp. 137-42).

When one considers that, within a couple of centuries of first encountering horses, the North American Indians had become some of the greatest horsemen in the world, it seems self-evident that the people of the ice age – who were every bit as intelligent as ourselves, and who lived in a world containing horse herds for many thousands of years – must have realised many times that one could do more with horses than simply throw a spear at them when one was peckish. Since it would have been easy to tame and raise foals, surely it would have dawned on them that these strong and robust animals could be employed to carry or drag the heavy equipment such as tents and hides that had to be transported between dwelling sites.

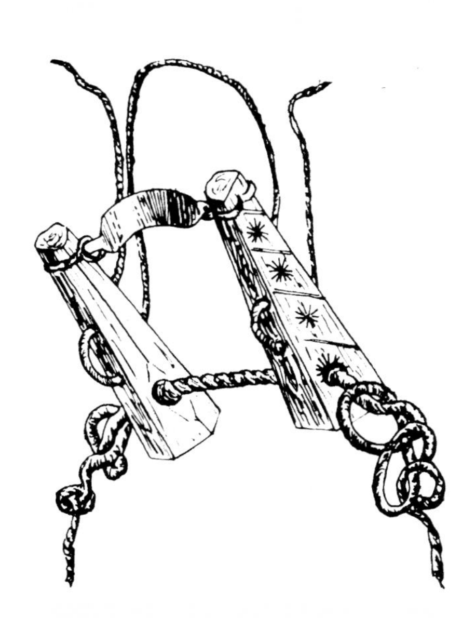

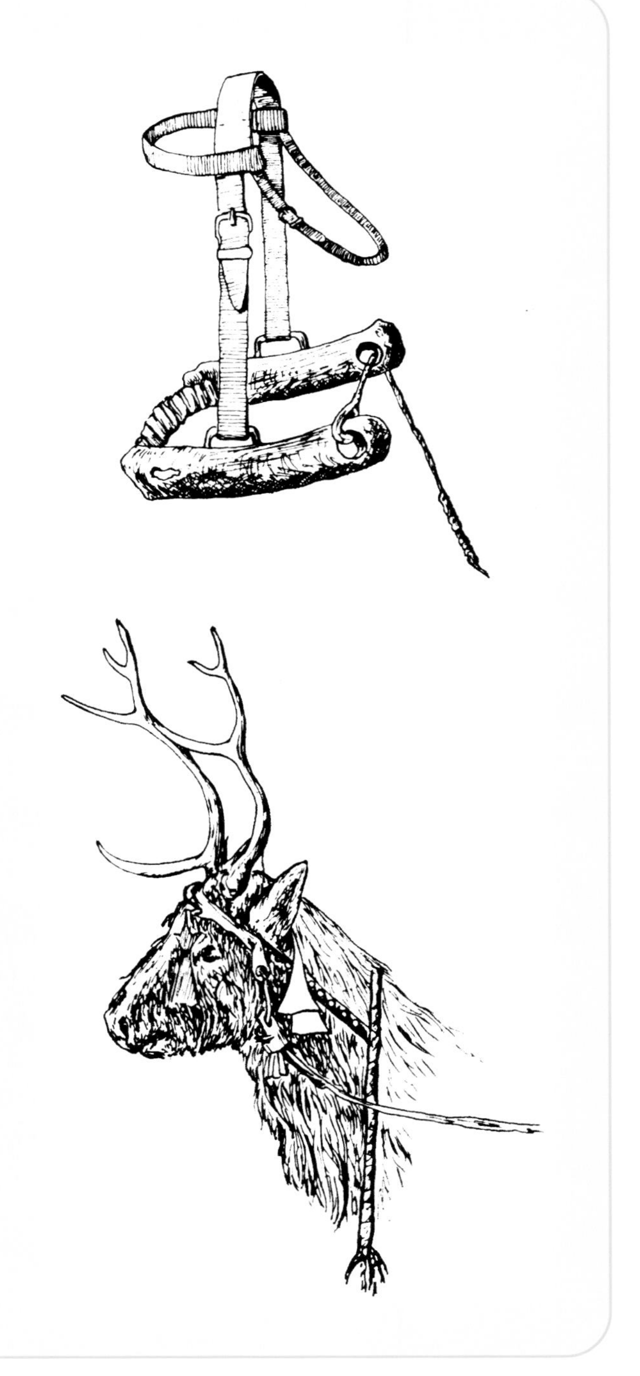

Figure 4.6. ▲ *a: Simple compression-bridles from Sardinia;* ► *b: Samoyed reindeer harness.*

In addition to the depictions of harnesses, there are other kinds of evidence which support this notion. First, ethnographic parallels strongly suggest that some of the many perforated antler batons may have formed part of such harnesses or bridles – as mentioned earlier (pp. 94-95), the wear in most of the perforations was clearly made by rope. Sardinians in recent times used similar batons to control horses by compressing the sensitive nasal area, and Samoyeds used very similar pieces in reindeer harnesses.

Second, a number of ice age horse incisors – notably from Le Placard and Enlène – bear a specific kind of anterior bevelled wear that has clearly been caused by 'crib-biting'. This 'stable vice' is a direct result of idleness and boredom, and is never encountered in

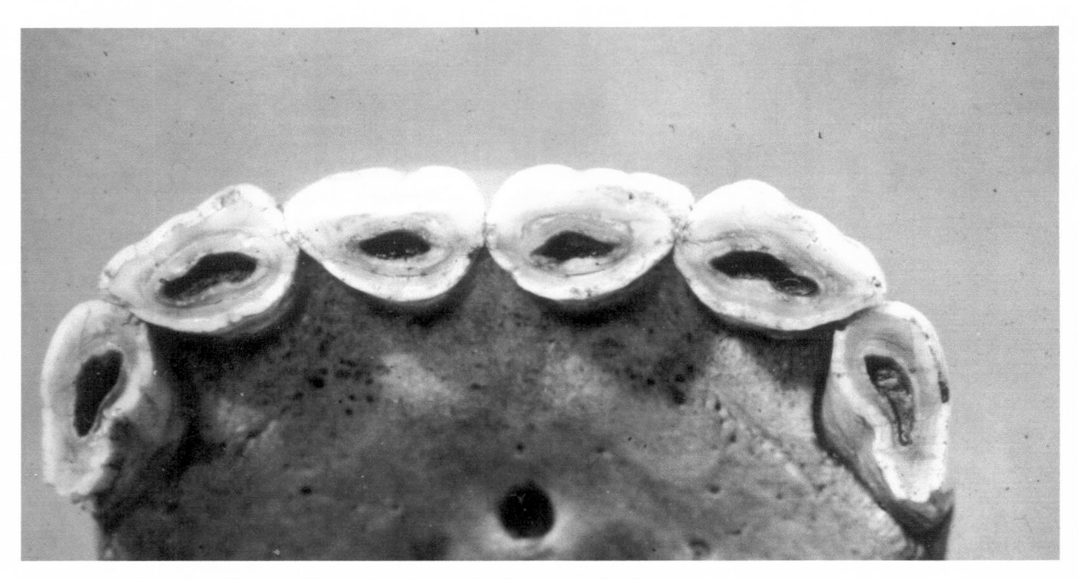

Figure 4.7. Horse jaw from Le Placard with bevelled wear at the front.

horses that run free. It is characteristic of horses that are tethered and confined for prolonged periods.

At Isturitz, the heavy reliance for millennia on reindeer, like that on horse, implies an efficient exploitation that was more intensive than opportunistic hunting. Edouard Piette, the pioneering 19th-century excavator of Gourdan in the Pyrenees, estimated that he had found the remains of at least 450 reindeer in his first two months, which led to a figure of well over 3000 in the portion of the site he dug. The deep stratigraphy pointed to an efficient and long-lasting exploitation – he believed in the domestication of reindeer here, and claimed to have found bones of a dog associated with reindeer and horse bones. He saw the reliance on reindeer at Gourdan and other sites as some kind of privileged association between people and herds, a '*vie en commun*', almost a kind of domestication.

Similarly, at the site of Duruthy (Landes), the excavator, Robert Arambourou, encountered what he believed to be a specialised exploitation of reindeer – of 66 individuals, 5 were fawns, 10 were large males, and the other 51 were either females or young males. Hence the occupants were probably culling surplus young males in the autumn in order to maintain a flourishing herd. Arambourou therefore thought these people had a lifestyle analogous to that of reindeer-herding Lapps.

In addition to such claims, there are a few specific clues to possible reindeer husbandry. For example, a few reindeer antlers have been found (e.g. at Bois-du-Roc, Charente) that seem to be from castrates, though some researchers are sceptical about this identification. The cave of Isturitz contained the injured metacarpal of a reindeer. It had a seriously infected multiple fracture, but the animal had survived for two years. It is possible that a reindeer could consolidate a multiple fracture of such a gracile bone without artificial aid, but it is highly improbable that a wild herbivore could have avoided all predators for such a period with such a handicap. In fact predation is highly selective for unhealthy individuals: wolves are known to concentrate on those animals which are most easily caught, and particularly on infirm stragglers. So this reindeer was 'predisposed to predation', and its two year survival strongly suggests some form of protection by people that may be symptomatic of a very close relationship between the cave's occupants and their principal resources.

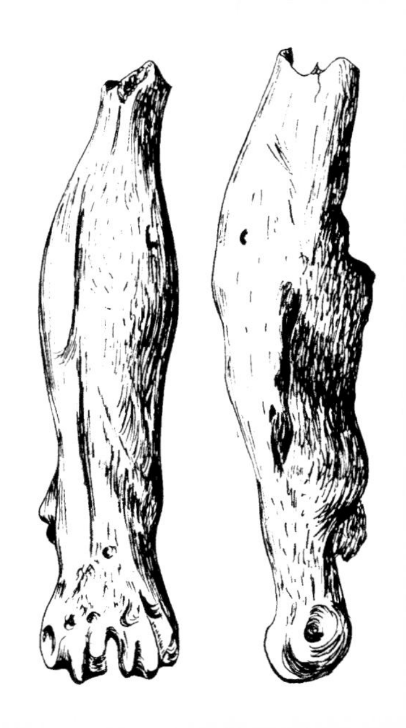

Figure 4.8. The Isturitz reindeer metacarpal.

Similarly, the skeleton was found of a young reindeer that fell into the Pyrenean cave of Les Trois Frères from above. It had an infected fracture of the mandible, with osteomyelitis, a large abscess, suppuration and an infected sinus. It had survived this condition for about two months, as a similar fracture of the maxilla had begun to mend. It would have had the greatest difficulty in feeding itself, and could not have masticated its food, which would have kept the sores open and irritated. How, therefore, did it escape predation for the two months before its fall? Predation is highly selective for unhealthy individuals – particularly in species such as the red and fallow deer, where herds actually reject diseased individuals. So, as with the reindeer at Isturitz, it appears that for some reason people protected and nurtured this crippled beast.

It is certainly true that dental anomalies and even mended fractures have occasionally been found in modern wild deer populations, but when one considers the variety of hungry predators that were around in the ice age, added to the fact that these specimens came from occupation sites, it seems reasonable to conclude that these individual animals had been protected.

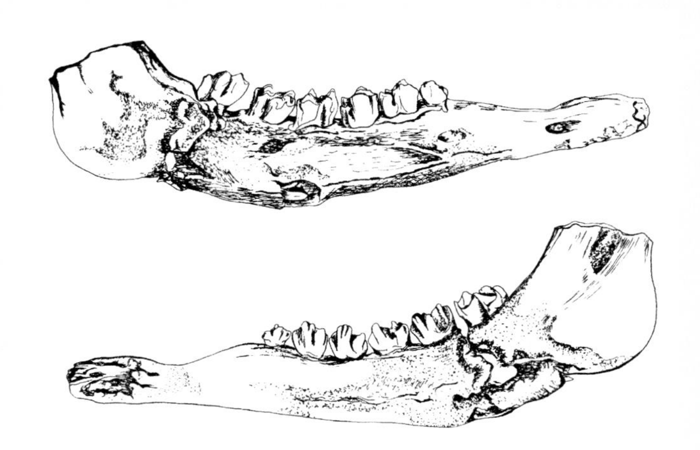

Figure 4.9. The reindeer jaw from Les Trois Frères.

There has never been a valid reason for rejecting *a priori* the idea of close animal control in the late Palaeolithic, and indeed, as shown above, there is a body of very varied evidence in favour of such a view. It seems perfectly feasible – indeed extremely likely – that some human groups in the last ice age travelled with pack animals, on horse-back, or in transport harnessed to horse or reindeer.

the 'M' coat-marking sign on the side (see fig. 4.4, p. 122), occasional stripes on legs and shoulder. However, recent genetic analysis has shown that the Przewalski is not a wild horse but a feral descendant of herded horses from a few millennia ago. The resemblances are thus coincidental, and the ice age horse is extinct.

Reining in the reindeer

Bison and aurochs (wild ox) were certainly exploited for food and raw materials in the last ice age – they are second only to horses in their frequency in the imagery – but they were not often a staple. One exception is the Gravettian open-air site of Amvrosievka (Ukraine), at the edge of a plain, where a huge accumulation of bones came from about a thousand bison – they were associated with spearpoints, as well as bladelets and micro-points which had probably been hafted onto weapons. Another example is Duruthy (Landes) where, in the middle Magdalenian, up to two-thirds of usable meat came from bison, which may thus indicate a specialization.

It is known that, in North America, Great Plains Palaeo-Indians often relied heavily on bison and their kill-sites contain dozens to hundreds of animals, yet they seem to have made little effort to maximise the yield of fat – major marrow bones were often ignored and there was little effort to boil grease from bones. Bison certainly provided plenty of lean meat, but fat is also of great importance, and it is crucial for hunter-gatherers to avoid what has been called 'rabbit starvation' – i.e. a diet with too much lean meat and/or too little fat.

Aurochs and bison were formidable animals, and since there is no evidence whatsoever of huge pit traps (a colossal undertaking with antler picks and scapula-shovels!) or of bison drives over cliffs (see above, p. 120), they had to be brought down with spears. One bison shoulder-blade from Kokorevo 1, Siberia, has a reindeer-antler spearpoint armed with a flint microbladelet stuck in it. Modern bison herds normally comprise a group of females and young around a bull, while the older males tend to live alone, only joining the herd at rutting time – so they are more vulnerable to predation. In the Pyrenean cave of Enlène, the faunal remains are dominated by bison (53%), followed by reindeer (29%) and horse (8%). The bison were mostly adults, but immature ones and foetuses were also found, so clearly some females were also killed. The ice age bison is now extinct but seems to resemble the modern European bison rather than the

American; the aurochs has been extinct since 1627, but efforts are underway to breed back to something like it.

Reindeer, by contrast, were of such importance in so many regions (especially in France) and phases of the last ice age that for a long time it was known as the 'Reindeer Age'. As mentioned earlier (p. 23), a family of seven would need a minimum of 25 lbs of meat per day, and since a tundra reindeer yields about 75 lbs, then one carcass would have been needed every 3 or 4 days. Some researchers have suggested that at least 150-200 reindeer per year would be necessary. Based on these figures, and assuming a sustained kill of about 10% of the reindeer population, a family of seven would need a minimum population of c. 1000 - 1500 reindeer to survive. Therefore a band of c. 25 people would require a standing population of 3500 - 5000 reindeer for their survival, and a tribe of 500 people would need 70,000 - 110,000 animals. But if they killed less intensively – under 10% – then perhaps 150,000 - 200,000 reindeer would be needed. However, a pure meat diet is inadequate to supply some essential vitamins like A or C – vitamin C could be obtained from plants or from the contents of reindeer stomachs.

In some sites, it is possible to assess in some detail how reindeer carcasses were processed. If parts of the same animal are found at different hearths, then clearly the food was being shared. If different animals are found at each hearth, then one can't be sure. At Pincevent (pp. 59-62) researchers measured 2613 bone fragments, and then tried to find matching pairs (left and right), based on degrees of fusion, etc. The best results came from front legs, especially metacarpal bones – fragments of one reindeer were found at three hearths, so clearly some animals were being shared around between dwellings.

Pincevent shows an intensive extraction of marrow and brains, with numerous skull fragments and teeth being found close to the big hearths. Exactly the same occurred at Verberie (Oise), a similar but smaller site of the same period in the Paris Basin. Both seem to have exploited the autumn migrations of the reindeer – the time when the best meat is available after the animals have built up fat reserves from the high-quality summer forage. At Verberie, there were five superimposed brief occupations, separated by flood deposits. The two hearths were bordered by stone blocks and had flint-knapping areas around them, as well as animal bone fragments – 99% of which were from reindeer. At least 16,000 reindeer remains were found in the site as a whole, from a minimum of 130 animals. Those aged one to two were killed within a few days or weeks in the autumn, at migration time. The occupants were selecting young adults in top form after the summer.

The site's butchering areas are marked by numerous intact vertebral columns, which contain little marrow and are a nuisance. They are located halfway between the two hearths, around two empty circular areas which are presumably where the tents stood. There are also coccyx and sternums, and carpals and tarsals – again, bones with no marrow. Metapodials (which contain lots of excellent marrow) are systematically absent. So these areas were clearly for initial butchering of the carcasses. Another smaller area was for boning the meat, and big flint blades there have use-wear showing that they were used for cutting meat. Observation of modern reindeer hunters in Siberia suggests that an entire animal can be cut up into manageable pieces in about 20 minutes.

It is important to note that connected vertebrae – which are low in nutrition – are so common at Verberie but almost absent at Pincevent; whereas femurs (which are highly nutritional) are frequent at Pincevent but highly under-represented at Verberie. In other words, it appears that Verberie was a site for the initial acquisition and butchering of carcasses – a place from which meat was transported – while Pincevent was a site to which meat was transported.

Different patterns can be seen in other places and phases. For example, in the Gravettian, at the Abri du Flageolet I (Dordogne), which was occupied in the winter, people were exploiting small groups of reindeer or individuals, especially adult females with their young. They seem to have been for immediate consumption, not stockage. Only some parts of the animals were brought back to the site – those rich in fat and marrow, especially the rear legs. The bits with little or no food value, like foot bones, are not found at the site – so the occupants only brought in what they needed. Conversely, at the Pyrenean cave of Enlène, reindeer carcasses were clearly brought in whole, and marks on bones show they were butchered in situ, which suggests that they were killed nearby. Both adults and young were killed, including numerous foetal remains. It is worth remembering that Les Trois Frères cave (the decorated annex to the living site of Enlène) yielded the fractured jaw of a reindeer, which suggests that animals here may have been protected (p. 127).

The reindeer is a migratory animal, and in situations where it constitutes the staple resource of a human group there arises a kind of symbiosis or social parasitism whereby people are compelled to adapt to living in the same manner as their prey, and to adopt a seasonally mobile way of life. The herd's movements prevent overgrazing, and migration is vital to the animals' health. Since all modern mainland populations of reindeer make some kind of

Figure 4.10.A deer vertebra from Montfort, pierced by a flint blade.

bi-annual migration, it is unlikely that the late glacial herds behaved very differently.

Ethnography suggests that human groups dependent at least seasonally on migratory reindeer herds can pursue one of three possible economies: they can follow them all year round (i.e. herd following, which is something like ranching); they may live permanently in the range occupied by the reindeer only in one season, where there are adequate resources for the seasons when herds are absent; or they may place themselves on migration routes and hope to kill sufficient animals during the two migrations to provide enough food for the whole year – as long as the herd movements are strictly limited and predictable. It is reckoned that a herd of 100 reindeer needs at least 60 sq km for its annual grazing requirements, and the annual territory of a family of four to five people must have been at least 300 sq km.

Some researchers have argued that ice age people would have intercepted reindeer herds, not followed them – migration-hunting is viable in the long-term when the herd's movements are limited by natural features and can be accurately predicted. As we have seen, this appears to have been the case at sites such as Pincevent and Verberie. But migration routes are notoriously unreliable, and can change abruptly due to factors such as pasture exhaustion, so perhaps this explains why these sites were only used for a relatively short period. It is this unreliability which causes risks to any human groups that are heavily dependent on reindeer, and which compels them to adopt a similar nomadic way of life.

Therefore most scholars believe that herd following was more common among ice age groups mainly dependent on reindeer, undertaking migrations between winter and summer ranges. Studies of teeth and antlers can pinpoint the season of occupation – e.g. if adult male antlers are mostly shed, while those of females and fawns are attached to the skull, this points to the winter. On this basis, the clusters of reindeer-dominated sites in the Dordogne and the Pyrenean foothills probably constituted the cold-season agglomerations of herd-followers who spent the summer with the reindeer in migrations of varying extent – to uplands or to coastal areas. Occasional animals stay in one range all year round, and old or infirm humans will also live a more sedentary life – this may explain why the Abri Pataud, as mentioned earlier (p. 120), contains reindeer representing all seasons. The overwhelming dominance of this species at the site – between 85 and 97% for millennia – suggests that the economic strategy was highly successful in the long term at safeguarding and conserving its staple resource, and it may even represent the careful management of essentially the same herds through time.

Modern Siberian reindeer herders have entered into a symbiotic relationship with their herds – however, taming a wild Siberian reindeer in recent times has never been possible, so it is extremely likely that the process of 'taming the wild' must have occurred many thousands of years in the past.

Red deer

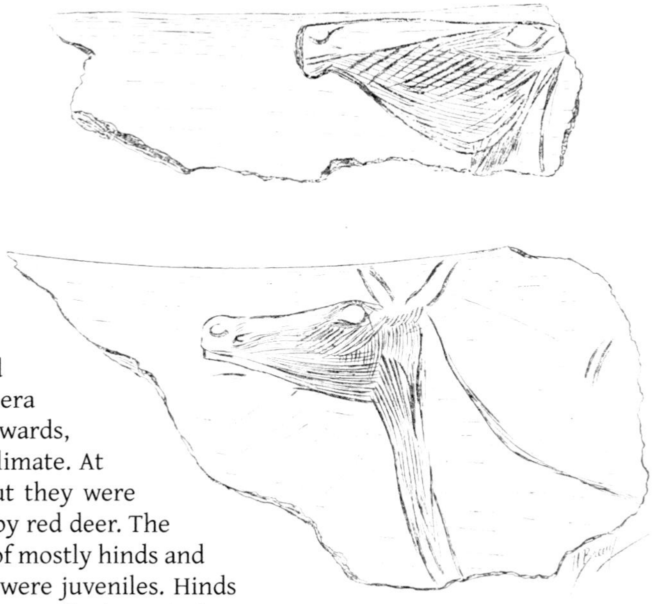

The reindeer was rarely depicted in cave art in France, despite its often huge economic importance; some of the finest images we have are found in northern Spanish caves (Tito Bustillo, Las Monedas, Altxerri) (p. 49), probably because the animal was a novelty and rarity here – this was the farthest south the species came. Instead, the ice age occupants of Spain mostly concentrated on the red deer. At the cave of La Riera (Asturias), occupied from c. 25,000 bp onwards, the economy changed along with the climate. At first horses and bovines dominated, but they were soon overtaken by ibex and eventually by red deer. The hunting of deer concentrated on herds of mostly hinds and fawns – 144 out of the 360 individuals were juveniles. Hinds were also prominent at the cave of Tito Bustillo (Asturias). Deer may have been hunted by mass drives or surrounds, year-round. The substantial numbers of prime-age deer point to some non-selective mass form of predation. Data from these two caves and others in the region support this view of systematic massive kills of red deer beginning as early as 23,000 bp.

Figure 4.11. Red deer engraved on red deer shoulder-blades, from Altamira.

Many people often equate red deer with the presence of lots of trees and hence with mild, humid conditions. But they are grazers as well as browsers, and in northern Spain they generally dominate at coastal plain sites like El Juyo, La Riera and Tito Bustillo regardless of the vegetation or climate, from 23,000 to 13,000 bp. The bones at La Riera were highly fragmented – 200,000 bone splinters were recovered – and maximally utilized for grease and marrow. It seems that nearly whole carcasses were often transported to the cave from nearby kill sites.

The ibex

In mountainous regions such as the Alps, Pyrenees and northern Spain, some groups focused their attention on the ibex. For example, the abundance of ibex bones in the cave of La Vache (Ariège) implies a long-term exploitation in the form of heavy seasonal culls and/or some form of control. The random hunting of single ibex – even today with gun and binoculars – is extremely difficult and exhausting. It is far more efficient – in terms of human energy and numbers of animals killed – to either ambush the herds or to drive them into natural corrals and cul-de-sacs for slaughter. This is also less disturbing to the herds – the remaining animals should not be panicked into abandoning the best grazing territories. Ibex soon come to tolerate the presence, the approach, and even the

Figure 4.12. Ibex drawn in the Salon Noir of Niaux (Ariège).

touch of humans without showing disturbance, so they can be controlled very easily, without fences or much effort. Dogs may even have been used (pp. 137-42). Ibex tend to move upwards when alarmed, so – as is still done by farmers in the Italian Alps – they can be quietly shepherded up and into enclosed spaces by 'beaters'.

The Magdalenian economy of La Vache probably rested on similar culls of ibex groups, or some kind of loose herding. The same has been suggested for the site of Las Malladetes in eastern Spain. In northern Spain, at the cave of La Riera (Asturias), located close to rocky escarpments, most ibex were killed shortly after birth (around May) as their milk teeth had not begun to wear. Perhaps the occupants surprised females who had separated from the herd to give birth.

The occupants of the cave of Les Eglises (Ariège), a site of the late Magdalenian, c. 12,000 bp, specialised in ibex and fish (see pp. 143-46). They made short stays in the late autumn and early winter – this is the rutting season when male and female ibex come together. The Magdalenians killed males and females of all ages. They were brought into the cave intact and were cut up in situ. The remains indicate systematic defleshing and marrow extraction, which suggests that they took the prepared meats away to a main residence elsewhere. One ibex represents about 130 lbs of meat (with 125 calories per 100 gm) and would feed a family for five days.

The mammoth

Although the public tends to associate ice age people with mammoths and assumes they were often hunted, in fact this appears to have happened very rarely. This is understandable – quite apart from the obvious dangers involved in tackling such a huge creature, why would anyone bother to do so when far better meat was available much more easily from deer, bison, horses, etc? As we have already seen (p. 69), most of the mammoth bones and tusks used in constructions were not produced by predation but collected from a wide area over long periods. It should be borne in mind that moving any portions of mammoths around would have required a tremendous amount of labour and effort.

Nevertheless, it is true that a handful of cases are known in Eurasia of mammoth hunting, and the same is true of North America in this period. For example, at Kraków, Spadzista Street (Poland), the remains of at least 86 mammoths were found, dating to 33,000 - 31,000 years ago. The presence of numerous hyoids (tongue bones), all bearing cutmarks, suggests that the site's occupants had feasted on roasted mammoth tongues (this is reminiscent of ethnographic accounts of Cheyenne killing whole herds of bison just for the tongues, a delicacy); and many of the mammoth bones were arranged into circular piles interpreted as the remains of meat caches.

At the Yana site in Arctic Siberia, dating to c. 33,000 - 31,000 bp, most of the bones are from mammoths, especially females, and stone points were found in a few young scapulas and pelvic bones. The hyoid bones were separate from the main accumulation, again suggesting the eating of tongues. This site has been interpreted as evidence of the hunting of mammoths of specific sizes, ages and sex. There seems to have been a concentration on juveniles and young adults at Krems-Hundsteig (Austria), around 31,000 bp – doubtless it was easier to kill youngsters and transport them, and perhaps their meat was tenderer and

Figure 4.13. a/b: Mammoth shoulder blade from Yana showing remains of projectile.

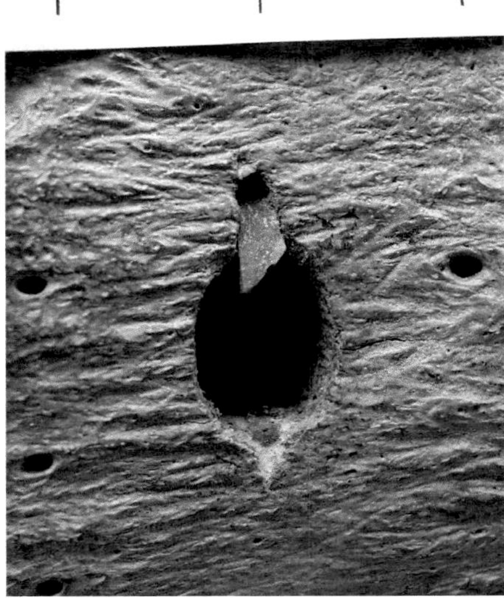

Figure 4.14. a/ ▶ b: Mammoth vertebra from Lugovskoe, pierced by a spear; fragments of the point remain embedded in the bone.

tasted better than that of adults – certainly, they would have had high-quality fat in some organs.

At the swampy site of Lugovskoe (Central Siberia), c. 22,000 - 17,000 bp, a mammoth vertebra was found which had been pierced by a spearhead made of greenish quartzite, fragments of which remained in the bone. The point had been removed or fallen out, and there was no sign of healing, so the animal probably died from the injury. As the vertebra is from the mid-chest region, the strike was probably aimed at the heart, and must have penetrated 10 cm of soft tissue as well as the scapula. Calculations suggest that the blow was applied with enormous strength, probably by means of a spearthrower from only 5 m away. For the hunter to approach so closely, it is likely that the mammoth was already caught in the sticky mud – perhaps people ambushed mammoths at places where they gathered, such as watering holes or salt flats. Stone tool fragments were also encountered in a mammoth rib at the Nikita Lake site (Arctic Siberia, c. 16,800 bp) and others at Kostenki 1 and Gontsy. At Kostenki 14, an ivory point was found embedded in a mammoth rib.

At other sites, mammoths may have been hunted rather than scavenged, but it is not always easy to establish the scenario. For example, at Milovice (Moravia), where tens of thousands of mammoth bones were found (see above, p. 69), only one bone bore any traces of butchering – but it is known that the defleshing of elephant bones often leaves no traces, so that is no guide to the cause of the accumulation. Nevertheless, isotopic analysis of some Gravettian human bones from Predmostí, Dolní Vestonice and Pavlov has revealed that these people consumed great quantities of mammoth meat, which accounted for about 60% of the protein source in their diet.

Carnivores and small game

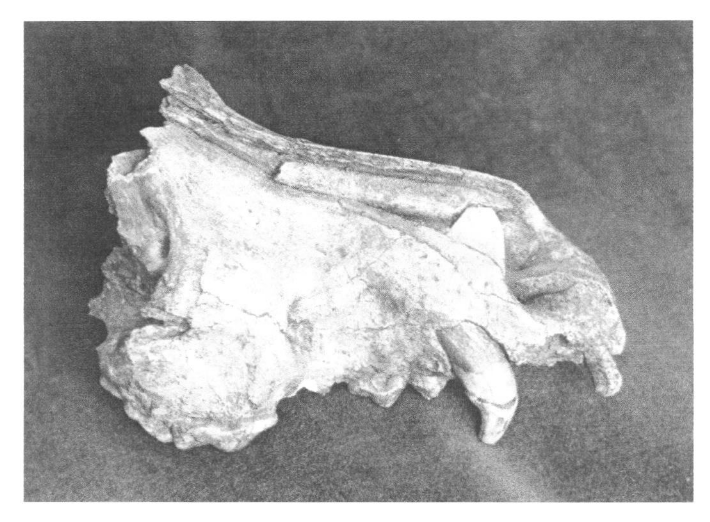

Figure 4.15. Wolf skull from Dolní Vestonice, with flint flake in its muzzle.

Carnivores were not hunted often – presumably the meat of herbivores was preferable, so they were doubtless exploited mostly for their pelts and fur (see above, p. 37). For example, at Mezin and Avdeevo whole or nearly whole skeletons of wolf and arctic fox were found with paws missing – they were presumably removed with the skins. Articulated paw skeletons have also been found separately. At Eliseevichi, the occupants killed six foxes under eight months, sixteen of one year, thirteen of two years, and five of three years – this suggests a desire for mature pelts, although carnivore bones were also used for tools and their teeth for jewellery (pp. 207-8). At Dolní Vestonice, a fragment of wolf skull had a flint flake still stuck in its muzzle.

Some small game (beaver, steppe marmot, pine marten) was also sometimes killed for fur. One assumes that traps, nooses and snares were used to catch them, and the same applies to rabbits and hares. On the Russian Plain, hares are found at more than 50% of sites – e.g. Gontsy had 16 individuals – their frequency is surpassed only by the gregarious herbivores, which indicates that they were systematically procured, not opportunistically.

Rabbits were much exploited in many Palaeolithic sites in eastern Spain and Portugal where they were a static and stable resource – i.e. a guaranteed food source when other resources were scarce. Their bones can be found in great abundance, and are often burned. However, since one red deer is the meat equivalent of 150 rabbits, and one ibex the equivalent of 100, it is clear that these small animals were a supplementary – though perhaps sometimes crucial – part of the diet. At the Gravettian cave of Lapa do Anecrial (Portugal), the fauna was massively dominated by rabbit

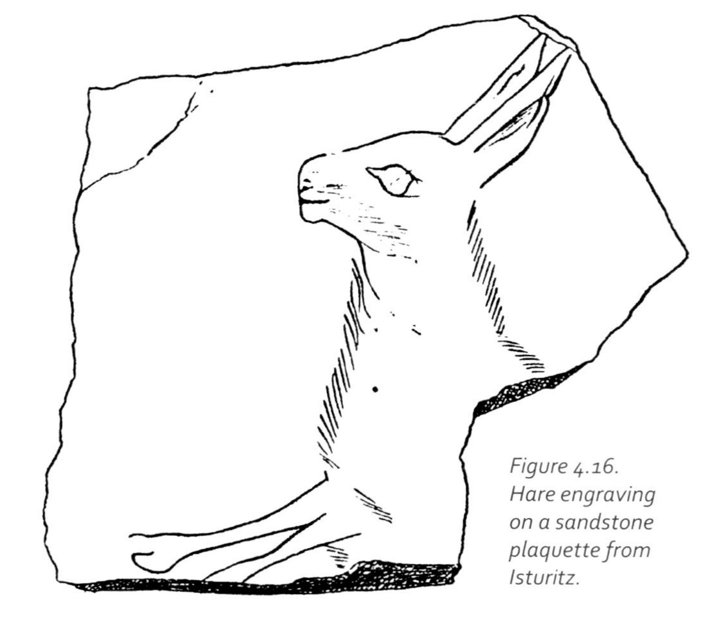

Figure 4.16. Hare engraving on a sandstone plaquette from Isturitz.

– at least 15 individuals. The lack of limb extremities suggests that the hides were removed with legs attached.

Ice age children would certainly have learned how to butcher animals and extract marrow from the bones. This is no easy task, however, and their apprenticeship probably commenced with smaller mammals, before moving on to larger and more valued packages of meat. A detailed analysis of butchered small carnivores and rabbit bones from the Magdalenian caves of Santa Maira and Cova de les Cendres found that rabbits had been as carefully filleted to remove the meat as had the larger animals like deer. This was striking, as it is unnecessary to fillet small animals like rabbits in order to consume the meat fresh. It was therefore proposed that the objective of separating the meat from the bones with such care was to preserve, dry and store the meat for future consumption. No doubt! It is highly unlikely that food would have ever gone to waste when a fresh supply was not guaranteed. However, there are so few calories and so little fat in rabbit meat that one wonders why such effort was made in processing these small animals – although the fur would be put to good use.

Embarking on a relationship with dogs

As mentioned elsewhere (p. 124), the existence of dogs in the last ice age was a subject of great debate in the late 19th century, a time when – in the French Pyrenees alone – claims were made of dog bones in a whole series of caves and shelters. Alas, none was subjected to detailed analysis, so we will never know if these claims were justified. In 1914, however, at Oberkassel, near Bonn (Germany), a 40-year-old Magdalenian man of c. 17,000 bp was found buried with a 25-year-old woman and a dog of 27-28 weeks. Recent analysis has shown that the dog had been gravely ill (probably distemper), and can only have survived with intensive human assistance.

Decades later, at Mallaha, a living site in Israel of c. 14,000 bp, a grave was found to contain an elderly adult of undetermined sex; its hand lay on the thorax of a puppy of about 4-5 months which had been buried with it. But it was unclear if this was a dog or wolf.

The task of elucidating when and where dogs first arose in the Palaeolithic has now fallen to osteometry and genetics, whose practitioners have not yet reached agreement, to say the least – though DNA has proved that the Oberkassel animal was definitely a domestic dog. Some specialists believe that the dog had already become separate from wolves in Eurasia by at least 30,000 years ago, while others prefer a date of c. 15,000. Either way, it is clear that the people of the last ice age had dogs for much, if not all, of the period that concerns us.

Geneticists believe that wolves have split into numerous 'clades' with specific traits – a clade is a grouping that includes a common ancestor. This situation has become even more complicated by dogs and wolves having, it seems, exchanged their genes over millennia – they continue to do so even today. As

Figure 4.17. a/b/c: The frozen puppy known as 'Dogor', c. 18,000 years old, found in permafrost at Sakha (Siberia) in 2018. 'Dogor' is the Yakut word for 'friend.'

a result, where and when wolves became domesticated is extremely difficult to ascertain, because of this continuous interbreeding between different 'clades' of wolves and other canids over tens of thousands of years. This means that the dogs that evolved from wolves during the last glacial period probably did not have the typical behaviour of – or the same genetic makeup as – the dogs and wolves that exist today, and ancient wolves would have been different from any 'modern' species existing today.

In the late 1990s genetic analyses confirmed that dogs had descended from ancient grey wolves, and in fact the two species share 99.9% of their DNA. However, exactly when this happened is still uncertain. Analysis of 1500 dogs from around the world (by one team of researchers) indicated that around

HOW AND WHY WERE WOLVES DOMESTICATED?

Many humans seem to have a deep-rooted fear of wolves; this has been well documented throughout history, which is somewhat surprising when one realises that dogs, derived from wolves, are our closest allies. According to many zoologists, wolves are not the vicious and dangerous species portrayed in films and legends, but, nevertheless, there is no denying that they are a top predator. Modern wolves are intensely social and intelligent creatures and are devoted to their 'pack family.' Scientists who study wolves report they are keen observers of their potential prey and not prone to kill unless hungry. They prefer to attack without risk to themselves and prey mostly on the injured and the very young and old.

Wolves often hunt in packs and can run down large animals and game. They hunt by scent. Even a large group of humans with hand weapons would stand little chance against a pack of wolves and, in the ice age, could only escape by climbing trees or taking refuge in a rock shelter or cave.

Modern wolves are adept at catching fish in their mouths, and are observed patrolling riverbanks during the salmon runs. It used to be thought that they cannot swim, but trained wolf-trackers have observed them swimming when they have to – although it seems they prefer not to get their tails wet! Wolves can run for miles, and can range over 1000 km looking for food. They use a variety of howls to communicate with their pack, and have a particular howl that lets other wolves know about a recent kill, or if one comes across food leftovers – perhaps early humans used this same method! These howls can be heard for miles, and invite other pack members to come and partake of the banquet. Often the kill is left in the sun to soften the carcass and tenderize the meat. Wolves can consume an enormous amount of food and then do not appear to concern themselves with eating again for several days.

One early suggestion of how wolves became domesticated was that hungry wolf cubs started hanging around human camps, scavenging for food, and at some point humans selected the friendly, more docile ones, discarding or culling the ones they couldn't tame. Regular feeding of these 'strays' may have led to enhanced dependency, and eventually humans and wolves formed a strong, mutually beneficial relationship. Of course, wolves will not have been the only animals hanging around – a recent study of the bone chemistry of foxes whose remains were found in cave sites of the Swabian Jura, c. 40,000 years ago, shows that they were eating a lot of reindeer, doubtless scavenged from carcasses near the camps.

An alternative idea is that groups of human hunters might have encountered wolves which were following the same herds and, recognizing each other's strengths, they began to co-operate as hunting allies. Perhaps our early ancestors were originally apprenticed to wolves, and learned their methods of selecting the 'easiest pickings' amongst a herd. This may have led to an extended period of co-operation, and later – even much later – a close relationship between the human and wolf developed.

We have at least two alternative theories: the first being that wolves and humans gradually learned to tolerate each other, and a bond eventually developed between the two. The second

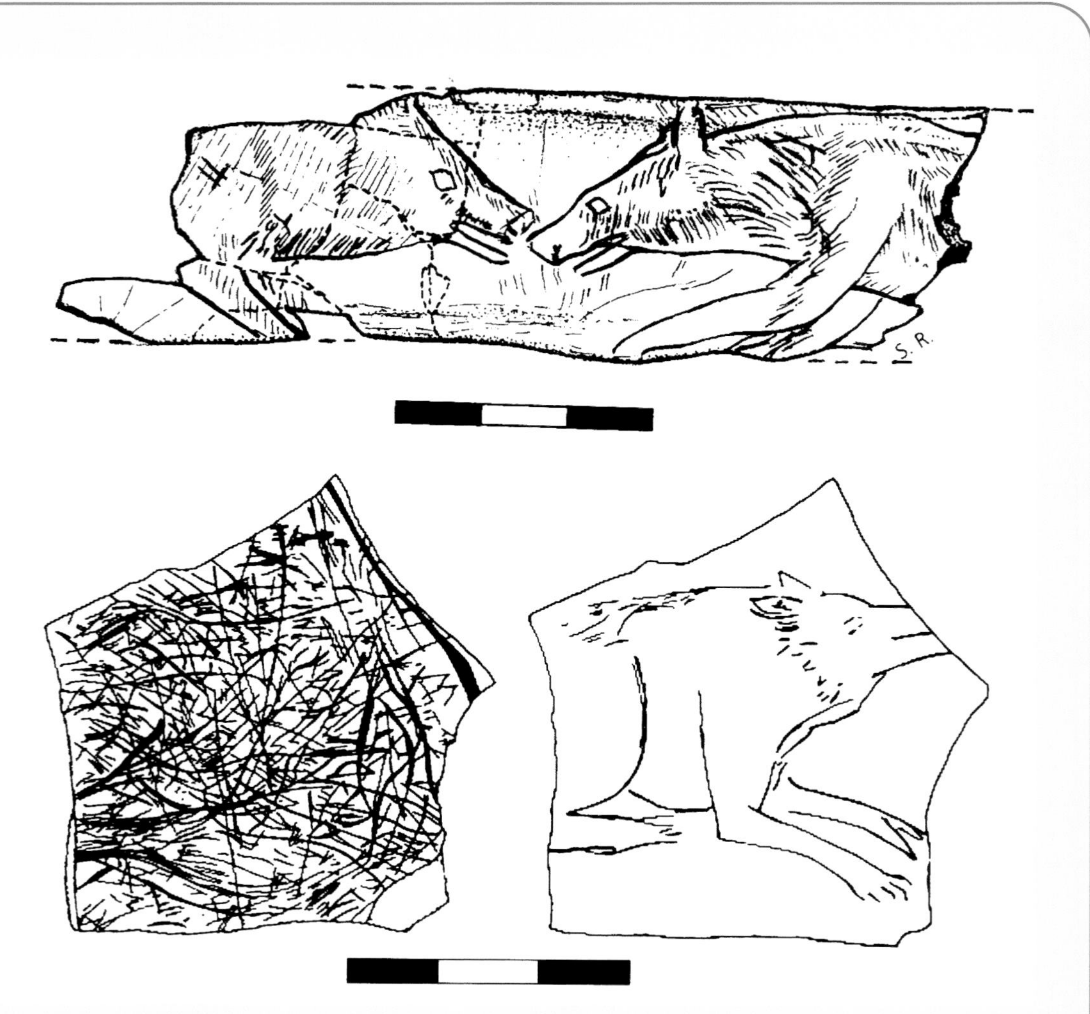

Figure 4.18. a: Tracing of engraving of wolves from La Vache (Ariège); b: Tracing of wolf engraving from La Marche (Vienne).

is that ice age people intentionally domesticated wolves to be their hunting allies, and to provide protection and companionship, to be a 'back-up' source of meat, and become a useful fur pelt when the animal had no further use. Or perhaps both scenarios occurred many times over the millennia and, as with many novel behaviours introduced during the last glacial period, this co-evolution had a stop-start history and occurred in stages so that the human and wolf, wolf-dog and human-dog relationship took a very long time to succeed.

The standard method used by dog trainers today comprises 'behaviour modification' techniques. This is when an animal learns to make associations, and by using negative or positive reinforcement, its behaviour is altered or 'modified' by the trainer, the purpose being to increase or decrease a particular behaviour. It is evident that at some point during the last ice age our ancestors had enough insight into wolf behaviour to encourage the traits they wanted (as guards and hunting allies), and discourage unwanted behaviour like running off with the family dinner! This skill should not be underestimated, and is another example of how very advanced our ancestors were in shaping the natural world around them to their advantage.

But what were the advantages of domestic dogs? There are many – help with hunting, herding and tracking; guarding dwellings, children and food; protection against predators; transporting loads and children; companionship and security; bed warmers; eating refuse and left-overs; entertainment – playfulness in dogs appeals to children and adults alike; the status of owning a 'top-dog' – perhaps they were even traded? And finally for food and fur pelts. Both wolves and dogs are extremely good at recognising humans (and objects), and individuals from these early communities and individuals in a pack of wolves may have developed strong relationships over time. Wolves and dogs are more alert than humans, their hearing is more sensitive: they can hear four times farther away, a higher frequency of sounds, and can differentiate sounds and locate the exact location of a sound, something that most humans have difficulty doing. A dog's sense of smell far outshines our own, and dogs are more easily aroused from sleep than humans, which may have been yet another advantage in the development of their relationship.

Arctic people have used dogs for almost as long as they have been living in that part of the world, and archaeological evidence has suggested their presence there for at least 17,000 years, although this remains contentious. In northern Siberia, 9000 years ago, people were making sleds that could have been pulled by dogs. Several dogs hitched to a sled (or large log) can pull a surprisingly heavy load, be it a carcass or anything a family wanted to take with them to another dwelling site. Experiments have shown that big dogs are easily taught to carry a large pack strapped to their back.

One remarkable research finding is that a dog's gaze increases human oxytocin levels! And, recently some researchers have proposed that women might have had a greater influence than men in the dog-human relationship and the domestication process. There are certainly many examples of a special relationship between dogs and women; for example, the Runa women of Ecuador's Upper Amazon believe their dogs are 'selves' because they think, get confused and can do stupid things. Runa women feel they can understand the different ways their own dogs bark and why, and believe their dogs can interpret the world around themselves just as humans can. Anthropologists have reported that the Munduruku women of Brazilian Amazonia treated their dogs like their own children, and it was common practice to suckle newborn pups at their own breast and place them in hammocks with their own young children.

In many societies the term 'person' is not equivalent to 'human.' Dogs have social minds too, and this has led to many cultures perceiving that dogs have agency, motives, an inner consciousness, a soul, can engage in social behaviour, and have their own identity or 'personhood.' This may go some way to explaining the early burials of dogs.

The Inuit are extremely reliant on their dogs for hunting and carrying, but also for locating a seal's breathing-hole in the ice and helping to hunt for polar bear and musk oxen. It has been reported that the Inuit hunter would rather lose a female family member (another mouth to feed), than the family dog that he depends on for hunting!

Figure 4.19. a: Engraved and bas-relief ibis on the ceiling of Church Hole, Creswell Crags (England); Magdalenian, 34 cm long and 13 cm high; b: Engraving of a duck from the Grotte de Gourdan (Haute Garonne).

16,000 years ago in China 'dogs' may have been bred by humans mainly for meat. Another team of researchers has concluded that dogs evolved from a now-extinct group of European or Asian wolves whose DNA lineage has not been found in modern wolf populations. Either the ancestor is extinct or has not yet been discovered.

Plucky bird hunters

Birds seem to have been of relatively little interest to ice age people – this is reflected in their imagery where birds are quite rare; apart from a few owls the depictions mostly comprise waterbirds such as swans, geese, ducks and herons – presumably the artists appreciated their sinuous and graceful forms.

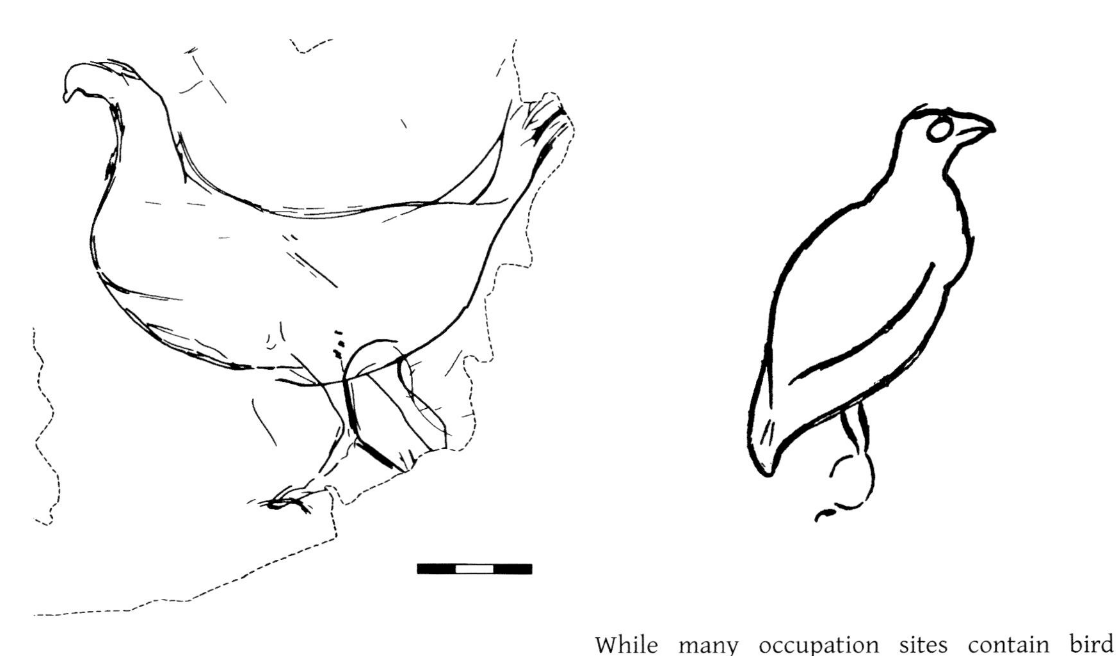

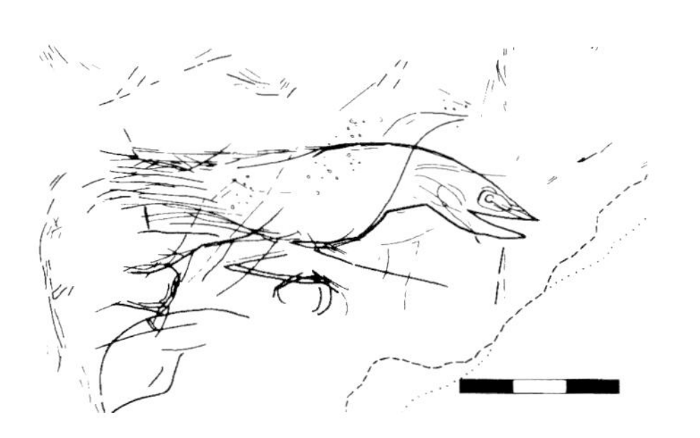

Figure 4.20. ▲ a: engravings of a lagoped and a corvid from plaquettes at Gönnersdorf; ► b: Engraving of a lagoped on a reindeer antler from Isturitz.

While many occupation sites contain bird bones (a few of which were used for musical instruments – see p. 230), and one or two have yielded eggshells (notably Pincevent, and caves in the Swabian Jura), birds seldom seem to have made a noteworthy contribution to the diet, presumably being exploited instead for raw materials and feathers. The major exception is lagopeds – the arctic or willow grouse (*Lagopus lagopus*) and the rock ptarmigan (*Lagopus mutus*). For example, 89% of the bird bones at Petersfels (Germany) were from lagopeds, and at Balcarova Scalka (Moravia) most of the 12,000 bird bones were also from these species. However, perhaps the best studied sites are two neighbouring Magdalenian caves in the Pyrenees – La Vache and Les Eglises.

In the inner chamber of La Vache, 95% of the bird bones were lagopeds – they were found clustered around hearths, and bore incision marks. The large 'Tribal Hearth' seemed to have a system for braising the birds within hot stones, still containing half a bird in connection. At Les Eglises, 100% of the bones are arctic or willow grouse, whereas only 75% of those at La Vache were of that species, the other 25% being rock ptarmigan.

As mentioned earlier (p. 133), the occupants of both these caves concentrated on ibex exploitation. If one assumes that the calories required by an average family at 0° C are c. 15,000 per day, one ibex (60 kg of meat, 125 calories per 100 gm) would feed a family for 5 days. But 200 ptarmigans (225 gm of meat,

168 calories per 100 gm) would be needed to do the same. Very few birds are present at Les Eglises, but La Vache yielded a minimum of 245 lagopeds – nevertheless these would feed a family for just over 6 days. In other words, the birds were clearly not a staple resource, more of a dietary supplement.

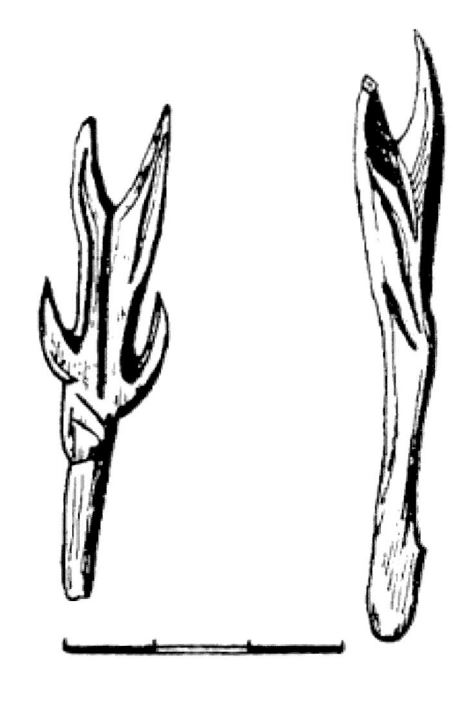

Figure 4.21. Bone points from La Vache, interpreted as 'bird arrows'.

Be that as it may, lagopeds seem to be the only birds that were the subject of organised fowling in the Palaeolithic: it was obviously easy to concentrate on these fairly large species whose ability to fly is not very developed. The people may have used missiles, slings or throwing sticks. The Caribou Inuit use bows and little harpoons, and some bone points at La Vache have been interpreted as bird-arrows of the type which avoids damage to feathers. Some bone implements at Balcarova Scalka closely resemble those of La Vache. But since the latter site's bird bones show no sign of wounds, it is far more likely that, as in the far north today, the hunting methods were well adapted to the birds' behaviour patterns: they are easily attracted by food (fresh willow buds/twigs) or deceived by appropriate sounds, and they prefer to run along an obstacle to seek an opening rather than fly over it – so the present-day standard methods of capture are snares, or nets stretched between bushes and trees along the birds' pathways. Both methods avoid damage to plumage.

In good weather a trapper can place c. 200 snares in a daily round, and whole flocks can be caught by nets. The birds are an easy catch and offer a change of diet; but though tasty, the delicate meat is very lean, and in the circumpolar area lagopeds represent only an inferior, emergency resource. A 19th-century text says that if a man eats nothing but ptarmigan he will die, since it is less nutritious than other meat. The birds are trapped by the elderly, the infirm, or women and children, and usually only as an occasional food in times of scarcity. However, the dietary value of their stomach contents is very high, being rich in vitamins – some humans even eat the birds' droppings for the high vitamin content.

Fishing on a small scale

Like birds, fish were almost never a staple. Although they do offer dietary elements lacking in small game – e.g. fish oils and fatty acids and vitamins – they were usually a minor and subsidiary resource. They had been exploited since at least Neanderthal times, but it was Solutrean people who seem to have begun using water resources more intensively – probably because they faced the much colder conditions of the last glacial maximum, which caused deforestation.

Freshwater fish only became really important in the Magdalenian. However, where marine fish are concerned, it is hard to assess the situation because so many coastal sites have been lost to us by the rise in sea-level. It is known that sea fish were already exploited in Neanderthal times, but their remains only appear in inland sites after the coast came closer – for example, Spain's Nerja Cave was 6 km from the Mediterranean coast at the glacial maximum, but by the Magdalenian this distance had shrunk to 1 km, and remains of marine resources had begun to be present in the site in some quantity – including thousands of fish bones and tens of thousands of mollusc shells.

Many species would have been available for most of the year, but growth rings in fish vertebrae reveal their season of death. Ice age sites mostly contain remains of freshwater fish – primarily salmon, trout, pike, carp and grayling – which is hardly surprising since the people mostly lived close to rivers and streams. On the other hand, the Abri Pataud was right next to the river Vézère, and very carefully excavated, but yielded very few fish remains, and, as mentioned earlier (p. 62), almost none were found at Pincevent despite its immediate proximity to the Seine and excellent conditions of preservation.

In the Pyrenees and Cantabria there is very little evidence for fishing before the Magdalenian. It is true that some modern hunter-gatherer groups show a distaste for fish. On the other hand, it is possible that much salmon was consumed but, as occurs among some Californian Indians, disrespect to the fish

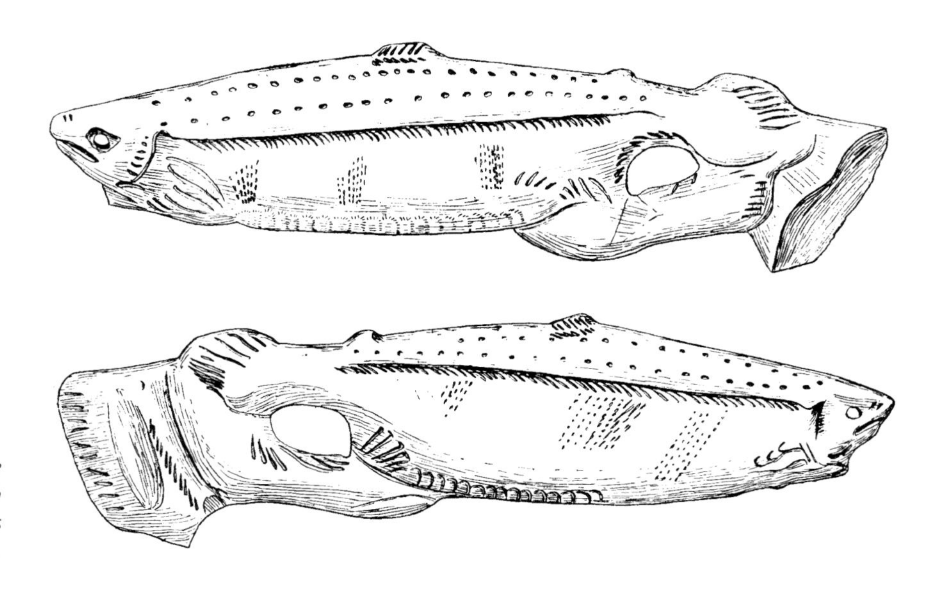

Figure 4.22. Bone carving of a fish from Lourdes (Hautes-Pyrénées).

was avoided by never discarding its bones – they were dried, pounded, ground in mortars and consumed. This was the 'First Peoples' way' of showing respect for the earth's 'gifts'.

It may be that these early communities had a strong connection with all the animals and the fish they relied upon, and that this became much more than an economic or nutritional relationship. Just as with many fishing people living today, there exists a long-standing 'tied-identity' between the fish and the indigenous cultures that rely on them for their survival. Communities living today along the North Pacific Rim, where salmon have been coming home to spawn for millions of years, depend on salmon for survival and celebrate the 'homecoming' of their 'sacred fish' with ceremonies each year to give thanks for the life they provide.

Although fish were a subsidiary resource in most places and phases of the ice age, a few examples of specialisation are known (see e.g. Ohalo II, below, p. 153). One such is the small Magdalenian Abri du Bois des Brousses (Hérault) where 660 fish vertebrae were found in and around a quadrangular stone structure, which was probably for drying or smoking the flesh. The site was occupied in the summer, and contained almost no mammal remains, so it was clearly very specialised. The species were carefully selected – there were a minimum of 82 trout, 21 graylings and 23 eels. The heads and tails were removed outside the site. The remains represent c. 100 kg of flesh. Experiments have shown that the fish could have been spread over wooden poles just above the fire. One month later the fish processed in this way showed no signs of deterioration and seemed edible.

At the Grotta di Pozzo, in central Italy's Apennine range, occupation layers dating to c. 15,000 - 14,000 years ago yielded abundant remains of large trout. Vertebrae and other post-cranial elements are strikingly underrepresented, in stark contrast to the numbers of skull elements, which suggests that the fish were partially processed here – i.e. the heads were removed – and then taken elsewhere for consumption.

The Pyrenean cave of Les Eglises yielded 520 vertebrae in an area of 20 sq m – from salmon and trout. They represented a minimum of 54 individuals, all of them big, from 50 cm to a metre and more. The heads were left at the river 100 m below, and only the bodies were carried up to the cave. This is understandable in view of their size – some Magdalenian salmon vertebrae were much bigger than the largest in France today! The cave's occupants seem to have caught most of them in November, and smoked/dried some parts of the fish to take to their main dwelling, wherever that was.

It is easy to catch salmon in the early winter when they are exhausted by a trip of almost a year and have reached their reproduction zone – they are present in high numbers, for egg-laying, and so are very visible and easy to harpoon. Some fish may have been caught by hand, others with hook and line; spears

ATLANTIC SALMON RUNS

During the last ice age, just before the summer arrived, and with regular predictability, millions of salmon would have returned from their distant offshore feeding grounds to spawn in the many rivers of southwest Europe where they were born. Huge fish, much bigger than the salmon we see today, would swim hundreds of miles inland through the rivers and deep into the forest areas of present-day France, Spain and Portugal. Through the mountainous landscapes the rivers took the fish swimming over- and under-ground, the porous karst rocks leaching nutrients into the water. Many of the rivers can disappear down holes and into caves, with the salmon following the water underground, often for miles, only to re-emerge in an entirely different valley. How strange this must have seemed to our ancestors – fish appearing from deep underground – one wonders if they understood the fishes' instinctive behaviour.

The salmon would be in the rivers and trapped in creeks for a considerable length of time, and there would have been ample opportunity for people to exploit such a wonderful calorie-loaded food resource – it was good for humans, and also good for bears and wolves (as mentioned earlier, p. 139, wolves have recently been observed catching salmon in a river). Brown bears weigh 300 kg, and when hungry would be a fearsome opponent even for spear-carrying humans. But it is quite possible that ice age people learned to share with and respect bears during the salmon-run season, just as in the remote Shiretoko Peninsula of northern Japan where brown bears and fishermen have learned to live alongside each other in order to take advantage of the annual salmon run.

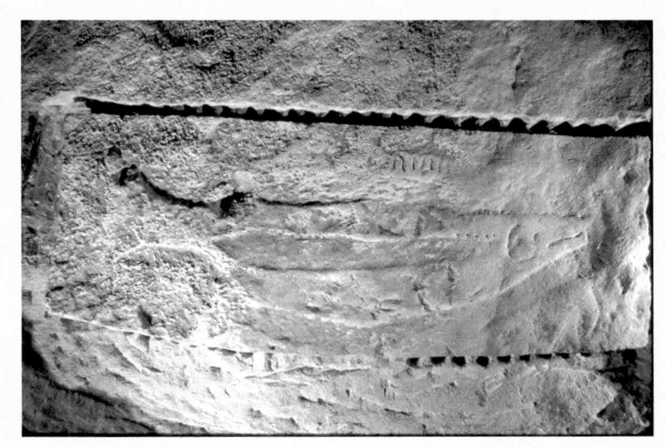

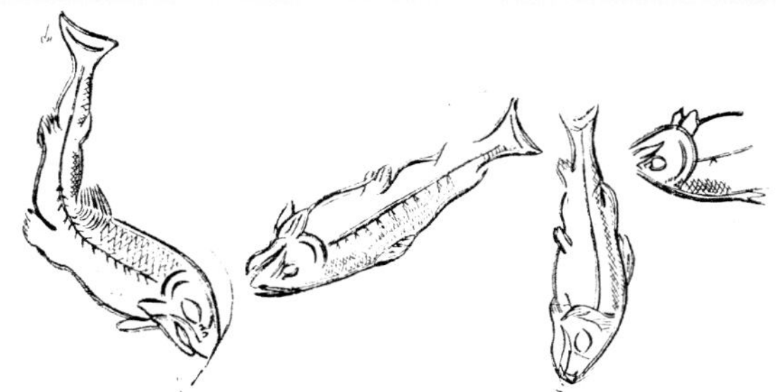

Figure 4.23. a: Bas-relief of an exhausted male salmon after spawning on the ceiling of the Abri du Poisson (Dordogne), over a metre in length; b: fish 'extracted' from a scene with deer engraved around a baton from Lortet (Hautes-Pyrénées).

Salmon return to the same places around the world, and at the same time every year; they only have a few weeks to spawn before many of them die, so preparing for their arrival would have been carefully planned in advance in order to maximise the catch. Some salmon get trapped in pools and low-level streams and then continue their migration upstream, but the higher water level means they have to leap-up to escape. Not only do many die from exhaustion, but humans – and bears – take advantage once again!

Female salmon are full of eggs, and are very nutritious and high in unsaturated fat and vitamins, especially vitamin D. The male salmon taste different. Salmon can be slow-roasted over a fire, smoked – did ice age people dine on smoked salmon? – and dried to keep for longer, and even frozen if conditions permit.

or harpoons or prongs; or nets, weirs and traps. A few fish-shaped bone objects are known which may have been lures, and a variety of what could be two- and three-pronged fishing gigs in reindeer antler and ivory.

These small pronged points would have been attached to a line with bait, and when taken by the fish they would jam in its gullet and hold until the fish could be landed. Small fish in shallow water can be caught with bare hands (or bear paws!) and a simple method – which requires patience and concentration – is to immerse one's hand in the water, wiggle one's fingers until the fish comes to be 'tickled', and then grab it firmly behind the open gills.

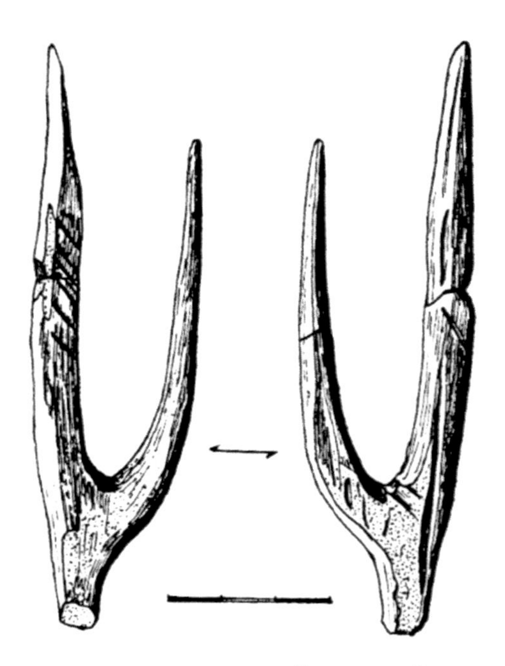

Figure 4.24. Bone point from La Vache, interpreted as a 'fish spear'.

Spearing with a barbed point would certainly have been one method used – several thousand supposed antler harpoons are known from the Magdalenian – but hitting a moving target in water is a skill that has to be taught and learned! Light refraction causes the 'line of sight' to be different; however, the corrections required can be learned with practice. Intensive catching would use cooperative methods like traps, nets and weirs. There is no way of knowing if these communities laid claims to fishing grounds and their surrounding areas, or if they had 'exclusion zones' for particular groups along the rivers.

Did they have small canoes? As we shall see (p. 89), this is virtually certain despite a complete lack of evidence. Making one would have been a major undertaking, and the wood would have been charred with fire, and doubtless waterproofed. Utilising fallen tree trunks that are wide enough to sit on could have sufficed, and they could have easily fished in the marshes with the aid of such primitive transport, especially with a paddle to steer. But they would have needed some knowledge about the deeper tidewaters and shore fringes, and the tidal times, in order to use rafts or boats in open waters.

Figure 4.25. A fish weir.

Obviously, people living on or near to the coasts were able to exploit marine fish too, such as bream, stingray and wrass. As mentioned earlier (p. 46), at the Last Glacial Maximum the coastline would have been 10 – 100 km further out in some areas, and so people from inland sites would have had a much greater distance to travel, but many communities could have had seasonal or permanent dwellings

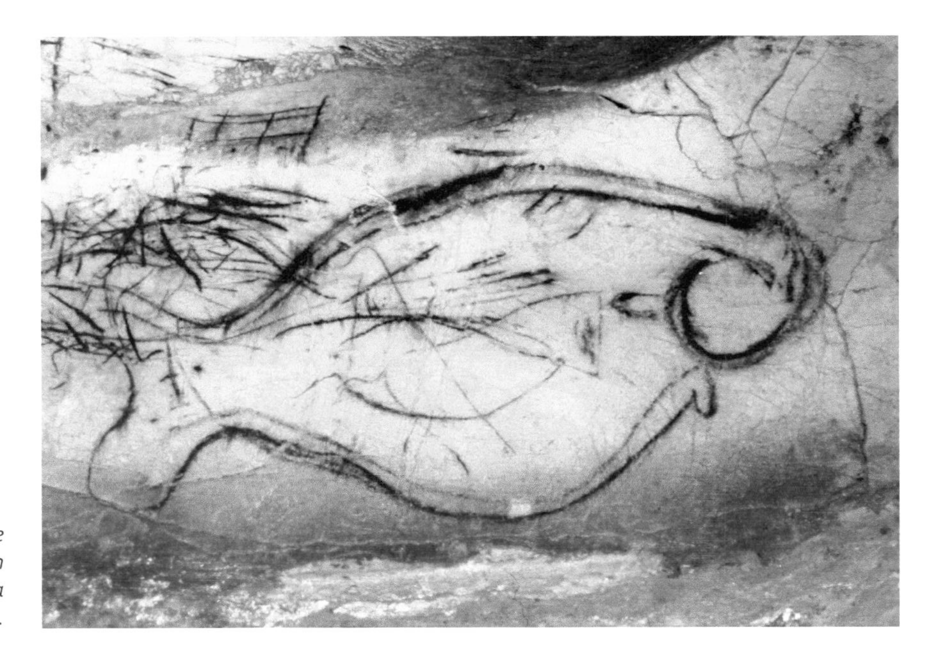

Figure 4.26. Large drawing of a fish in the cave of La Pileta, Spain.

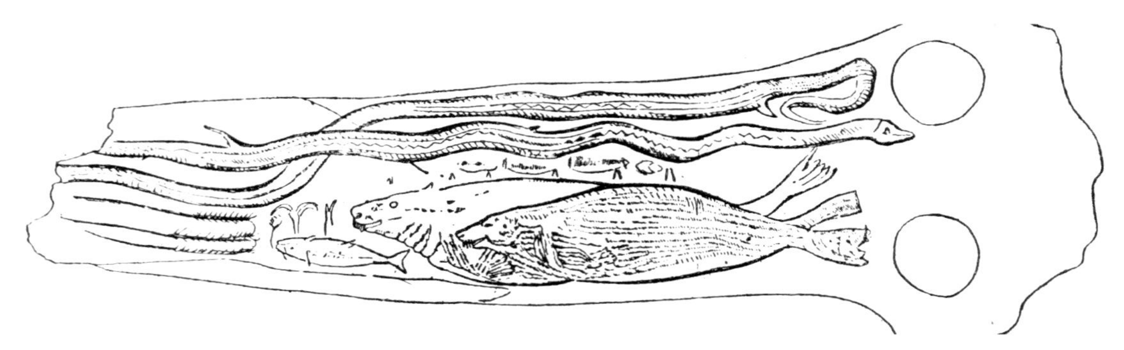

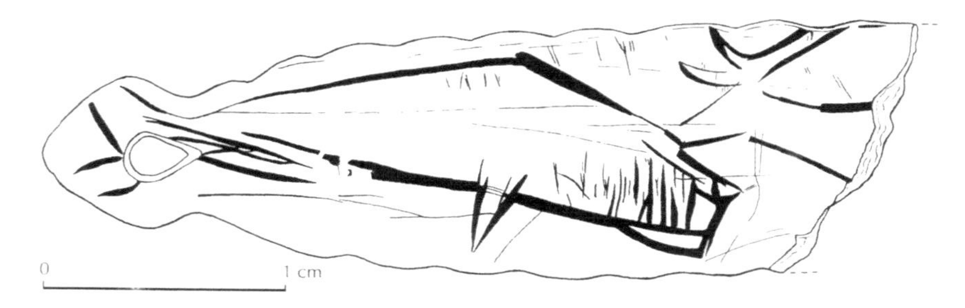

Figure 4.27.
▲ a: Drawing of the seals and other species on the baton of Montgaudier (Charente). Length: 30 cm. Magdalenian;
◄ b: the engraved whale and deer on a pendant from Bourrouilla (Pyrénées Atlantiques).

on the coast, which are now drowned and lost to us. Bone chemistry reveals the percentage of terrestrial and marine proteins in the diet, and analyses have shown that the latter increase at the end of the period – derived from fish and seafood on the coast, and from salmon inland.

Marine resources would have been collected from estuaries, tidal zones, coastal plains and numerous inlets along the rocky shorelines. Fish and molluscs would have been vital foods for these communities – mineral salts could be derived from crustaceans and shellfish. Seals or even a stranded whale might also provide an unexpected feast. We know that they were familiar with these creatures, as there are several fine engravings of seals in portable art, and also a few of whales, including one whale engraved on an actual cachalot tooth (p. 51). As we shall see later (p. 206-7), implements of whale bone were widely distributed in the Pyrenees and the north coast of Spain.

There were also seabirds and their eggs – four depictions of what may be auks have been found in France's Cosquer cave (p. 50). Seaweed can be chewed raw, or boiled to extract the iodine (a useful medicinal source); plankton is a great antioxidant; and small algae and all things 'fishy' are nutritious!

At the cave of Tito Bustillo (Asturias), the occupants mostly ate meat, but they also fished in the nearby estuary for sea trout and sole or flounder. At La Riera, sea bream was caught on the rocky coast. Most of the few depictions we have of sea fish are flatfish, which can be captured close to shore in shallows, e.g. in pools left by receding tides.

As mentioned earlier (pp. 50-51), at La Riera, from 21,000 bp onwards, over 19,000 relatively intact molluscs were found from 21 species, even though the site today is a two hour walk to the coast. Edible species comprised 97.5% of the collection, with only 2.5% being ornamental – and among the edibles, 92% were limpets (*Patella*). These can survive for three to four weeks if stored at 5-12° C under a protective covering of damp seaweed. Stored in the cave, they would have made a useful tiding-over food, and also a good trail food since molluscs stay fresh for several days.

Some shellfish could be eaten raw, but others are better cooked. Some can be opened with a knife, while others open in heat – either boiling water, or by roasting (e.g. burned specimens were found at El Juyo). Crustaceans could likewise be boiled. One wonders if ice age people ever boiled seawater to get salt....

Plant foods

Plants probably met 80% of ice age people's daily energy needs in temperate phases, and a minimum of 20% in cold ones. But actual plant remains are rarely preserved in most sites, so much of our knowledge has to be based on ethnography and on basic human requirements.

Humans need at least 1.5 litres of water per day, obtained from drinks and foods. We have no idea if ice age people made infusions, or alcoholic drinks from fermented berries, though they were certainly intelligent enough to do so. They must have obtained their mineral salts from numerous foods, especially plants and fruits, while carbohydrates came from wild plants, beans, roots and tubers, as well as wild fruits, berries, and perhaps honey. Vitamins could be obtained from fruits and wild plants like chicory or dandelions, while lipids came from unsaturated fats in fish oil and animal fat and marrow, and saturated fats from meat. Plenty of protein and vitamin B were available from a variety of fauna and flora, while plant proteins came from walnuts, hazelnuts and almonds – all of which have been found in ice age sites (see above, pp. 47-48).

Pine nuts and hazelnuts are high in protein – the Anasazi Indian populations of the southwest USA had the former as their main source of protein, and certainly pine nuts, hazelnuts and acorns were available during the Palaeolithic. Acorns are high in fat, potassium, iron and vitamins A and E and are a source of protein.

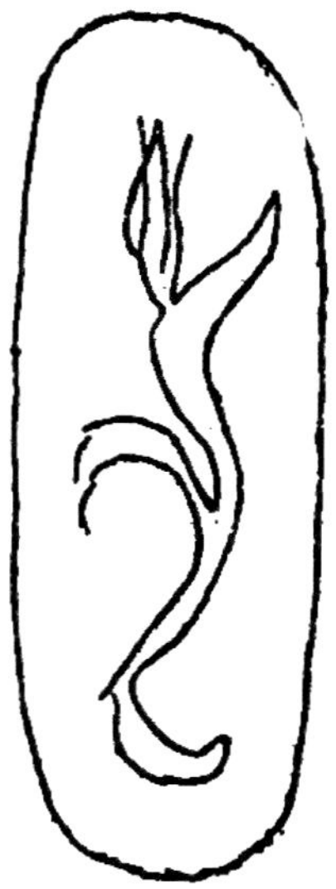

Figure 4.28. Engraving of a plant on a small pebble. C. 5 cm long, from Gourdan (Haute Garonne).

Clearly, a wide array of plants were available to our ancestors, with a vast range of uses. Some researchers, on the basis of data from over 50 modern hunter-gatherer groups, have suggested a rough average of 35% meat and 65% plants in the daily diet of our ice age people, though of course this will have varied from region to region and during different climatic phases. No plant foods will have been plentiful in the winter, but in the warmer seasons there were many to be had – especially wild berries and nuts.

It has been well documented ethnographically that hunter-gatherer communities miss no opportunity to collect roots, edible plants, fruit, etc, whenever they can get them. Nuts store well, and may have provided a lot of the protein in the diet, especially during the winter months. Foraging for particular foods demands patience; it also requires a high level of mental processing to find and collect the appropriate foods, and to identify and select non-poisonous plants and those required for medicinal purposes. Plant food must achieve maturity before it is edible, and these communities would have needed an excellent understanding of local plants – and their value to humans, especially as an all-meat diet is unhealthy over a prolonged period. Collecting 'safe to eat' plant foods would have been an important element in ice age children's 'need-to-know' curriculum, and it is very unlikely that these early communities only foraged as a back-up plan!

A few European sites have yielded actual remains of plant foods – for example, Miesenheim (see p. 47), Aurensan and El Juyo. Other sites contain tools which were probably used for processing plants – Duruthy had mortars and small grindstones, as well as 1500 flint blades, some of which showed traces of a gum for hafting and a sickle gloss on their cutting edge – a gloss which could only be caused by cutting plants.

Grindstones are often found in sites, and of course may have been used to grind all kinds of materials, but occasionally we can be sure that plant foods were involved; for example, analyses have detected starches on grinding stones from a number of Gravettian sites such as Kostenki XVI and Pavlov VI; similarly, at Bilancino II (Italy), the surfaces of a sandstone pestle and grinder yielded starch grains from cattail (*Typha*); in all these cases, it seems that flour was being produced. The Grotta Paglicci in Italy has likewise yielded a pestle-grinder from the Gravettian period (c. 28,000 bp). This sandstone cobble was found to bear numerous starch grains, primarily from oats, and it seems that a thermal treatment was carried out on the plant material before grinding took place. This may have been to dry the plants which makes grinding easier and faster in order to produce flour. One may suppose that the flour was then mixed with water, because hydration is necessary for cooking, and only cooking makes the starch digestible. In short, we have clear evidence of multi-step processing of plant foods in the ice age.

The dental analysis of the El Mirón lady (pp. 257-58) shows that she had a mixed diet including more resources from gathering than from hunting. It is clear that people ate more plant matter than had previously been imagined, and also ate seeds. Dandelion and goosefoot (chenopod) are both good substitutes for salt, and used to preserve food for longer. They can also be cooked and turned into a salt-ash, e.g. goosefoot pollen was excavated from the El Mirón burial site – it is loaded with calcium and also very salty. It can therefore be cooked and the ashes used as salt.

A CAMP OF FISHER-HUNTER-GATHERERS

Not much plant material has survived in the vast majority of ice age living sites known in Eurasia, but one camp, Ohalo II in Israel, was waterlogged and so has exceptional preservation of a wide range of materials. It therefore gives us a more rounded idea of life in the other sites.

The camp, in the Jordan Valley, dates to c. 19,000 years ago, and was submerged for millennia. It was exposed for three years (1989-1991) due to unusual low water-levels at the Sea of Galilee caused by prolonged drought and extensive pumping. The site was large – at least 1500 sq m – and its biggest structure was kidney-shaped, with remains of a wall constructed of plant material. The camp yielded large quantities of flints, charcoal, animal bones, and seeds and fruits. Fish bones were common in some places and rare in others. Acorns were common inside the big structure, but rare or absent elsewhere. A total of 130 shell beads (*Dentalium*) were found throughout the site – these were from either the Red Sea or the Mediterranean, and were obtained on trips to the coast or through exchange. As mentioned earlier (p. 90), the site also yielded fragments of charred, twisted fibres, 2-3 mm long, probably from cordage.

The faunal remains were rich and well-preserved, and included not only gazelles and deer but also birds, reptiles, rodents, turtles, hares and foxes. But the commonest resource was the thousands of fish vertebrae. The largest structure contained four piles of fish bones, including all skeletal elements. One pile included more than 1000 vertebrae, whereas other piles only had dozens. Since it is unlikely that the bones were piled on the floor – there were no pits – the excavators deduced that the fish were kept together, either tied with a cord or placed (dried, smoked or unprocessed) in a fibre container. The vertebrae in the piles are only 3-10 mm in diameter, and hence from small fish, 10-20 cm long, which were probably caught with fine nets or some form of trap.

Figure 4.29. Large (92 litre) woven basket from Muraba'at Cave, Israel, dating to c.10,500 years ago.

The botanical material comprised thousands of carbonized seeds and other plant parts which were retrieved by wet- and dry-sieving: they include some of the oldest grains of wild barley and wild wheat ever found, as well as more than 30 other species of plants. Analysis has shown that the barley, wheat and other plants were collected in the spring, while fruits were gathered in the autumn, so the site was probably occupied for more than six months at a time.

MODERN GATHERERS

There are many ethnographic examples of plant exploitation which can shed possible light on how this may have been done in ice age times. Here we present some information on the modern !Kung of southern Africa. The women and girls do the gathering, almost every day. They leave early in order to avoid the heat, and walk in single file, the oldest at the front and youngest at the back (girls start at the age of 6). Hence children quickly learn to identify plants and their uses. They will note the seasonal differences and the yearly round of flower, fruit, berry, cone, seed and nut and on which bush or tree they grow and in which places. Gathering the correct food

Figure 4.30. Hadza foragers.

also requires great skill in discriminating plants that are ripe/edible and not poisonous (especially fungi), and also in detecting tubers and roots underground.

Each person collects for her own family. They use only a staff, which is also a walking stick, and put everything into a big bag, made of antelope skin, which is carried on the back, thus leaving both arms free. They pick fruits (using the stick for the high ones), including those which have fallen to the ground, and dig for roots and tubers with the stick. The !Kung can carry 4-15 kg plus a young child, and walk for 1-5 hours per day. Berries are mostly eaten in the field. The men who go out hunting also gather nuts, tubers or honey. Gathering produces 60-80% of the group's food.

Ice age food processors

In this chapter we have presented a variety of evidence for how different species were exploited and butchered. One major and almost ubiquitous feature is the fragmentation of herbivore bones for marrow. In the early periods this was generally done by smashing, rather than with the method and precision visible in later periods. For example, at Isturitz the early reindeer fragments were bigger than in later phases, and even in the Magdalenian they became smaller through time. Does this indicate a growing need to extract maximum nutrition?

We have also mentioned – both in this section and in Chapter 2 – the existence of different kinds of fireplaces and associated structures which give clues to how foods were cooked or dried. It is clear that heated stones often played a role – for example, experiments have shown that food could have been cooked in utensils of wood, bark or leather close to – or hanging over – the fire without burning them (see box), or it could have been skewered on long spikes of wood and slowly baked over hot cobbles. At the Abri Pataud, it was found that reindeer bones were burnt at the epiphyses, but not the diaphyses – so the latter were protected by the flesh being cooked. It probably did not go unnoticed that roasting over a fire of juniper or laurel gives added flavour.

Water could be boiled in leather or hide containers, or in hollows lined with skins, into which hot stones were placed with wooden pincers (as some Eskimoan peoples do). As we have seen, some sites have accumulations of stones and pebbles reddened or fractured by thermal shock in and around the

THE ORIGINAL BOIL-IN-A-BAG MEAL

It has long been accepted that our ancestors cooked food using the 'roasting' method, although cooking over an open fire is tricky, and often leads to over-cooked and even burned food. We know ice age people could, and almost certainly did, make containers for storage out of skins and tree bark: birch bark is particularly suitable when available, but did they also use these containers for cooking? The answer is likely to be yes! It's quite possible that ice age chefs discovered the value of 'wet cooking,' that is boiling – or more correctly poaching – food as a way of softening meat, fish and vegetables, and thus increasing the digestibility and the nutritional value of these foods.

Aside from birch-bark containers, they could have used perishable hides or paunches (the animal's rumen or stomach) by placing them directly over hot cobbles, or over an open fire, attached to a wooden spit suspended across wooden posts stuck in the ground. The bark or animal hide containers would need to be filled with water, then heated to the point when the meat, fish, or edible plant material (even tubers and roots) is simmering but not boiling. Not only would this have softened the food, it would have preserved the vitamin C content lost through roasting. This method would also be superior as it deactivates toxins, releases starches (a good source of energy, fibre, calcium, iron and B vitamins), and enables the capture of fat and grease (the solid white residue) released during cooking – all enhancing the nutritional worth of the food.

Ethnographers have documented this method among some Sub-Arctic indigenous peoples of North America who suspended animal paunches over fires to cook the meat of the same animal. By carefully ensuring the fire was not too hot, the contents could last for a few days or even weeks.

hearths or in little hollows. Some of these hollows may have been earth ovens – for example, the Grotte des Scilles (Lespugue) had a pit with burned sides and limestone slabs at the bottom and top, while Kostenki also has several little hollows with burned sides around the main hearth – perhaps food was placed on embers?

Since they could certainly heat water, they presumably produced soups, stews or sauces. But did they eat with their fingers, or did they have utensils? In fact, there are some fine decorated spoons of reindeer antler at sites such as Fontalès and Gourdan, one made of a horse jaw from Pekárna, others in mammoth bone from Avdeevo, and an ivory specimen from Dolní Vestonice. A number of bone objects look like spatulas. One can therefore suppose that they were perfectly capable of making a whole range of cutlery – including forks – in wood which have not survived. Presumably food could be served onto flat or slightly concave stone plaques or wooden equivalents, they could drink out of horns, and they may also have had wooden cups of some kind. But we will never know who did the washing up!

To sum up, food procurement must have been a major mental and physical preoccupation for these early hunter-gatherers, and especially so – as we shall see in the next chapter – when it came to maintaining healthy women when they reproduced and nursed their young. In Chapter 5, we also try to present a realistic picture of what life would have been like for children growing up in the last ice age, and we explore how they would have learned the crucial skills and knowledge needed to survive the challenges they faced in their everyday lives.

Figure 4.31. Ivory spoons from Avdeevo, Russia.

PALAEOLITHIC RECIPES

A book appeared in Spain in 2016 which presented a wide variety of recipes that could have been produced from the resources available in the last ice age. Here is a possible example of our own:

Eggs with mushrooms

We have already seen (p. 143) that eggshells have been recovered from some sites and that some kinds of birds were heavily exploited. In southern Spain, partridges seem to have been a particular delicacy. Some effort must have been involved in gathering their eggs, since they lay them on the ground – only one clutch a year but up to a dozen at a time. It is important to note that their eggs are about 20% smaller than today's chicken eggs, and do not break in the same way. They taste something like duck eggs, which were also available.

Place a thin stone plaquette – shale, slate or whatever is available – to warm over the fire. When it is hot, place a few dollops of animal fat or marrow on it. When this is hot, throw on the pre-sliced mushrooms and allow them to cook.

Then prepare the eggs; they should not be too cold. With a sharp flint point, pierce the shell (but not too much so as not to break the fragile yolk), and carefully cut off the top of the shell little by little. Delicately pour the eggs onto the plaquette, beside the mushrooms, to cook until ready. This would make a tasty accompaniment to any leftover meat, fish or poultry!

Chapter 5

Ice Age People: From Womb to Tomb

Reproduction

Survival as a species obviously entails your children surviving, and this part of our book will pay particular attention to the commitment and contribution women made in ensuring the continuance of the human race and the wellbeing of their offspring over this extensive period. We can say with some confidence that childbirth and child rearing would have been a major investment for the *whole family group*, not just the parents – if indeed it was understood that men had a role in the process of conception!

We have challenged the long-standing model that fathers alone provided most of the food through hunting by arguing that women were just as capable of hunting as were men – in theory. However, the practicalities of childcare may well have often kept women close to the home base. We have, of course, no idea

Figure 5.1. A group of Magdalenians, reconstructions by Elisabeth Daynès.

about whether either role was considered more important than the other by ice age communities. We suspect not! We have also questioned the view that women alone were responsible for foraging for additional subsistence -- indeed foraging may have been far more than just an additional source of food.

The early part of this chapter will examine childcare, and the likely contribution made by fathers and the extended family group to this vital undertaking – obviously, without their dedication our species would not have survived the rigours and challenges of the last ice age. For example, who did the feeding and nursing, and who provided the direct care of infants and children? The traditional view – that women provided all the childcare, and the support from men was limited – may be at least partially correct; we can only turn to ethnographic data for insights into the possible division of childrearing between the sexes – apart from the obvious one of giving birth!

From here to maternity

A frequently asked question is 'was childbirth easier for women in the Stone Age?' The realistic answer is 'we don't know.' We can only assume that women experienced pain during delivery, and that some may have even found it a frightening experience. Women would have most likely given birth in rock shelters, caves or a temporary dwelling like a makeshift tent. This would be an unappealing option to modern women used to either home-comforts or high-tech labour wards; however, women from indigenous cultures give birth in much the same surroundings as our ancestors did without considering it a hardship. Hunter-gatherer women are by necessity fit and strong, and it may be that they were exceptionally so in the Upper Palaeolithic. Perhaps only the toughest men, women and their offspring survived the harshest periods of the ice age, and those that successfully reproduced had children who were best adapted to their environment.

Figure 5.2. The life-size female figures sculpted at Angles-sur-l'Anglin (Vienne).

We can only wonder what our ancestors – living 10,000, 20,000 or 30,000 years ago – thought about pregnancy and childbirth. How did they think babies were made? During gestation a child is part of its mother, slowly growing inside her, with the growth becoming increasingly obvious. We have not even an inkling of how our ancestors made sense of this. Of course they had intimate knowledge of, and were surrounded by, a variety of animals that had comparable reproductive journeys of their own, so what seemed part of the natural world may have simply been taken for granted.

Be that as it may, there is not a single depiction of animal copulation in the whole of ice age imagery, and not one clear depiction of human copulation either, or of any sexual behaviour. As we have already seen (p. 5) genitalia are rarely depicted on Palaeolithic humans, even the female figurines! On the other hand, there are numerous isolated motifs in both cave art and portable art – with a wide variety of shapes – which are traditionally interpreted as vulvas. This view is only definite when they are found in context within a recognisable female body (e.g. in the sculpted frieze of Angles-sur-l'Anglin). But isolated motifs are open to other interpretations – for example, some of them might plausibly be seen as hoof-prints or bird-foot prints (the recognition of animal and bird tracks must have been of great importance, so it would be no surprise if they were occasionally reproduced). There are also a far smaller number of recognisable isolated phalluses. What may be the clearest clues to an interest in sexual matters are found in natural shapes in some caves such as Gargas, La Lloseta or Roucadour – they contain natural clefts that resemble vulvas and which have been coated with red paint. It is reasonably sure that the resemblance was noted and used in the Palaeolithic – and the same doubtless applies to the many phallic stalagmites. One can therefore speculate endlessly about the symbolism linked with passing through such clefts within Mother Earth!

Figure 5.3. The 'vulva chamber' in Tito Bustillo (Asturias).

Pregnancies – when they occurred and how often – may have been determined *in some way* by the family group in these early cultures. Mobile tribes would have found long journeys over rough terrain especially arduous with a high ratio of infants and children to adults. Childbearing and childrearing are a major investment for the extended family group, and environmental challenges like unpredictable weather conditions would lead to fluctuations in the availability of food. Keeping their young provisioned would not be something they took for granted, and not being able to store food for long periods of time to offset food shortages in the future would be a serious challenge. Even if these family groups formed into larger bands for co-operative hunting and sharing food, there would be no guarantee from one season to the next that migrating herds would return to the same place at the same time as previously. Anxieties about food shortages would, one imagines, never be far from their thoughts.

There are regular and optimal seasons for most species to give birth; for example, the spring months when temperatures are rising, the land is no longer frozen, and more food becomes available. It is less likely, however, that hunter-gatherer females also followed a similar regular pattern, whereby their fertility was exactly regulated along with the changing seasons – although it is plausible that pregnancies were 'planned' (if they knew the cause!) or organised in some way to increase optimal outcomes. This remains speculative, of course, but given the huge investment any family group would have to make, it was unlikely to be a hit and miss affair, with infants born in the depths of winter when food resources would be at their minimum.

With this in mind, it's worth noting that a healthy diet is especially important during pregnancy to provide sufficient energy and nutrition to meet the mother's requirements, and those of her growing foetus, and later for breastfeeding. Specific deficiencies of vitamins and minerals like iodine and iron can affect the foetus profoundly. Iron is found in meat; iodine is present in fish and seafood, and iodine compounds can be extracted from seaweed. We can therefore surmise that a healthy diet *was* potentially available during the ice age, when meat and fish were in plentiful supply, but presumably they encountered difficult times as well, with short or long episodes when food may have become scarce. As iron-deficiency anaemia still affects about 60% of women in the developing world, and even 15% in the developed world, it is clear that a poor diet contributes to a suboptimal pregnancy and birth.

The phenomena of food aversions and food cravings during pregnancy, and what evolutionary function they serve, have only recently received serious attention, and the debate continues. Craving for foods rich in anti-oxidants or high in calories may be due in part to any losses caused by nausea and vomiting. Food aversions are probably linked to a physiological mechanism in pregnant women to avoid toxic foods containing pathogens that can be dangerous to the foetus. Particular foods such as fish and meat, and even plants that pose a high risk of containing toxins, are more likely to be avoided by pregnant women – but humans have other ways of detecting 'bad food' (taste, smell, and even the appearance of spoilt food), so it is interesting – and still remains something of a mystery – why and how this common occurrence has evolved in pregnant women. We can only wonder how this behaviour – if it was present so far back in our ancestry – was regarded by these early cultures. And, as we have already seen (p. 119), many cultures are happy to eat putrid food.

In the developed world, a healthy weight gain for a pregnant woman is considered to be 10-14 kg. This is associated with a low-risk gestation and childbirth and reduces the chances of a woman having an underweight infant at birth. In addition, maternal nutritional status at the time of conception is an important determinant of foetal growth and, from the second trimester to term, a pregnant woman needs approximately an extra 200 calories per day to maintain her unborn infant's development.

If we consider this in relation to a pregnant woman during the late ice age, the last couple of months of 'needing more' would also coincide with the period when her contribution of work (gathering, fishing, hunting, processing hides, etc) to the group might be much reduced, eventually leading to her dependence on others to support her needs. Again, we can only speculate how this process of 'calorie-loading' during pregnancy was enabled. Did the family group alter their food-sharing habits in some way to ensure a woman received a diet adequate to sustain her through the latter weeks of pregnancy? After childbirth, a woman would continue to need extra calories for breastfeeding her infant and, importantly, she would require a regular supply of fresh drinking water to maintain her milk production.

Breastmilk contains approximately 90% water, carbohydrates (mainly lactose), protein, and a range of vitamins and antibodies which are specific to the environment in which the mother and child live. Indeed, breastmilk can alter to meet changes in the weather – i.e. water content during hot weather – and to provide the nutritional needs of the individual child as it develops.

Childbirth can be tricky, and sometimes even a dangerous process, and one would imagine it was just as challenging, if not more so, during the last ice age. This view has, however, been challenged in the last decade. We will consider below the arguments for easier births in prehistory, but first we need to outline some of the inevitable risks women were likely to face in childbirth. In this way we can build a clearer picture of what the experience of this major life event might have been like, both physiologically and psychologically, for women during this early part of our ancestry.

Pregnancy and childbirth can be particularly risky for young and physically immature girls, and having begun menstruation is no indication that they are ready for pregnancy. There would have been no benefit to a small group of hunter-gatherers if their young women died from birth complications or their infants failed to survive, and one would expect that a prime age (even if not calculated in years) for becoming a mother would have been identified at some point. Repeated observation of suboptimal outcomes may have led to taboos or restrictions on young girls becoming pregnant. This is certainly the case within many living indigenous cultures, where menstruation occurs much later than in western societies. Among the !Kung hunter-gatherers, girls rarely reach menarche before the age of sixteen, and usually don't become mothers before nineteen.

Women must have menstruated in the last ice age, like women of today. It is likely that it was considered a nuisance, much as it is now – perhaps even more so, without modern conveniences. Indigenous groups around the world have devised many ingenious ways of managing their blood flow to avoid spoiling their clothing. Strips of old animal skins (often goat skin) or fibrous plant material such as big leaves are utilised; ice age people may even have woven suitable materials. By far the most innovative method is that used by women in Zambia who make dried dung 'patties' for this purpose. They collect fresh cow dung, grind it into a fine powder, and then shape it and wrap it in a skin or cloth. These 'patties' are highly absorbent, and after use are disposed of by being buried in the ground.

A successful birth by Caesarean section would seem highly unlikely – how could they have stopped the considerable bleeding? If the mother died with the infant still inside her, it would certainly have been possible to extract it with the tools and skills these early cultures had; but without a mother to nurse the infant, a baby's chances of survival would be very slim unless another breastfeeding woman was available (see below, p. 175). Other dangers the mother would face, like a breech birth or complications with the umbilical cord or placenta, excessive bleeding or postpartum haemorrhage, would in all probability result in her death. The baby's journey through the birth canal does not always proceed smoothly or quickly enough, which can make delivery difficult and even fatal for both the mother and her offspring.

THE OBSTETRIC DILEMMA

Coming out of the birth canal is a tight squeeze for all primates, especially human infants with their large heads and long bodies. Four million years of hominin evolution, starting when our early ancestor, the upright-walking Australopithecine, developed a bipedal posture, have led to the female pelvic anatomy becoming stronger and less flexible. This in turn has resulted in childbirth becoming painful and potentially dangerous, or, at the very least, quite a physical challenge for most women!

In the 1960s a theory known as the 'obstetric dilemma' seemed to give a reasonable explanation for the conundrum surrounding human childbirth. It proposes that a trade-off exists because the female pelvis has two competing roles – bipedal walking (which would favour a narrow pelvis), and giving birth to large-brained infants (which would favour a wide one). However, although foetal head size and maternal pelvic size appear to be important determinants in the potential for obstetric complications, recent research by specialists has led them to question this explanation and wonder why natural selection would lead to the persistence of such apparently adverse effects on either mother or offspring, or indeed both of them. Hence, this hypothesis alone is an insufficient explanation.

An alternative explanation is that natural selection could have worked in favour of women having larger pelvises if the need had been there. It is possible that the timing of childbirth is directly related to a woman's ability to continue nourishing her growing foetus. It is these energy demands that are the real difficulty for mothers, and not the tight fit between the baby's head and the birth canal. Human pregnancies are 37 days longer than they should be for an ape our size, and the last weeks of pregnancy push a woman close to the edge metabolically, as the growing foetus's own energy demands increase.

Pelvic formation and foetal growth patterns are both sensitive to diet and the 'thermal environment' – put simply, that's how physiologically adapted a population is to its natural climate. Some specialists suspect that the introduction of farming –- at the end of the ice age, around 12,000 years ago – made childbirth far more difficult, due to a dramatic change to a diet that was rich in carbohydrates rather than high in protein. This shift may have altered both a woman's stature and her pelvis size, and also, through a carbohydrate-rich diet, caused her developing infant to grow too large, leading to difficulties in delivery.

Bearing these factors in mind, we cannot assume that giving birth was more or less of a risk for women in prehistoric times. Recent findings indicate that in the developed world there has been a 15-25 % increase in infant size at birth over the last few decades, so it is reasonable to suggest that healthy newborns could have been smaller in antiquity and/or the gestation length shorter. Both of these factors would have led to less risk for mother and infant during childbirth.

However, we do have clear evidence of maternal and infant mortality, as shown by the examples below; what we don't know is how frequent and representative these cases are. Consequently we cannot assume a higher (or lower) mortality associated with pregnancy and parturition (giving birth) in the past.

The 'rare' cases presented below of infant burials serve to indicate the precarious nature of childbirth for early hunter-gatherer cultures, and also reveal the surprisingly complex behaviour surrounding the death and burial practices of our ice age ancestors. These remarkable finds may suggest that mother-and-infant deaths during childbirth were the exception – and that this unusual circumstance was the reason for the burial. It is impossible to know if archaeologists have been especially fortunate in finding these rare examples, or if there are many more burials of women that died in childbirth still to be discovered.

THE ABRI PATAUD

The prehistoric site of the Abri Pataud is in the middle of the village of Les Eyzies (Dordogne), and is one of the few classic excavation sites open to the public. The rock shelter contained about 10 m of sediment that has yielded a wealth of remains, prehistoric artwork, and a rock engraving known as the 'Venus of Pataud' (see appendix). The shelter is now part of the National Museum of Natural History.

Around 35,000 years ago, the shallow rock shelter was used for short stays only by its early occupants (Aurignacian hunter-gatherers), but over the following millennia, as the shelter eroded, people with the Gravettian tool kit settled here for longer periods. At the end of this phase (about 22,000 years ago) the shelter's roof collapsed, leaving just a narrow passageway between the rock face and fallen blocks of stone. Some time later, around 20,000 years ago, during the late Gravettian or early Solutrean occupation, Pataud became a small cemetery.

The ecological evidence produced by the excavation showed that in some periods this area had a temperate climate, not unlike that of today, but at other times it was a bitterly cold, bleak environment. The small ice age groups inhabiting the rock shelters of Les Eyzies would have depended on the rich resources the area offered them: a varied vegetation, a variety of animal herds and, just as vital, the nearby rivers with essential fresh water carrying a regular supply of fish. It seems likely that rock shelter settlements in the area would have been 'prime real estate' for hunter-gatherers and an ideal place to live during the last ice age!

Figure 5.4. The statue of the young girl in the Abri Pataud museum.

The Pataud shelter had almost completely collapsed by the time it was first excavated in May 1958. However, the narrow access through a tight 2 m wide corridor allowed the American excavator, Hallam Movius, to make his first important discovery: the skull of a young girl. The excavations continued, and in 1963 Movius and his team uncovered, near the original find, the remains of two young women, a newborn infant, and a child of about six months old.

This evidence suggested initially that both women were buried with their infants. The younger female, estimated to be around 16-18 years old, most likely died after childbirth. She was buried in a foetal position – that is, with her knees under her chin and placed on her right side with her neonate aged four to six weeks tucked closely beside her. The newborn comprised 16 fragments of ribs and a right leg. At some point later, the young woman's skull was removed from her remains and moved about 2-3 m away –- this was the skull that Movius had discovered five years earlier.

The second collection of remains belonged to a female between 20 and 25 years old, and included the bones of a six month old infant intimately mixed with hers. These comprised a crushed skull, vertebrae, ribs and two clavicles. Part of the child's skeleton rested on the woman's left arm. While this may be a burial, another simpler explanation may also be possible. The woman may have taken shelter inside the space and subsequently died with the infant in her arms. Her unfortunate death may not have occurred at around the same time as that of the other, younger woman; indeed their deaths may have been decades or even longer apart. It is important not to over-interpret burial scenarios or imagine symbolic behaviour through our own modern perspectives.

THE OSTUNI BURIAL OF A WOMAN AND HER INFANT

In 1991 during an archaeological dig in the small cave of Santa Maria di Agnano (Ostuni, Italy) the excavator, Donato Coppola, discovered a burial cavity dug into the hard ground inside the cave. It contained the archaeological remains of the nearly complete skeleton of a young (approximately 20 years old) woman who was in the advanced stages of pregnancy at the time of her death around 27,000 years ago. Her foetal skeletal remains – the head, six teeth, body and legs – were present and well preserved inside the mother's pelvic region. It has been estimated that she died at 31-33 gestational weeks.

The woman's skeleton was found in an excellent state of preservation; it was buried in a flexed position on her left side. Her right forearm was over her abdomen, and her left arm bent with the hand near her skull. She was richly adorned with hundreds of perforated seashells around her wrists and about her head. The head covering or mask of seashells was coated in a thick crust of red ochre. Placed near the left side of her head was a fragment of horse cranium. Inside the shallow burial cavity her skeleton had been surrounded by perforated seashells, horse and aurochs teeth, a red deer canine, and fragments of bone and flint.

The young woman's bones indicated she was fit and healthy at the time of her death, leaving us to wonder how she might have died and how to interpret the burial. The presence of 'dental stress episodes' suggests that both the mother and foetus were under severe physiological stress during the last two and a half months of pregnancy. These unknown stressors possibly resulted in the death of both the mother and the child.

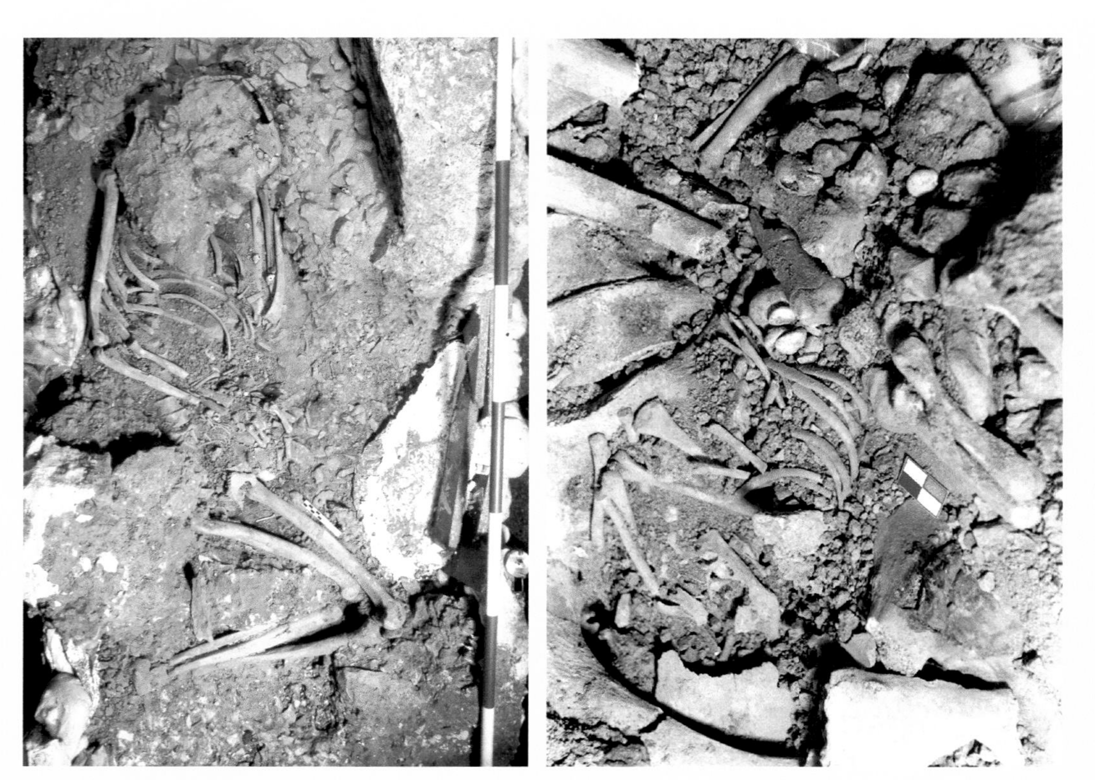

Figure 5.5. a/b: The Ostuni burial, with close-up of the pelvic area.

New research has drawn attention to some interesting taphonomic processes that shed light on the underrepresentation of infant remains in the archaeological record. Bones of infants and children are smaller, and the epiphyses have not completely ossified. These bones are also very porous and lack the strength of adult specimens. This makes them much more vulnerable in the ground (pressure, erosion, decomposition, etc) and also more easily damaged during an excavation. In addition, 'microbioerosion' (gut bacteria) can spread through a dead body within hours, and eventually completely degrade the remains of young children under the age of about five (as seen, perhaps, in the case of Arma Veirana, see below, p. 200). Interestingly, stillborn infants and those that died soon after birth have a greater chance of surviving in the archaeological record

THE CHILD BURIALS AT THE GROTTE DES ENFANTS

Balzi Rossi is a prominent dolomite cliff overlooking the Mediterranean Sea at Grimaldi, Italy, near the French border. Archaeological activity at the site started in the middle of the 19th century when Emile Rivière, a French doctor living in Cannes, took a keen interest in the archaeological material emerging from the site. Rivière made his first burial discovery in 1872, when he excavated the skeleton of an adult male. His attention then turned to a small cave along the Balzi Rossi cliffs that became known as the Grotte des Enfants. During this period of his excavations, from 1874-1875, he discovered the remains of two young children estimated to have died around 11,000 years ago.

In what would seem like an extraordinary move today, Rivière (who claimed ownership of the site) took it upon himself to have the whole burial area 'dug up' and transported to the Natural History Museum in Paris. This was not an uncommon practice at the time. Subsequently in 1990, the 'exhibit' was moved to the National Archaeology Museum just outside Paris. It should be noted that many of these early excavations took a different, less methodical and careful approach than those in recent times. So one cannot be completely confident that these infant burials were simultaneous, although the decorations seem to indicate this.

Rivière discovered the children buried close together at a depth of 2.7 m in the rock shelter, 10 m from the entrance. The skeletons were in extended positions with their skulls almost intact, and their ages, determined by their teeth, were estimated to be 3 years old and 18 months. The children's sex appeared to lean towards female. A re-examination of the remains in 2001 added information about how the younger infant died: a retouched bladelet stuck in its spine (vertebra T4) was the probable cause of death (p. 29). The older child had nothing obvious to explain its death. Ochre was not present, nor other grave goods in the burial pit, but there were hundreds of perforated seashells (*Cyclonassa neritea*) – somewhere in the region of 1700 shells, arranged in rows, appear to have been attached to a garment that is best described as a loin-cloth placed across the younger child's stomach (p. 110).

because they have not lived long enough for their bioerosive gut bacteria to develop.

Of course, distinguishing between a baby that was dead on delivery and one that died within a few days after birth is challenging for researchers, and we have no way of knowing if the incidence of stillbirths was higher or lower than it is today – although in all likelihood it was higher. According to data published by UNICEF in 2019 the global stillbirth rate was 13.9 per 1,000 total births.

THE PERINATAL SKELETON FROM WILCZYCE, POLAND

Excavations from 2000 onwards at an open-air hilltop site overlooking the Opatówka Valley, and close to the village of Wilczyce, yielded more than 30 female figurines in flint, along with the butchered bones of a variety of animals which were clearly exploited not only for meat but also for their fur pelts. The remains recovered suggest that the site was repeatedly used as an autumn/winter hunting camp during the late Magdalenian, around 13,000 bp.

It wasn't until 2005 that Bodil Bratlund identified infant bones among the faunal remains discovered earlier. An osteological examination of the skeletal finds showed that they were about 60% complete. The osteometric measurements of bones and dental formation of the perinate suggest it was around 38 weeks at its time of death. Estimates are inevitably based on recent human neonates, and so it is difficult to know what a full-term – and therefore a full-term birth weight – would have been during the ice age, and of course, as now, there would be variation. Genetic tests undertaken on fragments of the skeleton were inconclusive but suggestive of a female infant.

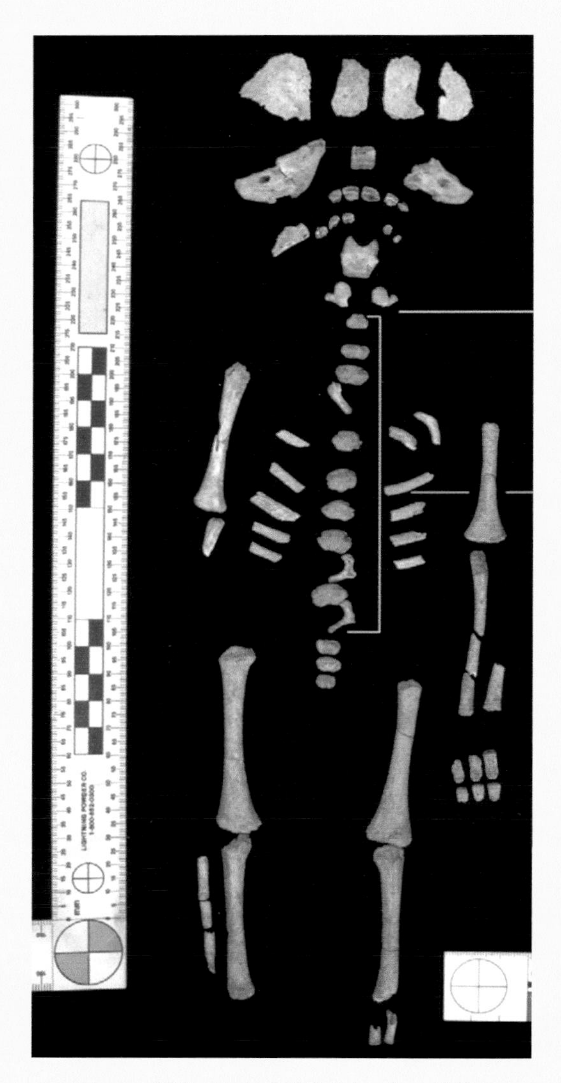

Figure 5.6. The perinatal skeleton from Wilczyce, Poland.

Several hundred sandstone slabs were recovered and were thought to have formed the pavements for the habitation structures on the site. The excavators suggested that the infant could have been interred under these slabs. This is particularly interesting, and differs from other burial practices in Europe during the Upper Palaeolithic.

The perinate seems to have been intentionally buried, along with a bundle of beads made from around 100 perforated arctic fox teeth, which were recovered from the same excavated area. The fox teeth seem to have been strung like a necklace and then placed in a bag and left as a burial offering with the infant remains. Although the body was found amongst the faunal waste beneath the dwelling, we should not assume that it was dumped with the garbage – one could just as easily argue that the family wanted her remains to be kept close by.

What we can say is that the Wilczyce post-mortem practice is very different to those described elsewhere, but it should come as no surprise that different regional communities and cultures across Europe, and over very extended time periods – not hundreds but thousands of years – have differences as well as similarities. It may be that infants who died either before, during, or soon after birth were not afforded particularly elaborate burial treatment. In all likelihood, the loss of an expected infant would have been considered no less traumatic and sad than it would today for a mother and her family. Of course, it is possible that even in these early cultures the 'status' of the infant, child or their parent may have been a factor in the kind of treatment they received (as seen in the La Madeleine child, pp. 107-9).

Another question that fascinates people is when twin births started in our ancestry. Given the small population numbers throughout Europe during the last ice age, it is unlikely our early ancestors encountered twin births very often, and when they occurred this must have been a rare and astonishing event for the mother and those present. We can only wonder what our ice age people must have made of having not one but two babies appear! Nevertheless, human twins were undoubtedly present in antiquity, although evidence for them in the fossil record has been elusive until recently.

In 2015 evidence of twins in an early Neolithic context (c. 7000 - 8000 bp) was published. The skeleton of a young woman and her two neonate remains, found in a hunter-gatherer cemetery at Lokomotiv, near Lake Baikal (Siberia), were re-examined. All three individuals died from complications associated with childbirth. The female was estimated to be 20-25 years old at death, and her two foetuses were full-term. Death appears to have occurred as a result of an obstructed labour, probably due to the first twin's breech position at birth. The foetus appeared to be partially birthed, and was not – or could not – be removed from the mother's body before she and the twins were interred. The Lokomotiv remains were, until recently, the oldest confirmed evidence of twins in the archaeological record; but we now have an even earlier example from the last ice age.

Twin births can be at a higher risk than singleton births as malpresentation of one or both twins is not uncommon, and, as noted earlier, the possibility of a Caesarean section birth or a forceps delivery would not have been an option available to women in prehistory.

IDENTICAL TWINS AT KREMS-WACHTBERG, AUSTRIA

In 2005 a team of excavators discovered the complete skeletons of two neonates at the periphery of the Krems-Wachtberg settlement, dating to around 30,000 - 31,000 bp. The infants were buried in an oval-shaped grave pit and embedded in red ochre. Intriguingly, the pit was not back-filled with soil but covered by a mammoth scapula – flaked to make it fit – supported by a fragment of mammoth tusk. Both neonates were strongly flexed and placed side by side with their heads to the north. One infant occupied a more central position in the grave and had three perforated mollusc shells (*Theodoxus*) and a perforated fox tooth that appear to have been worn as a necklace. The second infant was placed to the left of the first, and was furnished with a line of 53 mammoth ivory beads of similar size and shape that had probably been threaded together. These were placed over the infant's pelvis and its right hand was on top of them. As there was no sign of wear on their perforations it seems likely that the ivory beads were either a votive offering or a grave-good typical for the period.

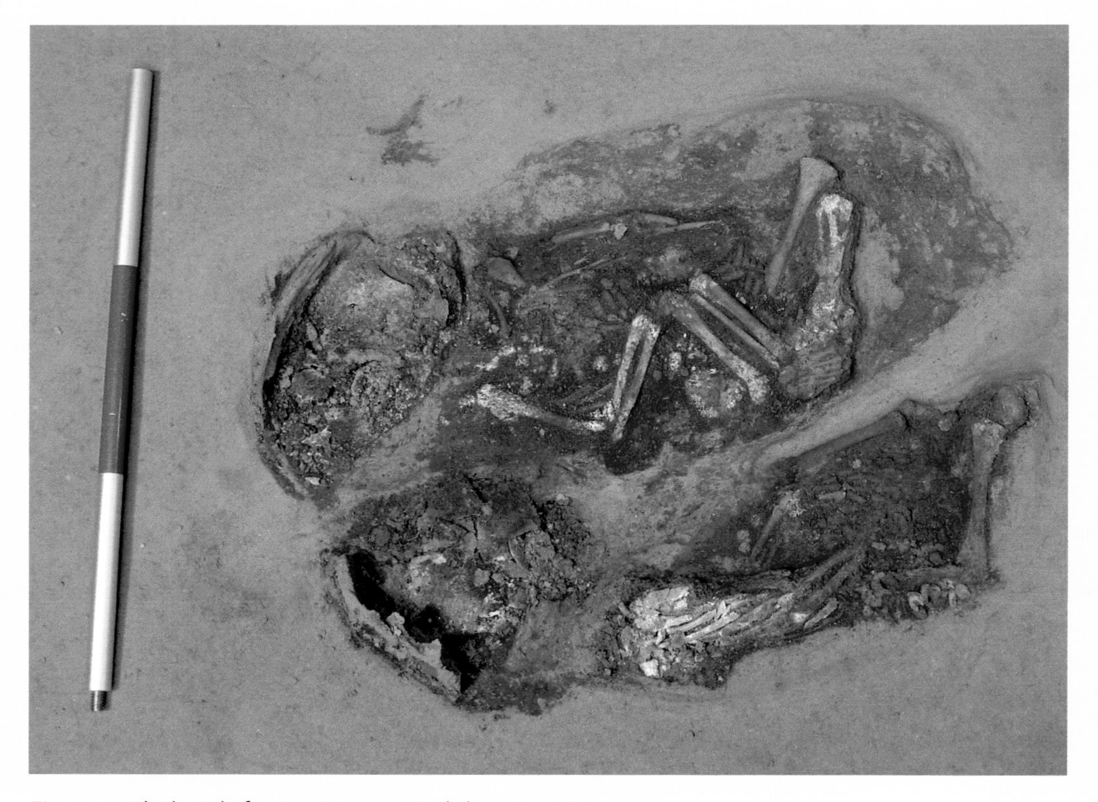

Figure 5.7. The burial of twins at Krems-Wachtberg (Austria).

Maria Teschler-Nicola and her team in Vienna have recently reanalysed the remains of the Krems-Wachtberg double burial and have revealed remarkable new findings. Results verified by aDNA analysis confirmed that the infants were in fact monozygotic male twins. Further analysis indicated that one neonate died around 39-40 gestational weeks, and the second infant died 6-7 weeks after birth.

Because the infants did not die at the same time, we can assume the grave would have had to be reopened to accommodate the second twin. This presumably was why it wasn't backfilled, but had a mammoth shoulder blade cover that would allow the grave to be re-opened; it also suggests that the second child's death may have been anticipated. The first infant had been embedded in red ochre, a not uncommon mortuary ritual at the time. This, along with the periglacial conditions during the period, may have delayed any deterioration of the first child's corpse by the time the grave was re-opened. The subsequent altering of the grave's layout and the placing inside of the additional infant, along with the ivory beads, give us a valuable insight into the mortuary behaviour of these early cultures.

This double infant male burial is the earliest reported case of a multiple birth, although it shouldn't be implied that this was the very first twin birth! It remains a mystery when or why multiple births first appeared in the human gene pool, or at what rate they occurred over our long ancestry. But the Krems-Wachtberg find demonstrates that a multiple birth, indeed a monozygotic twin birth, occurred 30,000 years ago.

Home delivery service

We have no clue as to whether female family members or men were present at births during the last ice age. But it's quite likely, as is the custom with most modern hunter-gatherers, that other women and even very young females were present during childbirth, to observe the practices and potential hazards involved, to assist if needed, or just to observe a sibling being born.

Until recently, childbirth was very different from our own first-world experience, which now usually takes place in a hospital with trained professionals to assist. There is a huge variety of traditional childbirth practices; for instance, they may involve a woman retreating into the forest with several other experienced women to assist (as with the Kaulong, Papua New Guinea, for example) because their men folk believe childbirth has a 'polluting effect.' A very different tradition exists when Ngarinyin Aboriginal women give birth: the women-helpers prepare a fire, collect water, leaves and herbs and dig a special pit for the mother-to-be to kneel in until she delivers her infant. The helpers sing, chant, rub her skin, and offer words of reassurance to soothe her. The father-to-be is taken some distance away by a group of older men. A hair belt is tied around his waist; he lies on the ground with his legs wide open and tightens the

Figure 5.8. One of the engraved Magdalenian plaquettes from Gönnersdorf (Germany), c. 12,600 bp, bears an image which has been interpreted by some researchers as a newborn infant connected to a female silhouette (with a flat abdomen and small breasts).

belt to assist his wife in labour. By simulating his partner's breathing in labour he believes he is attempting to transmit his 'energy' into her. These examples nicely illustrate that hunter-gatherer communities do not always share the same 'ideals' when it comes to childbirth practices.

Birth in most societies, including traditional herding or farming communities, is attended by non-specialist or trained helpers; for some small indigenous societies, childbirth is traditionally seen as a 'public event'! Certainly, it is rare in hunter-gatherer cultures for women to give birth alone. The !Kung people of southern Africa are unusual in this respect, citing 'physical courage' as the reason for going-it-alone when it comes to giving birth. However, interviews by ethnographers have revealed that, in reality, other women are often present during labour and birth, just to observe, or to assist should difficulties occur.

Having someone else present to give support, or to assist with the labour, would always increase the chances of a successful outcome for both mother and infant. This is especially so when guiding baby from the birth canal, and, depending on delivery position, being there to stop the newborn from falling to the ground! A key feature of human childbirth (although not unique – it has been observed in chimpanzees) is that the infant emerges facing backwards relative to the mother. This makes it extremely difficult physically for the mother to manage childbirth on her own.

Once the baby is delivered, someone has to wipe the fluids from its face and nostrils to start it breathing, check the umbilical cord is not wrapped around the neck (as sometimes happens), and cut it. Usually in traditional societies, if both appear well, the infant is placed on the mother's front so baby can find, by smell, its mother's breast and initiate suckling for itself.

A mother produces a hormone called oxytocin during labour: this is known as a 'bonding chemical' and encourages attachment between the mother and infant. Studies of existing hunter-gatherer cultures have found that everyone present at the birth, and especially those touching the infant or the mother, can be affected by the mother's oxytocin. Significantly, it appears that this birth hormone increases the emotional investment of those present at the birth in the infant's wellbeing.

After birth

Fresh water is absolutely essential for the mother after giving birth. Habitat choice, that is, choosing where to live, would undoubtedly have been influenced by the need to be close to a regular supply of fresh water (p. 98). And this seems to be the case, as most ice age living sites are in close proximity to rivers. A new mother needs to be well-hydrated to produce milk, and requires around 400-500 extra calories a day to successfully breastfeed her infant -- more if the mother soon returns to hard chores such as processing skins, foraging, or even hunting. The latter would involve travelling over rough terrain and walking some distance from the home base.

Babies at birth still have a huge amount of brain and nervous system development to undergo, predominantly in the first two years of life. Compared to other primates, they are underdeveloped when born due to the constraints of the female pelvis and the infant's head size (pp. 164-65), which means that during infancy babies' brains have huge energy needs to grow sufficiently; this high dependency places great demands on the mother. However, maternal milk is all the infant needs for its first six months of life, and nature has ensured that what a mother can provide is not just food, but also a sort of medicine providing the infant with immunity to a range of pathogens. It may have taken millions of years for human babies to evolve into a 'perfectly attractive infant,' that frequently elicits a caring and 'cooing' response from caregivers! There is no reason to doubt that the same holds true for the ice age.

Sharing the caring

An 'allomother' is anyone other than the biological mother that performs the functions *of a mother* and cares for the infant *in place of* the mother. This may be other female kin, a woman's own mother, the infant's father, or a non-relative babysitter. So alloparenting is not dependent on relatedness, although a mother is perhaps more likely to 'trust' a relative over other alloparents. Since infants are enormously dependent at birth, the best outcome for the newborn (and mother) is when the caring and responsibilities are shared by 'a community of others.' This early caring establishes the emotional ties with her extended family of caregivers, and as a consequence the child's survival becomes an investment for the whole group, not just the mother.

Research on the modern hunter-gatherer Hadza women of Tanzania revealed that women who are genetically related to the infant's mother can re-lactate when there is a hungry baby to be fed, and mum is unable to feed or is unavailable because of illness or death. Re-lactation was even possible for postmenopausal female relatives, and especially the infant's grandmother.

In most hunter-gatherer cultures, grandmothers, sisters, fathers, and other women and children help with infant care, but the mother is always the primary care giver until the child is about two years of age. There are very few examples of variation from this 'norm' amongst all of the surviving hunter-gatherer societies to date. This pattern of extended support must have been selected for through prehistory, and has presumably evolved because it increases the chances of infants surviving. It is probably the most efficient and pragmatic way of achieving an optimal outcome for communities with this lifestyle. A consequence of the active 'caring' for offspring by (mainly) other female members of a group is that women may have been highly valued in these early cultures, as their contribution, especially in the reproductive sphere, was essential to the survival of the group.

Postmenopausal women and the grandmother hypothesis

Homo sapiens females are not the only species to live beyond their reproductive capabilities. Many female primates also cease to menstruate before they die, but only human females continue to live for decades after they no longer reproduce. It has been proposed that this longevity in our species is due in part to their usefulness in increasing the survival chances of their daughters' offspring.

In hunter-gatherer societies today, when grandmothers are present, they are almost always involved in childcare and food provisioning for the family, and indeed the economic productivity of older post-menopausal women is usually very high. Grannies, it seems, may hold the key to our extended lifespan past fertility!

Emphasising the support women extend to each other in childrearing doesn't necessarily imply that ice age fathers spent hardly any time with their infants and young children. In close-knit indigenous groups, everyone inevitably spends a great deal of time together. For example, male Aka foragers in Central Africa develop strong intimate bonds with their offspring because they have regular and lengthy interactions with them. Even quite young infants and children are taken on hunting trips and remain in continuous direct contact with their fathers.

Family size and birth intervals

Hunter-gatherer women today who do not have contact with farmers or access to baby milk formula breastfeed their infants far beyond six months. Weaning is the cessation of breastfeeding, with a gradual reduction of suckling as solid food intake is increased. In these communities the average age of weaning is about three years, at which stage children can feed themselves with enough solid food to be properly nourished.

In indigenous cultures it may be several years before a particular child is fully weaned and another pregnancy commences, and this makes obvious good sense, because of the high costs involved in childbearing and childrearing. This cost-benefit ratio may have led ice age hunter-gatherer cultures to delay reproduction so as to invest more, both physically and emotionally, in each individual offspring. Delaying reproduction would be a highly adaptive strategy, not just for the growing child but everyone in the family group. This, of course, would be easier to achieve if they understood the process of conception!

It is possible for women to produce a child every year, but it is highly unlikely that our ice age ancestors had large families. This is certainly true of hunter-gatherers today. It has been suggested that this was an evolutionary adaptation giving women the physiological mechanism for delaying ovulation by prolonged breastfeeding – specifically, 'feeding on demand'.

Feeding on demand reduces the chance of a woman ovulating and thus lengthens birth spacing. Only in traditional cultures do we see infants given the on-demand option of being able to suckle at will – that is, *the infant chooses when,* and has direct and immediate access to its mother's breast. This usually means more frequent feeding but for less duration. Babies and small children sleep with their mothers and often feed while mother remains asleep. This continuous opportunity for nursing makes huge demands on the mother's energy, and if she returns to work either hunting or foraging and remains in continuous contact with her child, the physiological impact is not trivial. So, even if a woman resumes sexual activity, it is unlikely she will commence menstruating and ovulating until her child is weaned.

First foods for ice age infants

A mash of nuts (pine or acorn, roasted or ground) would have been available and gathered seasonally – for example, remains of highly nutritional pine nuts have been found in Nerja Cave. Nuts can be stored for months and are higher in protein, carbohydrate and fat than eggs, but a variety of bird and seabird eggs (there were no chickens around!) would no doubt have been collected regularly from nests. For example, when meat was scarce, nuts became the staple diet for the Anasazi Indian people, who for thousands of years populated the Great Basin area of America. As we have seen (p. 152), acorns were a major staple of the majority of later prehistoric Californian populations like the Chumash.

Cooked and pulped roots and a variety of plants would also be available in season. Some of these foods take effort to dig up, cook and prepare, but can be stored and even put in the ground over winter. Using cold storage would also have been a simple way of freezing meat and fish, as long as they were protected from scavengers.

The Ache hunter-gatherers of eastern Paraguay begin giving their children solid foods at 6-12 months. Delicacies such as armadillo fat or insect larvae are nutritious and perfectly healthy. It's very likely that ice age people gave their children animal bone marrow (a jelly-like substance in the middle of the bone), which contains more vitamins and minerals than the actual meat or fat. It's also high in calcium, so excellent for growing bones, and can be introduced to a baby as early as 6 months. Raw marrow is off-white and hard with a spongy texture but, when melted, it becomes rich and soft and tastes like a sweet, nutty-flavoured butter. It would have been in plentiful supply, especially in an animal's long bones, and we have already seen (pp. 155-56) that our ancestors went to a great deal of effort to extract every last bit of marrow from these bones.

The occupants of El Mirón (pp. 255-58) used stone boiling extensively to extract the fat from the bones of ibex and red deer; evidence of this practice was found in a shallow basin hearth dated to c. 15,000 bp. This technique is still used by hunter-gatherers today. The cobbles are heated in the hearth to melt and extract the fat. Any leftover grease can then be stored in the emptied intestines of animals from which the fat came.

Could they possibly have used horse or reindeer milk to supplement their infants' diet? Reindeer milk and ice cream have become a fashionable addition to diets in recent years, and certainly reindeer herders take advantage of the warm, nutritious drink, high in fat and protein, that is also easy to digest. However, it should be noted that horses and reindeer are difficult to milk, unlike cows, so the likelihood is pretty slim. Moreover, a female reindeer only produces a small amount of milk daily, so a great many would need to be corralled to make it worth the effort!

Pre-chewing of food by mothers has been observed in modern hunter-gatherers and may have been an option. Tribes such as the Efe, Yanomamo and Himba give their babies as young as three to four months old pre-masticated mouthfuls of food. This mouth-to-mouth method known as 'kiss-feeding' is provided by both mothers and allomothers. The food is mixed with the adult's saliva and then transferred to the infant's mouth by the adult's tongue.

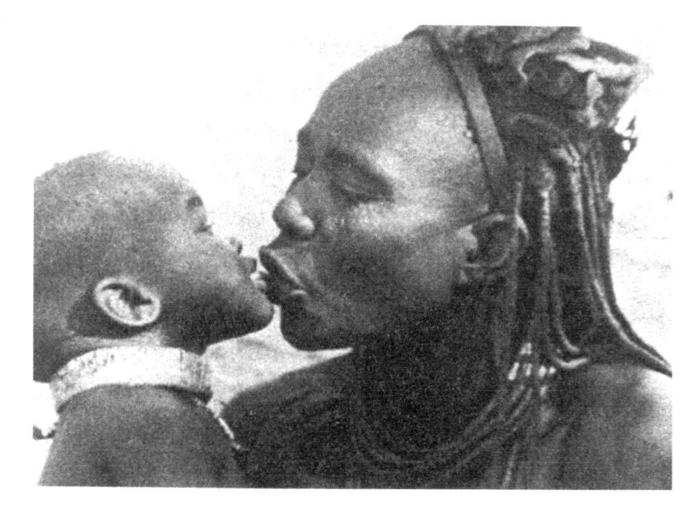

Figure 5.9. Kiss-feeding among the Himba of Namibia.

Weaning

Children may have been weaned when their teeth reached a certain stage of development (dental evidence suggests this may have been earlier for infants in prehistory), or by some established tradition, or if the mother resumed menstruation, which would indicate the possibility that she could become pregnant again. Of course, we can only speculate as to how much these ancient cultures understood about the mechanisms of conception - very little, one suspects. They may not even have understood the role of men as a necessary requirement for fertilisation, or the connection between having sex and pregnancy.

It is, however, highly probable that women did make a connection between their bleeding cycles and the waxing and waning of the moon, and this would enable them to keep track and predict when the next bleed would come. Anthropologists have noted this practice amongst a number of indigenous cultures, and it's not uncommon in societies with ancient traditions like the First Nation people of America for women to make a spiritual connection with the moon. As we shall see (pp. 219-20), some ice age engraved bone objects may have been linked to observation of lunar phases.

METHODS OF CARRYING AND TRANSPORTING INFANTS

Skin or fur slings were almost certainly utilised to carry infants across the mother's breast; this would allow the infant to feed on-demand when it was hungry or just for comfort. Additionally, when temperatures were at their lowest during the ice age some 20,000 years ago, keeping infants in a sling under outdoor clothing would insulate them against the cold. In some hunter-gatherer cultures infants remain attached to their mother using just such a method while she sleeps at night. Skin-to-skin contact allows the infant to feed when it wants, and be warm – thus increasing the chances of its survival through continuous contact with its mother.

The use of slings as a carrying method by contemporary hunter-gatherer women is much more prevalent in warmer climates, with cradleboards (p. 106) and swaddling more likely in colder regions. There are exceptions; for example, in sub-Polar regions, mothers traditionally have continuous skin-to-skin contact with their babies lying in a sling and kept insulated from the cold underneath a waterproof parka.

The invention of the 'sling' – made either of leather or fur – cannot be underestimated as a great leap forward for infant survival. Slings are rarely mentioned in the literature, as we have no trace of them in the archaeological record, but what a marvellous innovation! They would have been useful for carrying not only infants but all manner of other things like food, tools, fishing gear and weapons. Whoever came up with the simple but brilliant idea of a sling to transport things – and it may have a much longer ancestry than *H. sapiens* – was a truly pioneering innovator. Necessity is the mother of invention, and sometimes of inventions for mothers!

Figure 5.10. A Chamacoco mother and baby, Paraguay.

With her baby securely strapped to her, a woman would have been mobile again, and could return to gathering or even, perhaps, hunting (although a crying infant would have been a disadvantage in this pursuit!), gathering, or fishing. Surely this new-fangled baby-sling would catch on very fast with other women, who could now work or journey to a different home-site without the burden of carrying a baby or having to stop to feed it, secure in the knowledge that the infant was safe from any danger.

Figure 5.11. One of the engraved Magdalenian plaquettes from Gönnersdorf (Germany, c. 12,600 bp) depicts what seem to be four highly stylized women, one behind the other, with a small form behind the back of the second one. It is generally interpreted as the representation of a baby carried and tied to the back of a woman; and it has been pointed out that this woman has rounded breasts, while the others have pointed ones. Width of plaquette: 8 cm.

Who's your daddy? Paternity and avoiding incest

Clearly men and women mated, but we can discern nothing about their sexual behaviour from fossil evidence. Naturally, our ancestors had year-round potential for mating, but we have no way of knowing if this was restricted or if relationships were arranged in any way that limited sexual encounters. If our ancestors had no or little understanding of the role of males in conception (i.e. they didn't make the connection between copulation and pregnancy), can we then assume that they avoided interbreeding with mates who were too closely related?

It's possible that pregnant women didn't know, or were not concerned with, who the biological father was, especially if there were no restrictions on how many mates were available to a female. Nevertheless, even though the role of 'father' might not have been understood in the biological or genetic sense, the role of a man as 'protector' may have been the norm, and is not an unusual scenario in existing hunter-gatherer societies. Permanent roles for men may have been preferred for the welfare of the group, but it is equally possible that the 'job' could have been temporary, with men moving on to another group or community. The latter would help explain how the chances of interbreeding could be reduced.

Mating with close kin in humans can, and often does, lead to a range of genetic and health problems. There have been laws since Roman times – and even earlier, social taboos – prohibiting sexual relationships and marriage between closely related individuals, although various degrees of relatedness are permitted in some cultures; for example, first-cousin marriages. However, there is a great deal of cross-cultural variation in what relatedness is or is not permitted.

At some point in prehistory our ancestors must have dealt with this tricky problem by either young men or young women moving from their family group to find non-related mates. Exactly how and when this behaviour is likely to have started remains a mystery, and presumably there must have been periods when this was not possible, and inter-breeding may have occurred if communities became isolated and were unable to 'go further afield' to find a mate.

If inter-generational breeding occurred relatively frequently, then perhaps birth defects and disabilities would not have been uncommon in these early populations. It is certainly true, as we have seen, that individuals with noticeable developmental or degenerative abnormalities occur quite frequently in ice age burials, and account for about a third of the sufficiently well-preserved individuals. This has led to the suggestion that when 'unusual' individuals died, they may have been treated differently by their community, and afforded a more elaborate burial.

It seems likely that prehistoric people living in small groups would eventually have gained enough experience of infants born with defects to make the connection between close family matings and abnormalities either at birth or during the child's development. This crucial information would have been handed down through the generations, and we can be confident they paid attention to anything unusual – paying attention and making connections were the keys to their survival.

Who stays and who goes?

The most likely scenario during the last ice age was for related women to stay together as a group and support reproductive mothers in their efforts to rear children. Alternatively, having men 'stay put' in a community, and exchanging females with other groups, would create alliances, perhaps through hunting as a 'band' with other communities. This is called 'male philopatry,' and the view that this was the norm for the vast majority of early human cultures, including hunter-gatherers, has been widely supported – often dogmatically – by male researchers in the past.

However, a cross-cultural survey found that only 6 out of 48 hunter-gatherer groups were in fact patrilocal. It also seems that most hunter-gatherer societies today are flexible in their residence patterns, and couples often move around, live with different family groups over time, but in general stay with the woman's family when she is expecting a child.

It is often assumed that having a single commitment to one sexual partner, with some sort of contract, is a 'natural' state of affairs with a long history. However, in most foraging societies men and women are simply sex partners, and the offspring of these partnerships are the responsibility of the extended family or group. It's probably safe to assume that 'marriage customs', as we understand them, and the idealised 'nuclear family' of mother-father-and-children, were not the norm during prehistory.

It seems most likely that traditions changed over the many millennia of our prehistoric past, and there may have been periods when males or females were in 'short supply', and it was hard to find a mate within the local network of families. This may have led to elaborate customs regarding the exchange of young men and women with neighbouring bands of hunter-gatherers distributed over connecting territories. Ice age people were highly mobile and willing to travel long distances for particular resources and to exchange desirable goods. This will certainly have led to forming social contacts and social arrangements outside their home territory. Large aggregations or gatherings at 'supersites' like Isturitz and Le Mas d'Azil may have been the opportunity to find new mates, or future partners, or just have sexual encounters.

There are no clear images of copulation by either animals or humans in ice age imagery, which would lead one to suppose it was not a 'preoccupation' with prehistoric people but seen as a natural activity between the sexes, and not necessarily connected with females producing offspring. This is true for a number of indigenous people, for example some Aboriginal Australians, and the Trobrianders of Papua New Guinea, who had apparently not made this connection before coming into contact with Western anthropologists – although it is possible that the anthropologists had misunderstood! It is worth mentioning that any preliterate people who made the connection must have been able to count – at least up to nine!

Is there any evidence of infanticide?

Ethnographers of the late 19th century reported on the shocking frequency of infanticide amongst what used to be called 'primitive' societies. The Pelly Bay Netsilik Inuit in the Central Canadian Arctic were still practising female infanticide in the 1960s, according to ethnographic reports. Some researchers believed this practice was due, for the most part, to a concern for population growth, and the need for mothers to be mobile and productive. However, an alternative view proposed that it was more to do with male dominance over females, and a father's desire to have sons rather than daughters who would stay with their mother and be of little use as hunters. These preferences became accepted as 'the norm' over time, with the mother having the responsibility of disposing of the unwanted female infant to which she had just given birth!

Although internationally illegal, infanticide still exists in a small number of tribal communities around the world. Some researchers have proposed that infanticide would have been systematically practised during the Pleistocene period, due to the mothers in a mobile hunter-gatherer population being unable to meet the needs of closely spaced offspring.

There is no archaeological evidence for this happening, but we can't be sure that infanticide did not occur during times of stress when, for example, food shortages were experienced. This has happened with alarming frequency throughout history, when humans have been at the very limits of surviving during famines or sieges. It has also been suggested that 'imperfect' newborns and those with disabilities are unlikely to have been reared – but, as we have already shown (p. 33), this was not always true in the ice age.

Growing up

Children were a significant part of Upper Palaeolithic communities – perhaps even the largest part – and yet their existence had received little attention in archaeological and anthropological studies. Recently, however, a number of researchers have made useful contributions to the literature on the subject of growing up in the ice age. Nevertheless, it remains an area ripe for further exploration.

In the western world we use particular terms to define the biological stages of our human development, dividing our 'human life history' into five stages: infant, child, juvenile, adolescent and adult. These stages are not, however,

CAVORTING IN CAVES: THRILLS BUT NO SPILLS

Children were clearly not afraid to explore the far depths, narrow passages and tiny chambers of even the biggest caverns, whether alone (as at Aldène) or with adults (as at Le Tuc d'Audoubert). As we shall see (pp. 193-94), two young children played at leaving perfect footprints in the mud, hundreds of metres inside Niaux. This indicates that they not only had no fear of darkness or the strange unfamiliar subterranean world, but also that they must have been quite expert in the various lighting systems available to them (pp. 74-76). One can speculate that exploring in these dark, slippery places – often filled with tough climbs, tiny crawlways, obstacles, lakes or sheer drops – must have been a thrilling adventure, and an opportunity for displaying bravery or daredevil behaviour. And ice age people were clearly good at this, since not one unfortunate explorer's skeleton has ever been found lying on the floor of an Upper Palaeolithic cave, let alone one with broken bones. And yet they seem to have visited every nook and cranny of some major caves, sometimes risking their lives – for example the tiny, slippery decorated chamber in La Lloseta (Asturias) is an extremely tight squeeze to enter, and is at the edge of a drop down into Tito Bustillo cave, many metres below!

Figure 5.12. Elle Clifford in the crawlway of Le Tuc d'Audoubert.

Figure 5.13. a: The main chamber of the cave of Candamo (Asturias);

Figure 5.13. b: close-up of the decorated chamber high up (visible in the centre of the main photo), which is extraordinarily dangerous to reach, even today.

From an evolutionary point of view, it might seem that children's play is inefficient and costly; that is, it expends energy and increases their food requirements, and play can also increase the risk of an accident or injuries such as broken bones. However, we can be reasonably certain that children did play during this part of our prehistory, and that this was 'useful' to some extent – it is unlikely to have evolved and been selected for, unless it had some adaptive value for humans.

Contrary to the way we teach our own offspring to avoid touching and playing with dangerous objects, children growing up in the remote past may, from a very early age, have handled and carried around sharp tools, learning how to use them without injury to themselves or others. The Hadza believe that children *learn for themselves* what is dangerous, and adults allow very young children to handle sharp knives and blades as a necessity because tools are part of a forager's world in Hadza culture. Very young children thus quickly become effective tool users and proficient in many skills because they are allowed to play with knives and manipulate tools from an early age.

Figure 5.14. Maniq girl with a knife, Thailand.

observed in the same way by indigenous cultures, but developmental changes must have been noted by our hunter-gatherer ancestors. For example, the stage at which a child is weaned, the appearance or loss of teeth, learning to walk, or being old enough to light a fire, catch small animals or even use a spear may have been seen as landmarks in a child's life. In older children, stages may be marked by biological changes: the development of breasts, menstruation, or the growth of pubic hair or whiskers. It is not unusual in indigenous societies for the transition from childhood into adulthood to be marked by some sort of ceremonial 'rite of passage' or initiation ritual.

There are many different sorts of initiation ceremonies; some involve purification, or mastery of a difficult task; others require an intense or painful experience to show that the child (especially boys, but not exclusively) has courage and can endure pain.

It has been calculated that it takes around 13 million calories to feed a human infant through to the age of 18 years. That's a lot of food to find, cook and eat! We have already made the point that pregnancy and children are a 'high-cost' investment, but it doesn't stop there, as getting a child to adulthood also takes a huge effort for the extended family group. This would be especially so for those children with debilitating conditions like the youth from Romito (p. 33) and the youngster from Sunghir (pp. 24-28).

Human children mature slowly and are dependent on their mothers and the extended family for support, not only for food, but also to teach them the many skills required for their survival. Knowing how to make and use tools, light a fire, find suitable shelter, read the behaviour of animals and avoid predators, understand the surrounding landscape and various weather patterns, follow growing seasons and plant life – all of these would have been vital lessons. This expertise involves learning how to 'predict' in order not to miss any opportunity to secure a regular food supply.

However, it is far easier for prehistorians to reason *what* skills were required to survive the ice age than to establish *how* these lessons were transmitted. Were children 'told' what they needed to know, or was learning transmitted by observation and practice? What linguistic skills our early ancestors had acquired at this point remains something of a mystery (p. 213). Children growing up in a rich social context such as that provided by hunter-gatherer groups have the benefit of frequent attention, and can listen to conversations about daily life, future plans, gossip, and stories about ancestors and hunting exploits – all of which would undoubtedly be advantageous to their learning.

Ethnographers often report that, in surviving hunter-gatherer societies, there is little in the way of handed-down instructions to children, or teaching per se. Traditionally, children's learning is encouraged and developed by trial-and-error or by copying or mimicking their elders and acquiring their skills through direct experience and participation within the group. Young children can also learn opportunistically by exhibiting spontaneous behaviour (e.g. digging with sticks) or doing something by chance that is seen by adults as useful and therefore worth encouraging.

Did children learn to swim? We have no idea and can only ask the question. When people saw animals swimming across rivers they may have seen it as useful and given it a try. They needed to catch fish in fast flowing rivers,

FEMALE FIGURINES

Many of the ice age female figurines (pp. 9-11) are small enough to fit into a child's hand and may possibly have been teaching aids for youngsters. They were perhaps used to prepare girls for pregnancy and motherhood by teaching them to see these events as normal. Some could have been mascots or lucky charms. In some indigenous cultures, when a girl is old enough to have children she is given a doll to protect her and celebrate her fertility. Later this is given to her partner to help them conceive or to ward off a difficult childbirth.

If women were dressed all the time in heavy skins (perhaps even when they were asleep), then what opportunity did they have to look at themselves – or other women's naked bodies? There were no mirrors other than pools of water! Therefore some of the figurines could have been useful teaching aids to prepare females for menstruation, sex, pregnancy, childbirth and breastfeeding. However, if that is so, it is strange that not one figurine has the nipples depicted.

It has been proposed that some of the female figurines may symbolise 'the creating of life' in some way, that they represented a 'mother-earth ideal' of female fertility and the need to reproduce, or symbols of fertility, procreation and life – in short that women in the Upper Palaeolithic may have been admired for their reproductive powers. However, it seems far more likely that fertility was curbed during the ice age (p. 162).

The wide variation in the shapes of these statuettes strongly suggests they have different or multiple purposes. Each probably had its own symbolism and meaning, and this might have been conveyed to the viewer by the pose she holds, what parts of her body are accentuated (e.g. breasts or thighs), what she is wearing, or which decorative motifs and patterns are carved on her. Some have deliberate holes made in them and may have been worn as pendants or attached to clothing – polishing and wear facets confirm this. It is quite possible that these could have been made by females to represent something of great significance to women. We have no idea who carved them!

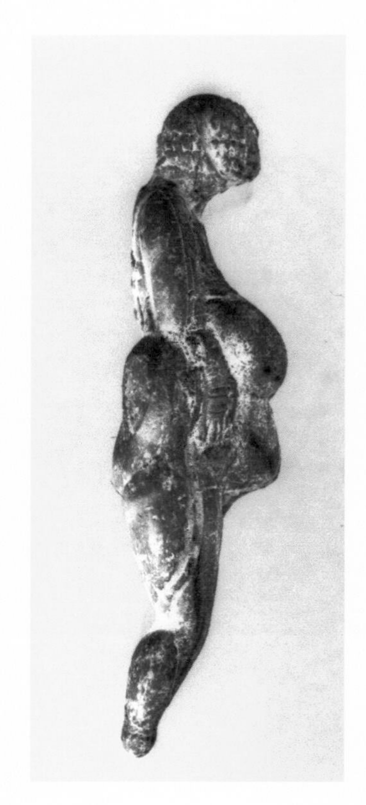

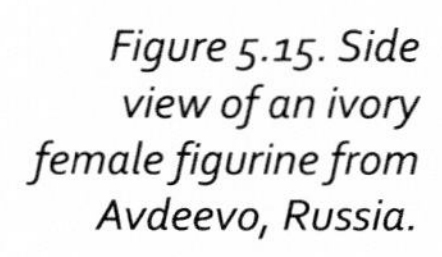

Figure 5.15. Side view of an ivory female figurine from Avdeevo, Russia.

collected marine products from the shoreline with the risk of getting cut off in rock shelters, and probably used small boats with the risk of falling in the water. So it is highly probable that they swam and washed in rivers and the sea (when the weather was at its warmest), but it would have been impossible to swim for long with heavy skin clothing on.

Hunter-gatherers rarely leave their children behind, and prefer to include them in all their activities away from home. The stereotypical view that only boys and fathers go on hunting trips together seems passé these days and, more importantly, the evidence does not support this notion. In many past and present indigenous populations, children of both sexes are taken on hunting trips, and it seems safe to assume that during the ice age all children needed to learn vital life skills in order to survive. It also seems that by merely observing adults and older children, young children can learn without the need of instructions. Children absorb the skills and knowledge they need almost by osmosis and by practising the various methods of chasing, trapping and catching animals through playing with other children.

Consequently, throughout the ice age, playing and learning subsistence skills could easily have been woven into daily life on gathering and hunting trips. On these excursions children would learn to track animals using signs, scents and sounds; navigate their way through the landscape; and be taught how to avoid any dangers.

Every culture has its own beliefs, language, signs and gestures, and even attitudes regarding the display of emotions. These behaviours are gradually taught to and absorbed by children, so that every child learns how to fit in with the accepted 'norms' of the group, including social behaviour, manners and habits, and rules of conduct.

Education and learning are part and parcel of our biological makeup and seem to have been designed by natural selection to enable young children to acquire their culture (in all its variants) through play and exploration. Most young animals play and chase, so it's probable that 'play' has deep evolutionary origins, and that children in the remote past had fun and played games. In some surviving hunter-gatherer societies (e.g. in the Kalahari), young children with miniature weapons like bows and arrows are encouraged to play-shoot at butterflies, toads and rodents. Eventually this leads to their becoming more skilled at killing small animals to add to the family diet. It is therefore reasonable to assume that miniature weapons or toy versions of tools and hunting equipment were given to children in the Palaeolithic. Evidence for this in the archaeological record would consist of functional miniatures of adult weapons and tools – for example, a little shovel carved from a mammoth bone was found in the burial of a four to five year old at Kostenki XV (Russia). The children buried at Sunghir (pp. 24-28) were accompanied by a number of ivory animal figurines and at least ten small ivory lances.

It is somewhat ironic that the one object from the Upper Palaeolithic that one might have assumed to be a toy – the ivory articulated 'doll' found at Brno in Moravia – came from the grave not of a child but of an adult male: the puppeteer, perhaps? Other than that, one can only speculate as to whether art objects were dolls (p. 188) or playthings. The very slim ivory female figurine from Laugerie Basse might be one such, as could the small figurines of children, women and birds from Mal'ta and Buret in Siberia (p. 103), the small crude terracotta figurine from Maininskaya in Siberia, or the terracotta statuettes from Afalou Bou Rhummel in Algeria, dating to between 18,000 and 11,000 years ago – but they could also be something more important, meaningful, ritual or mystical.

Figure ◀ 5.16. Ivory male doll, 13 cm tall and dating to c. 25,000 years ago, found in a grave at Brno (Czech Republic). Like those of a marionette, its head, arms and legs were once fastened to the body

It has been suggested that some of the many perforated shells found in ice age sites may have been used for babies' rattles. The stringing of perforated marine, freshwater, or terrestrial snail shells as a way of distracting and entertaining infants has been observed in many indigenous cultures. The fact that some Upper Palaeolithic youngsters seem to have worn a great deal of jewellery and decorated clothing, at least in the grave, has led to the suggestion that such

Figure ▼ 5.17. Terracotta human figure from Maininskaya (Siberia), 96 mm high, and dating to c. 16,500 years ago.

AN ENDURING MYTH: THE 'LION MAN'

One outstanding example of a popular and enduring myth about the ice age is the mammoth ivory statuette known as the 'Lion-Man', from Hohlenstein-Stadel (Germany). Found in 1939 in hundreds of small fragments, it was first reconstructed in 1969 and seen as a 'male statuette' with the head of either a feline or a bear. Over the years, as further reconstructions were carried out, some researchers decided that it was in fact a 'Lion Man', and this interpretation not only had popular appeal but has become firmly entrenched in the popular and academic literature. However, it is far more plausible that the figure represents a standing bear – bears often stand up like this – and it could in fact be the world's earliest 'teddy bear'!

Figure 5.18. Ivory statuette of the so-called 'Lion Man' from Hohlenstein-Stadel (Germany). Height: 31.1 cm.

embellishments were believed to have offered children and infants protection from harmful spirits. For example, the Xhosa of southern Africa adorn their babies and children with bracelets, armlets and anklets made from shells, seeds, and animal-bones.

The presumably humorous carvings at the end of antler spearthrowers depicting a fawn or young ibex excreting an enormous turd, with one or two birds perched on it (see pp. 227-28), could also have been playthings - but the amount of skill and effort put into carving antler in this way would argue more for valuable and prestige objects. It is extremely likely that ice age toys - which must have existed in great quantities - were primarily made of light and organic materials such as wood, bark, and basketry, and so have not survived. We have absolutely no way of deciding which other objects or tools might have belonged

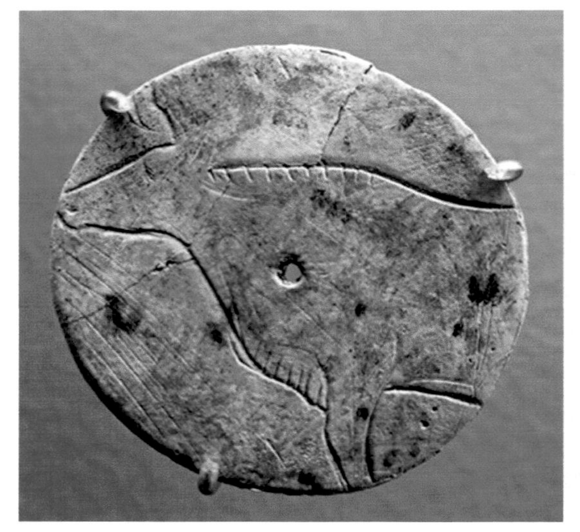

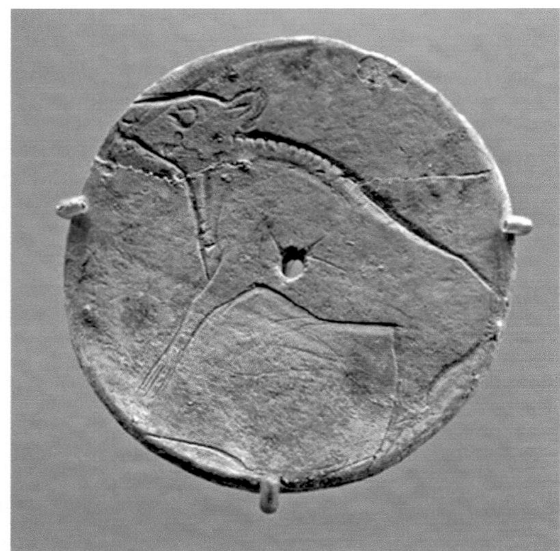

Figure 5.19. Engraved bone disc, with a central perforation, from Le Mas d'Azil (Ariège), with an aurochs on one side and a calf on the other. Magdalenian. Maximum diameter: 5 cm.

to children, unless they are found associated with them in graves – like the above-mentioned shovel.

Very few items have been found that are *clearly* children's playthings, but there is one category of object which may well have been made for the entertainment of youngsters. At Le Mas d'Azil in the French Pyrenees, archaeologists recovered a circular disc of bone, with an engraved image of a man and bear; it has a hole in the middle, presumably for a cord. When this was pulled, the disc would spin, and the image would seem to move -- in other words this seems to have been a very early 'thaumatrope'. Similar decorated pierced bone discs are also known from other sites in France, and appear to be optical toys that blend an image using motion. One can only imagine how thrilling these whizzing visuals must have been, and perhaps not just for children but all the family!

In addition ice age children probably collected curiosities like animal bones, feathers, pebbles, fossils and shells; collecting anything with striking features is ubiquitous in humans, and often starts in childhood. Both children and adults can have an urge to gather natural items from the landscape like stones, rocks, shells, or even things such as leaves and insects. Keeping insects and small animals as pets, although hard to prove, would have certainly been possible during the Palaeolithic.

Kids in caves – making a good impression

In addition to daredevil exploits (pp. 184-86), we have other kinds of evidence of children's activities underground. Almost all Palaeolithic footprints known so far have been found in caves in France, and the great majority are from children or adolescents. It seems that children, whether accompanied or alone, were not afraid to explore the narrow, twisted corridors and find their way around these

Figure 5.20. Prehistoric footprints of three children in the Réseau Clastres (Ariège).

dark and challenging places. Sadly, it has now become apparent that many footprints – as well as engravings on the clay floor – have been destroyed by later visitors to the caves or, in recent times, by investigators who, in their eagerness to search for art on the walls, have inadvertently damaged the evidence under their feet.

Why are almost all the footprints in caves those of youngsters? It is highly unlikely that they can all be explained by ideas about initiation ceremonies and the like. Instead, it can be far more plausibly explained by the fact that children are always wandering off, away from the main paths on which the more frequent traffic would obliterate adult footprints.

In the Grotte Chauvet (Ardèche), the footprints of a child, aged eight or nine, have been found at the back of the cave. They stretch for about 50 m, under a low ceiling, and the child may have been heading for a water source. The youngster was about 1.3-1.4 m high, and the width/length ratio of its prints suggests a boy. Two prints of a clay-covered right hand at the bottom of a decorated panel seem to have been made by the same child, since their size corresponds well with that of the footprints.

In the Réseau Clastres (Ariège), more than 500 prints have been found – they are not definitely Palaeolithic, but it is quite likely that they do date to that period. There are three trails side by side of small feet, 18 to 21 cm long, representing children who were probably 8 to 10 years old. They were walking normally, not running or jumping. In other caves there is evidence that they were not only totally relaxed in these dark depths, but even played there. At Niaux (Ariège) there is a large group of footprints in clay near the Galerie Profonde – 24 complete prints and 15 toe or heel marks. They represent two children, aged about 8 and 11, weighing between 27 and 30 kg, and between 1.33 and 1.39 m tall; they came at least twice to this low muddy area, and they spent some time and effort in carefully making the most perfect prints that they could.

Other indications of play activity can be detected: in the cave of Fontanet (Ariège) a little child of about five – who also left knee- and handprints – seems to have pursued a puppy or a fox into the cave's depths, since the animal's tracks are next to its prints. In the same cave there are also traces of adolescents playing together, throwing clay balls at each other. This is reminiscent of the

Figure 5.21. Prehistoric footprints in Niaux (Ariège), carefully and deliberately made by two young children.

Figure ◀ 5.22. Hand print of a young child in the cave of Fontanet (Ariège).

Figure ▼ 5.23. Some of the clay pellets on the wall of Toirano Cave.

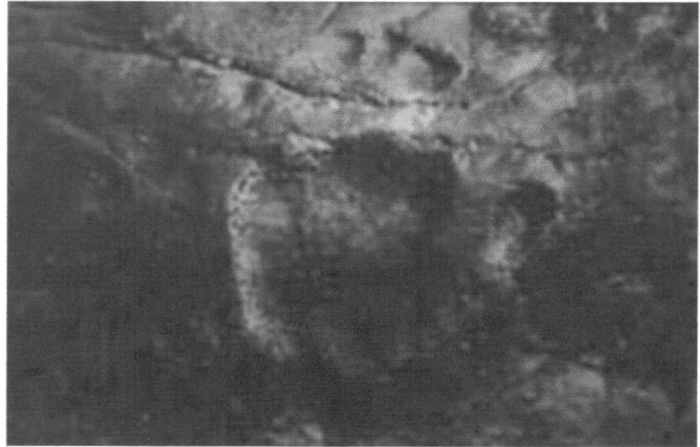

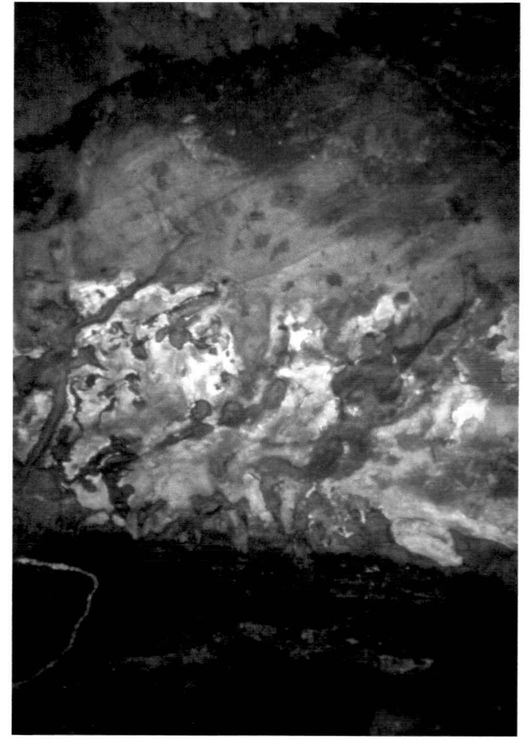

Italian cave of Toirano, where, in the innermost chamber, dozens of clay pellets were thrown at the back wall and also at a stalagmitic formation nicknamed the 'sphinx' – many pellets missed and lie on the cave floor; they are 3 to 7 cm in diameter. In Toirano, the activity dates to around 13,000 years ago, which is also the likely date of Fontanet on the basis of its art's style.

Finally, what is also probably play activity can be seen in Le Tuc d'Audoubert (Ariège), where

Figure 5.24. The two clay bison of the Tuc d'Audoubert (Ariège). Probably Magdalenian. The bison are 63 and 61 cm long respectively.

children clearly accompanied the artists who made the famous clay bison at the far end of the cave. Their small footprints can still be seen. The 'Heel Chamber', next to the clay bison, contains at least 183 heelprints, from children or adolescents moving around under a low ceiling (1.2 to 1.5 m high). It was originally estimated that these were made by five individuals; but a recent examination by Namibian Bushman trackers found that in the cave as a whole, no less than 14 individuals had left prints, half of whom were infants or adolescents. It is important to note that the Heel Chamber also contains a wealth of finger marks and simple drawings on its floor, which could be deeply mystical and significant (just as the heelmarks were long supposed to be some kind of ritual dance), but are perhaps more plausibly seen as the activities of bored children passing time while the adults were making the sculptures. Similarly, the placing of a cave bear skull on a rock in Chauvet cave has predictably been seen as evidence of a cave bear cult (p. 246), but of course it is just as likely that the skull arrived there by natural processes, that it was put there by a child amusing itself while the adults produced the art!

Children not only made fingermarks on the ground but also marked the walls and ceilings of caves. For example, on the famous ceiling of Pech Merle (Lot), almost all the markings were made by adults, but there are also two bands of lines that were clearly made by two small hands, those of either a woman or an adolescent. At this point the ceiling was 1.8 m up, and so quite reachable. These markings are known as flutings – simple lines made with one or more fingers, often the middle three fingers, by moving them over the soft clay or 'moonmilk' on the surface of the interior walls and ceilings inside limestone caves. This activity has created panels of long streams of 'flutings' that have survived, often in pristine condition, for thousands of years.

Recent studies have found that there is no perceptible difference between the finger widths of teenagers and adults, but there is a major difference between young children and older people. Very few children younger than two to three years can make fluted lines. In the French cave of Rouffignac, what may be Palaeolithic flutings (though their age is uncertain) include some made by children and others by teenagers or adults. It is noteworthy that the ceiling in places is just reachable by a man of 1.8 m stretching on his toes, so it is obvious that the children were lifted up to make the fingermarks. Why? Why does one not find adult flutings on high surfaces and children's flutings on lower ones, as would seem more likely?

Another case of an infant being lifted up has been found in the French cave of Cosquer (Bouches-du-Rhône), where a child's hand was pressed into the soft surface of a wall 2.2 m up, so it must have been either lifted up or sitting on an adult's shoulders. There is another handprint nearby, 2.4 m up, with an engraving of a possible sea animal between them. Elsewhere in the cave, traces of a child's four fingers covered in clay (total width 5 cm) can be seen on the moonmilk, in two instances, at a height of 1.9 m. Therefore at least one child – and perhaps several – had access to the deepest parts of this cave.

In the cave of Gargas (Hautes-Pyrénées), a child's or even a baby's hand was held to the wall by an adult while pigment was blown or spat over it. Elsewhere in the cave, a baby's hand was stencilled in black, and other hand prints and stencils of children are also known here.

Apart from the prints and markings surveyed above, the only examples of cave art which could plausibly be attributed to children are those in places which only small people could reach – for example, the decorated gallery of Fronsac (Dordogne) is only 35 cm wide; a passage of La Pasiega (Cantabria) filled with geometric motifs is also very difficult for an adult to enter, as is one of the side chambers of Bédeilhac (Ariège); and recently, experienced speleologists managed to push farther into Les Combarelles I (Dordogne) than ever before and found that Upper Palaeolithic people had got through to here and made drawings. If modern adult speleologists find it almost impossible to get through, then it is likely that the Palaeolithic explorers were either youngsters or very small and athletic adults.

A few researchers have claimed that much cave imagery may have been made by children, but the mastery of technique and form displayed in the figures made even in the most difficult places strongly suggests that adults were responsible – just as the amazing quality and the depth of knowledge of animal anatomy and behaviour displayed so prominently in most Palaeolithic images

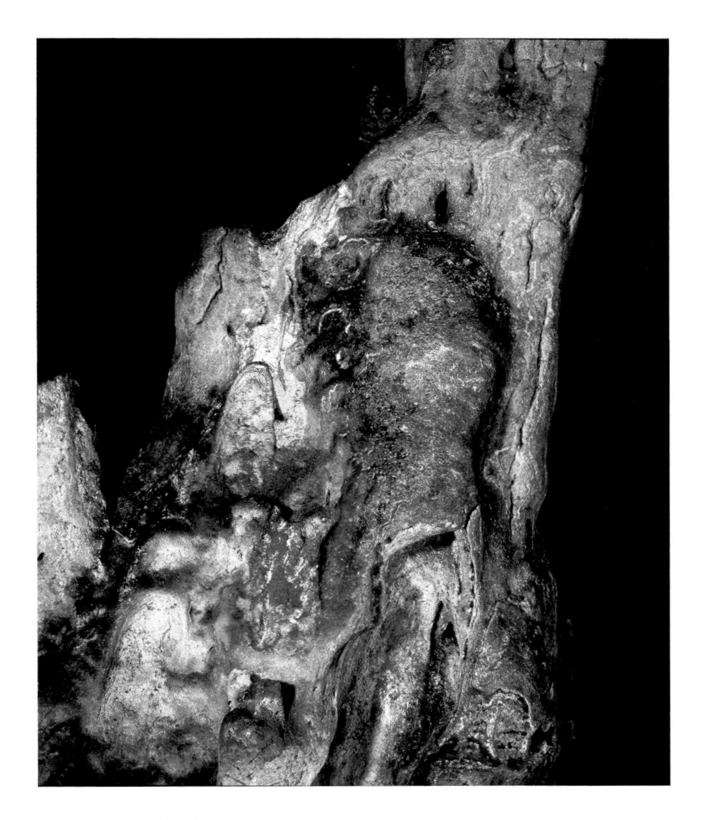

Figure 5.25. Vertical bison painted at El Castillo (Santander), utilising the shape of a stalagmite for its back, tail and hind leg. Probably Magdalenian. Length: 80 cm.

make it clear that experienced adults were the artists. It is certainly true that children can draw and paint from as young as three years of age, so it could be argued that the absence of figurative images made by them on rocks and cave walls confirms that the purposes of 'art' during the ice age were highly complex (p. 240), and not something children were able to communicate. In addition, engravings far outnumber paintings in ice age imagery, and it takes considerable strength, as well as skill, to engrave on stone.

Some caves and open-air decorated sites could have been 'classrooms' for children to learn; indeed, in a few caves what appears to be 'ideal' seating can be found directly opposite a display of artwork. The images were created and 'fixed' permanently so as to communicate and explain their significance, and the rocks and cave walls provided the perfect setting for retaining important information. Many of the decorated caves have festoons of stalactites hanging from the ceiling and stalagmites projecting upwards from the ground; many galleries are quite fantastic and create an atmosphere of wonder and awe – a world that simply does not exist outside. The irregular surfaces of cave walls, with their natural cracks and fissures, are the perfect foil for 'performance art'. Indeed, in some caves, concretions that look like a particular animal have been enhanced to look 'even more like' and emphasise the features of a particular animal – for example, the 'bison man' in El Castillo cave (Cantabria).

Painted murals of animals can almost come alive with the addition of the flickering light from torches or hand-held lamps; these create shadows that appear to move with the animals. Illuminated cave walls can often glisten with water exuding from the walls, and tiny particles of the quartz in the calcite rock sparkle when light moves over the surface. In this shadowy context, one can imagine how exciting the 'cinematic' effect of painted animals would have been to our distant ancestors, particularly if accompanied by storytelling and music. Indeed, the effect is no less thrilling for anyone fortunate enough to visit these awesome settings today. In some caves it seems obvious that the 'spectacle' within has been stage managed, most notably in Niaux's Salon Noir, the highest part of the cave, with a fully decorated 'backdrop' and fantastic acoustics. At Covaciella (Asturias),

Figure 5.26. Part of the main panel at Covaciella (Asturias). The bison at upper right measure 62 cm (left) and 76 cm (right) in length; the lower bison measures 69 cm. Magdalenian.

holes in front of the main decorated panel suggest that a screen existed here, perhaps to help dramatize the story-telling (see pp. 221-22)?

Death in the ice age – good grief!

Mobile people such as ice age hunter-gatherers may have had to deal with the death of a person while in transit from one living site to another. We can only imagine the difficult choice facing them – either abandoning the dead body en route, or carrying the remains to their destination camp. It is likely though, as in many of the situations humans have to deal with, that the 'process' of burial became formalised and ritualised in some way in their community. Formal burials imply funeral rites, but whatever meaning our early ancestors attached to the process is forever lost to us. It must remain a matter of speculation, despite claims to the contrary, whether or not these early cultures believed there was a life after death.

Bereavement psychology has grown as an area of interest in recent times, along with our understanding of the experience of loss and grief. The symptoms of grief are universal, and we can assume that a sense of sadness at the loss of a loved one goes far back in our evolutionary history. We can suppose with some confidence that rituals surrounding death and burial went some way to meeting the needs of those bereaved, by formalising or structuring death into a process of 'what to do and how to behave' in these circumstances. A 'gathering' of people gives support to those grieving; they can comfort the family and each other, express their sorrow, offer grave goods and indicate respect for a community's values and beliefs.

In a few cases, it seems clear that a memento of a deceased child was carried around. As mentioned earlier (p. 44), the Magdalenians put two holes into a newborn's parietal bone from the abri du Veyrier. The Pyrenean cave of Enlène yielded a perforated fragment of a child's mandible, covered in red ochre. It was very worn and polished, and had clearly served as a pendant for a long time. Two teeth were present – an incisor and first molar – and as the latter had erupted, the child must have been between 12 and 18 years old.

Ritualised burials appear to have emerged in Europe during the Gravettian, and there is a remarkable similarity in the funerary style that extends in this period from Western Europe to distant populations in Russia, which gives support to the notion that strong communication and trade networks existed between these populations (p. 207). In the words of Margherita Mussi, 'it is a fascinating thought that, more than 1000 generations ago, humans of Siberia may have been aware that many months of walking to the west – actually more than 8000 kilometres away - there were still people, different from themselves, yet in many respects similar.'

During the Middle Palaeolithic period – ca. 250,000 - 40,000 bp – when Neanderthals were the dominant humans living in Europe, approximately a quarter of individuals (purposely) buried were children, infants, and even foetuses. It has been suggested that the paucity of *Homo sapiens* child and infant burials during the Upper Palaeolithic – 40,000 - 10,000 bp, the last ice age – was

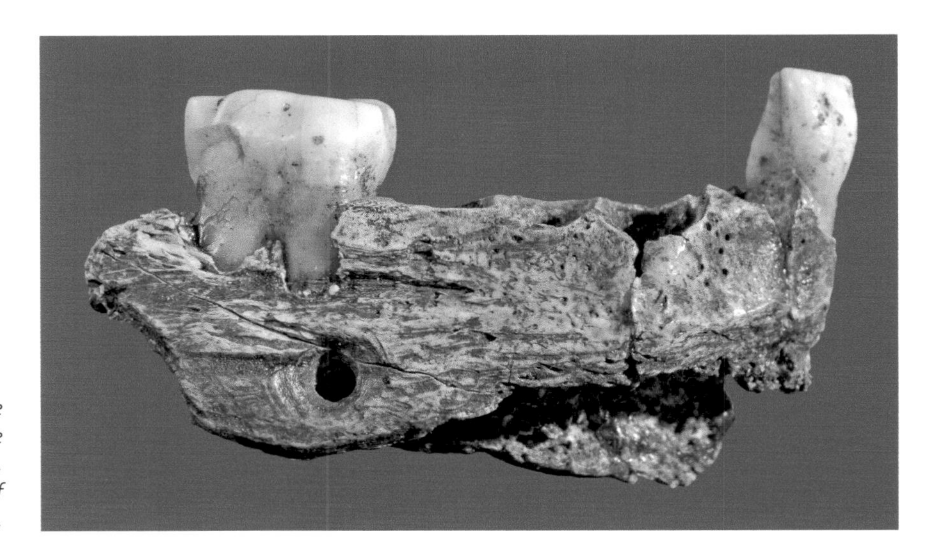

Figure 5.27. The pendant made from a child's jaw, from the cave of Enlène (Ariège).

related to the notion of 'personhood,' the idea being that some primary cultures do not consider that children exist as independent individuals until they are weaned from their mother. In hunter-gatherer societies this is usually when they can walk independently and keep up with adults – about three to four years of age – but one should bear in mind that numerical age is not relevant in these cultures and would not have been so in the distant past either.

However, there may well have been a point in time when children were buried like other family members, but the younger ones, like newborns or infants, were discarded without a sense of loss. Funerary practices are likely to have varied over these long time periods, and in different or incoming cultures; subtle changes in customs can eventually become extreme changes in a population's behaviour over time. Arrangements for death and mortuary practices and rituals to deal with it have changed markedly over the millennia of recorded history, as have beliefs and religious customs and conventions. Even the 'experience' of death for those still living, and beliefs in an afterlife, have altered through time and been transformed by different cultural influences.

We have already presented several examples (e.g. Sunghir, La Madeleine, Grotte des Enfants, Lagar Velho, etc) which show clearly that some, if not all, children were given elaborate interments. It is possible that these individuals had received 'special' treatment for a particular reason, and perhaps these examples are not representative of how children were usually treated in death by these early communities. On the other hand, one could argue that *all* children may have had special burials and high status simply because they were children, of huge importance to the communities due to the enormous effort invested in their upbringing – in other words, all children were special.

One recently discovered example lends support to this argument. A burial in the cave of Arma Veirana in north-west Italy, dating to immediately after the end of the ice age (c. 10,000 years ago), contained the badly preserved remains of an infant. Tooth development and post-natal enamel formation revealed that it died at an age of 40 to 50 days. Genetic analysis revealed that it was female. The body had been adorned with at least 66 perforated shell beads (*Columbella rustica*) and three perforated and polished shell pendants (*Glycimeris*). These seem to have been sewn onto a blanket, hood or other garment. Many of the beads are so worn that they were clearly not made for this burial. Nevertheless, their abundance indicates considerable material and emotional investment in the infant's burial, and suggests that the people of this time attributed personhood to near-neonatal girls – in other words, that baby girls were recognised as members of society.

The Romito dwarf (p. 33) was obviously supported and cared for by his family, but one can't discount the idea that some unwanted or disfigured infants were disposed of, either soon after birth or if they became a liability. A woman still nursing one infant, with little or no support from other females, may have had little choice but to reduce her burden, especially if food was difficult to procure.

Alternatively, infants may have been 'adopted' by another kin group that had lost or didn't have enough children. We will never know what psychological dilemmas they faced – or the choices they had to make. It's also possible there would have been variability in how the different cultural complexes dealt with these issues, and behaviours probably altered over time. Nor can we be sure how children were recognised in these early cultures, although the elaborate burials of infants and children give us no reason to suppose that mothers and close family felt less affection for their loved ones than we do.

That being said, in Western societies there exists a 'sense of ownership' regarding our 'own' offspring. This is steeped in our legal system, and it would be a mistake to assume our prehistoric ancestors necessarily felt the same way about their children. Offspring may have been 'shared' by the family group, especially if, as argued earlier, the extended family were 'co-operators' in the childrearing process. Indigenous populations often do not make the 'my/our' distinction, and all the children of their group or tribe are considered 'ours,' but one can safely assume that childrearing was of great importance to our Palaeolithic ancestors.

Although we will never know for certain what spiritual beliefs these ancient cultures held, it is possible that some cultures imagined there was a life after death – at least for some individuals – and that a burial was the beginning of a

THE YOUNG ITALIAN PRINCE

Arene Candide is a large cave system on the slopes of Monte Caprazoppa in Liguria, along the Mediterranean Coast. Inside the cave, archaeologists discovered a necropolis, the burials of twenty individuals from the very end of the ice age. The remains were of both sexes, ranging from young infants to the elderly, and were probably deposited in two separate periods.

In 1941-2, excavators uncovered the skeleton of an adolescent male, estimated to be 15-18 years old, in an intentionally-dug shallow pit whose edge was defined by large limestone blocks. He had been placed on his back in an extended position, on a bed of ochre, with his head facing south and the right forearm bent upwards. Ochre had then been scattered over the boy's remains. The estimated date of the burial is *ca*. 23,000 years bp.

The richness of the grave goods and jewellery led to the young male becoming known as Il Principe, or the 'Prince.' His headdress and face covering were embellished with hundreds of perforated *Nassa* shells and stag canines. Pendants of mammoth ivory, perforated *Cypraea* shells, and four intact perforated moose antler batons were placed around his chest area: three batons were engraved and the fourth, larger, baton was not. They were arranged around Il Principe's remains and possibly strung together about his shoulder. Most spectacular of all the grave goods was the 25 cm flint blade that was placed in his right hand.

Figure 5.28. The 'Prince' burial from Arene Candide, in Genoa Museum.

It was noted that the left part of the boy's jawbone was missing and a large mass of yellow ochre had been used to fill the space it left. This was used either to heal a wound or to cover up the unsightly area. If the youth had had a tooth abscess, and the infection had spread to the head and neck and then entered his blood stream, it may have caused enough damage to his internal organs to result in his death. The reason why his appearance was important enough to try and cover up his unsightly wound even after death is fascinating, especially as he had a decorated mask placed over his face! Yellow ochre is rare compared to red ochre, which was used profusely in burials throughout the Upper Palaeolithic, and it may have served a unique purpose in this burial and for those preparing his body.

journey that continued into a spiritual realm where they had to look their best and needed their personal possessions and grave goods with them.

We can only wonder how they explained the natural phenomena they experienced. Anthropologists who study primary cultures and the beliefs and cosmologies of indigenous people have left us in little doubt that their beliefs are extremely complex and have been shaped by a different perspective of reality and how the natural world operates. This different way of experiencing life and 'being' in the world is extremely difficult for us – in the Western world, with our own 'shared reality' – to comprehend. In the next chapter we shall explore further what we can reconstruct of ice age social life, organisation and communication.

Chapter 6

Keeping in Touch: Communication, Social Life and Organization

'Every animal leaves traces of what it was;
man alone leaves traces of what he created'
Jacob Bronowski, *The Ascent of Man*, 1973.

So far we have focused primarily on physical matters – what our ice age ancestors did to survive, how they sustained themselves by hunting and foraging, how they kept warm and made shelters, raised children, and buried some of their dead. We now turn to matters of the mind – how they communicated with each other and passed on their knowledge – a far more challenging task! Without the support of the written word, how did they ensure their culture's precious knowledge would be remembered, and transmitted to future generations?

It is obvious that human life cannot be reduced to habitat, food and crafts. In recent decades the involvement of First Nations people around the world in archaeological investigations has made researchers acutely aware of the importance of kinship relations, belief systems, relationships between individuals and groups, and the symbolic meaning of places and landscapes. And while many of these aspects of ice age life are impossible to deduce from archaeological evidence, we can nevertheless find some solid clues to their habits and thought processes.

Getting together

One of the most crucial aspects of hunter-gatherer life is the ability to get on with one's neighbours – cooperating and sharing resources when times are hard – while, at the same time, marking and guarding one's own group territory, in order to avoid taking wood or animal and plant resources which belong to others. We have no idea how territory was marked, although open-air rock art may have played a role here: for example, in Portugal's Côa Valley some of the bigger Gravettian pecked animal figures were placed where they could have been seen from a distance, and there is evidence (notably at the site of Faia) that originally there was red paint inside the pecked lines, which would have enhanced visibility. The sculpted friezes in rock-shelters like Cap Blanc and Angles-sur-l'Anglin, which were originally coloured, must also have been visible from some distance. There may, of course, have been numerous vivid paintings on prominent rock faces in the open air, but weathering will have destroyed them all over time.

Figure 6.1. The painted petroglyphs of aurochs heads at Faia (Côa Valley, Portugal.)

It is also possible that boundaries were marked in other ways – for example by wooden carvings which have long disappeared. In Siberia, however, one remarkable wooden carving has survived – the engraved anthropomorphic 'idol' of Shigir, found in 1894 (p. 89), which was 5.3 m tall, and has been dated to 11,600 bp. Made of larch, it has eight different faces, as well as geometric designs, and hints at a rich, complex symbolic and perhaps spiritual world.

As we have already seen, there must have been periodic gatherings of people from different areas, and perhaps the clearest evidence of this phenomenon is to be found in the two 'supersites' of the French Pyrenees: Isturitz (Pyrénées-Atlantiques) and Le Mas d'Azil (Ariège). Both are river tunnels, both have parietal art, both are important regional foci containing material from numerous periods, and both are ultra-rich in fine portable art objects.

Isturitz is the only major cave for miles around, so was probably a storehouse and meeting place, a socio-economic focus for people from a wide area. It was mainly used in the spring and autumn, but some people also stayed through the winter. The cave system comprises three superimposed decorated caves, and the upper cave (Isturitz itself) contained more portable art than all other caves in the whole Basque country combined. It was also a centre of production for small stone animal sculptures made of a sandstone from within a kilometre's radius, found in great numbers.

Figure 6.2. View of Le Mas d'Azil (Ariège) – the building provides the scale.

Both Isturitz and Le Mas d'Azil were clearly major workshops for their regions – as we have seen (p. 85), both had areas where antlers were accumulated and worked, and doubtless many other crafts involving flint and bone were also carried out in them on an important scale. There is also evidence for contact between them – for example, a sculpted fish at Le Mas d'Azil is almost identical to one at Isturitz. There are countless other examples of similarities between objects found in sites from Asturias to the Dordogne and beyond, especially in the Magdalenian, showing that people were in contact over great distances. There are also similarities in cave art – e.g. the Magdalenian bison of Covaciella (Asturias) and Santimamiñe (Basque country). The same applies to earlier periods – in the late Gravettian or Solutrean, the technique of drawing animals (mostly does) with an outline of red dots, displayed most remarkably in Covalanas cave (pp. 259-60), has been found in at least 14 caves in northern Spain, showing the temporary spread of a new idea, and perhaps the travels of one or more specialists.

The gatherings – perhaps annual at the local level, and less frequent at the regional level – must have been great occasions for socialising, making or renewing relationships, exchanging or bartering all kinds of tools, weapons, garments and adornments, swopping ideas and information, and last, but certainly not least, acquiring partners from outside the group.

How did people travel to and from such events? As we have already seen (pp. 123-28), they may well have used horses, reindeer or dogs to pull or carry equipment overland, but in some regions such as southwest France it would have been far more sensible and probably easier to travel by river. No ice age watercraft have survived – the oldest known are waterlogged Mesolithic dugouts from Denmark and Holland – but it is obvious that Upper Palaeolithic people were perfectly capable of travelling by water; for example, at Franchthi Cave (Greece), obsidian was found that had been brought from the island of Melos in the 12th millennium bp. In addition to dugouts, they may well have constructed rafts, or coracle-like boats of hides stretched over a wooden framework.

The clearest evidence we have for ice age movements comes from raw materials, fossils and shells that are found far from their sources. Some seashells travelled hundreds of kilometres from the Atlantic or Mediterranean to sites in the Pyrenees, Dordogne or northern France.

Dordogne sites (such as Laugerie-Basse, Abri Pataud, Abri Castanet) generally yield a high proportion of species from the Atlantic, particularly those which are common along the coast of Charente, but shells from the Mediterranean are also clearly represented. One finds the same ratio at the Atlantic end of the Pyrenees; but sites in the Central Pyrenees, such as Lespugue, at a distance of 200 km from either coast, contain a more even ratio, while further to the east, in Ariège (e.g. at Enlène), the proximity of the Mediterranean is reflected quantitatively in the shell collections, although even here Atlantic shells dominate slightly – this is no doubt because all rivers in the French Pyrenees (apart from those at the eastern extremity), like those of Dordogne, flow out to the Atlantic, and this must have determined to a considerable extent the movement of people and materials.

It is theoretically possible that all the shells came inland in an exchange network involving 'maritime peoples' for whom we have no evidence whatsoever thanks to the drowning of the coastlines of the last ice age through the rise in sea-level since that time. Certainly, a great deal of exchange went on; for example, Mediterranean shells have been found 1000 km away at German sites like Gönnersdorf and Andernach, while marine shells at Yudinovo (Russia) came from the Black Sea coast, a distance of at least 680 km. There is ample evidence throughout the Upper Palaeolithic for repeated contact with the coasts which involved not merely vague 'exchange networks' but also probably the seasonal movements of people, following herds, and dispersing or coming together in certain places at different times of year.

Figure 6.3. Perforated amber elk head, 4 cm long, from the open-air site of Weitsche, Germany, about 14,000 years old.

Fossil shells likewise travelled far – at Enlène they came from Aquitanian sources, over 200 km away. Sites on the Russian plain such as Mezin have fossil shells – mostly turned into beads – which are 300-800 km from their sources, and bits of amber from 100-200 km away.

In the Magdalenian, no less than 109 implements – mostly projectile points – of whale bone have been identified in 11 Pyrenean sites (no less than 63 of them at Isturitz). Exclusively of Atlantic origin, doubtless from animals stranded on the shore, they show that such implements were transported up to 350 km in an extended coastal-inland network. A further 54 whale bone points are known from 12 sites along the north coast of Spain, as far west as Asturias.

Highly prized stones like jasper, obsidian, pumice, steatite, pink sandstone or rock crystal often came from afar, presumably through exchange. In Russia, amber beads found at Dobranichevka were from at least 150 km away, while Voronovitsa had obsidian from at least 300 km away. Flint of good quality was also desirable – many Pyrenean Magdalenian sites mostly used the mediocre local flint but also contained blades and tools of Dordogne flint (from more than 200 km away), but no cores. For example, Le Mas d'Azil had a cache of three fine blades whose morphology and quality were not Pyrenean, and which were imports from the Dordogne. By contrast, at northern Magdalenian sites like Etiolles, Pincevent, Verberie, etc, the cores are there but the removed blades are not – so they were clearly traded, or taken with them when the sites' occupants went elsewhere.

Obviously, we will never know which specimens travelled directly from source to archaeological site, and which were exchanged or traded through space and time, and hence travelled in stages. One can find similar examples in other parts of the world in the same period – for instance, exchange networks of ostrich eggshell beads have been found in Lesotho, from c. 33,000 years ago, spanning hundreds of kilometres. They are thought to have been a medium of personal decoration and symbolic gift exchange that built relationships of mutual support and bound social networks together. One can only speculate as to whether some ornaments or prestige goods constituted some kind of 'money'!

Ice age bling

As mentioned earlier (p. 14), tattoos, body paint and scarification may well have existed in the ice age, but the only kind of bodily decoration for which we have direct evidence is jewellery. What has survived comprises all kinds of beads and perforated materials such as shells, teeth, fish vertebrae, fossils and exotic stones (including amber and steatite), but one can safely assume that they must also have used feathers and claws and talons, since we know that Neanderthals did so long before.

The animal teeth, perforated through the root, are mostly bovine and horse incisors and the canines of fox, stag, wolf, bear or lion – fox teeth are often the most abundant in the Aurignacian and Gravettian, especially in central and eastern Europe. For example, the adult male buried at Sunghir had two dozen perforated fox canines sewn on the back of his cap, and more were found with the two youngsters buried at the site. Over 50 perforated fox canines were found in Kostenki XVII and are dated to 32,000 years ago, while 150 covered the head of the child buried beside Kostenki XV. In Le Tuc d'Audoubert one can see cave bear jaws that were smashed by the Magdalenians to extract the canines.

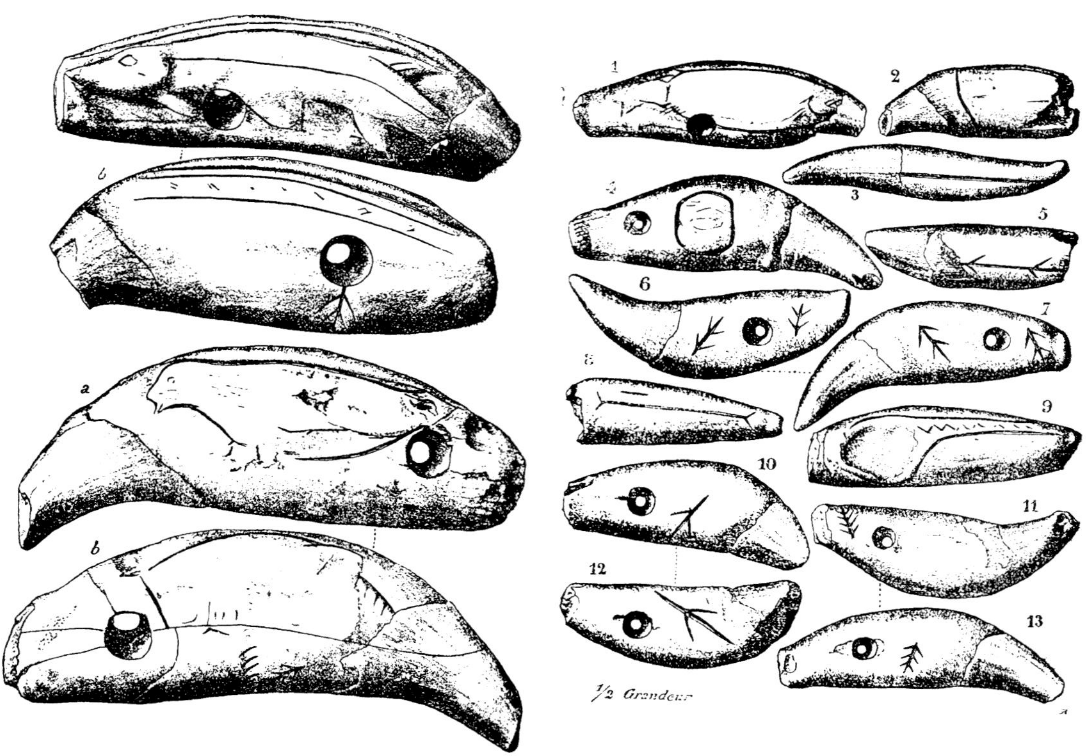

Figure 6.4. Engraved bear canines, including a depiction of a seal, from Duruthy (Landes).

At Duruthy (Landes), a skeleton was found with a necklace or belt of lion and bear canines, some of them bearing engraved motifs including a seal, a fish, 'harpoons', etc.

In western Europe, particularly in the Magdalenian, red deer stag canines were the favoured decoration; these prestige items were so rare that they were probably obtained through long-distance trade, and were a sign of wealth, as also among some North American Indian tribes in recent centuries. The best known are the 71 perforated specimens, dating to 15,570 bp (the biggest collection known from a single burial), found around the neck and chest of the woman buried at St Germain-la-Rivière (Gironde), 20 of which are engraved with crosses or parallel lines. Another collection of 196 deer canines came from a multiple burial of eight people, of both sexes, at Aven des Iboussières in southeast France, dating to around 10,200 bp; 49 of these items were decorated with notches. If these rare teeth were unobtainable, copies were sometimes made in bone, ivory or stone.

The popularity of canine teeth continued to the end of the Upper Palaeolithic, but in the Magdalenian there was an increase in the practice of sawing reindeer incisors: over 50 have been found at La Madeleine and Gönnersdorf, and over 200 at Petersfels (Germany). Their occasional discovery in rows shows that, as among some northern peoples in historical times, their roots were sawn

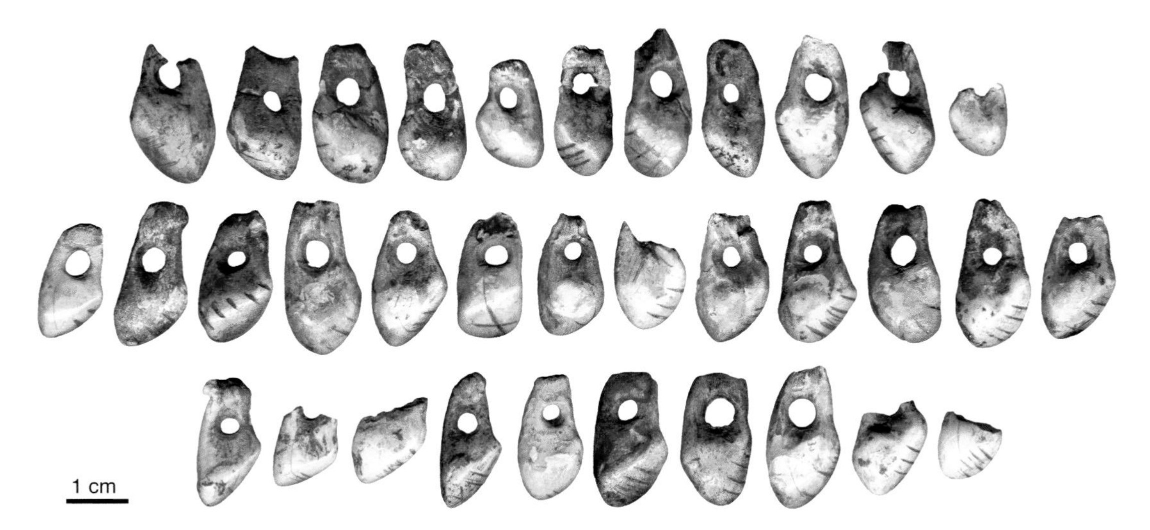

Figure 6.5. Perforated and engraved deer canines from the Magdalenian burial at St Germain-la-Rivière (Gironde).

through, and they were then cut from the mouth as a group, still held inside a strip of gum which was handy for hanging them as a string of 8 'pearls'. Occasionally, one encounters the teeth of other species used as pendants: eight perforated human teeth are known from sites in France (p. 44) and one from the Gravettian of Dolní Vestonice (Czech Republic). There are also pierced seal teeth from the Magdalenian of Isturitz.

One popular kind of ornament was the 'contours découpés' – bone cutouts. About 150 of them are animal heads (about two thirds of them horses) cut from a horse hyoid (bone of the tongue), the natural shape of which already bears some resemblance to a herbivore head. Many are perforated – some through the nostril or eye, presumably for figurative effect, and others probably to serve as pendants – and they have differing degrees of detail engraved on them: eyes, muzzle, coat, and so forth. Over 80% of them have been found in the French Pyrenees, although sites in Asturias and Cantabria have also produced a few very fine specimens of exactly the same type. No doubt the most outstanding find, hidden in a corner of the cave of Labastide (Hautes-Pyrénées), is what seems to be a necklace of 18 identical perforated heads, apparently of the isard (Pyrenean chamois) with its cold-season markings, together with one perforated bison head, all cut from horse hyoids; this remarkable ensemble was clearly made by a single artist of great talent.

It is worth noting that, like portable art as a whole, the distribution of 'contours découpés' is extremely uneven: of those in France, about two thirds come from three Pyrenean sites (the 'supersites' Mas d'Azil and Isturitz, plus Labastide because of its necklace); if those from Arudy are added, it means that over 75% come from only four sites. Cutout bone discs (rondelles or rodetes) – some of them perforated and engraved (p. 192) – are rather more widespread, but over half of them come from the Pyrenees, with Isturitz and the Mas d'Azil again

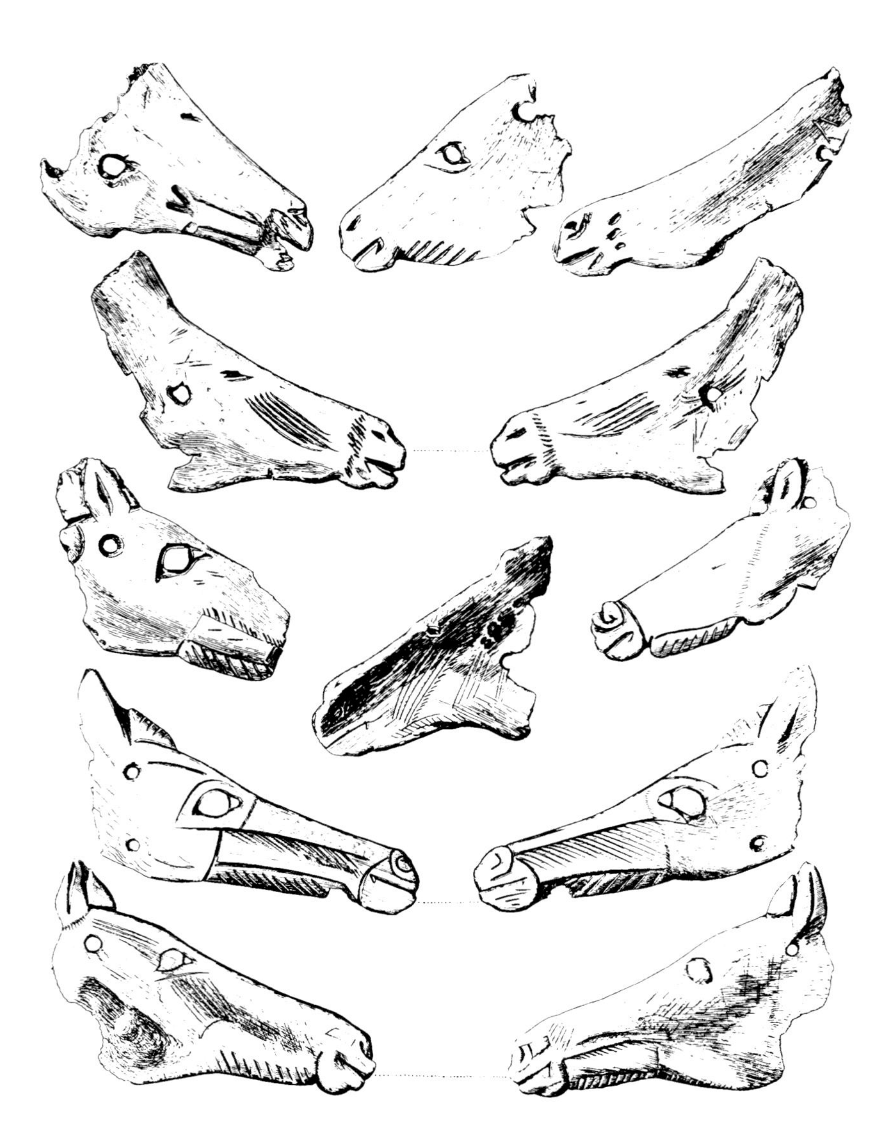

Figure 6.6. Bone 'contours découpés' of horse-heads from Isturitz.

the richest sites. Enlène has yielded four intact specimens, but more than 80 fragments!

As for shells, only a few species were selected: primarily small, globular gastropods (such as *Littorina* and *Cypraea*) which could easily be sewn to clothing; long forms (such as *Dentalia* or *Turritella*) which could easily be strung; and a few scallops (*Cardium*, *Pectunculus*). Many of these species are inedible, and their function was clearly decorative rather than nutritional. Most Upper Palaeolithic specimens were perforated with a pointed tool. They are often found in considerable quantity, even in early sites – there were 300 in the Aurignacian Cro-Magnon burial alone, and hundreds more in other burials –

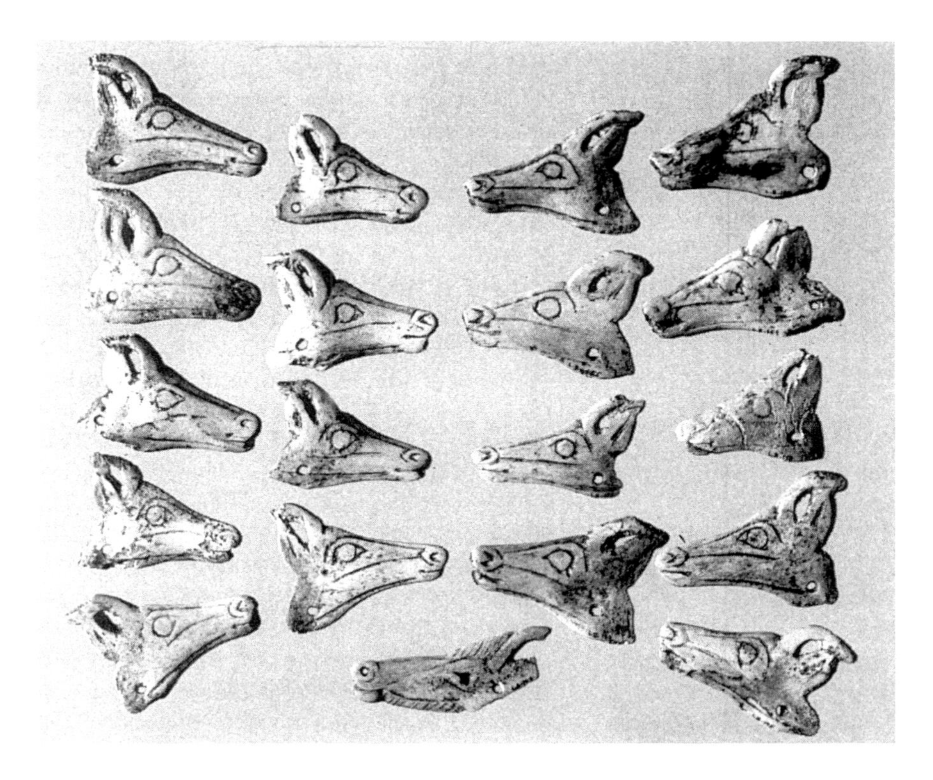

Figure 6.7. The necklace of isard heads, plus one bison head, from Labastide.

while living-sites such as Isturitz or the Abri Blanchard (Dordogne) contained hundreds of periwinkles. Fossil shells were also utilised, and sometimes came from great distances, as shown above. The shells of land molluscs were rarely used, no doubt because they are thinner and more fragile.

As we have seen (p. 110), beads and shells have frequently been found in great numbers in graves – on the head, neck, arms, legs, and sometimes all over the body. The three Sunghir bodies (pp. 24-28) also had ivory rings on their fingers. At Pavlov 7, fine ivory rings were found which were so fragile that they are unlikely to have been worn all the time. However, although most of the surviving jewellery has been found in graves, we know that it was not confined to the dead: necklaces and bracelets and anklets can be seen in depictions such as the Femme au Renne (Laugerie-Basse), two women at Isturitz, and at La Marche. One may speculate that ornaments indicated one's availability, age, clan or level in the hierarchy. Moreover, many beads and shells could have been attached, not to clothing, but to bags, baskets, musical instruments, tent walls, and so forth.

As with any other category of portable art, there is a marked differentiation in the distribution of ornaments: many sites in Europe (including some burials) have none or a few, and others have hundreds. The quantity of such objects doubtless depends on the intensity or recurrence of site occupation. But, a particular abundance may reflect the presence of independent, highly-skilled

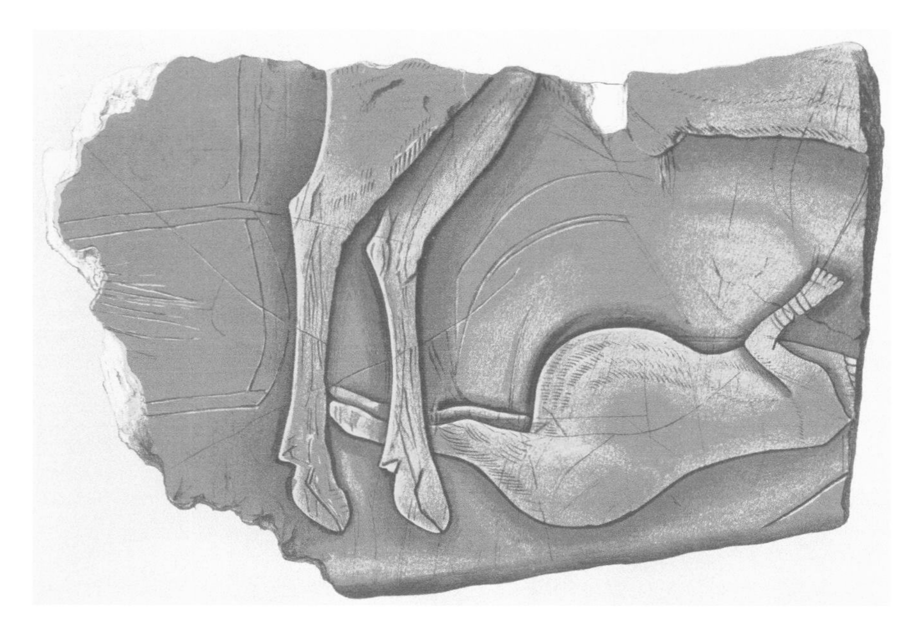

Figure 6.8. ◀ a: Drawing of the 'Femme au Renne' of Laugerie-Basse (Dordogne); ▼ b: Engraved bone from Isturitz (Pyrénées-Atlantiques) with two females (depicted either vertical or supine, judging from their breasts), one of whom has a barbed sign on her leg. Note the necklaces, bracelet and anklet. Magdalenian. Total length: 10 cm

and specialised craftsmen, as well as the varying functions of different sites (including clothing manufacture?), and perhaps even, where rich burials are concerned, some form of incipient hierarchy. This is particularly true of wealthy child burials, such as Sunghir (pp. 24-28) or the La Madeleine infant (pp. 107-9) – the children are most unlikely to have earned this prestige during their lifetime. On the other hand, as mentioned earlier (p. 200), one could argue that *all* children may have had special burials and high status simply because they were children.

People may well have used ornaments to identify with their group/community, with beads, shells and personal clothing acting as a status marker. Other aspects of differential distribution have emerged from a major study of Aurignacian jewellery. No less than fifteen regional groups were identified, but they were not dependent on availability of materials – for example, most of the mammal species whose teeth were used in southwest France also lived in Italy, but their teeth were not used there; and human teeth, on present evidence, were only used in southwest France in that period. So clearly the differences are purely cultural.

Language

If, as researchers believe, all these small communities did not share a language, they must have had symbolic ways (signs) of communicating information to each other. We cannot prove that they had a spoken language, but in view of the complexities inherent in many aspects of their lives, it seems safe to assume that they did. For example, there is no human society that refrains from gossiping, and gossip is likely to have been an important part of our ancestors' lives so they could keep track of other people in the group, share information about what others were doing and experiencing, and, through this vital knowledge, make inferences about the world around them.

It has been suggested by some researchers that language development was the key to our great leap forward. As utterances became longer and more complex (with more for the listener to process), this allowed for more complicated, flexible and creative thinking for planning future actions and for recalling past events. The ability to mentally simulate past and future scenarios and anticipate and predict future events – such as when the salmon will run, or seasonal and weather changes – brings a huge advantage: remembering past events allows humans to make the necessary plans in anticipation of the future events they have predicted.

If men were primarily responsible for hunting large game, this activity would have involved few verbal exchanges while the serious business of hunting was going on! Conversely, it follows that women, gathered together in domestic activities, or when collecting foods, would be talking 'constantly' with each other and their children. As a consequence this would result in women having been much more influential regarding the families' social organisation and the development of language per se.

We know absolutely nothing about their languages, but archaeology provides some insights into the kinds of information they needed to communicate to each other in order to be as efficient as possible in pursuing their challenging lifestyle.

Giving names to new ideas and imaginings is a very sophisticated way of thinking, as are myths. Myths are the part of a community's folklore concerned with 'sacred' stories or beliefs about their origins. Groups of people 'own' their folklore and beliefs, and these become encoded in myths over time. Our early ancestors may have composed verse, poetry, rhymes (and dances) as well as metaphors to preserve traditions. The ice age could have been a boom-time for metaphor – i.e. a figure of speech in which a word or phrase is applied to an object or action to which it is not literally applicable, such as 'have you *grasped* that idea?' – because so many new things were happening and connections were being made between things, both real and imaginary. Enhanced language abilities and the use of metaphor (something regarded as representative or symbolic of something else) must have led to asking meaningful questions

THERIANTHROPES

The strange depictions of fantastic or imaginary animals that sometimes appear in ice age imagery were probably metaphors for an important social message or belief that needed to be conveyed to a wider audience, or alternatively to a select few. But what name did they give to – and how would they have described – the complex therianthrope (part human, part animal) engraved and painted in Les Trois Frères? It is highly unlikely that the artist called it 'the sorcerer' or 'the horned god' like we do.

The Trois Frères figure is certainly strange: only the upright position and the legs and hands are really human. The rest is a mixture of different animals – the back and ears of a herbivore, the antlers of a reindeer, the tail of a horse, and the phallus in the position a feline would have it.

Having imagined this creature in all its complexity, they must have called it something equally complex. We have no idea what they believed about such 'supernatural beings', but since these unusual phenomena do not appear in Nature, they sprang from someone's imagination. Describing what they meant to others must have required an elaborate intellect, and the images were presumably used to convey a rich experience associated with a story, myth or metaphor to the viewer/listener, with a desire for it to be remembered. If acted out and in an exciting setting it would not easily be forgotten, as all the sensory apparatus had been invoked!

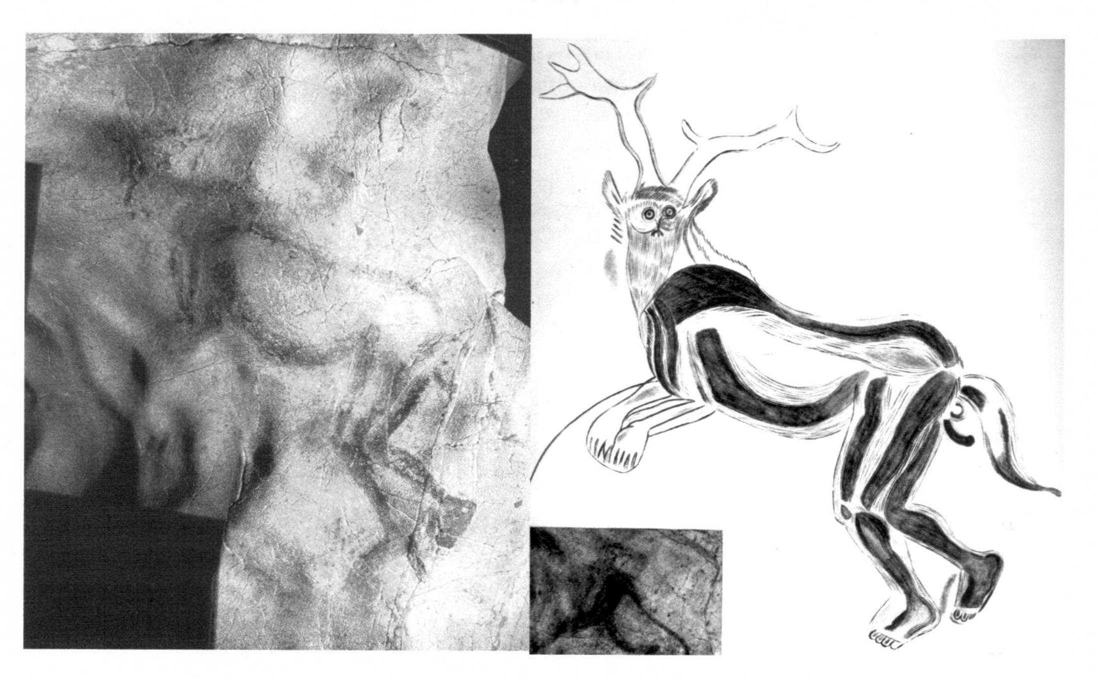

Figure 6.9. a: Photomontage of the painted and engraved 'sorcerer' of Les Trois Frères (Ariège). Probably Magdalenian. Length: 75 cm; b: Drawing of the 'sorcerer' in Les Trois Frères.

It is important to note that it took considerable effort to reach the 'sanctuary' where the Trois Frères figure is located. That cave was reached via that of Enlène – 235 m from Enlène's entrance is a 65 m-long corridor that leads to Trois Frères. It is impossible to stand up in it except at the end, and in three places one has to crawl! Yet it was much frequented and filled with archaeological material, including hundreds of plaquettes.

about the natural world – wondering why things happen the way they do – and coming up with explanations.

Myths and storytelling must also have been relied on heavily for the tremendous but crucial challenge of teaching someone the skill of predicting the future based on past experiences, even remote ancestors' experiences.

Thanks for the memory

It used to be thought that there was little innovation during the last ice age, and we hope that this book has gone some way to dispel this view. Some innovations can occur by accident or through mistakes that turn out to be useful – for example, finding Australia at least 50,000 years ago cannot have been a planned event because nobody knew it was there until they saw land!

What does seem clear is that people appear to have benefitted over this period of time from an improved memory capacity. There are many possible reasons why this could have happened. One early explanation was that Cro-Magnons 'invaded' Europe and rapidly replaced Neanderthals. This led to the founding of the Aurignacian culture and the 'golden age' of hunting and gathering. This view became a popular narrative both with prehistorians and the general public, and an image of our clever, brave and handsome noble savage ancestors quickly caught on. This view was also promoted by 19th-century scholars and archaeologists, and became known as the European replacement scenario.

This notion unfortunately led to all sorts of muddled thinking, especially in relation to human cognition, behaviour, symbolic ability, and language, particularly as no explanation was put forward as to why these early Cro-Magnon people had such enhanced abilities! Hopes of finding an increase in the Cro-Magnon skull size were dashed, especially as it turned out that cranial measurement is not so important when it comes to humans – what does matter is the organisational changes to neural networks within the brain. A number of theories about this development offer more credible explanations, but it should be remembered that the period spans 30,000 years and that's at least 1200 generations of humans – some might consider this was progress at a snail's pace!

One view is that the human brain developed due to improvements in diet quality and food nutrition. Another claims that changes in the neural structure of the human brain occurred due to a genetic mutation. Or it is just possible that humans found new external ways of storing knowledge, rules, and anything else they considered important enough to remember and communicate to each other. Enhanced language abilities and the use of metaphor would lead to asking meaningful questions about the natural world – why things happen the way they do – and coming up with explanations.

Of course any or all of the above factors could have interacted – and probably did so – to increase thinking, memory and verbal capabilities. For example, a better diet leads to an increase in brain functioning and innovative ways of remembering important information, while more efficient cooking practices would have led to improved digestion and increased energy for brain development. This would be especially important during an infant's weaning period when easily-digested bone marrow would have contributed to both brain size and physical development.

The 'genetic mutation' theory proposes that improved cognitive abilities and innovative thinking arose because of a change that affected the neural organisation of our ancestors' brains. The mental advantages would include enhanced working memory, intelligence, attention-span and memory storage; quicker information processing; better acquisition of language-vocabulary; and improved thinking and reasoning. 'Brain and culture' would have shaped one another over relatively short periods of time, and improvements would have been transmitted to future generations in memory-enhanced and innovative ways. However, not all specialists agree with this view, and some argue that any mental developments were not sudden or the result of a neural mutation, but rather that changes came about as part of a slow, gradual process over the many millennia of the Upper Palaeolithic.

Another view considers 'external' memory to be the issue of greatest importance – i.e. the use of symbolic representation and imagery to enhance memory and store information outside the brain. This, it is argued, was not due to a genetic change, but a cultural one that started and flourished with the invention of visual symbols and signs. Symbols convey a deeper and more complex meaning than a sign – signs usually convey something specific and unambiguous, but recognising the meaning of signs in nature, and having a permanent way of recording such signs, and not just by word of mouth, would have been a huge asset to the communal pool of knowledge.

Recording knowledge such as folklore, stories and myths, or just need-to-know information on cave- and rock-walls, portable artifacts, and a whole host of perishable items including clothing and their bodies was thus a means of 'externalizing' information storage for future recall. Having a symbol as cue for a memory, story or a need-to know thing, would have been a fantastic mnemonic

Figure 6.10. a: Geometric motifs in El Castillo (Cantabria);

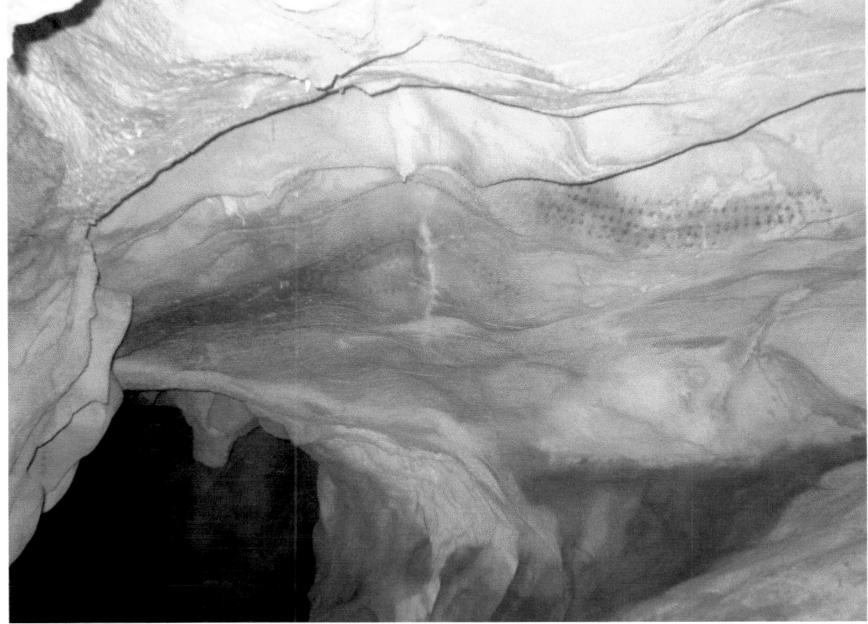

Figure 6.10. b: Geometric motifs in the cave of Chufín (Cantabria).

device! Over many generations, these relatively small communities would have *gradually* developed new representational devices that would have resulted in structural changes in the brain that allowed people to think, store and retrieve information much more successfully.

Figure 6.11. Horse and ibex figures, Penascosa (Côa Valley, Portugal).

These new ways of 'thinking and remembering' may have been a challenge that involved a great deal of imagination, original thinking, and complex mental manoeuvring. This would have been a very different method of remembering from the ones used by their predecessors, which must have depended almost entirely on 'working' memory, and without any way (that we know of) to store information externally. In short, everything their forerunners did, saw or heard had to be remembered by repeating it inside their heads (as thoughts) or as speech, stories or songs.

It is possible that all of these theories are correct and, if so, would have resulted in a phenomenal increase in people's ability to permanently record information, folklore and cultural memories that could easily be retrieved by future generations, and this would probably have increased a sense of group identity amongst those allowed access to these 'storage facilities.'

We now know that simple marks like blotches, dots, hand-stencils and geometric shapes were made in caves by Neanderthals, and this may have given our ancestors – who were doubtless quick to learn and adopt – an idea that this was a useful means of 'storing' and retrieving information that was 'good to know' and remember.

Big caves can be used as social spaces, and could have been a place to commune; the same applies to some of the major sites of open-air art like Portugal's Côa Valley. These were perhaps where people experienced a specific event together (a festival or a feast) – this would strengthen group ties and their collective memory and identity. Such gatherings also aid the retention and organisation of communal memories in a non-literate society without written records – a little like our taking photos of an event to help us remember it. Cultural memory is directed at fixed points in the past – sacred times, ceremonies – and these cultural memories are passed on to future generations who become the next keepers of the communities' or cultures' memories.

TELLING THE TIME

How did people know when it was time for regular gatherings or ceremonies? Clearly they must have had some means of keeping track of the passing of time.

It is possible that some of the engraved markings on portable objects, and especially on utilitarian items, may simply be decoration – although more may be involved even here, from marks of ownership to complex tallies and seasonal images. It is now clear that these highly intelligent people produced 'notations' – i.e. sets of marks accumulated as a sequence, perhaps from observation of astronomical regularities. Some linear sets of such marks (most notably a serpentine set on an Aurignacian object from Abri Blanchard) have plausibly been interpreted as possible examples of lunar notation: the most impressive and complex is a series of more than 1000 short incisions on an Upper Palaeolithic bone from the Grotte du Taï in eastern France. Microscopic analysis of a late Upper Palaeolithic bone from Tossal de la Roca, Spain, which has four series of parallel lines on each face, revealed that each set of its incisions was made by a

Figure 6.12. The Taï plaque, a rib fragment 8.8 cm long, with its complex, continuous serpentine accumulation of marks.

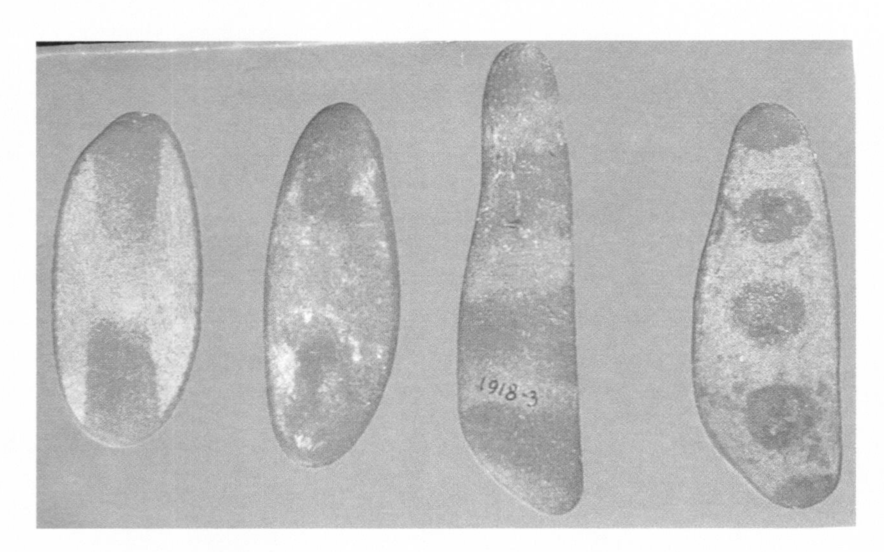

Figure 6.13. Selection of Azilian pebbles from Le Mas d'Azil (Ariège), each a few cm long.

different tool. There were also changes in the technique and direction of tool use between sets of incisions, which strongly suggests that these markings were accumulated over time, and thus may well be a system of notation. Furthermore, a technical analysis of the numerous markings engraved on an antler from La Marche, using criteria derived from experiments, suggested that the piece was an artificial memory system with a complex code based on the morphology and spatial distribution of the engraved marks.

These studies have focused attention on a type of marking which previously was ignored or dismissed as random; it is now clear that the marks are often coherent and ordered, and were carefully made over a period of time. Similarly, a study of the painted pebbles from the Azilian, the very end of the ice age, revealed that the 16 signs drawn on them were found in only 41 of the 246 possible binary combinations (indicating that some sort of 'syntax' was employed) and that there was a predominance of groups numbering from 21 to 29 or their multiples, which may again have some connection with lunar phases or lunations.

It is extremely probable that some of these prehistoric objects with engraved notches that conform to a pattern may relate to observations made by the carver about lunar phases. The phases of the moon – i.e. its waxing and waning – would certainly have been the principal means available to Palaeolithic people for measuring the passage of time. The night sky would have been much clearer and brighter during the ice age than it is today. People must have asked questions about the sky and invented stories to explain its phenomena.

Engraved bones like the ones cited above (some have deliberate holes suggesting they were worn) could also have been a convenient tool for ice age women wanting to keep track, for example, of their pregnancy and prepare for the birth. However, such a notion is entirely speculative, and these objects may have had another, or several other uses that we have yet to understand.

DRAMA IN CAVES

Caves can be places suitable for multi-sensory theatrical dramas, especially with the effects of smoking fires and smells – flickering light can make the painted images seem to move, and this, together with shadow-play, has the effect of 'bringing alive' or animating painted and engraved images. The most theatrical of all the caves is Niaux with its great decorated back-wall in the Salon Noir with its incredible acoustics (p. 234). The location of Tito Bustillo's main panel close to the thundering sound from the underground river is clearly no coincidence (p. 249).

Exploiting all the human senses in unusual surroundings is a highly charged and emotional experience for most people, from a High Mass in a cathedral to a large outdoor rock festival with a plethora of smells and different sounds – a visual drama plus the physical effects of standing in the same place for long periods. People are so crowded together they are touching, and in church even taste (the Eucharist) may be included. These – like birthday parties as children – are the sorts of experiences we are most likely to retain in the form of images and visual stories in our

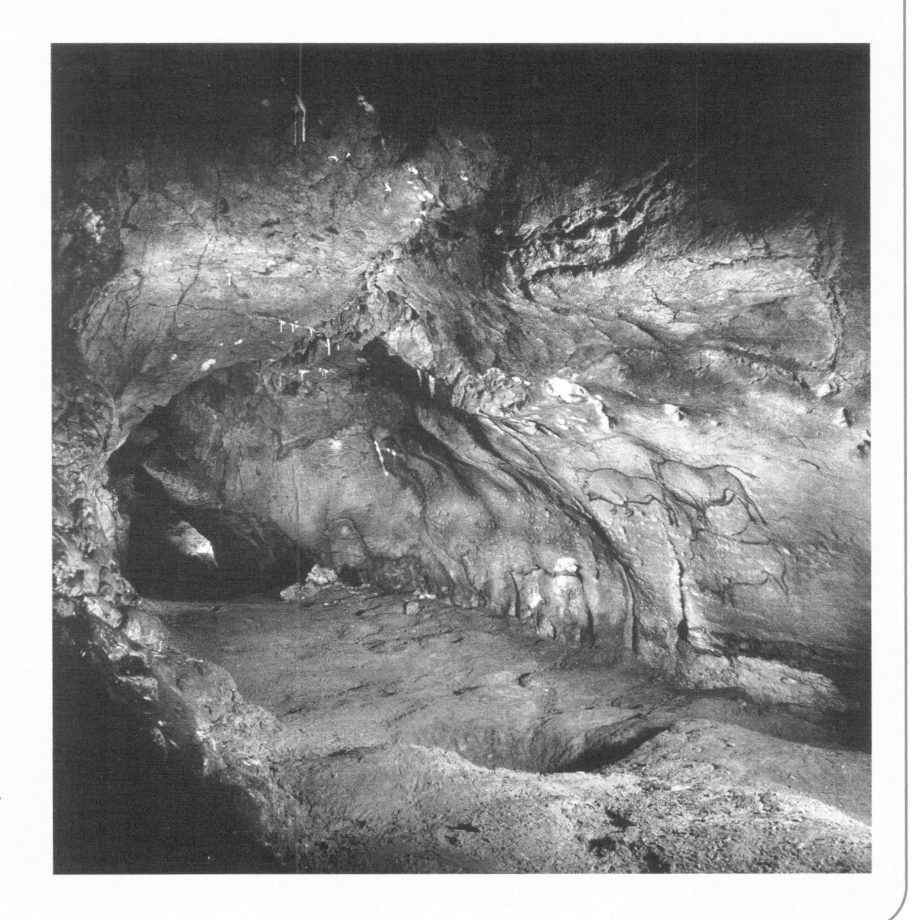

Figure 6.14. The bison frieze of Covaciella cave in its context.

lasting memories. Images along with an action or activity are easier to retain, and images plus 'doing' plus 'emotion' trump everything in terms of memorability.

Storytelling is very effective as a mnemonic device, especially when combined with images and in a dramatic setting. One possible example is the decorated cave of Covaciella (Asturias), where the striking bison images may have illustrated a story about bisons or used the bison as a metaphor for humans or something else. Some holes in the floor in front of the panel might have supported some kind of screen. Imagine telling children a story in a difficult-to-access place (where bears also hibernate), and the story is told with the important images hidden behind a screen until the denouement – when they are unveiled. This is exactly how medieval altarpieces were designed to work on the human psyche.

An even more dramatic example has been found in the 'anthropomorph chamber' of Tito Bustillo cave, and it may be the first representation of something resembling 'ourselves', although again, the true meaning it was meant to convey to the ice age viewer could be something much more abstract than we suppose. It seems likely, due to its hidden and inaccessible location, that only a select few were permitted to enter this chamber – perhaps to be told a mythical account of our selves and our origins. Of course, this idea may be fanciful, but most cultures have made an attempt to explain their 'beginning', and it is possible that this desire goes a long way back in human psychology! What is in no doubt is that this was the product of a mind that was capable of imagining, visualising, and producing a non-verbal abstract representation of their own thoughts, and the figures were like nothing they had seen in nature. Anthropomorphs, therianthropes (p. 214) and monsters are creatures that were not present in the real world but were created as 'supernatural' beings by human imagination.

Imagine the scene: after crawling and climbing, heart racing, you enter the smoke-filled chamber. Shadowy figures move around. There is a flickering glow of flames from a small hearth. You look up and see the glowing image of something familiar but not ....

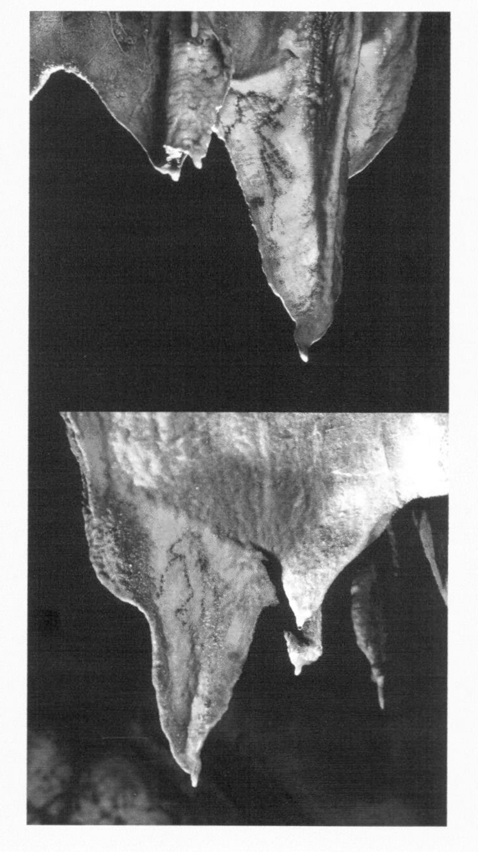

Figure 6.15. The anthropomorphs on the two sides of the drapery in the anthropomorph chamber of Tito Bustillo.

Since its discovery in 2001, very few visitors have been fortunate enough to experience this inaccessible and very 'private' place. An artificial wall was constructed during Palaeolithic times in this side-chamber of the cave, presumably to keep out all but a select few and to make access, and the tricky journey to the chamber, even more difficult.

Once in the chamber, it is striking how unusual the topography of the space is, and it has an awesome quality that is hard to put into words. One can only imagine what the ancient observer made of such a location, but it seems likely that the place, once found, was chosen for its difficult route and access, its secrecy, and the unexpected shapes and contours within the chamber. Centre stage, descending from the ceiling, and about 3 m above the present ground surface is an extraordinary natural rock formation. It dominates the chamber, and images have been painted in red on both sides of the almost translucent stalactite – a male anthropomorph on one side and a female on the other. What these figures represent we will never know – and perhaps the mystery was deliberate! Dating the calcite on which the paintings were made and the calcite that subsequently covered them places their execution between 37,000 and 29,000 years ago. Charcoal from the chamber's hearth has been dated to c. 37,000 bp. Most enigmatic is a deliberate structure that was probably used as a seating area for one individual to gaze upwards at the artwork.

Figure 6.16. Elle Clifford seated under the anthropomorph drapery.

There were doubtless special times and events for transmitting cultural memories. Gatherings around something exceptional connect people and the experience they share, be it rituals or celebrations or commemorating ancestors. Waterfalls, springs and lakes – even bogs and particular trees -- may have been thought to have special power, and the same might be true of caves or unusual rock formations.

The veneration of features of the natural landscape must go deep into the human past. Perhaps humans have a natural tendency to feel that certain places are unusual and 'special' or even awe-inspiring; and that an 'out of the normal' experience can occur near them. Ethnography shows us that people believe many things to be imbued with human intent – e.g. rocks may be seen as petrified people. The indigenous inhabitants of Australia interpret land formations as the intentional actions and journeys of the 'creator beings' during 'Dreamtime.' In traditional societies, landscape is not perceived as an inert backdrop to human life to be exploited for its resources, but as a network of interconnected sites associated with supernatural powers and mythological meaning. The landscape is seen as a giving environment, full of treasures; it is also full of symbolic meaning for the people who depend on its 'gifts.' For people who interact with the environment in this way it is easy for them to imagine and believe there are non-human powers that exist and have to be negotiated with in order to maintain a reciprocal arrangement. This interpretation is difficult to grasp by those of us whose history has followed a different trajectory.

The words *landscape / landscaef* were present in Old English, and imply surroundings that are separate from the viewer; this is markedly different from the experience of indigenous cultures that see themselves as belonging to and immersed in, their 'living and giving' surroundings. People that survive by hunting and gathering describe having an 'intense' relationship with their landscape, and feel they share their surroundings with the other inhabitants such as birds, animals, even insects and the vegetation they rely on to survive. They also feel a continuing relationship with their ancestors who have occupied the same land before them. The Native American tradition regards the land they live and hunt on as sacred.

Confronting a great expanse of wilderness of monumental hills, valleys, river bends, scrubby vegetation, few trees, and with snow covering the ground for much of the time may pose some difficulty to modern wilderness-adventurers trying to find their way around. Not so for the semi-nomadic hunter-gatherers who would know every detail of their surroundings, including the tracks and traces left by the many other–than-human creatures inhabiting the landscape. Any notable features would have been brought to the attention of youngsters, and tying these strategic landmarks to stories or myths would increase the probability of them being remembered.

Every landscape – even a desert – has features that are not always obvious to the inexperienced traveller, and it is highly likely that ice age people marked out their 'territory' with points or small details of importance such as the shape of a particular tree, an unusual stone outcrop or boulder, a particular clump of juniper bushes. These 'characters' would perhaps have been given names, just as we do today when something about our natural surroundings stands out.

In the American Southwest the Navajo Nation reservation of Monument Valley is a desert environment with mesas and buttes that all have names and ancient

Figure 6.17. a: The so-called 'map' at the back of Tito Bustillo (Asturias);

Figure 6.17. b: Tracing of the so-called engraved 'map' on the ivory plaque from Mezhirich (Ukraine);

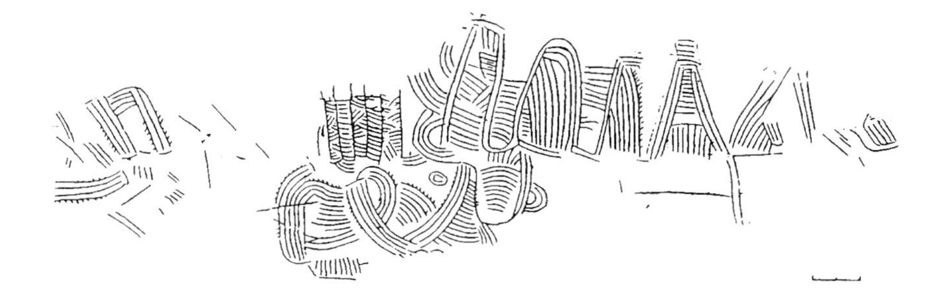

Figure 6.17. c: possible map engraved on a fragment of mammoth tusk from Pavlov (Moravia).

stories that are sacred to the Navajo people. We may see nothing exciting in a landscape, but ancient people seeing something unusual and noteworthy may have thought of a good story to explain what they saw. All this may well have developed to help people remember how to find their way home!

It is worth noting that a few ice age images have been interpreted as possible maps – one painted panel at the far end of Tito Bustillo is often considered to be a plan of the cave, and a few items of portable art have also been claimed to be maps: a stone from Limeuil with engraved meanders on it was thought to be a possible river map; an apparently abstract design engraved on a fragment of mammoth tusk from Pavlov has also been seen as a map; and the cave of Abauntz in the Spanish Pyrenees has recently yielded another possible example.

HAVING A LAUGH?

Story-telling in the ice age must have included some humour – but comedy is an elusive phenomenon which takes many forms. The need to laugh appears to be universal among humans, acting as a 'safety valve' for the emotions and a release of tensions, as well as a shared experience which can enhance social bonding and group membership – indeed, it has been called 'instant group therapy'. It is a pleasurable experience. We laugh instinctively at infants and children, and babies laugh at the unexpected and during play.

However, humour changes through space and time: today there are marked variations from place to place in the type of material considered funny. This problem becomes more acute when the dimension of time is included – nothing dates faster than comedy. What seems topical and witty today will produce a puzzled frown or a yawn tomorrow, and this elusive quality of humour increases with time. Inevitably, therefore, there are great difficulties in any attempt to assess the comedy of remote cultures, and especially that of prehistoric times.

All comedy has content and manner; the latter, involving delivery, timing and so forth, cannot survive in art. Prehistoric people undoubtedly laughed uproariously at tellers of funny stories, but all of that side of their humour has gone forever. What we are left with is the content, much of which we cannot recognise – for the simple reason that content draws heavily on contemporary trivia or on shared experiences. There is an added danger that what may seem funny to us in early art was intended to be serious or symbolic; for instance, one could imagine an alien reading the depictions of the Stations of the Cross as a hilarious comic-strip of one unfortunate individual having a really bad day!

Consequently, when seeking humour in the art of cultures earlier than our own, and particularly those with no writing to explain things, we are reduced to certain basic categories which seem to be common to all mankind. These are, on the whole, the types of humour aimed at the less sophisticated – what are today described as 'schoolboy' or 'lavatorial' humour:

exaggeration, inversion, satirical caricature, the grotesque/monstrous, scatology and, of course, sexuality. Intermingled with these themes is our apparently fundamental ability and need to laugh at the misfortunes of others – this is the essence of all slapstick humour and explains the global popularity of the silent comedies of old Hollywood. Under the mask of humour, society allows an infinite degree of aggression by everyone against everyone.

Figure 6.18. Apparent scene of bison (or musk-ox?) pursuing a human, carved in bas-relief around a block from Roc de Sers (Charente). Solutrean. The block is c. 35 cm thick, the human is 50 cm high, and the bison 54 cm.

One can be quite certain that there are innumerable examples of funny anecdotes to be found in the prehistoric art of the world but, without knowledge of the specific story that lies behind them, most, alas, will go unrecognized as being humorous. Hence, no recognizable slapstick is yet known in the earliest art because of its lack of perceptible narrative, although the bas-relief from the French ice age site of Roc de Sers of a human apparently being chased by a bison may conceivably belong in this category. Inversion, or a topsy-turvy world, can be found in cases where animals are shown in the guise of human beings; this kind of nonsense world turned upside down is found in other early cultures. Such humour seems to stem from our innate tendency to anthropomorphise animals, to regard them as 'little folk' and endow them with human abilities and qualities, and dress them up. However, there is no evidence from art that the people of the last ice age had this attitude – their rare depictions of what seem to be humans with animal heads are usually interpreted as 'sorcerers'.

Where scatology is concerned, the depiction of vomit and faeces is generally subject to taboos, and the humour thus lies in a flagrant flaunting of these rules. At least one case is known from the ice age: in the French Pyrenees, a whole series of almost identical antler spearthrowers are known, dating to about 12,000 BC. These show a young fawn or ibex looking over its shoulder at what appears to be a ridiculously large turd emerging from its anus; birds are perched on the turd (it should be noted, however, that some researchers believe this to be a birthing scene, although they cannot explain the birds!). The fact that fragments of up to ten examples have been recovered from different sites in addition to the two intact ones known

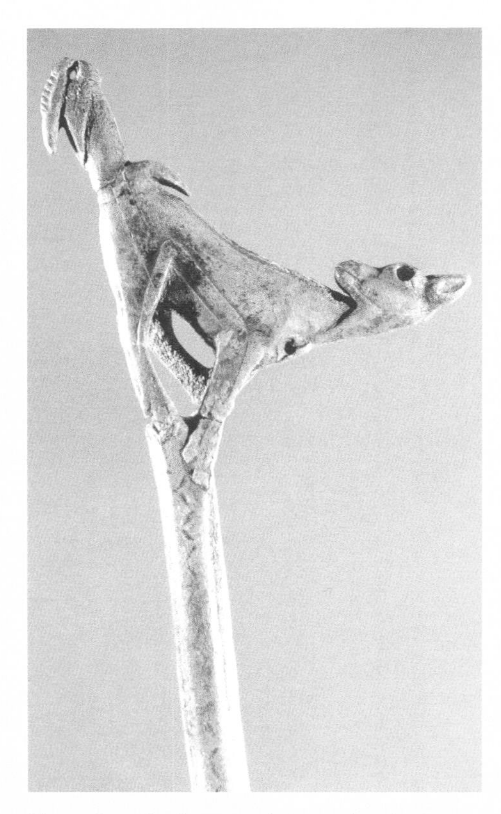

Figure 6.19. Antler spearthrower showing a young ibex or fawn with emerging turd, on which two birds are perched. Le Mas d'Azil (Ariège). Magdalenian.

means that scores, if not hundreds of specimens were originally produced, which implies that this joke – or humorous tale – was extremely popular in this period. A virtually identical scene (though without the turd) was depicted in Walt Disney's *Bambi*, produced before the discovery of these spearthrowers – thus implying that the image may be deeply embedded in the human psyche.

Erotic humour is by far the most popular of all types, both verbal and visual, and a very high percentage of all jokes are concerned with the sexual impulse. Once again this form of comedy is involved with the flaunting of taboos and, thereby, mocking the authority figures. Perhaps the earliest example of sexual humour occurs in the cave of Le Portel, France, and dates to the end of the last ice age. There is very little direct evidence for interest in sexuality as a whole in ice age imagery, and the occasional depictions of male or female genitalia were probably used in a ritual rather than a bawdy context. However, most scholars assume that the Portel figure is a bit of fun: a small stalagmite emerging from the cave wall was surrounded with the painted outline of a man, and a red dot was placed on the end of the 'phallus'.

There seem to be a few caricatures in the imagery of the last ice age; as we have seen, in addition to what appears a realistic portrait, there are a number of depictions of carefully differentiated human profiles on stone slabs from the French cave of La Marche, dating to *c.* 14,000 years ago (see pp. 6-7). It is clear from the remarkable detail in the animal pictures on the same slabs that these people were superb artists who could easily have captured a lifelike human face (even if, as some researchers believe, humans were far more difficult to draw than animals); the fact that they hardly ever did so is generally thought to indicate that there was some sort of taboo operating on accurate portraiture at this period. The La Marche heads may be clumsy attempts at portraits, or they may be purposely stylised, but it is equally likely that they are the earliest caricatures, and one or two have features and expressions which make this a particularly feasible explanation.

Figure 6.20. Figure of a human drawn around a natural phallus-like stalagmite protruding from the wall in Le Portel (Ariège). Probably Magdalenian. Height: 38 cm.

MUSICAL MOMENTS

It cannot be doubted that music was a feature of ice age life. Dance and song, whistling and hand-clapping leave no traces at all, and such things as reed-pipes, wooden instruments, and stretched-skin drums will have disintegrated; however, a few musical instruments have survived from the Upper Palaeolithic – there are about 30 'flutes', spanning the Aurignacian and Gravettian (c. 20), the Solutrean (3) and the Magdalenian; a few come from Germany, Hungary, Yugoslavia, Spain, Austria, and the former U.S.S.R., but most are from France, with 22 fragments from different layers in the supersite of Isturitz alone. Indeed, the majority of flutes are broken. The French ones are made of hollow bird bones, while the eastern specimens are of reindeer or bear bone; they have from three to seven finger-holes along their length, and are played like penny whistles rather than true flutes. Experiments with replicas by modern musicologists have revealed that, once a whistle-head is attached to direct the air-flow, one can produce strong, clear notes of piccolo-type, on a five-tone scale.

In recent years, it is the collection of early flutes from the caves of southwest Germany which has come to the fore: Hohle Fels has one made from a griffin vulture bone, as well as two made of ivory; Vogelherd has also yielded an ivory specimen, but the most remarkable ivory example is from Geissenklösterle which was found in more than thirty fragments. When reassembled, it emerged that it had been carved in two halves which were then joined together. This cave also has two specimens made of swan bone.

A few shaped, polished and engraved bird-bone tubes have been found which have no holes, and have been interpreted as trumpet-like 'lures' for imitating the call of a hind in the rutting season – one fine example from the Magdalenian site of Saint-Marcel even has a series of what look like deer ears engraved on it! Many perforated reindeer phalanges have been

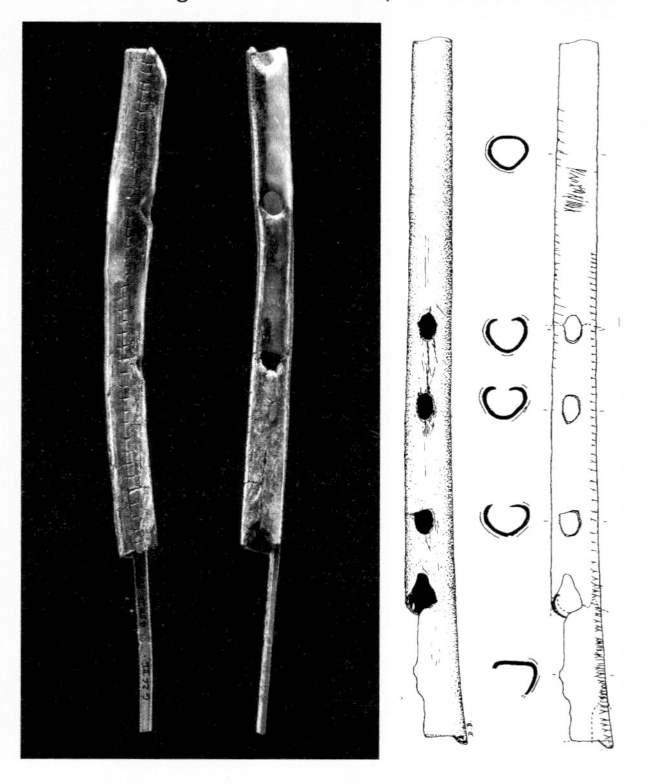

Figure 6.21. a: Mammoth-ivory flute from Geissenklösterle. Germany; ▶ b: drawing of a flute from Isturitz.

interpreted as whistles in the past, though often the hole was made – or at least started – by carnivore teeth or other natural breakage; those which were intentionally made do produce a shrill, powerful note. For example, Lartet found one at Aurignac in 1860, and managed to get a strident sound out of it. A few definite whistles in bird bone are also known, such as the Magdalenian specimens from Le Roc de Marcamps, Gironde, while perforated shells would have made good ocarinas. One large seashell from Marsoulas cave has recently been claimed to be a Magdalenian horn.

A number of oval objects of bone or ivory, with a hole at one end, have been interpreted as 'bull-roarers' ('rhombes', 'bramaderas'), a type of instrument which makes a loud humming noise when whirled round on a string – experiments have shown them to be particularly sonorous in caves. A very fine example made of reindeer antler is that from the cave of La Roche de Birol (Dordogne). The well-known parietal engraving from Trois Frères of a 'sorcerer' with a bison-head has often been interpreted as playing a musical bow, but this seems an extremely tenuous idea: since the lines go to its nose rather than mouth, then, if it were a musical instrument, it would have to be a nose flute! – and in any case these enigmatic marks could be all manner of things.

As for percussion, a number of mammoth bones, painted with red ochre, from the site of Mezin, near Kiev, dating to about 21,000 bp, have been claimed to be musical instruments – a hip-bone xylophone (osteophone?), skull and shoulder-blade drums, and jawbone rattles – and have been played by Soviet archaeologists, who even cut a record of their jam-session. However, some doubt has been cast on whether the supposed marks of surface damage, polish and wear on these objects really exist.

Figure 6.22. Engraved 'bull-roarer' with geometric/linear motifs and covered with red ochre, from La Roche at Lalinde (Dordogne). Magdalenian. Length: 18 cm, width: 4 cm.

Figure 6.23. 'Venus with horn' from Laussel (Dordogne). Probably Gravettian. Height: 44 cm.

Another category of instrument is the scraper or rasp (râcleur), and it has been speculated that the horn held by the 'Venus' of Laussel, with its parallel lines, may be a musical scraper.

Finally, there are possible lithophones in a number of caves: 'draperies' of folded calcite formations often resound when struck with a hard object (wooden sticks seem to produce the clearest and most resonant notes), and this seems to have been noticed by Palaeolithic people, since some of the lithophones are somewhat battered and are decorated with painted lines and dots which indicate the most resonant stalactites. Apart from Nerja, and possibly Tito Bustillo in Spain and Escoural in Portugal, as well as a couple of cases in the Pyrenees (Le Portel has draperies and columns bearing traces of ancient blows, while the Réseau Clastres has numerous broken concretions), all known examples are in the Lot region of France (Pech Merle, Les Fieux, Roucadour, etc); moreover, most of them are in or near chambers which could have held a large audience.

One doubtless hugely important factor in the selection of places in caves to decorate, and perhaps also in what to draw there, is the long-neglected aural aspect: the acoustics. In recent decades, detailed studies have been made of the acoustic properties of several caves, finding a strong connection between the locations of decoration and the areas of best resonance for men's voices. This notion has also been extended to the content of cave art, with the suggestion that the artists ingeniously used the caves' acoustics and echoes to conjure up the sounds made, for example, by moving herds of hoofed animals. It has been found by yelling and clapping or striking stones together that in deep caves like Lascaux and Font de Gaume echoes in the painted chambers produced sound levels between 23 and 31 decibels. In contrast, deep cave walls decorated with stealthy cats, like Lascaux's 'Cabinet des Félins' produce sound levels of only 1 to 7 decibels, whereas undecorated surfaces often are totally 'flat'. Although some of the interpretations linking these

Figure 6.24. Markings on the lithophone in the cave of Nerja.

findings to thundering ungulate herds or silent carnivores are less than convincing, and despite the fact that the acoustics of some caves and rock-shelters must have altered somewhat since Palaeolithic times, studies of this type are nevertheless valuable in that they are trying to revive something that one might imagine gone for ever – the dimension of sound that accompanied whatever rituals may have been carried out in these sites. In view of the obvious intelligence of the artists, as well as the fact that they took full advantage of the morphology of caves and especially of particular rock-shapes, it is extremely likely that they would have used any acoustic peculiarities to the full. There are, for example, good acoustics in the Grande Grotte of Arcy-sur-Cure, and the main chamber of Candamo; the terminal cavity in the Combel of Pech Merle contains nine dots and a sketchy mammoth, but it also has astonishing acoustic qualities which amplify any noise in the cave, and it was thus a very special place. However, the most spectacular and theatrical case is undoubtedly the Salon Noir of Niaux, a huge high chamber, where the art is laid out as if on the back wall of a big stage, and whose echoing acoustics are extraordinary.

Figure 6.25. Part of the Salon Noir in the cave of Niaux.

Images on the rocks

The most striking evidence for external memories in the ice age is the great quantity of rock art that has survived and been discovered so far. We know from Aboriginal informants in Australia that their rock art is multi-purpose – it is their equivalent of our encyclopedias, dictionaries, bibles, atlases, histories, storybooks and more. Open-air rock art of the ice age is still rare – it has only been known since 1970, and has only survived in a few suitable micro-climates. Only petroglyphs are known, since paintings will have disappeared rapidly. It is probable that open-air art was the norm during this period, and that vast quantities of it have been eroded or weathered away. More than a dozen sites have so far been found in Portugal, Spain, and the French Pyrenees where the animal engravings are certainly of this period, judging by their style, as well as the dating of archaeological deposits that cover some of the panels. Others have been found in Germany and even Egypt.

On the other hand, the imagery inside caves and rock-shelters has survived thanks to its protected and stable location, and it is best known because it has been studied intensively for almost 150 years. But at present we are aware of fewer than 450 decorated cavities spanning those 30,000 years – many of them containing few figures – which suggests that cave art was actually a quite marginal phenomenon. Nevertheless, caves must have made a major impression on the ice age mind – the bizarre formations of stalagmites and stalactites are totally unlike anything in the outside world, and must have been a source of wonder – as indeed they still are today! – as well as of stories needed to explain them. So it is hardly surprising that many cavities triggered a creative impulse.

Cave art comprises an astonishing variety and mastery of techniques. One basic and highly characteristic approach was the use of natural rock formations: the natural shapes of cave walls and stalagmites were employed in countless examples to emphasise or represent parts of a depiction – often producing 3D figures in the process, such as the bison drawn on the natural bosses on the Altamira ceiling.

The simplest form of marking cave walls was to run fingers over them, leaving traces in the soft layer of clay. This technique, perhaps the most ancient of all,

Figure 6.26. Section of the Altamira ceiling, showing standing figures on the flat surface and curled-up bison on the natural bosses in the rock. Magdalenian.

probably spans the whole period and may have been inspired by the abundance of clawmarks of cave-bears and other animals on the walls. In some caves, the finger-lines also include some definite animal and human-like figures. Engraving is by far the most common technique on cave walls, with incisions ranging from the fine and barely visible to broad deep lines. The tools used for engraving varied from crude picks to sharp flint flakes.

Work in clay was a regional speciality that is largely restricted to the Pyrenees: it ranges from finger-holes and tracings to engravings in the cave-floor and figures made on artificial banks of clay. The finest clay figures are two famous statues of bison in the cave of Le Tuc d'Audoubert and the headless bear which crouches like the Sphinx in the cave of Montespan, and which is made of about 1500 pounds of clay.

Wall-carvings are similarly limited in distribution, this time to the Périgord and Charente regions of Southwest France, where the limestone could be shaped, as well as northern England. But whereas clay figures are known only from the dark depths of caves, sculptures are always in rock-shelters or the brightly-lit front parts of caves. The figures were created with strong tools such as hammerstones and picks. Almost all the wall-sculptures have faint traces of red pigment and were originally painted, like much portable art.

The red pigment used on cave walls is iron oxide (haematite, or red ochre), while the black is usually manganese or charcoal. The main colouring materials were readily available, either casually collected as fragments or mined from known sources. Studies of pigments, particularly at the cave of Niaux in the French Pyrenees, have revealed the possible use of specific 'recipes' combining

Figure 6.27. The two clay bison of the Tuc d'Audoubert (Ariège) in their context, as the focal point of a small, low-ceilinged chamber. Probably Magdalenian. The bison are 63 and 61 cm long respectively.

Figure 6.28. Michel Lorblanchet spitting a hand stencil.

colouring material with 'extenders' such as talc or feldspath which made the paint go further. Analyses have also begun to detect traces of animal and plant oils used as binders to help fix the pigments to the rock surface, while experiments suggest that in some cases cave water was used for this purpose.

The simplest way to apply paint to walls was with fingers, and this was certainly done in some caves, but normally paint was applied with some kind of tool, though none has survived. Lumps of pigment may have been used as crayons, but since they do not mark the rock well, they were more likely to be sources of powder. Experiments suggest that animal-hair brushes or crushed twigs were the best tools to use. In some cases, paint was clearly sprayed, either directly from the mouth or through a tube, to produce dots as well as hand stencils (a way of leaving a hand print by placing the palm against the rock and blowing paint onto it and all around it).

The vast majority of figures drawn with pigment in the caves are simple outlines or have some infill – for example, some of the animals in the Chauvet Cave display a very sophisticated use of shading. The two-colour and multi-colour figures of the end of the ice age (such as the bison on the ceiling at Altamira) are rare in comparison with engravings and outlines.

Figures have been found not only on clay floors and on walls, but also on ceilings. Some, like the Altamira ceiling, were within easy reach, but for others a ladder or scaffolding was required. At Lascaux, holes cut into the wall of one gallery give some idea how the scaffolding was constructed (pp. 88-89).

Light was provided by fireplaces in some caves, but portable light was necessary in most cases. Since only a few dozen definite stone lamps are known from the whole period (pp. 74-76), it is likely that burning torches were generally used, which left little or no trace other than a few fragments of charcoal or black marks on the walls.

In wall art, unlike portable, there was no great limit on size, and figures range from the tiny to the enormous (over 2.5 m in some cases, with the great Lascaux bulls exceeding 5 m). Small figures are often found with large ones; the ground was almost never drawn, and there are no landscapes.

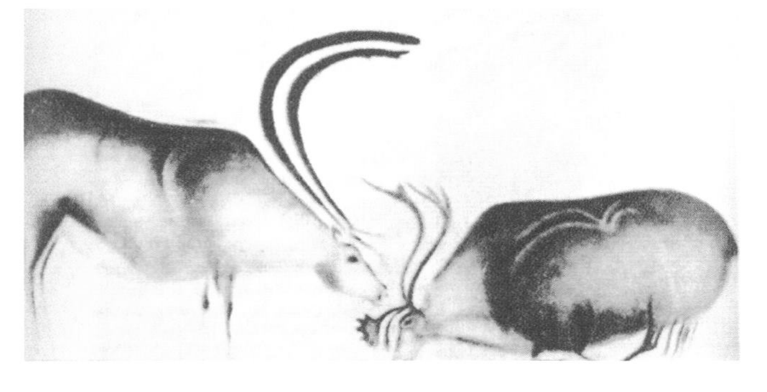

Figure 6.29. Tracing of engraved and painted figures depicting a male reindeer licking the brow of a female, Font de Gaume (Dordogne), Magdalenian.

For convenience, ice age drawings are normally grouped into three categories, although there is some overlap and uncertainty between them: animals, humans, and non-figurative or abstract (known as 'signs'). The vast majority of animal figures are adults drawn in profile, most of them easily recognisable, although many are incomplete or ambiguous, and a few are quite simply imaginary, such as the two-horned 'unicorn' of Lascaux. Schematisation, where a figure is reduced to its essential traits, is frequently seen in the isolated neck- and back-lines of horses, bison or mammoths.

The age of the animals can almost never be estimated, except for the very few juveniles known. The animals' sex is sometimes displayed directly, but almost always discreetly, so that secondary sexual characteristics such as antlers or size and proportions often have to be relied upon.

Most figures seem motionless – in fact, a few may be wounded, dying or dead – and animated drawings are rare, most of them appearing towards the end of the ice age. 'Scenes' are very hard to identify in ice age imagery, since it is often impossible to prove that figures are 'associated', rather than simply next to each other. Only a very few definite scenes are known.

One central fact is the overwhelming overall dominance of the horse and bison among ice age depictions, although other species (such as the mammoth or deer) may dominate at particular sites. Carnivores such as cats or bears are rare in most sites (with the exception of Chauvet); fish and birds are far more common in portable art than in wall art. Insects and recognisable plants are limited to a very few examples in portable art.

In short, ice age imagery is neither a simple catalogue of the animals in the artists' world, nor a random collection of artistic observations of nature. It has meaning and structure, with different species dominating in different periods and regions.

Depictions of people can be divided into definite humans, 'humanoids' and 'composites'. Definite humans are scarce in wall art (portable art accounts for over 75% of ice age human depictions), and there are very few women

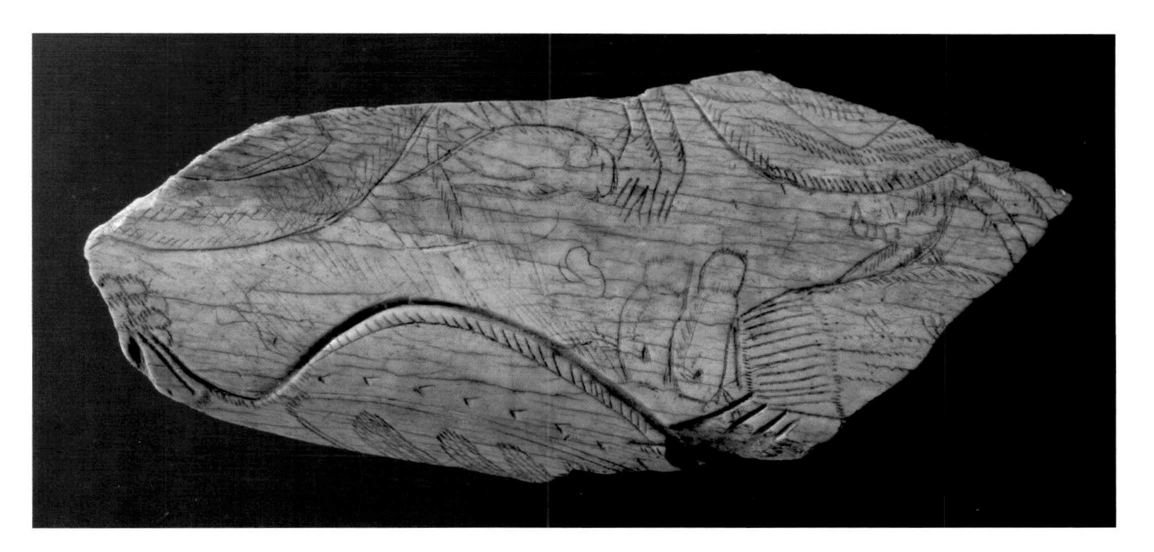

Figure 6.30. Engraving on bone of a grasshopper surrounded by birds. Enlène (Ariège).

resembling the 'Venus figurines' (pp. 9-11), which actually depict females of a wide span of ages and types and are by no means limited to the handful of corpulent specimens that are often claimed to be characteristic.

'Humanoids' comprise all those figures interpreted, but not positively identified, as being human: grotesque heads, 'masks', and 'phantoms' could be either animal or human. 'Composites' are figures that have clear and detailed elements of both. In the past all such figures were automatically and unjustifiably called 'sorcerers' and were assumed to be a 'shaman' or medicine man in a mask or animal costume. But they could just as easily be imaginary creatures, humans with animal heads. In any case, such composites (the most famous being the 'sorcerer' of Les Trois Frères, p. 214) are very rare, occurring in only a handful of sites.

The 'non-figurative' markings of the ice age have often seemed uninteresting or impossible to explain or define, but nowadays researchers believe that these marks may have been of equal, if not greater, importance to ice age people than the 'recognisable' figures. Non-figurative marks are two or three times more abundant than figurative, and in some areas far more. The category covers a tremendously wide range of motifs, from a single dot or line to complex shapes and to extensive panels of apparently unstructured linear marks. 'Signs' can be either totally isolated in a cave, clustered on their own panels, or closely associated with the figurative.

In the past, some shapes were assumed to be 'pictographic' (i.e. to represent objects) on the basis of what they 'looked like' – hence there arose terms like 'tectiforms' (huts), 'claviforms' (clubs), 'aviforms' (birds), etc. These are no longer taken literally, but used merely as rough guides to shape. However, it is impossible to know whether they are real objects or abstract designs or both.

The simpler motifs are more abundant and widespread, as one might expect, since they could be invented in many places and periods. The more complex forms, however, show great variability and are more restricted in space and time, to the extent that they have been seen as 'ethnic markers', perhaps delineating social groups of some kind. The marks were not set down at random, but follow some set of rules, like the animal figures. What those rules might mean is the thorniest problem in the study of ice age imagery.

The first and simplest theory put forward to explain the existence of art in this period was that it had no meaning: it was just idle doodlings, graffiti, play activity – mindless decoration by hunters with time on their hands. This 'art for art's sake' view arose from the first discoveries of portable art, but once cave art began to be found it rapidly became clear that something more was involved: the limited range of species depicted, their frequent inaccessibility and their associations in caves, the crowded and empty panels, the mysterious signs, the many figures that are purposely incomplete or ambiguous, all combine to suggest that there is complex meaning behind both the subject-matter and the location of ice age figures. There are patterns that require explanation, repeated patterns suggesting that the individual artists were subject to a widespread system of thought.

Figure 6.31. Ultraviolet photo of red 'claviform' sign in Les Trois Frères (Ariège) painted on a surface prepared by scraping. Probably Magdalenian. The claviform is 76 cm in length.

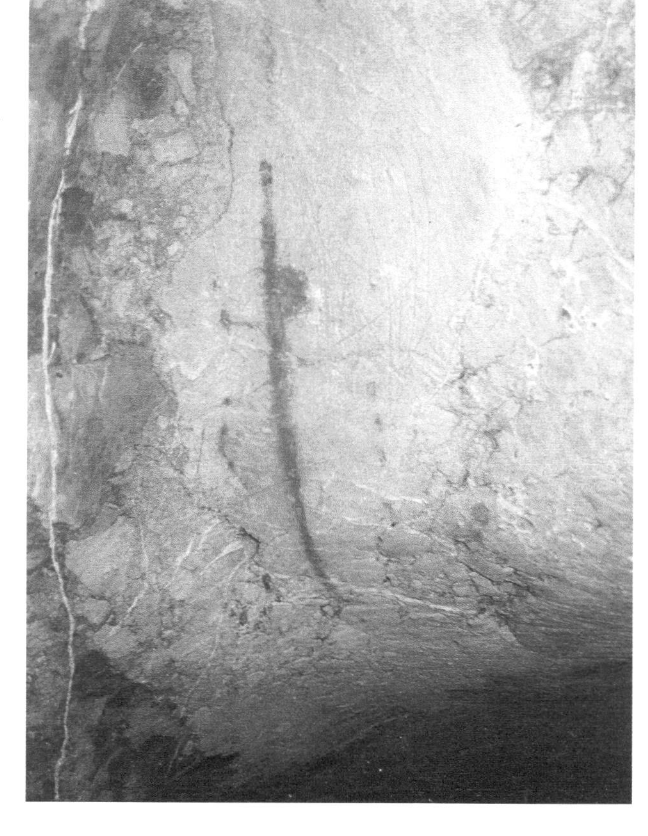

At the beginning of the 20th century, a new kind of theory took over: that the art was 'utilitarian' – that is, it had a definite function. These theories were based largely on newly published accounts of Australian Aborigines which inspired researchers to compare these 'primitive' users of stone tools with those of ice age Europe and thus to assume that the same purpose lay behind the art of both cultures. The Aborigines were said to perform ceremonies in order to multiply the numbers of the animals, and for this purpose they painted likenesses of these species on rocks. The analogy seemed perfect, and for decades all ideas and interpretations of cave art were subjectively chosen in this way out of the growing mass of ethnographic material from around the world.

'Sympathetic magic', including hunting magic, operates on the same basis as pins in a wax doll: the depictions of animals were produced in order to control or influence the real animals in some way.

Figure 6.32. a: Bison in Niaux's Salon Noir with marks often interpreted as missiles;

Figure 6.32. b: Tracing of some painted and engraved horses in the Panneau de l'Empreinte at Lascaux (Dordogne), showing extra eyes, ears, muzzles and legs. Probably Magdalenian. The 'multiple' horse covered in arrow-like marks is about 1 m in length.

Ritual and magic were seen in almost every aspect of ice age imagery – in breakage of decorated objects or depictions 'killed' ritually with images of spears or even physically attacked. 'Claviforms' were seen as clubs and 'tectiforms' as pit traps.

This subjectivity and wishful thinking led to many errors, as the theory was stretched and adapted to fit the evidence, or facts were carefully selected to fit the theory. Overall, there are very few ice age animal figures with 'spears' drawn on or near them, and most caves have no images of this type at all. The 'spears' (whatever they are) also occur on some human and humanoid figures. There are no clear hunting scenes. Moreover, the animal bones found in many decorated caves bear very little relation to the species depicted on the walls, and it is clear that the artists were not, by and large, drawing what they had killed or wanted to kill. This was not a 'hunters' art' in any simple sense.

Another popular and durable explanation of much ice age imagery is that it involves 'fertility magic': that is, that the artists depicted animals in the hope that they would reproduce and flourish to provide food in the future, a different kind of sympathetic magic. Once again, examples were selected which seemed to fit the idea, and researchers often saw what they wanted to find: animals mating, and an emphasis on human sexuality too. Yet few animals have their sex shown, and genitalia are almost always shown discreetly. As for copulation, in the whole of ice age imagery there are only a couple of possible examples, and they are extremely doubtful. Similarly, where humans are concerned, few figures have their genitalia marked, and the one or two claimed depictions of copulation are very sketchy and dubious.

It is clear that the greater part of ice age imagery is not about either hunting or sex, at least in an explicit sense. The next major theoretical advance, however, introduced the notion of a symbolic sexual element. In the 1950s two French scholars, Annette Laming-Emperaire and André Leroi-Gourhan, concluded that caves had been decorated systematically rather than at random. They based their interpretation on all the figures in a cave rather than on a selected few. Wall art was treated as a carefully laid-out composition within each cave; the animals were not portraits but symbols.

An investigation of how many figures of each species existed in each cave, together with their associations and their location on the walls, led Leroi-Gourhan to divide animals into four groups, based on the frequency of their depiction in cave art as a whole. He also divided caves into entrance zones, central zones and side chambers and dark ends. It appeared that about 90% of groups A (horse) and B (bison and wild ox) were concentrated on the main panels in the central areas, while most C figures (ibex, deer, mammoth) were near the entrance and on the peripheries of the central compositions, while D animals (carnivores, rhinos) clustered in the more remote zones. He then developed the concept of an ideal or standard layout to which each cave was adapted as far as possible: these were organised sanctuaries, with repeated compositions separated by zones marked with appropriate animals or signs.

Unfortunately, there are many exceptions to Leroi-Gourhan's 'rules' – and the very central and prominent cats and rhinos in Chauvet Cave, discovered after he died, have shown again how wrong he was. Moreover, his scheme worked on a presence/absence basis, not on abundance, so a single horse figure was seen as the equivalent of a mass of bison, or vice versa. Other variations such as colour, size, orientation, technique, and completeness were also ignored. Recent detailed studies, both of individual caves and of regional groups, stress that each site is unique and has its own 'symbolic construction' adapted to its own shape and size.

Leroi-Gourhan lumped all ice age cave art into his scheme and believed that it remained much the same for 20,000 years. There is certainly a degree of continuity over this timespan: caves are decorated with the same fairly restricted range of animals in profile and seem to represent variations on a theme.

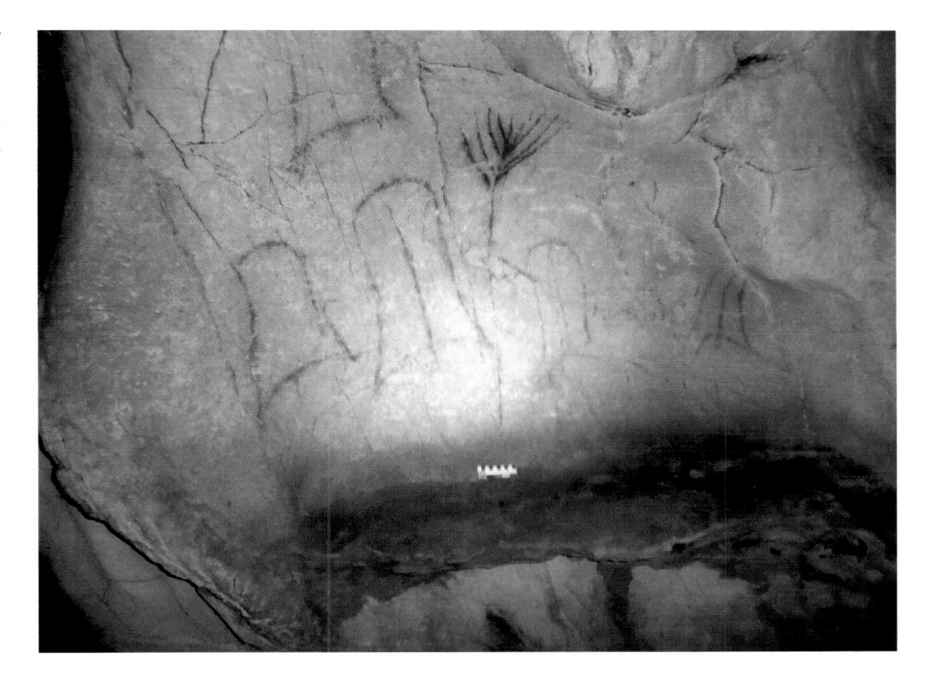

Figure 6.33. 'Signs' drawn in El Castillo: for Leroi-Gourhan the bell-like motifs probably represented vulvas while the plant-like motif was phallic.

Leroi-Gourhan's other key approach was his discovery of repeated 'associations' in the art, and his claim that there was a basic 'dualism'. Laming-Emperaire believed the horse to be equivalent to the female and the bison to the male; for Leroi-Gourhan it was the other way round. The numerically dominant horses and bison, concentrated in the central panels, were thought to represent a basic duality that was assumed to be sexual. This idea was then extended to the signs, which were considered male (phallic) and female (vulvar).

More recent studies have confirmed the fundamental role and opposition of horses and bison; it was also found that some 'associations' of animals are rare or non-existent – for example, one rarely finds depictions of bison with wild cattle, or bison with stags. In other words, Leroi-Gourhan may not have found a universally applicable formula, but he did discover order and repeated 'associations'. Laming-Emperaire eventually dropped this approach and instead adopted a theory reverting to 'totemism'; that is, she saw a decorated cave as a model of a group's social organisation, with animals of various sizes and ages representing either different generations or the mythical ancestors of different clans. This view was more flexible than that of Leroi-Gourhan, since it did not expect everything to remain stable through time and space, but rather to be different in each cave.

The work of these two scholars completely changed the way in which ice age imagery is studied. The images could no longer be seen as simple representations with an obvious and direct meaning, but as being full of conceptual ideas.

The most recent work on ice age imagery is splintering in many directions. One researcher, for example, has investigated the shape of wall-surface beneath each figure, finding in some caves that a high proportion of horses, deer and hand stencils are on concave surfaces, while an equally high percentage of bison and cattle are on convex; others are seeking detailed and firm methods by which to recognise the work of individual artists – we do not, of course, know the sex of the ice age artists (p. 21), and there is no justification for assuming that the art was all done by men and for men.

No single explanation can account for all of ice age imagery: it comprises at least two thirds of known art history, covering 30 thousand years and a vast area of the world; it ranges from beads to weapons and statuettes, from figures on blocks and rocks in the open air to complex signs hidden in the inaccessible crannies of deep caverns. Almost every basic artistic technique is represented, with everything from realism to abstraction. It is generally agreed that ice age imagery contains messages, no doubt of many kinds, but unfortunately we shall never know how to read them. Nevertheless, there is a great deal to be learned from their content, techniques, location and associations. Ice age images provide us with a fascinating glimpse into the world of our ancestors – the animals (some of them now extinct) which were of importance to them; their beliefs; and their remarkable aesthetic sense and breathtaking artistic skills.

What evidence is there for religion?

Many researchers have attributed most if not all cave imagery to religion, with possibilities ranging from totemism to animism. One theory – especially popular with the media – involved 'shamans'. In parts of Siberia the shaman is a very important figure, being a person with spiritual powers who combines the roles of healer, priest, magician, and artist as well as poet, actor and even psychotherapist! His most important function is to act as liaison between this world and the spirit world, a task usually performed by means of feigned 'trances'. Cultures with shamans usually have a zoomorphic view of the world, and things are seen and experienced in animal form. Hence, from this perspective, Palaeolithic images could be 'spirit animals', not copies of the real thing. In one theory of this kind, erroneously based on Siberian ethnography, it was suggested that many of the figures in Palaeolithic art were 'ongones', spirits that took the form of 'zoomorphs', 'anthropomorphs' and 'polymorphs', and that were asked to help in hunting, matters of health, and so on. Leroi-Gourhan (who was trained as an ethnologist and had a profound knowledge of true Siberian shamanism) reacted to this naive hypothesis by referring to 'facile equivalences' between the shamanism of eastern Siberia and some Palaeolithic data, seeing the analogy as far too general to be useful, and he firmly rejected any kind of linkage of the two phenomena. Sadly, this did not prevent a resurgence of shamanistic theories in the 1990s.

One formidable objection to the theories is that the meticulous and careful planning that is so blatant in the layout of imagery in many caves cries out against any idea of a random accumulation of images seen in 'trance'. Similarly the standardisation of style argues strongly against individual shamanic 'visions'. Specialists in neuropsychology revealed that the data used to create and promulgate the resurrected version of 'shamanism' – involving 'trance', 'altered states of consciousness', etc – were either outdated, distorted or completely erroneous. And there is not the slightest evidence for drug-taking in the last ice age.

Religions have clearly evolved over time, but when and how did they start? Is there anything in the archaeological record that indicates that our prehistoric ancestors were concerned with such matters? Skills were certainly handed down from one generation to the next – but what about myths, cults and religious beliefs?

A religion is generally thought to encompass a belief in supernatural events and beings or a life after death. Is it possible to see signs of religious behaviour or traces of cult practices and spirituality in the last ice age? 'Finding' religion and insights into the beliefs of prehistoric people in archaeological remains is mostly beyond our reach, yet this has not prevented researchers from imagining hunting rituals or shamanism in the period. It has often been assumed that the mere existence of deliberate burials – especially those with elaborate clothing and grave goods – proves a belief in an afterlife, and hence the presence of some kind of religion.

We don't know if the special individuals who were buried were given what we might call funerals, or whether any rituals relating to the dead were performed. Often graves have been over-interpreted – e.g. heads seen as purposely placed in particular directions aligned with east or west, or bodies in foetal position interpreted as ready to be re-born. Nearby fireplaces have likewise been seen as evidence of rituals, while animal bones supposedly indicate mourners partaking in a 'funeral' feast. Grave goods are generally interpreted as being needed for the next life or as 'gifts' for spirits/ancestors and the like. This may well be true in some cases, but we cannot be certain – there are many other possible reasons

JFK

Sometimes objects are placed with the dead simply because they belonged to them, or meant a great deal to them in life, or because the superstitious do not want the deceased's possessions to stay around. Some may indeed denote a belief in an afterlife, but we cannot differentiate these motives, particularly for prehistoric graves. As an example, consider the objects placed in John F. Kennedy's coffin by his family: first wedding anniversary gold cufflinks, a PT boat tie pin, some scrimshaw, a letter from Jackie, scribbled notes from his children, and rosary beads from his brother Bobby. How will a future archaeologist interpret this bizarre assemblage?

for placing garments and possessions with the deceased. Be that as it may, this does not exclude the emotional feelings of people burying their dead with the hope that they will one day encounter them again in some form or another.

If we turn to ethnographic sources for help, we risk, once again – as with 'shamanism' – falling into the trap of seeing Aboriginal people or indigenous Arctic populations as a good-fit comparison for ice age people. Clearly this is a dubious approach, as recent and living hunter-gatherers have had their own equally long trajectory through time along with all modern populations throughout the world. Just because living foraging and hunter-gatherer communities have myths and a spiritual history that have been handed down for longer than anyone can say, this does not necessarily mean that they originated with prehistoric people. Unfortunately this view has been assumed by many researchers into the origin of religious belief in the supernatural.

Theorists in the 1960s proposed that a system of religious symbols and beliefs was linked to hunter-gatherers' economic and social system and their natural surroundings – the religion of the hunt, for example, or the existence of 'bear cults.' Again, this view took hold because bear-cults still exist around the world, particularly in Arctic populations, be they reindeer herders or Eskimoan communities. Since bears existed in the Palaeolithic, rituals connected to bear hunting may well have begun in prehistoric times. But we have no proof – for example, in Chauvet Cave numerous bones of cave-bear are present naturally, and, as mentioned earlier (p. 195) one bear skull lies on an isolated rock. This has caused a great deal of ink to flow, with predictable speculations about a cave-bear cult and an 'altar', though of course it is just as likely that the skull arrived there through natural processes or was placed there by a bored child. In short, there is no reason to attribute this to mystical rather than natural or prosaic causes.

Surely we would have much more evidence of cave bear worship if it existed – more images, more bones and skulls moved around and stashed in caves rather than simply the bones of animals which sheltered and hibernated underground and died from natural causes. There are many bear bones and smashed skulls scattered in caves, but this could easily have been done by later generations of bears or other animals, or humans removing bear teeth for adornment, or children amusing themselves as mentioned above. In addition, caves often undergo periods of flooding which can result in the movement of archaeological remains such as animal bones, or even in several skulls ending up in one place with what seems like a peculiar or deliberate configuration.

Similarly some categories of object – most notably the female figurines (pp. 9-11) – are commonly interpreted as religious in some way, but once again there are many alternative possibilities. Almost all those found in Central and Eastern Europe (usually of mammoth ivory) have come from open-air settlements, and sometimes seem to have had a special role in the home. For example, one from Kostenki I was upright in a small pit, leaning against the wall, and facing the centre of the living area and the hearths; the pit was filled with soil mixed with red ochre and was capped by a mammoth shoulder-blade. Pits in other Russian sites have sometimes contained one, two or three such figurines, but we do not know if these pits were ritual or for storage. The statuettes have often been interpreted by Russian scholars as a mother- or ancestor-figure, a mistress of the house, or mother goddess.

Russian ethnography certainly provides food for thought in this regard. The Yamal Peninsula in the Siberian Arctic is still home, as it has been for thousands of years, to the 10,000 Yamal-Nenet nomadic people who herd 300,000 domestic reindeer across the frozen tundra. The Nenets' animist cosmology is centred on deities and ancestors that are represented by dolls, the most senior being the 'old woman of the chum' who protects their domestic space. These dolls are kept in a special place in the chum (yurt), and are carried around on sacred sledges. When the Nenets need to call on them for help, they and their sledges are fed vodka or fresh reindeer blood and prayed to like religious icons. There is extensive anthropological literature from numerous other cultures describing the manufacture and use of dolls that are revered and passed down like those of the Siberian Nenets.

However, the ice age statuettes have also been seen as fertility symbols, erotica, dolls (p. 188), children's toys, charms to ward off a difficult childbirth or even humorous figures made to take the fear of motherhood away! They have often been seen as representing prehistoric matriarchies; a 'mother-earth ideal' for women to be fertile and to reproduce; symbols of procreation and life. Women in the Upper Palaeolithic may well have been esteemed and admired for their reproductive, life-giving powers, but as we have seen (p. 162), fertility probably had to be curbed during the last ice age.

Some researchers have even suggested that the statuettes do not represent women at all, but rather a curved river or other landscape features. Certainly their diversity may indicate that these female figurines had a number of 'roles', or had different functions and served a variety of purposes. Each had its own symbolism and meaning, and this might have been conveyed to the viewer by the pose she holds, what parts of her body are accentuated e.g. breasts or thighs, what she is wearing or which decorative motifs and patterns are carved on her. In Renaissance art Christ's hands in their various positions conveyed a variety of messages to the viewer. This is not to suggest the figurines necessarily held any religious meaning – they may instead have been related to social or group identity. Their precise functions are extremely likely to have been complex and must remain forever beyond our grasp. Images of all kinds can convey deep meanings to the onlooker who shares the same language and culture as the artist.

It is also interesting to note that while these female figurines are found throughout Europe and in Russia, nothing similar has been found representing the male figure. Can we deduce from this that carved representations of males were of less significance to our Palaeolithic ancestors? It is doubtless safe to assume that over the extensive period of the last ice age humans believed that women, and women alone, were completely responsible for the 'making' of children. Men may at some point over that time have found an alternative source of 'creating' – maybe through artistic endeavours or male initiation ceremonies. The female figurines could have been manufactured by women for men, by men for women, or women for women (or even men for men) for their exclusive use. Or perhaps they were made by either men or women for children!

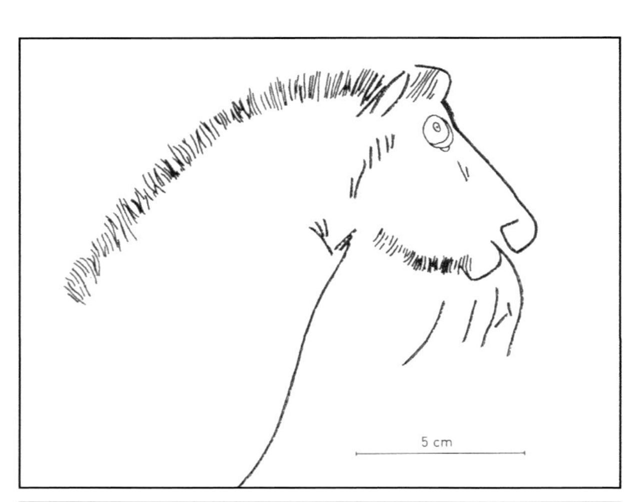

Figure 6.34. The hidden drawing of a horse-head in Pergouset (Lot), and a drawing showing the artist's position.

In fact there are only two kinds of evidence which point clearly to some kind of religious belief in the ice age. Not all images were necessarily mysterious or mystical – some cave images were 'public', made to be seen by other people, to the extent that concretions were broken to make the depictions more easily visible (e.g. at Candamo and Cougnac). But there were also many 'private' or 'hidden' images in some caves – their placing in highly inaccessible locations makes it clear that they were made, not for other people to see but presumably as offerings to something non-human: a god, spirit, ancestor, force of nature? The ultimate example is in the French cave of Pergouset, which has always been very difficult to enter. It takes a 130 m crawl to reach the engraved figures – this arduous journey (especially with a Palaeolithic lamp) could thus be seen as a kind of initiation, a tough physical ordeal. The cave contains a horse-head engraved in a fissure, placed there by the artist to prevent it being seen by any human – even the artist him/herself never saw it!

The other possible evidence consists of special objects carefully placed or hidden in special places. For example, in the small 'lioness chamber' of Les Trois Frères, a whole series of objects (flints, bones, a bear tooth and a burnt shell) were placed in fissures in this little 'sanctuary' dominated by one special feline image which seems to have been repeatedly pounded on the head and shoulders. The objects are most plausibly interpreted as 'ex-votos', offerings made to ask for – or to thank for – some kind of help?

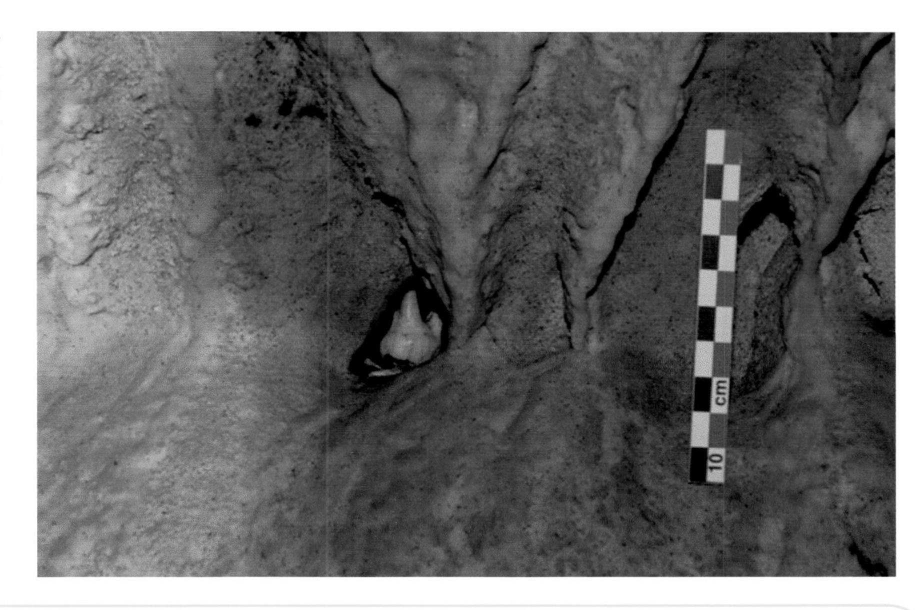

Figure 6.35. Bear tooth and flint tools in a niche in the 'Chapelle de la Lionne', Cave of Les Trois Frères (Ariège).

THE 'RITES OF SPRINGS'

It has been noticed that ice age cave art is frequently associated with 'bouches d'ombre', i.e. chasms or entrances to lower galleries, many of which have water in them – such as at Tito Bustillo, where one can hear the roar of the water from the main decorated panel; or at La Garma, where there may be a relationship between some images, such as a group of five hand stencils, and the sound of the river in another level of the karst, which can only be heard from the place where the images are located. This phenomenon may have been linked with myths concerning the underworld, the cult of the earth mother, and 'chthonic deities'; for example, at Pergouset, the engraved 'monsters' seem to emerge from a mysterious 'trou d'ombre', while at Ekain the farthest frieze of horses is located above two holes which lead to the dark and mysterious depths of the cave. At Le Travers de Janoye (Tarn) and Le Moulin (Lot), ibex and bison figures are linked to deep fissures into which the caves' waters disappear. Moreover, Pech Merle's 'bison-women' figures were placed under a block where water intermittently plunges down in a cascade from above and disappears into the earth less than a metre below them. It is worth noting that rushing water must have been among the very loudest and most impressive noises known to ice age people.

In countless regions and times caves have been associated with the womb, with ideas relating to maternity and birth, and with the entrance to the underworld. Boundaries are areas of confusion to human beings and, like the orifices of the body, are sacred places full of taboo; caves certainly constitute a boundary between the outside world and the underworld and thus have a special significance in many mythologies. Water plays a major role in virtually every known religion, and running water in particular is frequently looked upon as potent, dangerous, and linked with spirits. It is therefore highly probable that where running water visibly crosses the boundary of

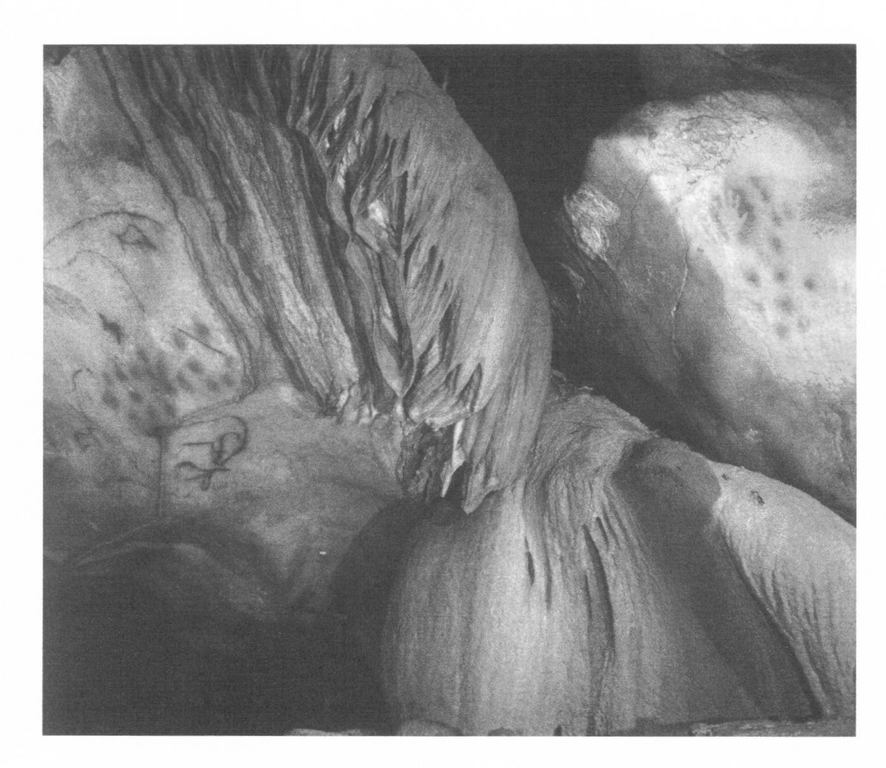

Figure 6.36. The 'bison-women' panel of Pech Merle (at left) in its context.

the underworld, in either direction, it may take on special significance – one could consider it 'abnormal water'. This effect would be heightened where water enters the earth in an impressive setting (as at Le Mas d'Azil, Labastide), or where it emerges as a spring – and especially a hot spring.

It has been suggested that these factors are likely to have played a role in whatever beliefs and rituals lie behind Palaeolithic parietal art – what might therefore be called the 'rites of springs'. Is it a coincidence, for example, that large clay models have only been found in two caves through which rivers flow (Le Tuc d'Audoubert and Montespan), and that both contained a headless snake skeleton? A large number of decorated caves are located very close to springs, and there is a marked correspondence between certain parietal sites and thermal/mineral springs; for example, the five or six decorated caves in the Monte Castillo overlook the village of Puente Viesgo, through which a geological fault runs, responsible for a number of hot springs which have been found suitable for medicinal purposes. It would be unsurprising if in the last ice age very special significance was accorded to springs which did not freeze and/or which were thought to have medicinal or magical powers.

Anything unusual such as hot springs may well have led to beliefs in supernatural agents causing these things to happen at particular places in the landscape or deep inside caves – things which were clearly extraordinary compared to the natural environment.

To sum up, ice age images had multiple functions – some were probably for decoration, others for storytelling and transmitting useful or vital information, and some were almost certainly religious in some way.

Is complex thought likely thousands of years in our deeper past? Certainly, our ice age ancestors were capable of complicated ideas and beliefs, but a sense of 'individual identity' is a process that is very much part of Western enculturation. 'Who am I?', 'What am I?' – these are probably not the sort of questions that would have concerned them. Our ancestors – like those few remaining indigenous populations that have survived intrusion from the modern world – lived in a wilderness that they felt no need to tame or shape to their own ends. They belonged to and were embedded in a pattern of life within the natural world that they knew they couldn't control or dominate – indeed such a notion probably never occurred to them. People who live on the margins of the developed world depend on one another for survival, and the basis of their existence was – and still is – group integrity and cohesion, relationships with each other, and their belonging to a 'place' and their relationship to that place. 'We' takes precedence over 'I', and this is how tribal life operates successfully. It seems highly probable that the same was true in the last ice age.

Conclusion

'The most important factor in survival is neither intelligence nor strength but adaptability.' – Charles Darwin

Over the course of this book's six chapters we have learned a great deal about our ice age ancestors – although it has involved tackling a giant jigsaw of information and evidence with many pieces missing. We have tried to fill in some of the gaps. But how far can we reasonably go with conjecture and supposition, given that it is vital to remain cautious when anything is difficult to establish or prove?

Current research is revealing archaeological evidence at an ever-accelerating pace – especially in areas where climate change is causing snow and permafrost to melt. At the same time, new and old finds are being re-examined in the laboratory, and a wide range of the latest scientific techniques are being applied. These are helping to consolidate some of our deductions about the past but are also eliminating some of the best-guess approaches we have hitherto relied upon. As we have seen (Chapter 1), this is particularly true of genetic analysis which has corrected some errors made previously in the sexing of human remains.

So what can we safely say about these early hunter-gatherers? We hope that we have been able to convey just how like us they seem to have been, despite the differences in technology and life-style. As far as we can tell, our ancestors looked, behaved and thought much like ourselves but in ways appropriate to the world they inhabited. We will never know what impression the often magnificent landscapes had on them, let alone the astonishing and otherworldly formations in deep caves. Presumably, their view of the surrounding environment and their sense of reality (i.e. what it meant to exist) must have been very different from our own. VERY different!

We have been able to piece together an impression – albeit an often sketchy one – of these early cultures, of the 1200 generations of men and women who spanned the 30,000 years studied in this book: what they looked like, where they chose to live, what they ate, how they clothed themselves and made implements and images. We have also made suggestions about how they organised themselves -- they certainly produced and manufactured goods, and traded their surplus commodities via long-distance connections.

We have assumed that men and women must have worked together to overcome the frequent and varied challenges that faced them during this immense period of time, and we have attempted to provide a picture of what it must have been like to grow up during the ice age. On the one hand we have clear evidence that some of these early communities supported the vulnerable and disabled – and perhaps even sick animals! On the other, we have no idea if people suffered from mental health problems, or what their feelings and emotions were like – for example, did they fall in love? Their imagery strongly suggests a respect – perhaps even feelings of tenderness or possibly veneration – for the animals on which they depended for so many vital resources. Also, we do not know which human actions and behaviours they judged to be acceptable or wrong; nor do we have the slightest inkling of their mythologies, or if they were religious in any way, beyond the few clues presented in the last chapter. As we have seen, the notion that 'shamans' were around in the ice age is completely unfounded.

Although many of our ancestors' characteristics and habits still exist in our own behavioural repertoire, it is highly probable that we have lost some of their skills and abilities. For example, they must have been able to mentally process and remember enormous quantities of unwritten information, such as how to move over large distances without getting lost. And even their basic survival skills – like lighting fires, finding resources and killing for food, or making clothing to insulate against the weather – are totally lost to the vast majority of modern people in the western world.

In addition, our ancestors must have been hyper-vigilant when it came to detecting dangers, many of which – such as attacks by predators – are no longer a problem today. Presumably they were also highly sensitive to situations that are perfectly natural but which were unusual and impossible to explain except through myths and legends – thunder, lightning, rainbows, echoes, and even freezing and thawing. Why did the sun rise in one place and descend in another? Why did the moon change shape and the stars move around? How did they explain dreams, let alone nightmares? Alas, we will never know how they made sense of all these things.

Can we take any warnings from our long history, not least about climate change? It is clear that, during the 30,000 years covered in this book, the climate and environment changed numerous times, with a particularly severe cold period at the Last Glacial Maximum (c. 20,000 years ago), and a perhaps equally devastating warming period at the end. And yet somehow our ancestors were resourceful and flexible enough to adapt to every change and survived! Will our 21st-century technology and knowledge enable us to do the same in the face of climate change?

It can be extremely difficult to reconstruct many aspects of everyday life in the last ice age, despite the often important contributions of experimentation – e.g. in working different materials. Most social and symbolic aspects of life remain completely inaccessible to the prehistorian. Hence for many intangible behaviours and customs we have inevitably had to resort to comparisons with historic or modern hunter-gatherer communities which have managed to maintain their existence despite the impact of negative intrusions from the modern world. What are the pros and cons of using comparative ethnography for this purpose? It is certainly a very rich source of possibilities and hypotheses. But we have stressed throughout the book that these recent people should never be seen as 'living fossils' and that the applicability of such information to the ice age remains extremely uncertain – it can only ever be speculation. It is extremely risky to pass from solid archaeological data to ethnological interpretation: if ethnographic analogies are used without care – as they very often have been in the past – hunches rapidly become certainties. It is extraordinarily tempting to project one's own beliefs and biases onto the mute data, and ultimately to invent new myths for the media – in other words, to produce prehistoric novels rather than a balanced, cautious account. We hope that we have avoided these temptations and pitfalls!

Case Study

El Mirón and Covalanas

To conclude our survey of ice age life, we present an account of two adjacent sites which together feature many of the varied aspects of the subject. They are located high up among the Cordillera Mountains in northern Spain, near the town of Ramales de la Victoria in eastern Cantabria.

Even today, when approaching from the valley below, one can easily spot the large west-facing opening of El Mirón cave in the steep, rocky cliff-face above. It is remarkably sheltered despite its large open vista, and it would have given its ice age residents a panoramic view of the open landscape with its steep escarpments and the valley below. Visitors from the many nearby caves and rock shelters could be seen approaching, as well as unwanted and dangerous predators and, most importantly, potential sources of food.

El Mirón literally means 'the voyeur', 'peeping Tom' or 'one who is staring fixedly' in Spanish, and these couldn't be more apt names for the vast cave mouth that dominates this part of the mountain. Its desirability as somewhere to live during the last ice age would also have been enhanced by its easy access to the nearby River Asón at the point where it meets the Calera and Gándara Rivers. In addition, the deep narrow valleys below El Mirón easily connect it to the Iberian coastline. Location is everything – and this was no less so during the last ice age. The cave mouth directly faces the prominent, triangular Pico San Vicente, a major landmark that looks just like the profile of Monte Castillo, the location of several major Palaeolithic living and decorated cave sites three valleys to the west of El Mirón.

Case Study Figure 1. El Mirón cave seen from afar

Choosing a home during the Upper Palaeolithic was never a haphazard affair – archaeologists have found the same highly desirable homes being occupied 'on and off' for thousands of years! El Mirón is one of those sites – evidence of occupation starts about 40,000 years ago and continues to occur all the way until the Bronze Age. The extensive excavations of Lawrence Straus, Manuel González Morales, and their team between 1996 and 2013 indicate that the cave was 'more or less in continuous use by humans in residence'.

Case Study Figure 2. Lawrence Straus outside El Mirón cave

During the Magdalenian period in this region, the climate was slowly and irregularly warming, but still colder than the present climate in Spain by on average about 5 degrees, and relatively dry at times as a great deal of the air's moisture was locked up in the ice fields of the Earth's northern hemisphere. The landscape would have had scattered stands of pine trees and junipers and occasional deciduous trees such as oak, elm, poplar, ash, beech or birch interspersed with grasslands and sagebrush. During the ice age the shoreline would have been about 5 km further away than it is today (i.e. *c.* 20 km.). There would have been no shortage of coastal rock-shelters that could provide overnight accommodation whenever people from El Mirón may have decided to exploit the abundant seafood and marine animals that the Cantabrian Sea had to offer, during either short visits or seasonal stays.

The cave's sunlit vestibule would have been a perfect vantage point for a vigilant observer on the lookout for that day's dinner. Along with a range of large game – always dominated by red deer and ibex – plus Atlantic salmon and other fish in the local rivers, there would also have been seasonal plant foods to harvest like tubers, starchy seeds and fungi.

Directly above El Mirón is the small, beautifully decorated cave of Covalanas with its remarkably well-preserved paintings. Both caves became known to archaeologists in 1903, although all early explorations of El Mirón were disappointing, including Lawrence Straus's own first visit in 1973. However, he was left with a lingering sense that there was something about the cave worthy of further investigation – a feeling, an intuition, that just wouldn't go away. One could see this as an example of 'having a nose' for a discovery, what the French call 'le pif'.

On his return in 1995 in association with González Morales, Straus was proved correct; during the long period during which the cave was excavated the team extracted tools, weapons and the remains of butchered animals revealing El Mirón's long, often repeated occupation beginning with sporadic use by Neanderthals.

Excavation revealed that, where the last ice age is concerned, the cave was used for brief occupations during the Gravettian and Solutrean periods, but much more extensively during the initial and early Magdalenian. The people made their living hunting mainly red deer and ibex – this was logical as the surrounding steep, rocky cliffs constitute classic ibex habitat, while the broad valley below was favourable for red deer. Masses of faunal remains were uncovered, generally with the long bones intensively broken, presumably to access the marrow. There were also the remains of many repeatedly used hearths, with fire-cracked rocks and charcoal sediments.

The numerous stone tools included scrapers and bladelets; the flint debris left over from manufacturing these implements was just abandoned in situ. Some of the stone was local, but most of the high-quality flint came from coastal Basque country outcrops c. 50 km away. Families living in the Asón Valley would have established it as their home territory but must have maintained relationships with other groups in nearby valleys. They clearly had trade links and obtained flint materials from areas as far away as Southwest France.

There were further signs of everyday life: antler spearpoints, often with engraved linear markings; a broken pendant made of slate with a horsehead engraving; shell beads (possibly grave goods); some eyed needles for sewing; and an antler spearthrower of a similar design to specimens found in contemporary sites in Southwest France near Bordeaux, where there are also grooved reindeer incisors like the one item from this species found in El Mirón. But the prize goes to the discovery of an engraved shoulder blade of a red deer stag in 2004. The images on it of a striated hind head and an aurochs are virtually identical to ones found in El Castillo, Altamira, El Juyo and other cave sites in Cantabria, and also similar to images on cave walls in the region. They could perhaps be seen as cultural markers defining the territory of a distinctive regional band that in turn had direct or indirect social and trade relations with other groups in territories to the west in Asturias and to the east in the Basque Country and beyond.

The Red Lady

However, in 2010 these earlier finds were overshadowed when the team made the spectacular discovery of the incomplete remains of a female who was to become known as 'the Red Lady of El Mirón'. Spectacular due to the nature of her burial but also because of her Early Magdalenian date, the 'Red lady' is the only adult ice age burial found anywhere in the Iberian Peninsula.

At the back of the cave's living area, 'the vestibule', covering 250 sq m, the excavators found a very large block of limestone that had fallen from the ceiling about 19,500 years ago, a few centuries before the burial. However, this did little to deter people from occupying the cave, and indeed this is where the excavators found the woman's corpse had been placed – in a natural depression in the metre-wide space between the cave wall and the limestone block.

Analysis revealed she was about 35- 40 years old when she died, and was buried sometime around 18,700 years ago. It is thought that she was originally buried on her left side with her back towards the stone block and facing the rear cave wall, and her skull was attached at the time of burial. At some later point, and after her flesh had naturally decomposed, her remains were disturbed by a carnivore. Sometime later still, her cranium and most of the unconnected long bones were removed, leaving over 100 mostly smaller bones from the entire skeleton, including the jaw bone deposited in the burial space. Her remains and/or her clothing had been heavily stained with red ochre either to preserve her corpse or as part of a burial ritual. In Magdalenian times it was apparently common to remove body parts such as skulls to other sites perhaps for display and veneration (as was the case in nearby El Castillo Cave in central Cantabria, where early excavations uncovered two isolated skull fragments).

Case Study Figure 3. The distinctive ochre on the block at El Mirón

The ochre was found to be rich in haematite crystals, giving it an intensely sparkling effect. The source of this distinctive material was found to be 20 km from El Mirón in a coastal zone outcrop – perhaps it had powerful symbolic value with reference to blood and its associations with human life, reproduction, and death. We can only speculate. This ochre is compositionally different from the 'normal', 'everyday' ochres that are very abundant in the occupation layers and that probably came from local sources. The flat surface of the limestone block facing the cave mouth was engraved with a series of lines including a V- shaped motif that could represent a female pubic triangle and might have indicated the presence of a female burial behind; the rear surface adjacent to the burial was then heavily stained with the same special red ochre. The nearby wall was covered with a mass of engravings including lines and a horse and possibly a bison image. The engravings on the block were successively covered over by later Magdalenian occupation layers. The artwork on the flat, originally 'inner', sheared-off surface of the block can thus be dated to the period between the time that the block had fallen from the cave ceiling and the time when it began to be covered over by layers of sediment that formed after the human burial.

Analyses revealed that the Red Lady was relatively healthy during her life; her teeth had no caries but were heavily worn. This could have been due to the practice of using her teeth as tools (para-masticatory use). Her dental calculus, microwear and stable isotopes revealed that she ate meat, fish, and plant foods (seeds and mushrooms). This lady was clearly highly respected, and the place chosen for her interment implies that her memory was meant to remain 'part' of the daily activities of the living.

The secret sanctuary

The small entrance of Covalanas cave is today well hidden in vegetation above El Mirón, and it would probably have been very hard, if not downright dangerous, to climb up to it. Yet someone – doubtless one or a few of the Solutrean occupants of El Mirón – discovered it and decided to decorate it. Covalanas was never occupied; it was used exclusively for decoration. It is one of a large number of cave art sites in the area immediately surrounding El Mirón.

The details of technique and content make it highly probable that all the figures on the cave's walls were made by a single person in one artistic episode, thought to have taken place in the Solutrean period (*c*.25,000 - 22,000 years ago), because of their style. The animal figures are all drawn with the same technique – done in outline with dots of red ochre. Some dots were clearly applied with fingers, others with the more flexible thumb; some dots are very separate, others juxtaposed. In any case, with this deceptively simple technique the artist managed to express a tremendous variety of posture, perspective and movement.

It is noticeable that the art occurs in the part of the cave that is narrowest and highest, and in total darkness. The placing of the figures clearly involved a great deal of careful planning. There are 17 female red deer, one muscular stag which has shed its antlers, an aurochs whose whole back line is the rock shape, and a large horse with flowing mane and a long tail. Although it seems to be a very personal and possibly private project by one artist – of sex unknown – it was

Case Study Figure 4. The best-preserved hind in Covalanas, made with red dots

probably meant to be seen by others, as shown by the use of anamorphosis: i.e. one hind figure was drawn in a distorted fashion, in order to look perfect as one approaches it from a distance.

Whenever the authors visit Covalanas, we like to imagine our ice age ancestors moving along and squeezing through the narrow passages; their hand-held torches or lamps would have cast light and shadows to create a rippling effect and make the magnificent display of figures move along with them. Seeing the scene of these animals unfold before their eyes would be like being immersed in a theatre of images and surely feel like high drama for our early ancestors – experiences that we too enjoy and fully participate in today. So great is the impact, that modern visitors to this cave are often overcome with emotion, and we have no reason to doubt that the effect of seeing Covalanas for the first time or on any subsequent visit would have been equally thrilling or moving for Ice Age people.

Appendix

The Fake 'Venus' of Abri Pataud

At the start of July 1958, the Les Eyzies local news press announced the discovery of the skull of the young woman at the Abri Pataud excavation. At the end of that August, following a violent and destructive storm that tore away the protective tarpaulin covering the dig, great disorder was caused to the archaeological site. Sheets of cardboard were laid down to protect the layers and some engraved rocks, and weighted down with blocks of limestone.

Three days later an even more sensational find was reported. A Miss Joan Bamberger, visiting from the Peabody Museum at Harvard, had been carefully excavating and then picked up one of the blocks of limestone. After brushing off the sediment and turning it over, she saw 'with emotion' a bas-relief carving of a beautiful female figure. Joan wrote its description in the excavation notebook: the figure, approximately 6 cm in length, has a small round head, pendant breasts, a right shoulder, beginning of upper right arm, elongated torso, rounded abdomen and hips, long thin legs ending in a point, and a distinct natural perforation below the pubic region. The Abri Pataud figurine's round swollen abdomen led later researchers to propose that it is a female in the late stages of pregnancy.

Case Study Figure 5. The 'Venus' of the Abri Pataud (Dordogne); the limestone block is 18 x 14 cm.

Despite the excavation director Hal Movius's discomfort that it wasn't found in situ, all further analysis by the team of investigators working at the site led him to feel confident about its Palaeolithic antiquity. It wasn't until a few days later that doubt was cast on its authenticity – although not finding the stone in its original stratigraphic context always left many of the team undecided.

While picnicking by the nearby River Vézère, Sheldon Judson, the team's geologist, still had lingering doubts and decided to carry out an experiment to see how easy it would be to make a bas-relief female figure that would fool an expert prehistorian. Using a local limestone block, a few flint blades and a rinse in muddy water, a fake 'Venus' was produced in the same style as the newly discovered one. A short time later, while the group were enjoying their dinner at the Cro-Magnon Hotel, Hal Movius was presented (without a word of explanation) with the fake Venus on a bed of cooked green beans. After his initial 'confusion and astonishment' Movius quickly accepted it as authentic. However, when confronted with the truth, he quickly tried to take it as a joke. The same evening took an even stranger turn when, while the group was having coffee, the Abbé Breuil turned up at the hotel and, despite Judson's protests, Movius showed Breuil the 'new' Venus. Breuil examined the piece very carefully, and then became very enthusiastic about its style and quality, assuming that the piece came from the excavation. According to contemporary accounts, he was carried away, finding it 'wonderful' that two Venus carvings were found at the excavation site and – despite Judson's claims that he was the author – Breuil was reluctant to accept the second as a fake, saying it was impossible for a young student, no matter how skilful, to produce such a masterpiece and that he, Breuil, was an expert in these things. After Judson had provided all the necessary proof Breuil became violently angry, and harsh words were exchanged. Movius defended the fakers for their experiment, which was aimed at establishing criteria for identifying an authentic work of art. It was not, he protested, a prank done in bad taste.

One unfortunate outcome of this hilarious episode was that it led many people in later years to confuse the two Venus figures and believe the 'original' figure found by Joan Bamberger to be the fake. Doubts really began circulating in the 1970s, resulting in Brigitte and Gilles Delluc's extensive reconstruction of the facts. Having contacted many of the original team who had excavated at the site (an investigation spanning 25 years, no less) they reported that the figure's origin and age are better established than many figures of the Gravettian period, and so the reason for the rumours surrounding its authenticity are most definitely due to the confusion caused by the second, fake Venus.

References

INTRODUCTION

de Beaune, S. A. 1995. *Les Hommes au Temps de Lascaux. 40000-10000 avant J.-C.* Hachette: Paris.

Bosinski, G. 1990. *Homo sapiens. L'histoire des chasseurs du Paléolithique supérieur en Europe (40 000 - 10 000 av, J.-C).* Editions Errance: Paris.

Cheynier, A. 1965. *Comment Vivait l'Homme des Cavernes à l'Age du Renne.* Editions Robert Arnoux: Paris.

Delluc, B. and Delluc, G. 2003. *La Vie des Hommes de la Préhistoire.* Editions Ouest-France: Rennes.

Pfeiffer, J. E. 1982. *The Creative Explosion. An inquiry into the origins of art and religion.* Harper and Row: New York.

CHAPTER 1

Bocquet-Appel, J-P. *et al.* 2005. Estimates of Upper Palaeolithic meta-population size in Europe from archaeological data. *Journal of Archaeological Science* 32: 1656-68.

Brody, H. 2001. *The Other Side of Eden. Hunter-gatherers, farmers, and the shaping of the world.* Faber and Faber: London.

Duhard, J-P. 1993a. Upper Palaeolithic figures as a reflection of human morphology and social organization. *Antiquity* 67, 83-91.

Geist, V. 1978. *Life Strategies, Human Evolution, Environmental Design. Toward a Biological Theory of Health.* Springer-Verlag: New York.

Haws, J. A. *et al.* 2020. The early Aurignacian dispersal of modern humans into westernmost Eurasia. *Proceedings of the National Academy of Sciences* 117 (41) www.pnas.org/cgi/doi/10.1073/pnas.2016062117

Kehoe, A. B. 1990. Points and lines, pp. 23-37 in (S. M. Nelson and A. B. Kehoe, eds) *Powers of Observation: alternative views in archaeology.* American Anthropological Association, Archaeological Paper 2. Arlington, VA.

Kehoe, A. B. 1991. The weaver's wraith, pp. 430-35 in (D. Waldes and N. D. Willow, eds) *The Archaeology of Gender. Proceedings of the 22nd Annual Conference of the Archaeological Association of the University of Calgary.* University of Calgary Archaeological Association: Calgary.

Maier, A. *et al.* 2016. Demographic estimates of hunter-gatherers during the Last Glacial Maximum in Europe against the backdrop of palaeoenvironmental data. *Quaternary International* 425: 49-61.

Nadel, D. *et al.* 1994. 19,000-year-old twisted fibers from Ohalo II. *Current Anthropology* 35 (4): 451-7.

Nelson, R. K. 1983. *Make Prayers to the Raven.* University of Chicago Press: Chicago.

Nougier, L. R. 1959. *Géographie Humaine Préhistorique*. Paris.

Patou-Mathis, M. 2020. *L'Homme Préhistorique est aussi une Femme*. Allary Editions: Paris.

Roebroeks, W. *et al.* (eds) 2000. *Hunters of the Golden Age: The Mid-Upper Palaeolithic of Eurasia (30,000-20,000 BP).* University of Leiden Press: Leiden.

Rozoy, J-G. 1996. Le Magdalénien supérieur en Europe: Ecologie, démographie, regions, pp. 290-92 in *La Vie Préhistorique.* Editions Faton: Dijon.

Schmidt, I. *et al.* 2021. Population estimates for the Final Palaeolithic (14,000 to 11,600 years cal. BP) of Europe – challenging evidence and methodological limitations, pp. 221-37 in (L. Mevel *et al.*, eds) *On the Move. Mobility of People, Objects and Ideas during the European Upper Paleolithic.* Société Préhistorique française: Paris.

Soffer, O. 1985. *The Upper Paleolithic of the Central Russian Plain.* Academic Press: Orlando.

Straus, L. G. 2019. Just how dense on the Cantabrian landscape were Solutrean people? Current speculations, pp. 1-25 in (I. Schmidt *et al.* eds) *Human Adaptations to the Last Glacial Maximum. The Solutrean and its Neighbors.* Cambridge Scholars Publishing.

Tallavaara, M. *et al.* 2015. Human population dynamics in Europe over the Last Glacial Maximum. *Proceedings of the National Academy of Sciences* 112 (27): 8232-37.

Tanner, A. 1979. *Bringing Home Animals.* Institute of Social and Economic Research, Memorial University of Newfoundland: St John's.

The Lapedo child

Zilhão, J. and Trinkaus, E. (eds) 2002. *Portrait of the Artist as a Child. The Gravettian Human Skeleton from the Abrigo do Lagar Velho and its Archaeological Context.* Instituto Português de Arqueologia, Trabalhos de Arqueologia 22, Lisbon.

La Marche

Pales, L. and de St Péreuse, M. T. 1976. *Les Gravures de La Marche: II, Les Humains.* Ophrys: Paris.

Female figurines

Delporte, H. 1993. *L'Image de la Femme dans l'Art Préhistorique.* (2nd ed.). Picard: Paris.

Duhard, J-P. 1991. The shape of Pleistocene women. *Antiquity* 65, 552-61.

Duhard, J-P. 1993. Réalisme de l›Image Féminine Paléolithique. Cahiers du Quaternaire 19, C.N.R.S.: Paris.

Trinkaus, E. 2005. The adiposity paradox in the Middle Danubian Gravettian. *Anthropologie* 43 (2): 101-09.

Cap Blanc

Bahn, P. G. 2012. The Cap Blanc lady, pp. 120-25 in (P. Bahn, ed.) *Written in Bones. How human remains unlock the secrets of the dead.* Firefly: Toronto/Buffalo.

Dahlberg, A. and Carbonell, V. 1951. The dentition of the Magdalenian female from Cap Blanc, France. *Man* 61: 49-50

Tracks and traces

Bennett, M. R. *et al.* 2020. Walking in mud: remarkable Pleistocene human trackways from White Sands National Park (New Mexico). *Quaternary Science Reviews* 249: 106610

Bustos, D. *et al.* 2018. Footprints preserve terminal Pleistocene hunt? Human-sloth interactions in North America. *Science Advances* 4: eaar7621

Králik, M. and Novotny, V. 2005. Dermatoglyphics of ancient ceramics, pp. 449-97 in (J. Svoboda, ed.) *Pavlov I Southeast. A Window into the Gravettian Lifestyles.* Institute of Archaeology: Brno.

Králik, M., Novotny, V. and Oliva, M. 2002. Fingerprint on the Venus of Dolní Vestonice. *Anthropologie* 40 (2): 107-13.

Webb, S. 2021. An echo from a footprint: a step too far, pp. 397-412 in (A. Pastoors and T. Lenssen-Erz, eds) *Reading Prehistoric Human Tracks.* Springer Nature: Cham, Switzerland.

Webb, S. *et al.* 2006. Pleistocene human footprints from the Willandra Lakes, southeastern Australia. *Journal of Human Evolution* 50: 405-13.

Genders – rigid or fluid?

Claassen, C. and Joyce, R. A. 1997. *Women in Prehistory. North America and Mesoamerica.* University of Pennsylvania Press: Philadelphia.

Ehrenberg, M. 1989. *Women in Prehistory.* British Museum Publications: London.

Hollimon, S. E. 1997. The third gender in Native California: Two-Spirit undertakers among the Chumash and their neighbors, pp. 173-88 in C. Claassen and R. A. Joyce, eds) *Women in Prehistory. North America and Mesoamerica.* University of Pennsylvania Press: Philadelphia.

Women hunters

Brown, J. K. 1970. A note on the division of labor by sex. *American Anthropologist* 72: 1073-78.

Estioko-Griffin, A. 1985. Women as hunters: The case of the eastern Cagayan Agta group, pp. 18-32 in (P. B. Griffin and A. Estioko-Griffin, eds) *The Agta of Northeastern Luzon: Recent studies.* San Carlos: Cebu City, Philippines.

Estioko-Griffin, A. and Griffin, P. B. 1981. Woman the hunter: the Agta, pp. 121-51 in (F. Dahlberg, ed.) *Woman the Gatherer.* Yale University Press: New Haven.

Haas, R. *et al.* 2020. Female hunters of the early Americas. *Science Advances* 6, no. 45: 1-10.

Hedenstierna-Jonson, C. *et al.* 2017. A female Viking warrior confirmed by genomics. *American Journal of Physical Anthropology* 164: 853–60.

Lombard, M. and Kyriacou, K. 2020. Hunter-gatherer women. *Oxford Research Encyclopedia of Anthropology.* https://doi.org/10.1093/acrefore/9780190854584.013.105

Villotte, S. and Knüsel, C. J. 2014. "I sing of arms and of a man...": medial epicondylosis and the sexual division of labour in prehistoric Europe. *Journal of Archaeological Science* 43: 168-74.

Diet

Delluc, G., Delluc, B. and Roques, M. 1995. *La Nutrition Préhistorique.* Pilote 24: Périgueux.

Sunghir

Alexeeva, T. I. and Bader, N. O. (eds) 2000. *Homo sungirensis. Upper Palaeolithic man: ecological and evolutionary aspects of the investigation.* Scientific World: Moscow.

Trinkaus, E. and Buzhilova, A. P. 2018. Diversity and differential disposal of the dead at Sunghir. *Antiquity* 92 (361): 7–21.

Trinkaus, E. *et al.* 2014. *The People of Sunghir.* Oxford University Press: New York.

Violence

Bello, S. M. *et al.* 2011. Earliest directly-dated human skull-cups. *PLoS ONE* 6 (2): e17026

Bello, S. M. *et al.* 2015. Upper Palaeolithic ritualistic cannibalism: Gough's Cave (Somerset, UK) from head to toe. *Journal of Human Evolution* 82: 170-89.

Crevecoeur, I. *et al.* 2021. New insights on interpersonal violence in the Late Pleistocene based on the Nile valley cemetery of Jebel Sahaba. *Scientific Reports* 11: 9991. https://doi.org/10.1038/s41598-021-89386-y

Cro-Magnon

Charlier, P. *et al.* 2018. Did Cro-Magnon 1 have neurofibromatosis type 1? *Lancet* 391: 1259.

Thillaud, P. L. 1985. L'homme de Cro-Magnon et ses maladies, pp. 66-73 in Les Maladies de nos Ancêtres, *Les Dossiers Histoire et Archéologie* 97.

Romito

Bahn, P. G. 2012. The Romito dwarf, pp. 164-66 in (P. Bahn, ed.) *Written in Bones. How human remains unlock the secrets of the dead.* Firefly: Toronto/Buffalo.

Frayer, D. W., Macchiarelli, R. and Mussi, M. 1988. A case of chondrodystrophic dwarfism in the Italian Late Upper Palaeolithic. *American Journal of Physical Anthropology* 75: 549-65.

Teeth

Frayer, D. W. and Russell, M. D. 1987. Artificial grooves in the Krapina Neanderthal teeth. *American Journal of Physical Anthropology* 74: 393-405.

Humphrey, L. T. *et al.* 2014. Earliest evidence for caries and exploitation of starchy plant foods in Pleistocene hunter-gatherers from Morocco. *Proceedings of the National Academy of Sciences* 111 (3): 954-59.

Villotte, S., Ogden, A. R. and Trinkaus, E. 2018. Dental abnormalities and oral pathology of the Pataud 1 Upper Paleolithic human. *Bulletins et Mémoires de la Société d'Anthropologie de Paris* 30 (3): DOI:10.3166/bmsap-2018-0020

Diseases

Armelagos, G. 2009. The Paleolithic disease-scape, the hygiene hypothesis, and the second epidemiological transition, pp. 29-43 in (G. A. W. Rook, ed.) *The Hygiene Hypothesis and Darwinian Medicine.* Birkhäuser: Basel.

Armelagos, G. *et al.* 1996. Disease in human evolution: the re-emergence of infectious disease in the third epidemiological transition. DOI:10.5479/10088/22354

Cardona P., Català, K. and Prats, C. 2020. Origin of tuberculosis in the Paleolithic predicts unprecedented population growth and female resistance *Scientific Reports* 10, Article 42.

Chisholm, R. H., Trauer, J. M., Curnoe, D. and Tanaka, M. M. 2016. Controlled fire use in early humans might have triggered the evolutionary emergence of tuberculosis. *Proc. Natl. Acad. Sci. USA* 113: 9051–56.

Cockburn, T. A. 1971. Infectious diseases in ancient populations. *Current Anthropology* 12 (1): 45-62.

Dastugue, J. and de Lumley, M. A. 1976. Les maladies des hommes préhistoriques du Paléolithique supérieur et du Mésolithique, pp. 612-22 in (H. de Lumley, ed.) *La Préhistoire française*, vol. I:1. CNRS: Paris.

Sparacello, V. S. *et al.* 2018. New insights on Final Epigravettian funerary behavior at Arene Candide Cave (Western Liguria, Italy). *Journal of Anthropological Sciences* 96: 1-24.

Velo, J. 1984. Ochre as medicine: a suggestion for the interpretation of the archaeological record. *Current Anthropology*. 25 (5): p. 674.

Arcy parasite

Bouchet, F. *et al.* 1996. Palaeoparasitology in a Pleistocene context: initial observations in the Grande Grotte at Arcy-sur-Cure (Department of the Yonne, France). *Comptes Rendus de la Société française de Parasitologie, série III* 319: 147-51.

Burials

Bégouën, H., Bégouën, L. and Vallois, H. 1937. Une pendeloque faite d'un fragment de mandibule humaine (Epoque magdalénienne), pp. 559-64 in *Compte rendu, 12e Congrès Préhistorique de France, Toulouse-Foix*. Paris.

Kacki, S. *et al.* 2020. Complex mortuary dynamics in the Upper Paleolithic of the decorated Grotte de Cussac, France. *Proceedings of the National Academy of Sciences* 117 (26): 14851-56.

Le Mort, F. 1982. Actions intentionnelles sur les os humains, in *La Mort dans la Préhistoire*. Dossiers Histoire et Archéologie 66, September.

Mussi, M. 1996. Rituels funéraires dans les sépultures gravettiennes des Grottes de Grimaldi et de la Grotte delle Arene Candide: une mise au point, pp. 833-46 in (M. Otte, ed.) *Nature et Culture, Colloque de Liège, Dec. 1993*. ERAUL 68: Liège.

Pettitt, P. 2010. *The Palaeolithic Origins of Human Burial*. Routledge: London.

Svoboda, J. 2008. The Upper Paleolithic burial area at Predmostí: ritual and taphonomy. *Journal of Human Evolution* 54 (1): 15-33.

Trinkaus, E. *et al.* 2019. Pieces of people in the Pavlovian: burials, body parts and bones in the earlier Upper Palaeolithic. *Human Remains and Violence* 5 (1): 70-87.

Ullrich, H. 1996. Reconstruction of close biological relationships in Palaeolithic burials, pp. 765-96 in (M. Otte, ed.) *Nature et Culture, Colloque de Liège, Dec. 1993*. ERAUL 68: Liège.

The Dolní Vestonice trio

Klíma, B. 1987. Das jungpaläolithische Massengrab von Dolní Vestonice. *Quartär* 37/38: 53-62.

Klíma, B. 1995. *Dolní Vestonice II: Ein Mammutjägerrastplatz und seine Bestattungen*. The Dolní Vestonice Studies, vol. 3. Etudes et Recherches Archéologiques de l'Université de Liège 73.

Svoboda, J. A. 2020. *Dolní Vestonice-Pavlov. Explaining Paleolithic Settlements in Central Europe*. Texas A&M University Press: College Station.

Trinkaus, E. and Svoboda, J. (eds) 2006. *Early Modern Human Evolution in Central Europe. The People of Dolní Vestonice and Pavlov*. Oxford University Press: Oxford.

CHAPTER 2

Bahn, P. G. 1984. *Pyrenean Prehistory*. Aris and Phillips: Warminster.

Bahn, P. G. 2016. *Images of the Ice Age*. Oxford University Press: Oxford.

Bégouën, R. *et al.* 2019. *La Grotte d'Enlène. Immersion dans un habitat magdalénien*. In Fine: Paris.

Jelínek, J. 1975. *Encyclopédie Illustrée de l'Homme Préhistorique*. Gründ: Paris.

Olive, M. and Taborin, Y. (eds) 1989. *Nature et Fonction des Foyers Préhistoriques*. Mémoires du Musée de Préhistoire d'Ile de France No. 2. Nemours.

Palma di Cesnola, A. 2001. *Le Paléolithique Supérieur en Italie*. Jérôme Millon: Grenoble.

Soffer, O. 1985. *The Upper Paleolithic of the Central Russian Plain*. Academic Press: Orlando.

Zubrow, E., Audouze, F. and Enloe, J. (eds) 2010. *The Magdalenian Household: Unraveling Domesticity*. State University of New York Press: Albany.

The changing climate

Seltzer, A. M. *et al.* 2021. Widespread six degrees Celsius cooling on land during the Last Glacial Maximum. *Nature* 593: 228-32.

Flora and fauna

Cleyet-Merle, J-J. 1990. *La Préhistoire de la Pêche*. Editions Errance: Paris.

Duke, D. *et al.* 2021. Earliest evidence for human use of tobacco in the Pleistocene Americas. *Nature Human Behaviour* https://doi.org/10.1038/s41562-021-01202-9

Leroi-Gourhan, Arl. and Girard, M. 1979. Analyses polliniques de la grotte de Lascaux, pp. 75-80 in (A. Leroi-Gourhan and J. Allain, eds) *Lascaux Inconnu*. XIIe Suppl. à Gallia Préhistoire. C.N.R.S.: Paris.

Leroi-Gourhan, Arl., Schweingruber, F. H. and Girard, M. 1979. Les bois de Lascaux, pp. 185-88 in (A. Leroi-Gourhan and J. Allain, eds) *Lascaux Inconnu*. XIIe Suppl. à Gallia Préhistoire. CNRS: Paris.

Lister, A. and Bahn, P. 2007. *Mammoths* (3rd edition). Frances Lincoln: London / University of California Press: Berkeley.

Martínez-Varea, C. M. *et al.* 2019. *Corema album* archaeobotanical remains in western Mediterranean basin. Assessing fruit consumption during Upper Paleolithic in Cova de les Cendres (Alicante, Spain). *Quaternary Science Reviews* 207: 1-12.

Who could live...

Legge, A. J. 1972. Cave climates, pp. 97-103 in (E. S. Higgs, ed.) *Papers in Economic Prehistory*. Cambridge University Press: Cambridge.

Use of deep caves

Andrieux, C. 1979. Problèmes soulevés par l'action des circulations d'eau et d'air sur le climat des cavités souterraines dans les massifs karstiques, pp. 127-40 in (D. de Sonneville-Bordes, ed.) *La Fin des Temps Glaciaires en Europe*. CNRS: Paris.

Cave comforts

Cueto, M. *et al.* 2016. Under the skin of a lion: unique evidence of Upper Paleolithic exploitation and use of Cave Lion (*Panthera spelaea*) from the Lower Gallery of La Garma, Spain. PLos ONE 11 (10): e0163591

Leroi-Gourhan, A. 1981. Pollens et grottes ornées, pp. 295-97 in *Altamira Symposium*. Ministerio de Cultura: Madrid

Rottländer, R. C. A. and Schlichtherle, H. 1979. Food identification of samples from archaeological sites. *Archaeo Physika* 10: 260-67.

Sievers, C. *et al.* 2022. Plant bedding construction between 60,000 and 40,000 years ago at Border Cave, South Africa. *Quaternary Science Reviews* 275: 107280

Carry on camping

Bahn, P. G. 1983. New finds at Pincevent. *Nature* 304: 682-83.

Bodu, P. 1991. Pincevent site magdalénien, pp. 60-67 in *Les Premiers Chasseurs dans la vallée de la Seine*. Les Dossiers d'Archéologie 164.

Bosinski, G. 1981. *Gönnersdorf. Eiszeitjäger am Mittelrhein*. Rhenania-Verlag: Koblenz.

Combier, J. (ed.) 1982. *Les Habitats du Paléolithique Supérieur. Actes du Colloque International, Roanne-Villerest 1982.*

García-Diez, M. and Vaquero, M. 2015. Looking at the camp: Paleolithic depiction of a hunter-gatherer campsite. *PLoS ONE* 10 (12): e0143002

Gaucher, G. and Julien, M. 1980. A Pincevent reconstitution des tentes de chasseurs de rennes, pp. 46-51 in *Revivre la Préhistoire*, Dossiers de l'Archéologie 46.

Jenny, J. *et al.* 1989. Nature et function des foyers magdaléniens d'Hauterive-Champréveyres (Suisse), pp. 181-87 in (M. Olive and Y. Taborin, eds) *Nature et Fonction des Foyers Préhistoriques.* Mémoires du Musée de Préhistoire d'Ile de France No. 2. Nemours).

Julien, M. and Karlin, C. (eds) 2014. *Un Automne à Pincevent. Le campement magdalénien du niveau IV20.* Mémoire 57, Société Préhistorique française: Paris.

Leroi-Gourhan, A. and Brézillon, M. 1972. *Fouilles de Pincevent: essai d'analyse ethnographique d'un habitat magdalénien (la section 36).* VIIe supplement à Gallia Préhistoire. 2 vols.

Olive, M. 1988. *Une habitation magdalénienne d'Etiolles. L'unité P 15.* Mémoires de la Société Préhistorique française 20, Paris.

Soulier, P. 2021. *Pincevent (1964-2019). Cinquante-cinq années d'ethnologie préhistorique.* Mémoire de la Société Préhistorique française 68. Paris.

Building with mammoths

Iakovleva, L. *et al.* 2012. The late Upper Palaeolithic site of Gontsy (Ukraine): a reference for the reconstruction of the hunter-gatherer system based on a mammoth economy. *Quaternary International* 255: 86-93.

Klein, R. G. 1973. *Ice-Age Hunters of the Ukraine.* University of Chicago Press: Chicago.

Lister, A. and Bahn, P. 2007. *Mammoths* (3rd edition). Frances Lincoln: London / University of California Press: Berkeley.

Oliva, M. (ed.) 2009. *Sídliště mamutího lidu, u Milovic pod Pálavou: otázka struktur s mamutími kostmi / Milovice, site of the mammoth people below the Pavlov hills: the question of mammoth bone structures* (Studies in Anthropology, Palaeoethnology and Quaternary Geology 27, ns 19). Moravské Zemské Muzeum: Brno.

Pidoplichko, I. G. 1998. *Upper Palaeolithic Dwellings of Mammoth Bones in the Ukraine.* BAR International Series 712. Oxford.

Fire

Ballet, O. *et al.* 1979. Etude technique de poudres colorées de Lascaux, pp. 171-74 in (A. Leroi-Gourhan and J. Allain, eds) *Lascaux Inconnu.* CNRS: Paris.

Bordes, F. 1969. Traitement thermique du silex au Solutréen. *Bulletin de la Société Préhistorique française* 66: 197.

Collina-Girard, J. 1998. *Le Feu avant les Allumettes.* Editions de la Maison des Sciences de l'Homme: Paris.

Collins, M. B. 1973. Observations on the thermal treatment of chert in the Solutrean of Laugerie-Haute, France. *Proceedings of the Prehistoric Society* 39: 461-66.

Legoupil, D. 1989. Le feu chez les Indiens "canoeros" (nomades marins) de Patagonie: un exemple ethno-archéologique, pp. 123-27 in (M. Olive and Y. Taborin, eds) *Nature et Fonction des Foyers Préhistoriques.* Mémoires du Musée de Préhistoire d'Ile de France No. 2. Nemours.

McCauley, B. *et al.* 2020. A cross-cultural survey of on-site fire use by recent hunter-gatherers: implications for research on Palaeolithic pyrotechnology. *Journal of Paleolithic Archaeology* 3: 560-78.

Perlès, C. 1977. *Préhistoire du Feu.* Masson: Paris.

Pomiès, M. P. *et al.* 1999. Préparation des pigments rouges préhistoriques par chauffage. *L'Anthropologie* 103 (4): 503-18.

Théry-Parisot, I. and Costamagno, S. 2005. Propriétés combustibles des ossements: données expérimentales et réflexions archéologiques sur leur emploi dans les sites paléolithiques. *Gallia Préhistoire* 47: 235-54.

Have you got a light?

de Beaune, S.A. 1987. *Lampes et Godets au Paléolithique.* XXIIIe Supplément à Gallia Préhistoire. Paris.

de Beaune, S.A. 2000. Les techniques d'éclairage paléolithiques: un bilan. *Paleo* 12, 19-27.

Medina-Alcaide, M. A. *et al.* 2021. The conquest of the dark spaces: an experimental approach to lighting systems in Paleolithic caves. *PLoS ONE* 16 (6): e0250497. https://doi.org/10.1371/journal.pone.0250497

CHAPTER 3

Bahn, P. G. 1984. *Pyrenean Prehistory*. Aris and Phillips: Warminster.

Bahn, P. G. 2016. *Images of the Ice Age*. Oxford University Press: Oxford.

Bégouën, R. *et al.* 2019. *La Grotte d'Enlène. Immersion dans un habitat magdalénien.* In Fine: Paris.

Palma di Cesnola, A. 2001. *Le Paléolithique Supérieur en Italie*. Jérôme Millon: Grenoble.

Zubrow, E., Audouze, F. and Enloe, J. (eds) 2010. *The Magdalenian Household: Unraveling Domesticity.* State University of New York Press: Albany.

Toolmaking

Bird, C. F. M. 1993. Woman the toolmaker: evidence for women's use and manufacture of flaked stone tools in Australia and New Guinea, pp. 22-30 in (H. du Cros and L. Smith, eds) *Women in Archaeology. A feminist critique*. Occasional Papers in Prehistory 23, Australian National University: Canberra.

The flint stones

Paris, C. *et al.* 2019. Les gisements gravettiens d'Amiens-Renancourt 1 etv 2 (Somme, France): premières données palethnologiques, pp. 97-115 in *Préhistoire de l'Europe du Nord-Ouest: mobilités, climats et identités culturelles.* 28e Congrès, Société Préhistorique française.

Pigeot, N. 1986. Apprendre à débiter des lames: un cas archéologique d'éducation technique dans l'habitation U5 d'Etiolles. *Bulletin de la Société Préhistorique française* 83 (3): 67-69.

Taborin, Y. 1991. Le gisement d'Etiolles, pp. 68-71 in *Les Premiers Chasseurs dans la vallée de la Seine*. Les Dossiers d'Archéologie 164.

Mastic

Allain, J. and Rigaud, A. 1989. Colles et mastics au Magdalénien, pp. 221-23 in (M. Olive and Y. Taborin, eds) *Nature et Fonction des Foyers Préhistoriques.* Mémoires du Musée de Préhistoire d'Ile de France No. 2. Nemours).

Broglio, A. 1996. Les sépultures épigravettiennes de la Venetie (Abri Tagliente et Abri Villabruna), pp. 847-69 in (M. Otte, ed.) *Nature et Culture, Colloque de Liège, Dec. 1993.* ERAUL 68: Liège.

Leroi-Gourhan, A. 1983. Une tête de sagaie à armature de lamelles de silex à Pincevent (Seine-et-Marne). *Bulletin de la Société Préhistorique française* 80: 154-56.

Feats of clay

Bougard, E., 2010. *The use of clay in the Upper Palaeolithic of Europe. Symbolic Applications of a Material.* British Archaeological Reports International series 2069, Oxford.

Gonysevova, M. 1999. Fabrication expérimentale d'artefacts gravettiens en terre cuite et essai de reconstitution de la variante d'un "four" (Moravie, République Tchèque). *L'Anthropologie* 103 (4): 519-29.

Vandiver, P. B. 2022. Upper Paleolithic ceramic figurines and similarities to some late Pleistocene pigment and pottery materials and technologies of Eurasia. *Quaternary International* 608-609: 8-32.

Vandiver, P. B. *et al.* 1989. The origins of ceramic technology at Dolní Vestonice, Czechoslovakia. *Science* 246: 1002-8.

Using hard bits of animal

d'Errico, F. *et al.* 2018. The origin and evolution of sewing technologies in Eurasia and North America. *Journal of Human Evolution* 125: 71-86.

Hahn, J. *et al.* (eds) 1995. *Le Travail et l'Usage de l'Ivoire au Paléolithique Supérieur.* Istituto Poligrafico e Zecca della Stato, Libreria dello Stato: Rome.

Khlopachev, G. A. and Giria, E. U. 2009. *Secrets of the Ancient Carvers of Eastern Europe and Siberia: Treatment techniques of ivory and reindeer in the Stone Age (Based on archaeological and experimental data).* Nauka: St Petersburg. [in Russian, with English summary]

Newcomer, M. H. 1980. Savoir utiliser les outils préhistoriques, pp. 18-22 in *Revivre la Préhistoire*, Dossiers de l'Archéologie 46.

Wood

Aranguren, B. *et al.* 2018. Wooden tools and fire technology in the early Neanderthal site of Poggetti Vecchi (Italy). *Proc. Nat. Acad. Sc.* 115 (9): 2054-59.

Bergman, C. A. 1993. The development of the bow in Western Europe: a technological and functional perspective, pp. 95-105 in (G. L. Peterkin *et al*, eds) *Hunting and Animal Exploitation in the Later Palaeolithic and Mesolithic of Eurasia.* Arch. Papers of the American Anthropological Association No. 4.

Delluc, B. and Delluc, G. 1979. L'accès aux parois, pp. 175-85 in (A. Leroi-Gourhan and J. Allain, eds) *Lascaux Inconnu.* CNRS: Paris.

Langley, M. C. *et al.* 2020. Bows and arrows and complex symbolic displays 48,000 years ago in the South Asian tropics. *Science Advances* 6: eaba3831

Leroi-Gourhan, A., Schweingruber, F. and Girard, M. 1979. Les bois, pp. 185-91 in (A. Leroi-Gourhan and J. Allain, eds) *Lascaux Inconnu.* CNRS: Paris.

Lombard, M. 2011. Quartz-tipped arrows older than 60ka: further use-trace evidence from Sibudu, KwaZulu-Natal, South Africa. *Journal of Arch. Science* 38: 1918-30.

Rios-Garaizar, J. 2018. A Middle Palaeolithic wooden digging stick from Aranbaltza III, Spain. *PLoS ONE* 13(3): e0195044. https://doi.org/10.1371/journal.pone.0195044

Rozoy, J-G. 1978. *Les Derniers Chasseurs.* 3 vols. Bull. de la Société Archéologique Champenoise. Charleville.

Terberger, T. *et al.* 2021. The Shigir idol in the context of early art in Eurasia. *Quaternary International* 573: 14-29.

Innovations with fibres and plants

Adovasio, J. M., Soffer, O. and Page, J. 2007. *The Invisible Sex.* HarperCollins: New York.

Bahn, P. G. 1985. Utilisation des ressources végétales dans le Paléolithique et le Mésolithique des Pyrénées françaises, pp. 203-12 in *Homenatge al Dr Josep Corominas. Quaderns del Centre d'Estudis Comarcals de Banyoles* 1.

Bahn, P. G. 2001. Palaeolithic weaving: a contribution from Chauvet. *Antiquity* 75: 271-72.

Chauvet, G. 1910. *Os, ivoires et bois de renne ouvrés de la Charente. Hypothèses palethnographiques.* E. Constantin: Angoulême.

Ehrenberg, M. 1989. *Women in Prehistory.* British Museum Publications: London.

Glory, A. 1959. Débris de corde paléolithique à la grotte de Lascaux (Dordogne). *Mémoires de la Société Préhistorique Française* 5: 135-39.

Kehoe, A. B. 1990. Points and lines, pp. 23-37 in (S. M. Nelson and A. B. Kehoe, eds) *Powers of Observation: alternative views in archaeology.* American Anthropological Association, Archaeological Paper 2. Arlington, VA.

Kehoe, A. B. 1991. The weaver's wraith, pp. 430-35 in (D. Waldes and N. D. Willow, eds) *The Archaeology of Gender. Proceedings of the 22nd Annual Conference of the Archaeological Association of the University of Calgary.* University of Calgary Archaeological Association: Calgary.

Kilgore, C. and Gonthier, E. 2014. Premières découvertes sur les techniques de fabrication de cordages à partir de rouets (*Bâtons-percés*). Evidences sur le mobilier et l'art pariétal du Paléolithique supérieur (Magdalénien). *L'Anthropologie* 118 (3): 347-81.

Lucas, C. *et al.* 2019. Investigating the use of Paleolithic perforated batons: new evidence from Gough's Cave (Somerset, UK). *Archaeological and Anthropological Sciences* 11: 5231-55.

Nadel, D. *et al.* 1994. 19,000-year-old twisted fibers from Ohalo II. *Current Anthropology* 35 (4): 451-7.

Soffer, O. *et al.* 2000. The 'Venus' figurines: textiles, basketry, gender and status in the Upper Paleolithic. *Current Anth*ropology 41: 511-37.

Soffer, O. *et al.* 2000a. Palaeolithic perishables made permanent. *Antiquity* 74: 812-21.

Vanrell, L. and Olive, M. 2021. Autres traces d'activités humaines dans la grotte, pp. 52-53 in (L. Vanrell and M. Olive, eds) *La Grotte Cosquer. Trente ans de recherches.* Dossiers d'Archéologie 408, Nov/Déc. Faton: Dijon.

Animal skins and clothing

Charles, R. 1997. The exploitation of carnivores and other fur-bearing mammals during the North-Western European late Upper Palaeolithic and Mesolithic. *Oxford Journal of Archaeology* 16 (3): 253-77.

Gilligan, I. 2018. *Climate, Clothing, and Agriculture in Prehistory*. Cambridge University Press: Cambridge.

Keeley, L. H. 2010. The probable division of labor in Magdalenian hide working, pp. 227-34 in (E. Zubrow *et al.*, eds) *The Magdalenian Household: Unraveling Domesticity.* State University of New York Press: Albany.

Lbova, L. 2016. Anthropomorphic figurines of Ice Age Art in Siberia: new data and perspectives on the function of prehistoric mobile art. *Expression* 12: 16-25.

Poplin, F. 1980. Le dépeçage des animaux, pp. 24-32 in *Revivre la Préhistoire*, Dossiers de l'Archéologie 46.

Soffer, O., Adovasio, J. M. and Hyland, D. C. 2000. The "Venus" figurines: textiles, basketry, gender and status in the Upper Palaeolithic. *Current Anthropology* 41 (4): 511-37.

La Madeleine

Vanhaeren, M. and d'Errico, F. 2001. La parure de l'enfant de La Madeleine (Fouilles Peyrony). Un nouveau regard sur l'enfance au Paléolithique Supérieur. *Paleo* 13: 201-40.

Best foot forward

Ledoux, L. 2019. *L'Ichnologie Préhistorique et les Traces d'Activités au Sein des Cavités Ornées. Les grottes de Fontanet (Ariège) et de Cussac (Dordogne).* Doctoral thesis, University of Bordeaux.

Pastoors, A. *et al.* 2015. Tracking in caves. Experience based reading of Pleistocene human footprints in French caves. *Cambridge Archaeological Journal* 25 (3): 551-64.

Trinkaus, E. 2005. Anatomical evidence for the antiquity of human footwear use. *Journal of Archaeological Science* 32: 1515-26.

Trinkaus, E. and Shang, H. 2008. Anatomical evidence for the antiquity of human footwear: Tianyuan and Sunghir. *Journal of Archaeological Science* 32: 1515-26.

CHAPTER 4

Bahn, P. G. 1983. Late Pleistocene economies of the French Pyrenees, pp. 168-86 in (G. Bailey, ed.) *Hunter-Gatherer Economy in Prehistory. A European Perspective*. Cambridge University Press: Cambridge.

Bahn, P. G. 1984. *Pyrenean Prehistory*. Aris and Phillips: Warminster.

Bahn, P. G. 2007. Hunting for clues in the Palaeolithic. *Antiquity* 81: 1086-88.

Bailey, G. (ed.) 1983. *Hunter-Gatherer Economy in Prehistory. A European Perspective*. Cambridge University Press: Cambridge.

de Beaune, S. A. (ed.) 2007. *Chasseurs-cueilleurs: Comment vivaient nos ancêtres du Paléolithique supérieur*. CNRS: Paris.

Geist, V. 1978. *Life Strategies, Human Evolution, Environmental Design. Toward a Biological Theory of Health*. Springer-Verlag: New York.

Jelínek, J. 1989. *Sociétés de Chasseurs. Ces hommes qui vivent de la nature sauvage*. Gründ: Paris.

Speth, J. D. 2017. Putrid meat and fish in the Eurasian Middle and Upper Paleolithic: are we missing a key part of Neanderthal and modern human diet? *PaleoAnthropology* 2017: 44-72.

Zubrow, E., Audouze, F. and Enloe, J. (eds) 2010. *The Magdalenian Household: Unraveling Domesticity.* State University of New York Press: Albany.

The boomerang

Bahn, P. G. 1987. Return of the Euro-boomerang. *Nature* 329: 388.

Bahn, P. G. 1995. Flight into pre-history. *Nature* 373: 562.

Evers, D. and Valde-Nowak, P. 1994. Wurfversuche mit dem jungpaläolithischen Wurfgerät aus der Oblazowa-Höhle in den polnischen Karpaten. *Archäologisches Korrespondenzblatt* 24: 137-44.

Valde-Nowak, P. *et al.* 1987. Upper Palaeolithic boomerang made of a mammoth tusk in south Poland. *Nature* 329: 436-38.

Solutré

Combier, J. (ed.) 2016. *Solutré, Volume du 150e anniversaire*. Centre de Recherches de Solutré, Académie de Mâcon.

Horses

Bahn, P. G. 1982. Homme et cheval dans le Quaternaire des Pays de l'Adour, pp. 21-26 in *Les Pays de l'Adour, Royaume du Cheval,* Guide-Catalogue, Musée Pyrénéen: Lourdes.

Gaunitz, C. *et al.* 2018. Ancient genomes revisit the ancestry of domestic and Przewalski's horses. *Science* 360: 111-14.

Animal control

Bahn, P. G. 1976. Les bâtons troués--réveil d'une hypothèse abandonee. *Bulletin de la Société Préhistorique de l'Ariège* 31: 47-54.

Bahn, P. G. 1978. The 'unacceptable face' of the West European Upper Palaeolithic. *Antiquity* 52: 183-92.

Bahn, P. G. 1980. Crib-biting: tethered horses in the Palaeolithic? *World Archaeology* 12, October: 212-17.

Bahn, P. G. 1984. Preneolithic control of animals in Western Europe: the faunal evidence, pp. 27-34 in (C. Grigson and J. Clutton-Brock, eds) *Animals and Archaeology: 4 - Husbandry in Europe,* Proceedings of the 4th International Congress of Archaeozoology, London, April 1982; British Arch. Reports, International series no. 227.

Kuntz, D. 2018. Relations homme/renne au Paléolithique: la question de la domestication et de ses critères d'identification, pp. 1-16 in (A. Averbouh *et al.* eds) *L'Aquitaine à la fin des temps glaciaires.* PALEO, numéro special.

Pales, L. and de St Péreuse, M. T. 1966. Un cheval-prétexte: retour au chevêtre. *Objets et Mondes* 6: 187-206.

Piette, E. 1906. Le chevêtre et la semi-domestication des animaux aux temps pléistocènes. *L'Anthropologie* 17: 27-53.

Reining in the reindeer

Audouze, F. 1996. Les lieux de découpe des rennes à Verberie, pp. 12-17 in *Revivre le Passé grâce à l'archéologie*. Dossiers d'Archéologie 216.

Bahn, P. G. 1977. Seasonal migration in South-west France during the late Glacial period. *Journal of Archaeological Science* 4: 245-57.

David, F. *et al.* 2010. Slaughter and carcass processing of reindeer in Siberia. Patterns and distribution of tasks – comparisons between prehistoric and ethnoarchaeological cases, pp. 245-68 in (E. Zubrow *et al.*, eds) *The Magdalenian Household: Unraveling Domesticity.* State University of New York Press: Albany.

Enloe, J. G. 2010. Fauna and site structure at Verberie. Implications for domesticity and demography, pp. 22-50 in (E. Zubrow *et al.*, eds) *The Magdalenian Household: Unraveling Domesticity.* State University of New York Press: Albany.

Enloe, J. and David, F. 1989. Le remontage des os par individus: le partage du renne chez les Magdaléniens de Pincevent (La Grande Paroisse, Seine-et-Marne). *Bulletin de la Société Préhistorique française* 86 (9): 275-81.

Speth, J. D. 2020. Paleoindian bison hunting on the North American Great Plains – two critical nutritional constraints. *PaleoAnthropology* 2020: 74-97.

Sturdy, D. A. 1975. Some reindeer economies in prehistoric Europe, pp. 55-95 in (E. S. Higgs, ed.) *Palaeoeconomy.* Cambridge University Press: Cambridge.

The red deer

Clark, G. A. and Straus, L. G. 1983. Late Pleistocene hunter-gatherer adaptations in Cantabrian Spain, pp. 131-48 in (G. Bailey, ed.) *Hunter-Gatherer Economy in Prehistory. A European Perspective.* Cambridge University Press: Cambridge.

Straus, L. G. 1992. *Iberia Before the Iberians: The Stone Age Prehistory of Cantabrian Spain.* University of New Mexico Press: Albuquerque.

The ibex

Bahn, P. G. 1979. La Paléoéconomie magdalénienne du Bassin de Tarascon (Ariège). *Bulletin de la Société Préhistorique de l'Ariège* 34: 37-46.

Straus, L. G. 1987. Upper Paleolithic ibex hunting in Southwest Europe. *Journal of Archaeological Science* 14: 163-78.

The mammoth

Agam, A. and Barkai, R. 2018. Elephant and mammoth hunting during the Paleolithic: a review of the relevant archaeological, ethnographic and ethno-historical records. *Quaternary* doi:10.3390/quat1010003

Bocherens, H. and Drucker, D. G. 2021. Isotopic insights on ecological interactions between humans and woolly mammoths during the Middle and Upper Palaeolithic in Europe, pp. 349-62 in (G. E. Konidaris *et al.*, eds) *Human-Elephant Interactions from Past to Present.* Tübingen Paleoanthropology Book Series – Contributions in Paleoanthropology 1. Tübingen University Press: Tübingen.

Demay, L. *et al.* 2021. Upper Pleistocene hominins and wooly mammoths in the East European plain, pp. 201-33 in (G. E. Konidaris *et al.*, eds) *Human-Elephant Interactions from Past to Present.* Tübingen Paleoanthropology Book Series – Contributions in Paleoanthropology 1. Tübingen University Press: Tübingen.

Lister, A. and Bahn, P. 2007. *Mammoths.* (3rd ed.). Frances Lincoln: London / University of California Press: Berkeley.

Carnivores and small game

Almeida, F. *et al.* 2007. An Upper Paleolithic Pompeii: technology, subsistence and paleoethnography at Lapa do Anecrial, pp. 119-39 in *From the Mediterranean basin to the Portuguese Atlantic shore: Papers in Honor of Anthony Marks. Actas do IV Congresso de Arqueologia Peninsular, Faro Setembro 2004.* Universidade do Algarve: Faro.

Soffer, O. 1985. *The Upper Paleolithic of the Central Russian Plain.* Academic Press: Orlando.

Villaverde, V. *et al.* 1998. The Upper Paleolithic in Mediterranean Spain: a review of current evidence. *Journal of World Prehistory* 12 (2): 121-98.

Villaverde, V. *et al.* 2012. The end of the Upper Palaeolithic in the Mediterranean Basin of the Iberian Peninsula. *Quaternary International* 272/3: 17-32.

Embarking on a relationship with dogs

Baumann, C. *et al.* 2020. Fox dietary ecology as a tracer of human impact on Pleistocene ecosystems. *PLoSONE* 15(7): e0235692

Chambers, J. *et al.* 2020. Dog-human coevolution: cross-cultural analysis of multiple hypotheses. *Journal of Ethnobiology* 40 (4): 414-33.

Davis, S. J. M. and Valla, F. R. 1978. Evidence for domestication of the dog 12.000 years ago in the Natufian of Israel. *Nature* 276: 608-10.

Germonpré, M. *et al.* 2009. Fossil dogs and wolves from Palaeolithic sites in Belgium, the Ukraine and Russia: osteometry, ancient DNA and stable isotopes. *Journal of Archaeological Science* 36: 473-90.

Janssens, L. *et al.* 2018. A new look at an old dog: Bonn-Oberkassel reconsidered. *Journal of Archaeological Science* 92: 126-38.

Schleidt, W. M., and Shalter, M. D. 2018. Dogs and mankind: coevolution on the move – an update. *Human Ethnology Bulletin* 33: 15-38.

Shipman, P. 2021. *Our Oldest Companions: The Story of the First Dogs.* Harvard University Press: Cambridge, Mass.

Plucky bird hunters

Bahn, P. G. 1979. La Paléoéconomie magdalénienne du Bassin de Tarascon (Ariège). *Bulletin de la Société Préhistorique de l'Ariège* 34: 37-46.

Eastham, A. 2021. *Man and Bird in the Palaeolithic of Western Europe.* Archaeopress: Oxford.

Laroulandie, V. *et al.* 2020. Bird procurement by humans during the Middle and early Upper Paleolithic of Europe: new data for the Aurignacian of southwestern France. *Quaternary International* 543: 16-24.

Fishing on a small scale

Aura, J. E. *et al.* 2010. Treinta años de investigación sobre el Paleolítico superior de Andalucía: la Cueva de Nerja (Málaga, España), pp. 149-72 in (X. Mangado, ed.) *El Paleolítico Superior. Novedades del Siglo XXI.* Universitat de Barcelona: Barcelona.

Bazile, F. 1991. Habiter le Languedoc au Paléolithique supérieur, pp. 72-79 in *L'Homme de Cro-Magnon*. Les Dossiers d'Archéologie 156.

The brown bears and the fishermen (*BBC: Japan, Earth's Enchanted Islands*) 2015. https://www.bbc.co.uk/programmes/p02trsmt

Cleyet-Merle, J-J. 1990. *La Préhistoire de la Pêche*. Editions Errance: Paris.

García, C. and Martinez, J. J. 1988. The Atlantic salmon in the rivers of Spain with particular reference to Cantabria, pp. 179-209 in (D. Mills and D. Piggins, eds) *Atlantic Salmon: Planning for the Future*. Croom Helm: London. DOI:10.1007/978-94-009-1235-9_10

Jochim, M. A. 1976. *Hunter-Gatherer Subsistence and Settlement: a predictive model.* Academic Press: New York.

Le Gall, O. 1992. Les Magdaléniens et l'ichtyofaune dulçaquicole, pp. 277-85 in (J-P. Rigaud *et al.*, eds) *Le Peuplement Magdalénien*. Editions du Comité des Travaux Historiques et Scientifiques: Paris.

Mussi, M. *et al.* 2008. Tempi e modi del ripopolamento dell'Appennino Centrale nel Tardiglaciale: nuove evidenze da Grotta di Pozzo (AQ), pp. 111-31 in (M. Mussi, ed.) *Il Tardiglaciale in Italia - Lavori in corso.* BAR International Series 1859, Archaeopress: Oxford.

Roche, J. and McHutchison, M. (eds) 1998. *First Fish - First People. Salmon Tales of the North Pacific Rim.* University of Washington Press: Seattle.

Plant foods

Lippi, M. M. *et al.* 2015. Multistep food plant processing at Grotta Paglicci (Southern Italy) around 32,600 cal B.P. *Proceedings of the National Academy of Sciences* 112, No. 39: 12075-80.

Revedin, A. *et al.* 2010. Thirty thousand year-year-old evidence of plant food processing. *Proc. Nat. Acad. Sciences* 107 (44): 18815-19.

Tyldesley, J. A. and Bahn, P. G. 1983. Use of plants in the European Palaeolithic: a review of the evidence. *Quaternary Science Reviews* 2: 53-81.

Ohalo

Nadel, D. 1996. The organization of space in a fisher-hunter-gatherers camp at Ohalo II, Israel, pp. 373-88 in in (M. Otte, ed.) *Nature et Culture, Colloque de Liège, Dec. 1993.* ERAUL 68: Liège.

Nadel, D. and Hershkovitz, I. 1991. New subsistence data and human remains from the earliest Levantine Epipalaeolithic. *Current Anthropology* 32 (5): 631-5.

Nadel, D. *et al.* 1994. 19,000-year-old twisted fibers from Ohalo II. *Current Anthropology* 35 (4): 451-7.

Ice age food processors

Carbonell, E. and Bellmunt, C. S. 2016. *Recetas Paleo. La dieta de nuestros orígenes para une vida saludable.* Libros Cúpula: Barcelona.

Speth, J. D. 2015. When did humans learn to boil? *PaleoAnthropology* 2015: 54-67.

CHAPTER 5

Blaffer Hrdy, S. 2009. *Mothers and Others: The Evolutionary Origins of Mutual Understanding.* The Belknap Press of Harvard University Press: Cambridge, Mass.

Konner, M. 2010. *The Evolution of Childhood: Relationships, Emotions, Mind.* The Belknap Press of Harvard University Press: Cambridge, Mass.

Taylor, T. 1996. *The Prehistory of Sex.* Fourth Estate: London.

From here to maternity

Bahn, P. G. 1986. No sex, please, we're Aurignacians. *Rock Art Research* 3: 99-120.

Delluc, G. and B. 2006. *Le Sexe au Temps des Cro-Magnons.* Pilote 24: Périgueux.

d'Errico, F. 2009 The oldest representation of childbirth, pp. 99-109 in (P.G. Bahn, ed.) *An Enquiring Mind. Studies in Honor of Alexander Marshack.* American School of Prehistoric Research Monograph series. Oxbow Books, Oxford.

The obstetric dilemma

Dunsworth, H. M. 2018. There is no "obstetrical dilemma": towards a braver medicine with fewer childbirth interventions. *Perspectives in Biology and Medicine* 61 (2): 249-63.

Wells, J. C. K., DeSilva, J. M. and Stock, J. T. 2012. The obstetric dilemma: an ancient game of Russian roulette, or a variable dilemma sensitive to ecology? *American Journal of Physical Anthropology* 149, No S55: 40-71.

The Abri Pataud

Movius, H. L. (ed.) 1975. *Excavation of the Abri Pataud, Les Eyzies (Dordogne)*. American School of Prehistoric Research, Bulletin 30. Cambridge, Mass.

The Ostuni burial

Coppola, D. and Vacca, E. 1996. Les sépultures paléolithiques de la Grotte de Sainte Marie d'Agnano à Ostuni (Italie), pp. 797-810 in (M. Otte, ed.) *Nature et Culture, Colloque de Liège, Dec. 1993*. ERAUL 68: Liège.

Nava, A. *et al.* 2017. Virtual histological assessment of the prenatal life history and age at death of the Upper Paleolithic fetus from Ostuni (Italy). *Scientific Reports* 7: 9427. DOI:10.1038/s41598-017-09773-2

The Grotte des Enfants

Gambier, D. 1996. Pratiques funéraires au Paléolithique supérieur. L'exemple de la sépulture des enfants de la Grotte des Enfants (site de Grimaldi-Italie), pp. 811-31 in (M. Otte, ed.) *Nature et Culture, Colloque de Liège, Dec. 1993*. ERAUL 68: Liège.

The Wilczyce burial

Irish, J. D. *et al.* 2008. A late Magdalenian perinatal human skeleton from Wilczyce, Poland. *Journal of Human Evolution* 55: 736-40.

Twins

Lieverse, A. R., Bazaliiskii, V. I. and Weber, A. W. 2015. Death by twins: a remarkable case of dystocic childbirth in Early Neolithic Siberia. *Antiquity* 89: 23-38.

The twins of Krems-Wachtberg

Teschler-Nicola, M. *et al.* 2020. Ancient DNA reveals monozygotic newborn twins from the Upper Palaeolithic. *Communications Biology* https://www.nature.com/articles/s42003-020-01372-8

Sharing the caring

Hewlett, B. S. *et al.* 2000. Internal working models, trust and sharing among foragers. *Current Anthropology* 41: 287-97

Postmenopausal women

Hawkes. K. *et al.* 1998. Grandmothering, menopause, and the evolution of human life histories. *Proceedings of the National Academy of Sciences* 95: 1336-39.

Family size and birth intervals

Hewlett, B. S. and Lamb, M. E. (eds) 2017. *Hunter-Gatherer Childhoods: evolutionary, developmental and cultural perspectives*. Routledge: Abingdon.

First foods

Robinson, D. W. 2010. Land use, land ideology: an integrated geographic information systems analysis of rock art within south-central California. *American Antiquity* 75 (4): 792-818.

Methods of carrying and transporting infants

Fisher, E. 1979. *Woman's Creation. Sexual Evolution and the Shaping of Society.* McGraw-Hill: New York.

Russell, P. M. 1987. *Women in Upper Paleolithic Europe*. M.A. Thesis.

Who stays and who goes?

Alverez, H. P. 2004. Residence groups among hunter-gatherers: a view of the claims and evidence for patrilocal bonds, pp. 420-42 in (B. Chapais and C. M. Berman, eds) *Kinship and Behaviour in Primates*. Oxford University Press: Oxford.

Infanticide

Birdsell, J. B. 1968. Some predictions for the Pleistocene based on equilibrium systems among hunter-gatherers, pp. 229-40 in (R. B. Lee and I. DeVore, eds) *Man the Hunter*. Aldine: Chicago.

Freeman, M. A. 1971. Social and ecologic analysis of systematic female infanticide among the Netsilik Eskimo. *American Anthropologist* 73: 1011-18.

Growing up

Bahn, P. G. 2015. Children of the Ice Age, pp. 167-87 in (G. Coskunsu, ed.) *The Archaeological Study of Childhood: Interdisciplinary Perspectives on an Archaeological Enigma.* The Institute for European and Mediterranean Archaeology Distinguished Monograph Series 3: SUNY Press: Albany, NY.

Bell, H. R. 1998. *Men's Business Women's Business: The Spiritual Role of Gender in the World's Oldest Culture.* Inner Traditions International: Rochester, Vermont.

Grey, P. 2011. The evolutionary biology of education: how our hunter-gatherer educative instincts could form the basis for education today. *Evolution: Education and Outreach* 4: 28–40.

Kaplan, H. *et al.* 2000. A theory of human life history evolution: diet, intelligence and longevity. *Evolutionary Anthropology* 9 (4): 156-85.

Langley, M. C. 2017. Magdalenian children: projectile points, portable art and playthings. *Oxford Journal of Archaeology* 37 (1): 3–24.

Langley, M. C. and Litster, M. 2018. Is it ritual? Or is it children? Distinguishing consequences of play from ritual actions in the prehistoric archaeological record. *Current Anthropology* 59 (5): 616-43.

Lbova, L. 2021. The Siberian Paleolithic site of Mal'ta: a unique source for the study of childhood archaeology. *Evolutionary Human Sciences* 3: e9.

Nowell, A. 2021. *Growing Up in the Ice Age*. Oxbow; Oxford.

The 'Lion Man'

Clifford, E. and Bahn, P. 2018. If the cat fits... a new look at the so-called 'Lion Man' from Hohlenstein-Stadel. *Die Kunde* 69: 99-120.

Clifford, E. and Bahn, P. 2020. The bear necessities: a new view of the so-called 'Lion Man'. *Current World Archaeology* 100, March/April: 24-29.

Wehrberger, K. (ed.). 2013. *The Return of the Lion Man. History, Myth, Magic*. Ulmer Museum. Thorbecke Verlag: Ostfildern.

Cavorting in caves

Lancey, D. F. 2017. *Raising Children: Insights from Other Cultures*. Cambridge Univ. Press: Cambridge.

Kids in caves

Bégouën, R. *et al.* 2009. *Le Sanctuaire Secret des Bisons. Il y a 14 000 ans dans la caverne du Tuc d'Audoubert...* Somogy éditions d'art, Paris.

Garcia, A. 2001. Les empreintes et les traces humaines et animales, pp. 34-43 in (J. Clottes, ed.) *La Grotte Chauvet. L'Art des Origines*. Le Seuil: Paris.

Pales, L. 1976. *Les Empreintes de Pieds Humains dans les Cavernes. Les Empreintes du Réseau Clastres de la Caverne de Niaux (Ariège)*. Archives de l'Institut de Paléontologie Humaine 36. Masson: Paris.

Pastoors, A. *et al.* 2021. Episodes of Magdalenian hunter-gatherers in the Upper Gallery of Tuc d'Audoubert (Ariège, France), pp. 211-49 in (A. Pastoors and T. Lenssen-Erz, eds) *Reading Prehistoric Human Tracks. Methods and Material.* Springer: Cham, Switzerland.

Pfeiffer, J. E. 1982. *The Creative Explosion. An inquiry into the origins of art and religion.* Harper and Row: New York.

Sharpe, K. and Van Gelder, L. 2004. Children and paleolithic "art": Indications from Rouffignac Cave. *International Newsletter On Rock Art* 38: 9-17.

Sharpe, K. and Van Gelder, L. 2006. Evidence for cave marking by Palaeolithic children. *Antiquity* 80: 937-47.

Death in the ice age – good grief!

Hodgkins, J. *et al.* 2021. An infant burial from Arma Veirana in northwestern Italy provides insights into funerary practices and female personhood in early Mesolithic Europe. *Scientific Reports* 11:23735 https://doi.org/10.1038/s41598-021-02804-z

Mussi, M. 1996. Rituels funéraires dans les sépultures gravettiennes des Grottes de Grimaldi et de la Grotte delle Arene Candide: une mise au point, pp. 833-46 in (M. Otte, ed.) *Nature et Culture, Colloque de Liège, Dec. 1993.* ERAUL 68: Liège.

Mussi, M. *et al.* 2000. Echoes from the mammoth steppe: the case of the Balzi Rossi, pp. 105-24 in (W. Roebroeks *et al.* eds) *Hunters of the Golden Age: The Mid-Upper Palaeolithic of Eurasia (30,000-20,000 BP).* University of Leiden Press: Leiden.

Pettitt, P. 2010. *The Palaeolithic Origins of Human Burial.* Routledge: London.

Sparacello, V. S. *et al.* 2018. New insights on Final Epigravettian funerary behavior at Arene Candide Cave (Western Liguria, Italy). *Journal of Anthropological Sciences* 96: 1-24.

CHAPTER 6

Bahn, P. G. 2016. *Images of the Ice Age.* Oxford University Press: Oxford.

Brody, H. 2002. *The Other Side of Eden, Hunter-Gatherers, Farmers and the Shaping of the World.* Faber and Faber: London.

Porr, M. and Bell, H. R. 2012. 'Rock-art', 'animism' and two-way thinking: towards a complementary epistemology in the understanding of material culture and 'rock-art' of hunting and gathering people. *Journal of Methodological Theory* 19: 161-205.

Getting together

Bahn, P. G. 1982. Inter-site and inter-regional links during the Upper Palaeolithic: the Pyrenean evidence. *The Oxford Journal of Archaeology* 1: 247-68.

Bahn, P. G. 1984. *Pyrenean Prehistory.* Aris and Phillips: Warminster.

Bégouën, R. *et al.* 2019. *La Grotte d'Enlène. Immersion dans un habitat magdalénien.* In Fine: Paris.

Garate Maidagan, D. 2010. *Las Ciervas Punteadas en las cuevas del Paleolítico. Una expresión pictórica propia de la cornisa cantábrica.* Suplemento 33, Munibe. Sociedad de Ciencias Aranzadi: San Sebastian.

Lefebvre, A. *et al.* 2021. Interconnected Magdalenian societies as revealed by the circulation of whale bone artifacts in the Pyreneo-Cantabrian region. *Quaternary Science Reviews* 251: 106692

Pétillon, J-M. 2013. Circulation of whale-bone artifacts in the northern Pyrenees during the late Upper Paleolithic. *Journal of Human Evolution* 65: 525-43.

Stewart, B. A. *et al.* 2020. Ostrich eggshell bead strontium isotopes reveal persistent macroscale social networking across late Quaternary southern Africa. *Proceedings of the National Academy of Sciences* 117 (12): 6453-62.

Taborin, Y. 1985. Les origines des coquillages paléolithiques en France, pp. 278-301 in (M. Otte, ed.) *La Signification culturelle des Industries Lithiques.* British Arch. Reports, International series No. 239, Oxford.

Taborin, Y. 1992. Les espaces d'acheminement de certains coquillages magdaléniens, pp. 417-29 in (J-P. Rigaud *et al.*, eds) *Le Peuplement Magdalénien.* Editions du Comité des Travaux Historiques et Scientifiques: Paris.

Terberger, T, *et al.* 2021. The Shigir idol in the context of early art in Eurasia. *Quaternary International* 573: 14-29.

Ice age bling

Taborin, Y. 1987. *La Parure en Coquillage au Paléolithique.* 29e Suppl. à Gallia Préhistoire. CNRS: Paris.

Taborin, Y. 2004. *Langage Sans Parole. La Parure aux Temps Préhistoriques.* La Maison des Roches: Paris.

Vanhaeren, M. 2010. *Les Fonctions de la Parure au Paléolithique Supérieur: de l'individu à l'unité culturelle.* Editions Universitaires Européennes: Sarrebruck.

Vanhaeren, M. and d'Errico, F. 2003. Le mobilier funéraire de la dame de Saint-Germain-la-Rivière (Gironde) et l'origine paléolithique des inégalités. *Paleo* 15, 195-238.

Vanhaeren, M. and d'Errico, F. 2006. Aurignacian ethno-linguistic geography of Europe revealed by personal ornaments. *Journal of Archaeological Science* 33, 1105-28.

Language

Deacon, T. W. 1998. *The Symbolic Species. The Co-evolution of Language and the Brain.* W.W. Norton and Co.: New York and London.

Deutscher, G. 2006. *The Unfolding of Language. The Evolution of Mankind's Greatest Invention.* Arrow Books, Random House: London.

Lakoff, G. and Johnson M. 2015. *Metaphors We Live By.* University of Chicago Press: Chicago and London.

Therianthropes

Bahn, P. G. 2016. *Images of the Ice Age.* Oxford University Press: Oxford.

Bégouën, R. *et al.* 2014. *La Caverne des Trois-Frères. Anthologie d'un exceptionnel sanctuaire préhistorique.* Somogy, Editions d'Art: Paris.

Thanks for the memory

Donald, M. 1991. *Origins of the Modern Mind: Three Stages of Evolution and Cognition.* Harvard University Press: Cambridge, Mass

Donald, M. 2001. *A Mind so Rare. The Evolution of Human Consciousness.* Norton and Co.: London.

d'Errico, F. 1998. Palaeolithic origins of artificial memory systems: an evolutionary perspective, pp. 19-50 in (C. Renfrew and C. Scarre, eds) *Cognition and Material Culture: the Archaeology of Symbolic Storage.* McDonald Institute Monographs: Cambridge.

McGilchrist, I. 2010. *The Master and his Emissary. The Divided Brain and the Making of the Western World.* (Chapter 7. Imitation and the Evolution of Culture). Yale University Press: New Haven and London.

Pfeiffer, J. E. 1982. *The Creative Explosion. An inquiry into the origins of art and religion.* Harper and Row: New York.

Solso, R. L. 2003. *The Psychology of Art and the Evolution of the Conscious Brain.* The MIT Press: London.

Telling the time

d'Errico, F. 1995. A new model and its implications for the origin of writing: the La Marche antler revisited. *Cambridge Archaeological Journal* 5: 163-206.

d'Errico, F. and Cacho, C. 1994. Notation versus decoration in the Upper Palaeolithic: a case-study from Tossal de la Roca, Alicante, Spain. *Journal of Archaeological Science* 21: 185-200.

Marshack, A. 1972. *The Roots of Civilization.* Weidenfeld and Nicolson: London. (2nd edition, 1991, Moyer Bell: New York).

Marshack, A. 1991. The Taï plaque and calendrical notation in the Upper Paleolithic. *Cambridge Archaeological Journal* 1, 25-61.

Drama in caves

García-Diez, M, Ochoa, B. and Rodríguez Asensio, J. A. (eds) 2015. *Arte Rupestre Paleolítico en la Cueva de la Covaciella (Inguanzo, Asturias).* Gobierno del Principado de Asturias; Oviedo.

Millara, A. and Angulo, J. 2010. *Conoce Tito Bustillo.* Amigos de Ribadesella: Ribadesella.

Polledo González, M. 2011, *El Arte Paleolítico de Tito Bustillo: Cazadores y artistas en la cueva del Pozu'l Ramu*, Mensula Ediciones: Pola de Siero, Asturias.

Having a laugh

Alpert, B. O. 1992. Des preuves de sens ludique dans l'art au Pléistocène Supérieur. *L'Anthropologie* 96 (2-3): 219-44.

Bahn, P. G. 1997: *The Cambridge Illustrated History of Prehistoric Art.* Cambridge University Press.

Lombo Montañés, A. 2014. Interpretación de retruécanos, imágenes de doble sentido y bromas en el arte paleolítico. (The interpretation of puns, jokes and double meaning images in Palaeolithic art). *Complutum* 25 (1): 35-46.

Musical moments

Bahn, P. G. 2015. Bow and errors, pp. 59-65 in (H. Stebergløkken *et al.*, eds) *Ritual Landscapes and Borders within Rock Art Research. Papers in Honour of Professor Kalle Sognnes.* Archaeopress: Oxford.

Buisson, D. 1990. Les flûtes paléolithiques d'Isturitz. *Bulletin de la Société Préhistorique française* 87: 420-33.

Conard, N. J. *et al.* 2009. New flutes document the earliest musical tradition in southwestern Germany. *Nature* 460: 737-40.

Dauvois, M. 1989. Son et musique paléolithiques, in *La Musique dans l'Antiquité, Les Dossiers d'Archéologie* 142, Nov: 2-11.

Dauvois, M. 1994. Les témoins sonores paléolithiques extérieur et souterrain, pp. 11-31 in (M. Otte, ed.) *«Sons Originels», Préhistoire de la Musique*. Actes du Colloque de Musicologie, Dec. 1992. ERAUL 61: Liège.

Dauvois, M. and Boutillon, X. 1990. Etudes acoustiques au Réseau Clastres: Salle des Peintures et lithophones naturels. *Bulletin de la Société Préhistorique Ariège-Pyrénées* 45: 175-86.

Fritz, C. *et al.* 2021. First record of the sound produced by the oldest Upper Paleolithic seashell horn. *Science Advances* 7: eabe9510

Morley, I. 2013. *The Prehistory of Music. Human Evolution, Archaeology, and the Origins of Musicality*. Oxford University Press: Oxford.

Reznikoff, I. and Dauvois, M. 1988. La dimension sonore des grottes ornées. *Bulletin de la Société Préhistorique française* 85: 238-46.

Waller, S. J. 1993. Sound reflection as an explanation for the content and context of rock art. *Rock Art Research* 10: 91-101.

Images on the rocks

Bahn, P. G. 2016. *Images of the Ice Age*. Oxford University Press: Oxford.

Clifford, E. 2014. Images of the Ice Age: Caves and Mythological Worlds. Thesis submitted for the Degree of Master of Science in Early Prehistory. The University of York Archaeology Department.

Leroi-Gourhan, A. 1968. *The Art of Prehistoric Man in Western Europe*. Abrams: New York.

Leroi-Gourhan, A. 1982. *The Dawn of European Art*. Cambridge University Press: Cambridge.

Religion

Bahn, P. G. 2011. Religion and ritual in the Upper Palaeolithic, pp. 344-57 in (T. Insoll, ed.) *The Oxford Handbook of the Archaeology of Ritual and Religion*. Oxford University Press: Oxford.

Bégouën, R. and Clottes, J. 1981. Apports mobiliers dans les cavernes du Volp (Enlène, Les Trois-Frères, Le Tuc d'Audoubert), pp. 157-88 in *Altamira Symposium*. Ministerio de Cultura: Madrid.

Boyer, P. 2001. *Religion Explained. The Human Instincts that Fashion Gods, Spirits and Ancestors*. Vintage Books Random House: London.

Delporte, H. 1993. *L'Image de la Femme dans l'Art Préhistorique*. (2nd ed.). Picard: Paris.

Helvenston, P. and Bahn, P. 2005. *Waking the Trance Fixed*. Wasteland Press: Kentucky, USA.

Insoll, T. (ed.) 2011. *The Oxford Handbook of The Archaeology of Ritual and Religion*. Oxford University Press: Oxford.

Jennett, K, D. 2008. *Female figurines of the Upper Palaeolithic*. Hons. Thesis. digital.library.txstate.edu (PDF available on-line)

Leroi-Gourhan, A. 1964. *Les Religions de la Préhistoire*. PUF: Paris.

Patte, E. 1960. *Les Hommes Préhistoriques et la Religion*. Picard: Paris.

Wunn, I. 2000. Beginning of religion. *Numen* 47: 417-52. Leiden.

JFK

Gillon, S. M. 2009. *The Kennedy Assassination – 24 Hours After*. Basic Books: New York.

The 'Rites of Springs'

Bahn, P. G. 1978. Water mythology and the distribution of Palaeolithic parietal art. *Proceedings of the Prehistoric Society* 44: 125-34.

Bahn, P. G. 1980. 'Histoire d'Eau': L'art pariétal préhistorique des Pyrénées. *Travaux de l'Institut d'Art Préhistorique de Toulouse* 22: 129-35.

de la Rasilla Vives, M. and Duarte Matías, E. 2018. Casualidad o estrategia? Las aguas termales y minero-medicinales en la configuración de los yacimientos con arte rupestre paleolítico de Asturias y su correlato cantábrico. *Nailos* 5: 17-41.

CASE STUDY

El Mirón and Covalanas

García Diez, M. and Eguizabal Torre, E. 2003. *La Cueva de Covalanas.* Consejería de Cultura: Santander.

González Morales, M. R. and Straus, L. G. 2009. Extraordinary early Magdalenian finds from El Mirón Cave, Cantabria (Spain). *Antiquity* 83: 267-81.

Straus, L. G. and Gonzalez Morales, M. (eds) 2012. *El Mirón Cave, Cantabrian Spain.* University of New Mexico Press: Albuquerque.

Straus, L. G., Gonzalez Morales, M. and Carretero, J.M. (eds) 2015. "The Red Lady of El Mirón Cave": Lower Magdalenian Human Burial in Cantabrian Spain. Special issue of *Journal of Archaeological Science* 60: 1-137.

Seva Román, R. *et al.* 2019. Sources of the ochres associated with the Lower Magdalenian "Red Lady" human burial and rock art in El Mirón Cave (Cantabria, Spain). *Journal of Archaeological Science Reports* 23: 265-80.

APPENDIX

The fake 'Venus' of Abri Pataud

Delluc, B. and G. 2000. La vénus sculptée de l'abri Pataud (Les Eyzies): oui! *Bulletin de la Société Historique et Archéologique du Périgord* 127: 43-72.

Figure credits

Chapter 1

Figure 1.1. a-d: Courtesy J. Zilhão
Figure 1.2. a: After Pales and de St Péreuse
Figure 1.2. b: After Airvaux and Pradel
Figure 1.3. Courtesy G. Pinçon
Figure 1.4. After Breuil
Figure 1.5. After Minellono
Figure 1.6. a: Photo J. Vertut, P. Bahn collection
Figure 1.6. b: Photo P. Bahn
Figure 1.6. c: After Lbova
Figure 1.7. a: Photo J. Vertut, P. Bahn collection
Figure 1.7. b: Photo P. Bahn
Figure 1.7. c: Photo E. Daynès
Figure 1.8. a: Photo A. Marshack, P. Bahn collection
Figure 1.8. b: Photo courtesy M. Králík and Z. Nerudová
Figure 1.9. Photo courtesy M. Bennett, Bournemouth University
Figure 1.10. Photo A. Kehoe
Figure 1.11. Photo P. Bahn collection
Figure 1.12. a-d: Courtesy the late N. Bader
Figure 1.13. a: Photo B. and G. Delluc
Figure 1.13. b: Photo P. Froesch
Figure 1.14. a: Photo D. Frayer
Figure 1.14. b: Photo P. Bahn
Figure 1.15. Photo P. Bahn
Figure 1.16. a: Photo courtesy the late J. Jelínek
Figure 1.16. b: Photo A. Marshack, P. Bahn collection
Figure 1.17. Photo P. Bahn

Chapter 2

Figure 2.1. After Bosinski
Figure 2.2. Photo from the late Arlette Leroi-Gourhan
Figure 2.3. a: Photo M. Girard.
Figure 2.3. b: After Marshack.
Figure 2.4. Photo P. Bahn
Figure 2.5. Photo L. Vanrell
Figure 2.6. After de Saint Périer
Figure 2.7. Photo J. Vertut, P. Bahn collection
Figure 2.8. Photo P. Bahn
Figure 2.9. Photo N. Aujoulat, courtesy N. Jhaveri
Figure 2.10. Photo P. Bahn
Figure 2.11. Photo R. Bégouën
Figure 2.12. a: After Pinçon et al.

Figure 2.12. b: Photo P. Bahn
Figure 2.13. After García-Diez and Vaquero
Figure 2.14. a: After Leroi-Gourhan.
Figure 2.14. b. Photo P. Bahn
Figure 2.15. Photo P. Bahn
Figure 2.16. Photo courtesy G. Bosinski
Figure 2.17. Photo courtesy G. Bosinski
Figure 2.18. After Rogachev
Figure 2.19. After Boriskovski
Figure 2.20. a: Photo D. Sacchi. b. Photo P. Bahn
Figure 2.21. After Pidoplichko
Figure 2.22. After Oakley
Figure 2.23. Photo R. Bégouën
Figure 2.24. Photo J. Vertut, P. Bahn collection
Figure 2.25. Photo B. and G. Delluc

Chapter 3

Figure 3.1. After Breuil.
Figure 3.2. Photo S. Lancelot, INRAP
Figure 3.3. Photo R. Bégouën
Figure 3.4. After Leroi-Gourhan
Figure 3.5. Photo J. Zilhão
Figure 3.6. a: Photo courtesy the late A. Leroi-Gourhan;
Figure 3.6. b: After Abramova;
Figure 3.6. c/d: Photos B. and G. Delluc
Figure 3.7. Photo A. Marshack, P. Bahn collection
Figure 3.8. After Bouvier
Figure 3.9. Photo R. Bégouën
Figure 3.10. a/b: After Bouvier
Figure 3.11. Photo courtesy the late Arlette Leroi-Gourhan
Figure 3.12. After Breuil
Figure 3.13. Photo A. Heikel 1894.
Figure 3.14. a/b: Photos courtesy the late Arlette Leroi-Goiurhan
Figure 3.15. a: Photo J. Adovasio
Figure 3.15. b: After Soffer et al.
Figure 3.16. Photo L. Vanrell
Figure 3.17. Photo E. Daynès
Figure 3.18. After Lartet and Christy
Figure 3.19. Photo E. Clifford collection
Figure 3.20. Photo E. Clifford collection
Figure 3.21. Photo B. and G. Delluc
Figure 3.22. After Gaussen
Figure 3.23. Photo J. Vertut, P. Bahn collection
Figure 3.24. After Marshack
Figure 3.25. a/b/c: Photos L. Lbova
Figure 3.26. Photo E. Clifford

Figure 3.27. Photos L. Lbova
Figure 3.28. Photo E. Clifford collection
Figure 3.29. Photo A. Marshack, P. Bahn collection
Figure 3.30. Photo M. Vanhaeren
Figure 3.31. Lithograph by J. Pilloy, 1898
Figure 3.32. Courtesy of the late N. Bader
Figure 3.33. Photo L. Ledoux

Chapter 4

Figure 4.1. Photo J. Vertut, P. Bahn collection
Figure 4.2. Photo P. Bahn
Figure 4.3. P. Bahn collection
Figure 4.4. Photo J. Vertut, P. Bahn collection
Figure 4.5. a: After Pales
Figure 4.5. b/c: Photo and drawing, J-D. Larribau
Figure 4.5. d: After Plenier
Figure 4.5. e: After Clot and Cantet
Figure 4.6. a/b: After des Ormeaux
Figure 4.7. Photo P. Bahn
Figure 4.8. After de Saint Périer
Figure 4.9. After Pales
Figure 4.10. After Cartailhac
Figure 4.11. After Breuil
Figure 4.12. Photo B. Caland
Figure 4.13. a/b: Photos P. Nikolskiy
Figure 4.14. a/b: Photos E. Mashchenko
Figure 4.15. Photo courtesy the late J. Jelínek
Figure 4.16. After Passemard
Figure 4.17. a/b/c: Photos S. Fedorov
Figure 4.18. a: After Marshack; b: after Mélard
Figure 4.19. a: Photo Creswell Crags Research Team; b: after Piette
Figure 4.20. a: After Breuil and Bégouën
Figure 4.20. b: After Bosinski
Figure 4.21. After Malvesin-Fabre et al.
Figure 4.22. After Breuil
Figure 4.23. a: Photo A. Marshack, P. Bahn collection
Figure 4.23. b: After Breuil and de St Périer
Figure 4.24. After Malvesin-Fabre et al.
Figure 4.25. Photo E. Clifford collection
Figure 4.26. Photo J. Vertut, P. Bahn collection
Figure 4.27. a: After Breuil; b: photo and drawing courtesy of the late A. Roussot
Figure 4.28. After Piette
Figure 4.29. Photo Y. Berman
Figure 4.30. Photo courtesy the late Frank Marlowe
Figure 4.31. Photo P. Bahn

Chapter 5

Figure 5.1. Photo E. Daynès
Figure 5.2. Photo courtesy G. Pinçon
Figure 5.3. Photo P. Saura
Figure 5.4. Photo P. Bahn
Figure 5.5. a/b: Photos E. Vacca
Figure 5.6. Photo courtesy J. Irish
Figure 5.7. Photo C. Neugebauer-Maresch. (C) ÖAI-ÖAW (Austrian Academy of Sciences)
Figure 5.8. After Marshack and d'Errico
Figure 5.9. Photo E. Clifford collection
Figure 5.10. Photo E. Clifford collection
Figure 5.11. Photo G. Bosinski
Figure 5.12. Photo P. Bahn
Figure 5.13. a/b: Photos P. Saura
Figure 5.14. Photo K. Hakami
Figure 5.15. Photo A. Marshack, P. Bahn collection
Figure 5.16. Photo A. Marshack, P. Bahn collection
Figure 5.17. Photo P. Bahn
Figure 5.18. Photo Ulm Museum
Figure 5.19. Photo J. Vertut, P. Bahn collection
Figure 5.20. Photo J. Vertut, P. Bahn collection
Figure 5.21. Photo J. Vertut, P. Bahn collection
Figure 5.22. Photo J. Vertut, P. Bahn collection
Figure 5.23. Photo P. Bahn
Figure 5.24. Photo R. Bégouën
Figure 5.25. Photo P. Saura
Figure 5.26. Photo P. Saura
Figure 5.27. Photo R. Bégouën
Figure 5.28. Photo P. Bahn

Chapter 6

Figure 6.1. Photo M. Reis
Figure 6.2. Photo P. Bahn
Figure 6.3. Photo Landesmuseum, Hanover
Figure 6.4. After Lartet and Chaplain-Duparc
Figure 6.5. Photo M. Vanhaeren
Figure 6.6. After de Saint Périer
Figure 6.7. Photo A. Marshack, P. Bahn collection
Figure 6.8. a: After Piette
Figure 6.8. b: Photo J. Vertut, P. Bahn collection
Figure 6.9. a: Photo J. Vertut, collection Bégouën
Figure 6.9. b: After Breuil
Figure 6.10. a/b: Photos P. Bahn

Figure 6.11. Photo P. Bahn
Figure 6.12. Photo A. Marshack, P. Bahn collection
Figure 6.13. Photo J. Vertut, P. Bahn collection
Figure 6.14. Photo P. Saura
Figure 6.15. Photos R. de Balbín
Figure 6.16. Photo P. Bahn
Figure 6.17. a: Photo R. de Balbín
Figure 6.17. b: After Gladkih et al.
Figure 6.17. c: After Marshack
Figure 6.18. Photo J. Vertut, P. Bahn collection
Figure 6.19. Photo J. Vertut, P. Bahn collection
Figure 6.20. Photo P. Bahn
Figure 6.21. a: Photo University of Tübingen; b: after Buisson
Figure 6.22. Photo J. Vertut, P. Bahn collection
Figure 6.23. Photo J. Vertut, P. Bahn collection
Figure 6.24. Photo P. Bahn
Figure 6.25. Photo B. Caland
Figure 6.26. Photo P. Saura
Figure 6.27. Photo J. Vertut, collection Bégouën
Figure 6.28. Photo P. Bahn
Figure 6.29. After Breuil
Figure 6.30. Photo R. Bégouën
Figure 6.31. Photo J. Vertut, collection Bégouën
Figure 6.32. a: Photo B. Caland
Figure 6.32. b: After Glory
Figure 6.33. Photo P. Bahn
Figure 6.34. Drawing by M. Lorblanchet
Figure 6.35. Photo R. Bégouën
Figure 6.36. Photo M. Lorblanchet

Case studies

Case study Figure 1. Mirón: Photo L. Straus.
Case study Figure 2. Mirón: Photo L. Straus
Case study Figure 3. Ochre photo R. Seva
Case study Figure 4. Covalanas: Photo P. Saura
Case study Figure 5. Pataud: Photo B. and G. Delluc

Index